By the time of the Calvinist Reformation, the cities of Holland had established a very long tradition of social provision for the poor in the civic community. Calvinists, however, intended to care for their own church members, who were by definition "within the household of faith," through the diaconate, a confessional relief agency. This book examines the relationship between municipal and ecclesiastical relief agencies in the six chief cities of Holland – Dordrecht, Haarlem, Delft, Leiden, Amsterdam, and Gouda – from the public establishment of the Reformed Church in 1572 to the aftermath of the Synod of Dort.

The author argues that the conflict between charitable organizations reveals competing conceptions of Christian community that came to the fore as a result of the Dutch Reformation. He analyzes how civic and church leaders faced these tensions and how the general settlements led to a unique blend of religious pluralism and confessional identity in seventeenth-century Holland.

This is the first comparative study of poor relief in Holland, which contributes to our understanding of the Reformation throughout Europe.

CHARLES H. PARKER is Assistant Professor of History, Saint Louis University.

CAMBRIDGE STUDIES IN EARLY MODERN HISTORY

The reformation of community

CAMBRIDGE STUDIES IN EARLY MODERN HISTORY

Edited by Professor Sir John Elliott, University of Oxford
Professor Olwen Hufton, University of Oxford
Professor H. G. Koenigsberger, University of London
Dr. H. M. Scott, University of St. Andrews

The idea of an "early modern" period of European history from the fifteenth to the late eighteenth century is now widely accepted among historians. The purpose of Cambridge Studies in Early Modern History is to publish monographs and studies which illuminate the character of the period as a whole, and in particular focus attention on a dominant theme within it, the interplay of continuity and change as they are presented by the continuity of medieval ideas, political and social organization, and by the impact of new ideas, new methods, and new demands on the traditional structure.

For a list of titles published in the series, please see end of the book

The reformation of community

Social welfare and Calvinist charity in
Holland, 1572–1620

CHARLES H. PARKER

CAMBRIDGE
UNIVERSITY PRESS

PUBLISHED BY THE PRESS SYNDICATE OF THE UNIVERSITY OF CAMBRIDGE
The Pitt Building, Trumpington Street, Cambridge CB2 1RP, United Kingdom

CAMBRIDGE UNIVERSITY PRESS
The Edinburgh Building, Cambridge, CB2 2RU, United Kingdom
http://www.cup.cam.ac.uk
40 West 20th Street, New York, NY 10011–4211, USA
http://www.cup.org
10 Stamford Road, Oakleigh, Melbourne 3166, Australia

First published 1998

Printed in the United Kingdom at the University Press, Cambridge

Typeset in Ehrhardt 10/12 pt   [VN]

A catalogue record for this book is available from the British Library

Library of Congress cataloging in publication data

Parker, Charles H., 1958–
The reformation of community: social welfare and Calvinist
charity in Holland, 1572–1620/Charles H. Parker
p.   cm. – (Cambridge studies in early modern history)
Includes bibliographical references and index.
ISBN 0 521 62305 7 (hardback)
1. Gereformeerde Kerk in de Nederlanden – Charities – History – 16th century.
2. Gereformeerde Kerk in de Nederlanden – Charities – History – 17th century.
3. Reformed Church – Netherlands – Charities – History – 16th century.
4. Reformed Church – Netherlands – Charities – History – 17th century.
5. Charities – Netherlands – History.   6. Public welfare – Netherlands – History.
7. Netherlands – Church history – 16th century.   8. Netherlands –
Church history – 17th century.   I. Title.   II. Series.
BX9474.2.P37   1998
284'.2492'09031 – dc21
98-3782 CIP

ISBN 0 521 62305 7 hardback

To Jean and Drew

Contents

Illustrations, tables, and appendices

Acknowledgements

One of the most rewarding aspects of doing the research and writing for this study has been the opportunity to come in contact with many learned, vibrant, and generous people who have taken the time to help me along the way. They have offered suggestions, read my work, corrected many of my errors, and encouraged me at critical points. About ten years ago, I decided to undertake a study of charitable institutions in Holland from the late middle ages through the Reformation period. At that time, I knew little about poor relief or the Low Countries. And Dutch would be yet another language to learn. This book, then, really bears witness to the mentoring that takes place in the world of academic scholarship. The helpful guidance of so many scholars has made this a better book than it otherwise would have been, just as their kindness has made the experience a rich one for me personally. It is a great pleasure for me to thank, by way of acknowledgement, a few of the people who played an instrumental role in the development of this project.

I should first thank James D. Tracy, my mentor at the University of Minnesota. It was he who first suggested to me that comparative study of poor relief in Holland would reveal some important characteristics of Dutch religious culture from the late middle ages to the early seventeenth century. Professor Tracy oversaw my graduate work and dissertation (out of which this book grew) at every point. Despite his own crowded schedule, he always made time to answer my questions, talk with me, and give me advice. He has provided a thorough, yet constructive critique of my work, and he has given a vast amount of his time to me. Most importantly perhaps, the standards of scholarship and professional integrity that he has set for himself have served as a model for me and many other young scholars. I am also grateful to the History Departments at the University of Minnesota and at Auburn University for giving an unlikely applicant a chance to succeed. My professors and my graduate school colleagues forced me to defend my views, to clarify my ideas, and sometimes to modify them. Stanford Lehmberg and Klaas van der Sanden at Minnesota and Donna Bohanan at Auburn made time for me and believed in me. I also owe a great deal to Glen Eaves whose enthusiastic lectures first drew me to the Reformation period.

My colleagues in the History Department at Saint Louis University have created an atmosphere conducive to learning and to friendship. I am grateful that they have given me a place to do research as well as to teach. Members of the Interdisciplinary

Research Group in the Arts and Sciences at Saint Louis University have also made useful comments on portions of the book and offered a place to exchange ideas across disciplines. Ellen Autenthie in the interlibrary loan department has performed many miracles by bringing a number of very old books to me.

A number of other scholars have had a strong hand in the development of my understanding of poor relief and the religious culture out of which it grew. Professors Philip Benedict, Donald Critchlow, Robert Du Plessis, Philip Gavitt, Thomas Madden, Ray Mentzer, Andrew Pettegree, Darlene Pryds, Lee Wandel, and David Wisner have read and made comments on all or significant portions of this project. Each provided various substantive criticisms, made organizational suggestions, and challenged me to think more comparatively about charity and welfare. During my research stays in the Netherlands, Professors J. J. Woltjer and A. Th. van Deursen made themselves available to me and gave me the benefit of their knowledge of the Dutch archives. They gave me counsel at moments of crisis and helped me avoid dead-end paths. They also read my dissertation and offered a number of helpful suggestions. On a personal level, Llewellyn Bogaers, Angelique Dietz, Michael Flynn, and Hanneke van Wijk gave food, shelter, and friendship to a very lonely American graduate student.

Despite the generosity of a great host of people, my research and writing on poor relief could not have taken place without significant financial support. A Fulbright Fellowship, jointly administered by the Institute of International Education and the Netherlands–America Commission for Educational Exchange, in 1990–91 gave me access to the Dutch archives. Summer grants by the Andrew Mellon Foundation at Saint Louis University (1996), the Newberry Library Consortium (1995 and 1996), and the National Endowment for the Humanities (1997) enabled me to complete the research and gave me extended periods of time to write.

I would also like to thank the editors and the Press Syndicate at Cambridge University Press for taking on this project. I greatly appreciate all of their work in service of this book. The editors of the following journals were very generous to allow me to use previously published material. "Moral supervision and poor relief in the Reformed Church of Delft, 1579–1609," *Archiv für Reformationsgeschichte* 87 (1996), 334–61, and "The moral agency and moral autonomy of church folk in post-Reformation Delft, 1572–1620," *Journal of Ecclesiastical History* 48 (1997), 44–70, form the basis of chapter 5. Portions of "Poor relief and community in the early Dutch Republic," in *Always Among Us: A History of Private Charity and Public Welfare*, Donald T. Critchlow and Charles H. Parker, eds. (Lanham, Md., 1997), pp. 13–34, and "Dordrecht," in *The Oxford Encyclopedia of the Reformation*, Hans J. Hillerbrand, ed. (New York, 1996), vol. II, pp. 1–2, appear in chapter 6.

As I close, I would like to express my deep gratitude to my family for their affection, patience, and understanding for the past ten years. My parents, Charles and Dolores Parker, have been among my most enthusiastic (and certainly my longest) supporters. Finally and above all, my wife Jean and my son Drew have been my dearest companions during these past eleven years. They have allowed me the time to think, research, and write. Among countless other sacrifices, Jean took on the role of single mother for nine months in 1990–91 and for two months in 1997, while I was in the Netherlands. They not only have been highly supportive, but they have enriched my life and work in so many ways. The fictional character Max Havelaar remarked that his wife "divided his troubles and multiplied his joys." Jean and Drew have done that for me. This book is dedicated to them.

Abbreviations

AGN	*Algemene Geschiedenis der Nederlanden* 12 vols., Utrecht, 1949–58
GAA. Kerkeraad	*Gemeente Archief te Amsterdam. Archief van de Nederlands Hervormd Gemeente te Amsterdam, Protocollen van de Bijzonderen Kerkeraad, 1578–1621*
GAA. Keurboek	*Gemeente Archief te Amsterdam. Archief van de Burgermeesteren, Keurboeken*
GAA. Memorialboek	*Gemeente Archief te Amsterdam. Archief van de Burgermeesteren, Groot Memorial Boek vande Burgermeesteren*
GAA. Predikanten	*Gemeente Archief te Amsterdam. Kerkeraad, Register van Predikanten, Ouderlingen, ende Diaconen, 1578–1734*
GAA. Thesaurien	*Gemeente Archief te Amsterdam. Archief van de Thesaurien Ordinaris*
GAA. Vroedschapresoluties	*Gemeente Archief te Amsterdam. Archief van de Vroedschap, Resolties van de Vroedschap*
GAD. ACC	*Gemeente Archief te Delft. Archief van de Kerkeraad van de Nederlands Hermormd Gemeente, Verzameling van Arent Corneliszoon Crusius*
GAD. Burgermeesteren	*Gemeente Archief te Delft. Archief van de Vroedschap, Burgermeesteren*
GAD. Kamer	*Gemeente Archief te Delft. Archief van de Kamer van Charitate*
GAD. Kerkeraad	*Gemeente Archief te Delft. Archief van de Kerkeraad van de Nederlands Hervormde Gemeente, Handelingen van de Algemene Kerkeraad*
GAD. Keurboek	*Gemeente Archief te Delft. Archief van de Vroedschap, Keurboek*
GAD. KrCor	*Gemeente Archief te Delft. Archief van de Kerkeraad van de Nederlands Hervormde Gemeente, Ingekommen stukken, minuten en afschriften van uitgegane stukken*
GAD. Memorialboek	*Gemeente Archief te Delft. Archief van de Vroedschap, Memoriaelboeck van de Burgermeesteren*

List of abbreviations

GAD. Memorialen	*Gemeente Archief te Delft. Archief van de Diaconie en Kamer van Charitate, Memorialen*
GAD. Regle	*Gemeente Archief te Delft. Archief van de Kerkeraad van de Nederlands Hervormde Gemeente te Delft, Kerkeraad Reglementen en Instructie*
GAD. Resolutieboeck	*Gemeente Archief te Delft. Archief van de Vroedschap, Resolutieboeck van Veertigen*
GAD. Wetresoluties	*Gemeente Archief te Delft. Archief van de Vroedschap, Resolutien van de Heeren van de Wet*
GADR. Kerkeraad	*Gemeente Archief te Dordrecht. Archief van de Kerkeraad*
GAG. Vroedschapboeken	*Gemeente Archief te Gouda. Oud Archief te Gouda, Vroedschapboeken*
GAH. Kerkeraad	*Gemeente Archief te Haarlem. Oud Archief van de Kerkeraad, Acta van de Kerkeraad*
GAH. Kerkeraad, Predikanten	*Gemeente Archief te Haarlem. Oud Archief van de Kerkeraad, Acta van de Kerkeraad, Predikanten*
GAH. Vroedschapresolutien	*Gemeente Archief te Haarlem. Netresoluties van de Haarlemse Vroedschap*
GAL. Kerkeraad	*Gemeente Archief te Leiden. Archief van de Kerkeraad, De Bouck des Kerckenraets, 1584–1590*
NAGN	*Algemene Geschiedenis der Nederlanden*, new series, 15 vols., Haarlem, 1977–83

Introduction

AUTHORITY, COMMUNITY, AND CHARITY

In the early weeks of November 1573, the leaders of the fledgling Calvinist congregation in the city of Delft took a bold step forward.[1] They had decided that the congregation was now ready to hold its first formal election for elders and deacons since the city government had lifted the ban on Reformed worship in August 1572. But this election was no mere formality; it would establish an official Calvinist organization in the new church. The Delft magistrates, however, were not keen on Calvinism; they had accepted the fact of a public Reformed Church only as a temporary consequence of their surrender to a Beggar army.[2] From August 1567 to July 1572, the city government had cooperated, albeit sometimes reluctantly, with a renewed Spanish campaign to combat heresy. Out of a concern for how the non-Reformed magistrates might respond, the "brothers" dispatched Arent Corneliszoon, a pastor, and Huyg Jacobszoon van der Dussen, an elder, to announce the election to the burgomasters.

The choice of these delegates was strategic: Corneliszoon was the son of a former burgomaster; van der Dussen was a notable brewer and a church warden (*kerkmeester*).[3] The social position of these two men would help allay the fears of the burgomasters and grant the church a degree of legitimacy. At the same time, however, the Calvinist leaders wanted to make it clear that this announcement was not a request; it was a declaration. They resolved: "the brothers will announce this decision to the burgomasters . . . not in order to subject the freedom and the rule of the church to the [political] authority, but only to warn and admonish [them] not to take offense at this election though it is a new and unseen thing."[4] The strategy worked, at least for the moment; the Delft burgomasters treated this declaration as a request to which they consented.[5]

[1] At that time there were about 180 members of the Reformed Church in Delft: H. J. Jaanus, *Hervormd Delft ten tijde van Arent Cornelisz. (1573–1605)* (Amsterdam, 1950), p. 33.
[2] J. C. Boogman, "De overgang van Gouda, Leiden, Dordrecht, en Delft in de zomer van 1572," *Tijdschrift voor Geschiedenis* 57 (1942), pp. 105–8.
[3] Jaanus, *Hervormd Delft*, pp. 94–100; Reinier Boitet, *Beschryving der stadt Delft* (Delft, 1729), p. 308; A. Ph. F. Wouters and P. H. A. M. Abels, *Nieuw en ongezien: kerk en samenleving in de classis Delft en Delfiland, 1572–1621*, 2 vols. (Delft, 1994), vol. I, p. 563.
[4] *GAD. Kerkeraad* (November 9, 1573).   [5] *Ibid.*

Though this turn of events represented a triumph for local Calvinists, the Delft burgomasters, like all magistrates in Holland, were not particularly given to "new and unseen things." On the contrary, contemporaries attached the greatest value to ancestral liberties, customary privileges, and historic traditions. Since 1559 Dutch regents had already seen enough new things to last them a lifetime. They had witnessed the revival of the dreaded inquisition hunting for heretics, the emergence of Calvinist evangelists preaching "hedge-sermons" to growing crowds, the wave of iconoclastic mobs plundering church property, the influx of Spanish military officials taking reprisals against local citizens, and the appearance of armies making demands on local governments.[6] And now, new Calvinist congregations in cities like Delft were asserting their independence.

Only to avoid more turmoil, the Delft burgomasters conceded a measure of jurisdiction over the ministries of the Reformed congregation to church officers. Yet they were careful to warn the consistory that it was not to meddle in any political affairs.[7] To be sure, this interchange was a slight episode compared to the tumultuous events that had engulfed Calvinists and civic leaders. But it was also an omen of the coming strife in the transition from a society closely associated with the Catholic Church to a Protestant republic. This new church, with its strident confessional demands, had just displaced an ancient faith in some very old cities. As a result, there would be many unseen things bringing conflict to the cities of Holland in the late sixteenth and early seventeenth centuries.

One of the issues that sheds light on this critical transition in Dutch history is the tension between municipal poor relief and Reformed charity in Holland. Focusing on the six "great cities" of Holland (Dordrecht, Haarlem, Delft, Leiden, Amsterdam, and Gouda),[8] this study uses poor relief to examine competing visions of Christian community that came into conflict as a result of the Dutch Revolt and Reformation. At issue was the relationship between the Reformed diaconate (the church college responsible for charity) and civic poor relief agencies. Calvinists intended to establish an independent diaconate whose primary priority would be to relieve the needs of poor church members. Opponents of Calvinism, however, expected church deacons to work under municipal authority and objected to favoring the church poor over everyone else. This broad struggle was not simply a "churchstate" conflict, for the respective factions were not consistently synonymous with membership in a particular governing body. Lay elders and deacons

---

[6] For general accounts of the Dutch Revolt, see Geoffrey Parker, *The Dutch Revolt* (Ithaca, 1977), and Pieter Geyl, *The Revolt of the Netherlands 1555–1609*, 2nd edn. (London, 1958).

[7] See *GAD. Kerkeraad* (November 9, 1573).

[8] This designation arose as the provincial States of Holland acquired greater formal authority in the late fifteenth and early sixteenth centuries. Due to their economic importance to the province, each of these six cities was allowed to cast one corporate vote on matters coming before the provincial assembly. Other small cities were also represented in the States, but the votes of the "great cities" and the single vote of the nobility were the only ones that really mattered: H. de Schepper, "De burgerlijke overheden en hun permanent kaders 1480–1579," in *NAGN*, vol. v, p. 324.

were often magistrates and many church officers came from the ranks of the social elite.[9]

Although "authority" assumed the prominent place in these deliberations, disputes over "authority" connoted a deeper disagreement over what actually constituted the Christian community during this momentous period in Dutch history. That is, quarrels over the borders between civil and ecclesiastical jurisdictions arose out of a more fundamental controversy about the very nature of society.[10] Despite the variety of local arrangements in these cities, this general struggle reveals the distinct blend of confessional identity and religious pluralism that characterized post-Reformation Holland.

Therefore, the interaction that took place between consistories and magistrates in these six cities from 1572 to 1620 is best understood as a protracted effort to reconcile disparate conceptions of community. Those antagonistic to the confessional features of diaconal charity attempted to coopt it within municipal welfare networks. To that end, they worked to exercise civil authority in the election of deacons, to oblige church officers to treat all recipients equally, and often to merge diaconates with municipal poor relief agencies. As the famous Synod of Dort adjourned in 1619, the struggles over poor relief organization came to a close in these six cities. Although the particular institutional settlements varied significantly, these negotiations reveal the

---

[9] G. Groenhuis, *De predikanten: de sociale positie van de gereformeerde predikanten in de Republiek der Vereenigde Nederlanden voor 1700* (Groningen, 1977), pp. 62–6; A. Th. van Deursen, *Bavianen en slijkgeuzen: kerk en kerkvolk ten tijde van Maurits en Oldenbarnevelt* (Assen, 1974), pp. 83–4.

[10] On a wide range of topics from poor relief, to popular festivals, to religious processions, to civil punishments, social historians have emphasized the religious underpinnings of civic society. Some of the important studies in this immense literature include Natalie Zemon Davis, "The reasons of misrule," in her *Society and Culture in Early Modern France* (Stanford, 1975), pp. 97–123; Davis, "The sacred and the body social in sixteenth-century Lyon," *Past and Present* 90 (1981), pp. 40–70; John Bossy, "The mass as a social institution, 1200–1700," *Past and Present* 92 (1983), pp. 29–60; Bossy, "Review article: holiness and society," *Past and Present* 75 (1977), pp. 119–37; Bossy, "Blood and baptism: kinship, community and Christianity in western Europe, fourteenth to the seventeenth century," in *Sanctity and Secularity: The Church and the World*, Derek Baker, ed. (Oxford, 1973), pp. 129–43; Pieter C. Spierenburg, *The Spectacle of Suffering: Executions and the Evolution of Repression from a Pre-industrial Metropolis to the European Experience* (Cambridge, 1984); R. W. Scribner, "Civic unity and the reformation in Erfurt," *Past and Present* 66 (1975), pp. 29–60; Scribner, "Ritual and popular religion in Catholic Germany at the time of the reformation," *Journal of Ecclesiastical History* 35 (1984), pp. 47–77; Peter Burke, *Popular Culture in Early Modern Europe* (New York, 1978). Furthermore, the links between communal values and religious practice have been a central theme in scholarship on the urban Reformation in the German territories. See Bernd Moeller, *The Imperial Cities and the Reformation: Three Essays*, H. C. Erik Midelfort and Mark U. Edwards, Jr., eds. (Durham, N.C., 1982); Thomas A. Brady, Jr., *Ruling Class, Regime and Reformation in Strasbourg 1520–1555* (Leiden, 1978); Heinz Schilling, "Calvinistische Presbyterien in Städten der Frühneuzeit: eine kirchliche Alternativeform zur bürgerlichen Repräsentation? (Mit eine quantifizierenden Untersuchung zur Holländischen Stadt Leiden)," in *Städtische Führungsgruppen und Gemeinde in der werdenden Neuzeit*, W. Ehbrecht, ed. (Cologne, 1980), pp. 385–444; Steven Ozment, *The Reformation in the Cities: The Appeal of Protestantism to Sixteenth-Century Germany and Switzerland* (New Haven, 1975); Kaspar van Greyerz, "Städt und Reformation: Stand und Aufgaben der Forschung," *Archiv für Reformationsgeschichte* 76 (1985), pp. 6–63; Pieter Blickle, *Gemeindereformation: die Menschen des 16. Jahrhunderts auf dem Weg zum Heil* (Munich, 1987).

process by which this leading province in the northern Netherlands acquired such an unusual character. It was both a decentralized republic heavily influenced by orthodox Calvinism, and a multi-confessional society that protected religious dissidents.

CIVIC CULTURE AND CONFESSIONALISM IN EUROPE AND HOLLAND

The struggles over poor relief not only reveal the dynamic interplay between confessional Calvinism and civic culture in Holland, but they also have implications for scholarship on religious culture and social welfare in early modern Europe. The case of Holland is instructive because common European patterns played themselves out in a unique way in this important province. Since negotiations over poor relief in Holland were directly related to confessional conflict, it is necessary first to examine how the prevailing trends of confessional formation in continental Europe manifested themselves in the northern Netherlands.

By the 1560s, as Calvinism was just beginning to make an appearance in the Low Countries, most other European states were undergoing a process of what historians now describe as "confessionalization."[11] According to this model, the three major religious traditions (Catholicism, Lutheranism, and Reformed Protestantism) had each already formulated their own respective statements of orthodoxy into explicit doctrinal creeds. Any possibilities of reconciliation or even conciliation among Catholics, Lutherans, and Calvinists were long past. After the Peace of Augsburg, the vigorous theological controversies of the early sixteenth century had ossified into a struggle for political dominance in Europe until the end of the Thirty Years War.

As rulers declared their allegiance to one of the three major creeds, they found that religious orthodoxy also squared nicely with political centralization. They promoted these dual aims by imposing social discipline on their subjects and by punishing non-conformity within territories under their authority. Although accompanied by destructive warfare, most notably in France and the Empire, confessionalization facilitated the rise of strong centralized states wedded to religious orthodoxy.

Confessional conflicts also left an indelible imprint on Holland, though they developed in an unusual fashion and the political effects they produced were very different from the rest of Europe.[12] Unlike other areas, Holland's cities actually

---

[11] For a survey of this literature and its implications for the Netherlands, see Benjamin J. Kaplan, *Calvinists and Libertines: Confession and Community in Utrecht 1578–1620* (Oxford, 1995), pp. 5–12.

[12] The older literature on what may be regarded as the Dutch equivalent to confessionalization has centered around how and to what the extent the Republic actually became Protestant. Pieter Geyl first posited the view that most Netherlanders did not embrace Calvinism willingly; rather, it was forced on them by social and economic pressure. The Catholic historian, L. J. Rogier, expanded upon Geyl's thesis by arguing that Calvinists used poor relief, public education, and political disenfranchisement to compel people to join the Reformed Church. According to Rogier, Calvinism was most successful in areas where Catholic parish ministries were weak and corrupt. Even then, it took the Reformed Church until 1650 before it could claim a majority membership: Geyl, *The Revolt of the Netherlands*, pp. 215–16; L. J. Rogier, *Geschiedenis van het katholicisme in de Noordelijke Nederlanden*

increased their political power at the expense of national and provincial authorities over the course of the sixteenth and seventeenth centuries. The major episode in this trend, the Revolt, was the Dutch response to the absolutist agenda of the Spanish crown and the religious discipline of the Counter-Reformation. Tensions mounted in 1559 when Phillip II's regency government (in Brussels) inaugurated a complete reorganization of the diocesan structure in the Low Countries. This "bishoprics scheme" expanded the number of dioceses from four to fourteen and dramatically increased the number of inquisitors in the provinces. There was little doubt that these inquisitorial offices would be filled by clerics who took Tridentine Catholicism to heart and who would wage an all-out war on heresy.[13] For the Dutch nobility and urban magistrates, both of whom showed little enthusiasm for confessional Catholicism, these measures violated the assortment of local privileges that they had gained over a long period of time.[14]

As a general rule, however, city governments in the province of Holland, despite strong anti-Spanish sentiment, were not in favor of rebellion. Outright defiance would lead to war, and war would threaten the free flow of river traffic upon which their economies depended. Magistrates despised the high-handedness of Spanish authorities, but this loathing did not translate into any passion for political insurrection or religious reformation.[15] It was primarily the Sea Beggars, led by William of Orange and supported by Calvinist activists, who were the major adversaries of Spanish authority. After six years of trouble including widespread iconoclasm, Spanish occupation, and harsh taxes Gouda, Dordrecht, Delft, and Leiden were forced under military pressure to join the side of the rebellious provinces in 1572.[16] Haarlem and Amsterdam came into the rebel orbit permanently in 1577 and 1578, respectively.[17]

After this transition (known to the Dutch as the *overgang*), magistrates in these cities proved that they would also resist any political encroachment from a stadholder, a provincial Estates, or a Calvinist synod. As a result of fierce local determination, the Revolt accelerated a process of oligarchization in the cities and contributed to a dominating municipal presence in the provincial Estates. This vital province exhibited the most decentralized provincial governance in northern Europe in the sixteenth and seventeenth centuries.

in de 16e en 17e eeuwen, 3 vols. (Amsterdam, 1945–7), vol. I, pp. 438–79. J. A. de Kok also endorsed Rogier's contention about poor relief in *Nederland op de breuklijn Rome-Reformatie* (Assen, 1964), pp. 63–88, 183–92. More recently, A. Th. van Deursen has suggested that the highly uneven regional growth of Calvinism and the meager resources of the church in most places would have severely limited any such ambitions: van Deursen, *Bavianen*, pp. 102–27. Current scholarship (cited in n. 24) tends to confirm van Deursen's doubts and focuses on the interplay between city governments and Calvinist consistories.

[13] Rogier, *Katholicisme*, vol. I, pp. 201–445; Kaplan, *Calvinists and Libertines*, pp. 8–11.

[14] See J. J. Woltjer, "Dutch privileges, real and imaginary," in *Britain and the Netherlands*, J. S. Bromley and E. H. Kossman, eds. (London, 1975), pp. 19–35.

[15] Jonathan I. Israel, *The Dutch Republic: Its Rise, Greatness, and Fall 1477–1806* (Oxford, 1995), p. 171.

[16] Boogman, "De overgang."   [17] Israel, *The Dutch Republic*, pp. 192–3.

Due to these fortuitous circumstances, the patricians who governed the cities of Holland had been able to avoid Catholic confessionalization and its centralizing proclivities. And they had become afraid that Calvinists were trying to do the same thing. The Estates of Holland and Zeeland rewarded Calvinists for their unwavering support by making the Reformed faith the public religion of the rebellious provinces in 1572. Due to resistance from municipal delegates to the States, this Calvinist Church never acquired the status of a formal state church. The States of Holland and Zeeland designated the Reformed Church as the "privileged" ecclesiastical institution. City governments paid the salaries of ministers and Reformed worship services were held in the parish churches. But church membership was strictly voluntary and the former properties of the Catholic Church (parish and monastic) came under the control of civil authorities.[18] Thus, citizenship or residency in civil society was not synonymous with church membership in a Reformed eucharistic community. Furthermore, the closed oligarchies that governed the cities of Holland sought to expand their political power and to keep a close check on the affairs of local Reformed churches.[19]

Thus, confessional conflict in Holland had a unique Dutch flavor that pitted the particularistic and pluralistic policies of urban magistrates against the confessional ambitions of Calvinist leaders. As a result of these historical conditions, the tension between what scholars have called the sectarian tendencies and the public character of the Calvinist Churches of the Dutch Republic came into open conflict from 1572 to the 1618–19 Synod of Dort.[20] During this phase of the Dutch Reformation, there was widespread disagreement and considerable negotiation over the place of the new church in civil society. Many city magistrates found common cause with a small, but vocal cadre of ministers who opposed the confessional character of the Dutch Reformed Church. This "Libertine" faction in Holland considered the church a public church for all people. These opponents of Calvinism made it clear that magistrates, as the "Christian authority," should govern church affairs. From this standpoint, the confessional demands of Calvinism smacked of an ecclesiastical tyranny that Netherlanders had only recently overthrown.[21] Consequently, Libertines worked to undermine an independent

---

[18] A. Th. van Deursen, "Kerk of parochie? De kerkmeesters en de dood tijdens de Republiek," *Tijdschrift voor Geschiedenis* 89 (1976), pp. 531–5. Numerically, the Reformed church grew very slowly and claimed only about 20 percent of the population by 1620: J. J. Woltjer, "De plaats van de calvinisten in de Nederlandse samenleving," *Zeventiende Eeuw* 10 (1994), p. 16; Fred A. van Lieburg, "From pure church to pious culture: the further reformation in the seventeenth-century Dutch Republic," in *Later Calvinism: International Perspectives*, Fred W. Graham, ed. (Kirksville, Mo., 1994), p. 412.

[19] James D. Tracy, "The Calvinist church of the Dutch Republic, 1572–1618/19," in *Reformation Europe: A Guide to Research* II, William S. Maltby, ed. (St. Louis, 1992), pp. 261–2.

[20] Alastair Duke, "The ambivalent face of Calvinism in the Netherlands, 1561–1618," in *International Calvinism 1541–1715*, Menna Prestwich, ed. (Oxford, 1985), pp. 112–13; van Deursen, *Bavianen*, pp. 13–33.

[21] Benjamin J. Kaplan, "'Remnants of the papal yoke': apathy and opposition in the Dutch Reformation," *Sixteenth-Century Journal* 25 (1994), pp. 659–62.

ecclesiastical structure (such as synods and classes), eliminate church discipline, and subdue an independent diaconate (the church college responsible for poor relief).[22]

Calvinists, the dominant force in the Dutch Reformed Church since the early 1570s, understood their church to be a pure eucharistic community and thus attempted to regulate access to communion, discipline wayward members, and superintend an independent diaconate. The neglect of these ministries would compromise the integrity of biblical religion and invite the wrath of God. With a different understanding of "Christian authority," Calvinists enjoined magistrates to support the church's ministries and combat heterodoxy without interfering in their internal religious affairs.

From the establishment of the Reformed Church in 1572 until 1619, the provincial Estates and the Reformed leadership attempted to settle many issues relating to the borders between temporal and ecclesiastical authority. Matters such as public worship, administration of church property, marriage, and baptism were negotiated on a national or provincial level. The reorganization of charitable institutions, though, was one issue that higher authorities left for local city magistrates and consistorial authorities to resolve. As such, the topic of poor relief provides a prism to examine the attempts to reconcile a civic vision of Christian community with a eucharistic one in the chief cities of the province.

POOR RELIEF IN EUROPE AND HOLLAND

Thus far, studies on Dutch charitable institutions have had little impact on poor relief scholarship from the late middle ages to the seventeenth century. Perhaps this lack of influence is a result of the considerable shortage of non-Dutch scholarship on poor relief in Holland. Beyond Simon Schama's treatment of charity in his cultural exposé of the Dutch Golden Age and A. Th. van Deursen's recently translated description of popular culture in the seventeenth century, there has been no extensive treatment of poor relief in Holland in the English language.[23] While charitable institutions in Holland have made cameo appearances in a variety of Dutch studies, there has been no comparative monograph on poor relief in Holland in any language.[24] This void is

---

[22] "Libertine" was a general pejorative used by orthodox Reformers for a variety of people and groups who opposed consistorial discipline: Kaplan, *Calvinists and Libertines*, p. 14.
[23] Simon Schama, *The Embarrassment of Riches: An Interpretation of Dutch Culture in the Golden Age* (Berkeley, 1978), pp. 14–24, 174–5, 570–87; A. Th. van Deursen, *Plain Lives in a Golden Age: Popular Culture, Religion and Society in Seventeenth-Century Holland*, Maarten Ultee, trans. (Cambridge, 1991), pp. 44–66. See also Sheila D. Muller, *Charity in the Dutch Republic: Pictures of Rich and Poor for Charitable Institutions* (Ann Arbor, Mich., 1985).
[24] Dutch scholarship on poor relief has been limited to individual cities. See Christina Ligtenberg, *Armezorg te Leiden tot het einde van de 16e eeuw* ('s-Gravenhage, 1908); Ch. A. van Manen, *Armenpflege in Amsterdam in ihrer historischen Entwicklung* (Leiden, 1913); Joke Spaans, *Haarlem na de reformatie: stedelijke cultuur en kerkelijk leven, 1577–1620* ('s-Gravenhage, 1989), pp. 163–89; John P. Elliott, "Protestantization in the Northern Netherlands, a case study: the classis of Dordrecht, 1572–1640,"

curious, since the Dutch have been on the cutting edge of welfare policy for the past three hundred years.

What the immense scholarship on poverty and charity in Europe has done quite effectively is to outline the institutional development and spread of poor relief reform over the course of the sixteenth century.[25] The movement to reorganize charitable institutions was initially an urban phenomenon that built on a number of reforms in the fourteenth and fifteenth centuries.[26] Sparked by rising levels of poverty and disenchantment with traditional forms of charity, a number of Protestant cities in the Empire, as well as Catholic cities in the southern Low Countries and Italy (Venice), began to establish a comprehensive network of poor relief in the 1520s.[27] The key features of this program included eliminating begging, consolidating all parish foundations under the authority of a municipal agency, laicizing charitable institutions, and creating public works projects. Inherent in this system was a more rigid classification of the poor that corresponded to institutional relief categories. Civil officers offered relief to the "deserving" domiciled poor, and housed the sick, the aged, and orphans in specific institutions, while they banned "undeserving" vagrants and unskilled non-residents from their cities.[28] In 1534 the city government of Lyons established an *aumône générale* (general almshouse) that became the prototype for centralized municipal poor relief in sixteenth-century Europe.[29] By the end of the

Ph.D. thesis, Columbia University (1989), pp. 345–417; R. B. Evenhius, *Ook dat was Amsterdam: de kerk de hervorming in de gouden eeuw*, 5 vols. (Amsterdam, 1965–71), vol. I, pp. 100–6, vol. II, pp. 73–8; H. ten Boom, "De diaconie der gereformeerde kerk te Tiel van 1578–1795," *Nederlands Archief voor Kerkgeschiedenis NS* 55 (1975), pp. 32–69; ten Boom, *De reformatie in Rotterdam 1530–1585* ('s-Gravenhage, 1987), pp. 25–38, 65–8, 198–202; C. A. Tukker, *De classis van Dordrecht van 1573 tot 1609: bijdrage tot de kennis van in- en extern leven van de gereformeerde kerk in de periode van haar organisiering* (Leiden, 1965), pp. 78–86, 181–2; Wouters and Abels, *Nieuw en ongezien*, vol. I, pp. 311–417, vol. II, pp. 203–88. A. Th. van Deursen's *Bavianen* pointed out the diversity of welfare arrangements between local magistrates and Reformed church officers (see pp. 102–26). Despite the value of this excellent study, van Deursen concentrated primarily on developments with the Calvinist church and not their municipal contexts.

25 See Jean-Pierre Gutton, *La Société et les pauvres en Europe (XVIe–XVIIIe siècles)* (Paris, 1974), pp. 104–6; J. Nolf, *La Réforme de la bienfaisance publique à Ypres au XVIe siècle* (Ghent, 1915), pp. xl–xliii; P. Bonenfant, "Les Origines et le charactère de la réforme de la bienfaisance publique aux Pays-Bas sous le règne de Charles-Quint," *Revue Belgique de philologie et d'histoire* 6 (1927), pp. 219–20, 225–6; F. R. Salter, ed., *Some Early Tracts on Poor Relief* (London, 1926), pp. 6–22.

26 Brian Pullan, *Rich and Poor in Renaissance Venice: The Social Institutions of a Catholic State* (Cambridge, 1971), pp. 198–215; Brian Tierney, *Medieval Poor Law: A Sketch of Canonical Theory and Its Application in England* (Berkeley, 1959), pp. 131–2. Robert Jütte (in *Poverty and Deviance in Early Modern Europe* [Cambridge, 1994], p. 102), on the other hand, has concentrated on the "new bureaucratic spirit" of the sixteenth century and thus has viewed these changes as a watershed in the history of social welfare.

27 See nn. 25 and 26, as well as Carter Lindberg's *Beyond Charity: Reformation Initiatives for the Poor* (Minneapolis, 1993), pp. 128–60.

28 Jütte, *Poverty and Deviance*, pp. 143–50.

29 Natalie Zemon Davis, "Humanism, heresy, and poor relief in sixteenth-century Lyon," in Davis, *Society and Culture*, pp. 17–64. See also Jean-Pierre Gutton, *La Société et les pauvres: l'exemple de la généralité de Lyon, 1534–1789* (Paris, 1971); R. Gascon, "Economie et pauvreté aux XVI et XVII siècles: Lyon exemplaire et prophétique," *Études sur l'histoire de la pauvreté*, M. Mollat, ed. (Paris, 1974), pp. 747–60.

century, most cities in Europe either had completely reorganized parish charity along these lines or had adopted many of these principles.[30]

If there is a general consensus over the components of this reform movement, there has been much disagreement over its causes. Until the late nineteenth century, the dominant and largely unchallenged view was that the Lutheran Reformation was the most important driving force behind welfare reorganization. Reform certainly coincided with Reformation in Wittenberg, Nuremburg, Augsburg, and other Protestant cities. And Martin Luther himself denounced the salvific motivations of Catholic charity, criticized clerical corruption in religious foundations, and condemned begging. Luther went beyond simply promoting poor relief reform; he also assisted magistrates in Wittenberg and Leisnig in drafting reform ordinances in 1519 and 1523, respectively. From this standpoint, poor relief reform illustrated a Protestant social vision that diverged sharply from the self-serving charitable institutions of medieval Catholicism.[31]

In the 1880s, two Catholic historians, Georg Ratzinger and Franz Ehrle, challenged the Lutheran claims to originality and the negative stereotypes this view imposed on Catholic charity. In particular, they argued that Catholic magistrates in Nuremburg and Ypres had already begun poor relief reform before the advent of Protestantism.[32] This challenge set off a protracted and often polemical exchange among Lutheran and Catholic historians over where reform occurred first and its relationship to Protestantism and Christian humanism.[33] Writing in the 1920s, the Catholic historian Paul Bonenfant conceded that reform took place first in the

---

[30] This does not mean, though, that decentralized forms of poor relief became extinct at the end of the sixteenth century. In Catholic countries, confraternal charity existed well into the eighteenth century. And during the Counter-Reformation, private religious foundations even made a comeback. In most areas these religious institutions either worked alongside centralized municipal agencies, cooperated with them, or took over the entire range of parish poor relief. For an excellent summary of the literature on Counter-Reformation charity, see Jütte, *Poverty and Deviance*, pp. 125–39.

[31] See Otto Winckelmann, "Über die ältesten Armenordnung der Reformationszeit," *Historische Vierteljahrschrift* 17 (1914/15), pp. 361–440; Ernst Troeltsch, *The Social Teaching of the Christian Churches*, 2 vols., 2nd edn., Olive Wyon, trans. (New York, 1960), vol. I, pp. 133–8. For this approach in later twentieth-century historiography, see Harold Grimm, "Luther's contributions to sixteenth-century organization of poor relief," *Archiv für Reformationsgeschichte* 61 (1970), pp. 222–34; Carter Lindberg, "'There should be no beggars among Christians': Karlstadt, Luther, and the origins of Protestant poor relief," *Church History* 46 (1977), pp. 313–34; Lindberg, "The liturgy after the liturgy: welfare in the early reformation," in *Through the Eye of a Needle: Judeo-Christian Roots of Social Welfare*, Emily Albu Hanawalt and Carter Lindberg, eds. (Kirksville, Mo., 1994), pp. 177–91.

[32] Franz Ehrle, *Beiträge zur Geschichte und Reform der Armenpflege* (1881); Ehrle, "Die Armenordnungen von Nürnberg (1522) und von Ypern (1525)," *Historische Jahrbuch* 9 (1888), pp. 450–79; Georg Ratzinger, *Geschichte der Armenpflege*, 2nd edn. (Freiburg-im-Breisgau, 1884).

[33] Most scholars continue to acknowledge the humanitarian values of northern humanism as an important factor in the promotion of reformed poor relief, even if their articulated programs were subsequent to the creation of the new institutions: Henri Pirenne, *Histoire de Belgique*, 3 vols., 2nd edn. (Brussels, 1912), vol. III, pp. 288–90; Winckelmann, "Armenordnungen," pp. 376–84. See also Geoffrey Elton, "An early Tudor poor law," *Economic History Review*, 2nd series, 6 (1953), pp. 55–7. A very good discussion of this debate (which informed the outline of this paragraph) can be found in Elsie Ann McKee, *John Calvin on the Diaconate and Liturgical Almsgiving* (Geneva, 1984), pp. 94–106.

Lutheran city of Nuremburg, but he argued that Catholic magistrates in Ypres did not recognize anything Lutheran in the Nuremburg reforms.[34]

More recent research in the twentieth century has effectively demolished the nineteenth-century Lutheran model. Originally published in 1968, Natalie Zemon Davis's seminal study of the *aumône générale* in Lyons exposed the common social concerns that motivated both Protestants and Catholics to work together in establishing a new centralized relief system there.[35] Noting that Lyons was not an isolated example, Davis concluded that changes in the structure of charity "did not break along religious lines."[36] Rather, "The context for welfare reform . . . was urban crisis, brought about by a conjuncture of older problems of poverty with population growth and economic expansion."[37] Appearing three years later, Brian Pullan's *Rich and Poor in Renaissance Venice* demonstrated that many components of the relief programs of the 1520s and 1530s had been implemented as early as the fourteenth and fifteenth centuries.[38] Legislation against vagrancy and the establishment of centralized charitable hospitals emerged in England and northern Italy long before the Reformation. Even as early as the twelfth century, canonists cautioned benefactors against giving charity indiscriminately. Consequently, many of the cardinal principles within late medieval Catholic charity established precedents for sixteenth-century welfare.[39] While Pullan attributed the impetus for the new 1525 poor law in Venice to influences from other cities, some of which were Lutheran, he concluded, "It is, however, doubtful how far such schemes ought to be identified with Lutheranism."[40] Conversely, he stressed the gradual evolution of sixteenth-century reform and argued that there were few practical differences in charitable institutions in Protestant and Catholic lands.[41] Furthermore, the studies of Linda Martz and Maureen Flynn have shown that poor relief reform came to Spain, which was largely untouched by the Reformation.[42] Even though Protestantism was not the sole cause of the new social welfare ordinances, there is general agreement today among most scholars that Protestantism provided a strong impetus for reform, especially in centralizing relief under civil administration. In Holland, however,

---

[34] Bonenfant, "Origines," 6 (1927), pp. 216, 220–3.

[35] Davis, "Poor relief," p. 58. In *Beyond Charity*, pp. 68–172, Carter Lindberg has recently reasserted the argument for the central importance of Lutheran theology in the origins of poor relief reform. With respect to the debate over Protestantism and poor relief reform, however, Lindberg's argument simply reiterates the older Lutheran perspective.

[36] Davis, "Poor relief," p. 60. [37] *Ibid.*, p. 59. [38] Pullan, *Rich and Poor*, p. 198.

[39] *Ibid.*, pp. 198–202.

[40] *Ibid.*, p. 255. Two other excellent monographs on poor relief in Italy are Sandra Cavallo, *Charity and Power in Early Modern Italy: Benefactors and Their Motives in Turin, 1541–1789* (Cambridge, 1995), and Philip R. Gavitt, *The Ospedale degli Innocenti, 1410–1536* (Ann Arbor, Mich., 1990).

[41] Pullan, *Rich and Poor*, pp. 11–12, 104, 197. Pullan does note that Catholic charity continued to concern itself with the salvation of benefactor and recipient: Brian Pullan, "Catholics and the poor in early modern Europe," *Transactions of the Royal Historical Society*, series 5, 26 (1976), pp. 25–30.

[42] Linda Martz, *Poverty and Welfare in Hapsburg Spain: The Example of Toledo* (Cambridge, 1983), pp. 61–158; Maureen Flynn, *Sacred Charity: Confraternities and Social Welfare in Spain, 1400–1700* (Ithaca, 1989), pp. 75–141.

Dutch Calvinists resisted civil control over all forms of poor relief. The hostile milieu in which Calvinist congregations found themselves in the 1560s had forced them to develop cohesive communities dependent on mutual support. As a result, inherently confessional views of community informed charitable activity in these congregations. These perspectives were filtered through the experiences and contacts of Dutch Reformers in the refugee churches of Emden and London. As exiled leaders returned to Holland and members came out of hiding, they attempted to implant these ministries into cities that had a strong tradition of magisterial involvement in social welfare.

If twentieth-century scholarship has undermined the singular contribution of Lutheranism to the origins of poor relief reform, it was Davis's analysis of the *aumône générale* in Lyons and Pullan's work on Venetian charitable institutions that laid the basis for a new research agenda on sixteenth-century welfare. Since the 1970s a substantial number of articles, monographs, and surveys have examined economic conditions in sixteenth-century Europe, investigated the desperate conditions of the poor, analyzed the institutional forms of welfare, and explored the contacts between rich and poor.[43] While these studies have treated a wide range of overlapping issues, they have been framed in three general historiographical traditions.

On the macro-historical level, scholars interested in the transition from feudalism to capitalism regard sixteenth-century welfare as an instrument to accommodate the needs of a nascent capitalist economy.[44] In his masterful survey of civilization and capitalism, Fernand Braudel blamed structural changes in the European economy for the widespread underemployment that pushed many into pauperism. Welfare functioned merely to supplement the meager wages of residents who could work, while anti-begging legislation had as its goal driving out non-residents or punishing them for being unemployed. For Braudel, these measures created a new form of slavery that merchant capitalism bequeathed to early modern Europe.[45]

---

[43] For a useful bibliography of this literature, see Jütte, *Poverty and Deviance*, pp. 217–28.

[44] For example, see Fernand Braudel, *Civilization and Capitalism, Fifteenth–Eighteenth Century*, 3 vols., Sian Reynolds, trans. (New York, 1981), vol. II, pp. 506–11; Immanuel Wallerstein, *The Modern World-System I: Capitalist Agriculture and the Origins of the European World-Economy in the Sixteenth Century* (New York, 1974), pp. 254–5; Catharina Lis and Hugo Soly, *Poverty and Capitalism in Pre-Industrial Europe* (Atlantic Highlands, N.J., 1979); H. Soly, "Economische ontwikkeling en sociale politiek in Europa tijdens de overgang van middeleeuwen naar nieuwe tijden," *Tijdschrift voor Geschiedenis* 88 (1975), pp. 584–97; R. H. Tawney, *Religion and the Rise of Capitalism* (New York, 1926), pp. 262–4. With a distinctly different aim, Eric Jones has contended that social welfare policy was one of the unique features that distinguished Europe from the rest of the world: Eric L. Jones, *The European Miracle: Environments, Economies, and Geopolitics in the History of Europe and Asia*, 2nd edn. (Cambridge, 1987), p. xiii.

[45] Braudel, *Civilization and Capitalism*, vol. II, pp. 506–11; also, Immanuel Wallerstein in *Modern World-System*, p. 254, quotes G. N. Clark, *The Wealth of England from 1496 to 1760* (London, 1946), pp. 84–6, to assert that the English poor laws were designed to provide an adequate supply of labor, to steady the class structure, and to stabilize the location of industry.

Perhaps the most forceful representatives of this approach in recent European historiography are Catharina Lis and Hugo Soly. Guided by Braudel's structuralism and by a neo-Marxist perspective, Lis and Soly have provided the most forceful argument that the labor market shaped poor relief in pre-industrial Europe.[46] In their synthesis of pre-industrial poverty and capitalism, they took issue with the "deterministic character" of neo-Malthusian models. They replaced it with a determinism of their own: class formation. In their view, "poverty can be fully understood only as the consequence of an established structure of surplus-extractive relations."[47] With regard to early modern poor relief, they argued that "a social policy was brought into being with two dominant functions: control of the relatively superfluous population and regulation of the labor market."[48] According to Lis and Soly, capitalism required a different method of dealing with poverty in order to sustain a low-wage labor supply, to promote production, and to ensure social stability.[49]

The value of this approach has been to link poor relief reform to complex economic problems in a broadly comparative way. The spread of new welfare policies, however, did not always correspond to the formation of a large-scale market economy. Poor relief reform took root in areas of Spain that lagged behind northern Europe in the extensive formation of a capitalist economy. Disputes over details aside, the various forms of this argument collapse the assorted cultural influences on charity in the diverse communities of western Europe into a bourgeois drive for greater productivity. In addition, they assume consistent strife between rich and poor, even though such antagonism was not normative. In Holland, economic hardship certainly compelled magistrates to take stronger measures to deal with poverty, but they did so out of a religious framework that constrained their range of alternatives. In addition, many of the elements of sixteenth-century welfare occurred gradually over the course of the fourteenth and fifteenth centuries, long before any part of Europe had a rationalized labor market. These cities were economic entities under patrician rule, and elites promoted the ideal that the municipality was an organic Christian community bound together by mutual concerns for salvation and prosperity.

Enveloped within this cultural ethos, poor relief in the cities of Holland conformed to the ideal that all inhabitants of the city were bound together in a sacred

---

[46] A similar argument for public welfare in the United States was made several years earlier by Frances Fox Piven and Richard A. Cloward in *Regulating the Poor: The Functions of Public Welfare* (New York, 1971). Interestingly, their brief treatment of the sixteenth century (pp. 9–16) was based to a large extent on Natalie Davis' study of the *aumône générale*. I would like to thank Donald T. Critchlow for bringing the former work to my attention.

[47] Lis and Soly, *Poverty and Capitalism*, pp. xii, 215. Three of the most able advocates of these neo-Malthusian models were M. M. Postan, *Essays on Medieval Agriculture and General Problems of the Medieval Economy* (Cambridge, 1973); Wilhelm Abel, *Massenarmut und Hungerkrisen im vorindustriellen Europa: Versuch einer Synopsis* (Berlin, 1974); and Emmanuel Le Roy Ladurie, *The Peasants of Languedoc*, John Day, trans. (Urbana, Ill., 1974).

[48] Lis and Soly, *Poverty and Capitalism*, p. 220.   [49] *Ibid.*, p. 221.

and civic community under the authority of the magistracy. The communal character of poor relief in Holland grew out of the medieval church's understanding of poverty and charity. Yet the administration of poor relief was not the primary prerogative of ecclesiastical leaders. For, as early as the fourteenth century, magistrates in these cities assumed fundamental control over parish poor relief and even exercised a strong role in monastic charity. Concerned with the economic welfare of the city, magistrates regarded charity to be a civic responsibility and a religious duty within the cultural framework of medieval Christianity.[50]

A second trend in scholarship on early modern poor relief has focused specifically on the social control mechanisms in welfare legislation. A central feature of early modern social history was the drive by political and church authorities to create a well-ordered society. This concern for order demanded greater control over religious doctrine, family life, social interaction, and sexual relations. Disciplining the common folk cut across confessional lines, as Protestant and Catholic leaders waged an extensive war on popular culture in their lands. According to Philip Hoffman, both Reformations promoted "a harsh new ethic that extolled modesty, thrift, diligence, and self-control."[51] Gerhard Oestreich connected this disciplining effort to the rise of absolutism, fortified by Neostoicism and Calvinism. Consequently, "the result was the enhancement of social discipline in all forms of life."[52] For their own religious reasons, Calvinist ministers throughout Europe also participated in this broad pattern of social control, as they attempted to regulate the morals of the rank-and-file membership.[53] The success of Reformed discipline has

---

[50] Adriaan H. Bredero, *Christenheid en christendom in de middeleeuwen: over de verhouding van godsdienst, kerk, en samenleving*, 2nd edn. (Kampen, 1987), p. 277; Abel Athouguia Alves, "The Christian social organism and social welfare: the case of Vivès, Calvin, and Loyola," *Sixteenth-Century Journal* 20 (1989), pp. 5–7.

[51] Philip Hoffman, *Church and Community in the Diocese of Lyon, 1500–1789* (New Haven, 1984), p. 2. See also Robert Muchembled, *Culture populaire et culture des elites* (Paris, 1978); Jean Delumeau, *Le Catholicisme entre Luther et Voltaire* (Paris, 1971); James R. Farr, "The pure and disciplined body: hierarchy, morality, and symbolism in France during the Catholic reformation," *Journal of Interdisciplinary History* 21 (1991), pp. 391–414.

[52] Gerhard Oestreich, *Neostoicism and the Early Modern State*, Brigitta Oestreich and H. G. Koenigsburger, eds., David McLintock, trans. (Cambridge, 1982), p. 7.

[53] Heinz Schilling's work on discipline in Emden should caution scholars against assuming that civic and religious authorities pursued the same agenda. His quantitative study of the Calvinist discipline demonstrates the distinction between punitive state discipline of crime and the Calvinist discipline of sin: Heinz Schilling, "'History of crime' or 'history of sin'? Some reflections on the social history of modern church discipline," in *Politics and Society in Reformation Europe: Essays for Sir Geoffrey Elton on His Sixty-fifth Birthday*, E. I. Kouri and Tom Scott, eds. (London, 1987), pp. 289–310. Other important studies of Calvinist discipline include: Robert M. Kingdon, "The control of morals in Calvin's Geneva," in *The Social History of the Reformation*, L. P. Buck and J. W. Zophy, eds. (Columbus, Ohio, 1972), pp. 3–16; Kingdon, "The control of morals by the earliest Calvinists," in *Renaissance, Reformation, Resurgence*, Peter de Klerk, ed. (Grand Rapids, Mich., 1976), pp. 95–106; François Méjan, *Discipline de l'Eglise Réformée de France annotée et précédée d'une introduction historique* (Paris, 1947); Janine Estèbe and Bernard Vogler, "La Genèse d'une société protestante: étude comparée de quelques registres consistoraux languedociens et palatins vers 1600," *Annales ESC* 31 (1976), pp. 362–88; R. Po-Chia Hsia, *Social Discipline in the Reformation: Central Europe 1550–1750* (New York, 1989), pp. 124–6.

led Heinz Schilling to conclude that Calvinism contributed to the "formation of a modern mind."[54]

Influenced by studies on criminology and Michel Foucault's model of the "Great Confinement," many scholars taking this line of inquiry understand early modern social welfare policy to be a part of an overarching program to acculturate the poor to bourgeois cultural standards.[55] According to Foucault, the institutions of correction which arose between the seventeenth and the nineteenth centuries had as their goal the confinement of social deviants from the rest of society. The guiding principle behind confinement was the union of knowledge and power. Elites used their power to incarcerate degenerates so that they would learn the discipline of work, their antidote for most social ills.[56] Thus, Foucault interpreted social welfare policies, whether punitive or affirmative, as the implementation of bourgeois discipline onto the poor who were, by this definition, socially deviant.

Based on Foucault's concepts of power, knowledge, and classification, social historians have shown how city governments responded to social instability by reasserting their authority over the poor, by stigmatizing moral deviance, and by repressing non-productive survival strategies.[57] Civil ordinances provided assistance and some training to the "deserving" poor, but they criminalized idle folk, non-residents, vagrants, and beggars in order to isolate them from the local community. Thus, the social discipline approach to early modern welfare emphasizes the vertical power relationship between authorities and marginal folk, the renewed elite demand for moral order, and the classification of the poor into distinct categories.

These studies clearly demonstrate that elites were often more concerned with social stability than social welfare and that the poor could expect greater control over their lives as a result of poor relief reforms. Again, the situation in Holland presents a somewhat different scenario: discipline was not simply a vertical power relationship. Since membership in the Reformed Church was voluntary, those who chose to become members accepted the demands of ecclesiastical discipline, at least in principle. Known as *liefhebbers* (sympathizers), many people chose to attend worship services and to participate to varying degrees in church life without ever becoming church members. Everyone in a city was welcome to frequent church

---

[54] Heinz Schilling, *Civic Calvinism in Northwestern Germany and the Netherlands, Sixteenth to Nineteenth Centuries* (Kirksville, Mo., 1991), p. 40.

[55] For a few examples, see Donna T. Andrew, *Philanthropy and Police: London Charity in the Eighteenth Century* (Princeton, 1989); Robert Jütte, "Poor relief and social discipline in sixteenth-century Europe," *European Studies Review* 11 (1981), pp. 25–52; H. C. M. Michielse, "Policing the poor: Juan Luis Vivès and the sixteenth-century origins of modern social welfare administration," *Social Service Review* 64 (1990), pp. 1–21; Robert Schwartz, *Policing the Poor in Eighteenth-Century France* (Chapel Hill, N.C.,1988); Spierenburg, *Spectacle of Suffering*.

[56] See Michel Foucault, *Madness and Civilization: A History of Insanity in the Age of Reason*, Richard Howard, trans. (New York, 1965), pp. 38–64; and Foucault, *Discipline and Punish: The Birth of the Prison*, Alan Sheridan, trans. (New York, 1977).

[57] Jütte, *Poverty and Deviance*, pp. 158–77.

services, but the communion table was reserved exclusively for those who met the rigorous requirements of religious discipline. Herman Roodenburg's study of discipline in Amsterdam has shown that members were all too familiar with the activities of their Reformed neighbors and were more than happy to inform the consistory of any suspicious activity.[58] Poor relief recipients who committed misdeeds could forfeit their place on the deacons' register, but even these most vulnerable folk exerted a strong degree of agency. Just as church officers conditioned assistance on the basis of future behavior, recipients themselves conditioned behavior on the basis of future assistance. Disciplining poor folk in Holland, therefore, was a negotiated process in which both the consistory and poor relief recipients attempted to manipulate diaconal charity for their own ends.

Both of these two historiographic traditions (economic instrumentality and social discipline) share the basic assumption that the reforms of the sixteenth century introduced a dichotomy between religious charity and civic welfare. For example, W. K. Jordan has claimed that the motivation for philanthropy became more social than spiritual. Analyzing over 50,000 English wills, he argued that charitable bequests for the poor supplanted pious bequests for the repose of one's soul, which for Jordan indicated that English society became more concerned with social problems in this world than with spiritual anxieties in the afterlife.[59] Institutional studies of poor relief underscore this pattern. As governments, especially in Protestant areas, developed a sense of social responsibility, they established rational (i.e., non-religious) systems of provision. According to Robert Jütte, it was the Protestant Reformation that "paved the way for the development of a new social policy which favoured secular systems of poor relief."[60]

Consequently, according to this model, public assistance prevailed over religious charity, which ultimately led to all sorts of experiments to deal with poverty. From the seventeenth through the nineteenth centuries, workhouses, asylums, and prisons confined the "undeserving" poor, while proscriptive laws and workfare programs attempted to force people to work. In the twentieth century, national governments became the custodians of the poor through massive welfare programs the future of which, these days, is in doubt.

This model is problematic because a strict dichotomy between public assistance and private charity is far too simplistic, certainly for the sixteenth and seventeenth centuries. It also neglects the important contributions that private and religious enterprises have made in early modern social welfare policy. A third historiographical trend is now beginning to call this dichotomy into question by exploring the interaction between religious charity and public assistance. Kathryn Norberg, in

---

[58] Herman Roodenburg, *Onder censuur: de kerkelijke tucht in de gereformeerde gemeente van Amsterdam, 1578–1700* (Hilversum, 1990), pp. 350–69.

[59] W. K. Jordan, *Philanthropy in England 1480–1660: A Study of the Changing Pattern of English Social Aspirations* (London, 1959), p. 15.

[60] Jütte, *Poverty and Deviance*, p. 108.

her wide-ranging study of poverty and charity in Grenoble from 1600 to 1814, shows how a variety of Catholic charitable organizations reflected a Counter-Reformation spirituality throughout the seventeenth century.[61] Two female con-fraternities, the Order of Madeline and the Order of Orphans, perpetuated the medieval sacral understanding of poverty and their members performed pious works for the poor as part of their strict moral and religious code. The Company of the Holy Sacrament contributed to this sense of religiosity by rigorously imposing a moral order onto the poor.[62] Thus, Norberg's study indicates how the religious outlook and social vision of elites in Counter-Reformation Grenoble influenced their treatment of the needy.

Taking a similar approach in her study of charity in Zamora, Maureen Flynn also revealed the continuing vitality of sacral ideals in confraternal charity up to the middle of the eighteenth century. Flynn argued that the "sacredness of charity" underlay all the activities of Zamoran confraternities. As elsewhere in Catholic Europe, the charitable works of these organizations were a collective attempt to aid in the salvation of members, both alive and deceased. The ritual enactment of charity constructed the social order in Zamora by defining relationships between individuals at different social levels. Given the vigor of these confraternities, it is no wonder that centralized programs of poor relief did not take hold in Zamora.[63] Situated in a very different religious milieu, Lee Wandel's study of poor relief in Reformation Zurich shows that the treatment of the poor helped define the basis of a new Protestant Christian community. The poor were visible images of Christ's mercy, and charitable giving dramatized how a Reformed society practiced brotherly love.[64] In a period characterized by the emergence of capitalism and social discipline, religious understandings of order and community continued to be guiding principles in the form of charitable organizations.

Scholars of modern social welfare history are also calling attention to the importance of religious charity. Anthony Brundage has recently explained that religious charities worked at the local level to mitigate the harsh effects of the 1834 Poor Law in Victorian England. As for welfare in the United States, Dorothy M. Brown and Elizabeth McKeown have pointed out that local Catholic leaders have collaborated with public welfare organizations and have integrated their religious foundations into state-sponsored welfare programs since the nineteenth century. Currently, Catholic Charities receives 40 percent of its budget from the United

[61] Cissie Fairchilds has also noted that, even though poor relief institutions in Aix-en-Provence followed the 1534 Lyonnais program, the impulses for charity continued to be religious in nature. Thus, a Counter-Reformation social vision was the ideological component of charity in Aix. See Cissie C. Fairchilds, *Poverty and Charity in Aix-en-Provence, 1640–1789* (Baltimore, 1976), pp. 18–37.
[62] Kathryn Norberg, *Rich and Poor in Grenoble, 1600–1814* (Berkeley, 1985), pp. 20–59.
[63] Flynn, *Sacred Charity*, pp. 44–114.
[64] Lee Palmer Wandel, *Always Among Us: Images of the Poor in Zwingli's Zurich* (Cambridge, 1991), pp. 170–3.

States government.[65] Religious charity has been more than a passing phase in the historical development of social welfare.

These excellent studies are but a few examples of a growing recognition of the strong communal dynamic of charity in early modern and modern times. This study of Holland attempts to show that religious charity remained an integral part of municipal poor relief in a period in which social provision supposedly became increasingly secular. Calvinist deacons collaborated with or worked under the authority of municipal almoners (sometimes not very happily) to care for the poor. The Dutch case calls attention to the complex relationship between civic culture and religious life which ordered the institutional forms of poor relief in Holland.

The central institutional problem in poor relief was the relationship between Reformed diaconates and municipal welfare agencies. Orthodox Calvinist church leaders understood diaconal charity to emanate from their eucharistic community, which they called the "household of faith." This condition necessitated independence from municipal control so that deacons, under the watchful eye of the consistory, could care for the poor in their eucharistic community. Based on the model of the apostolic church, this ethic placed the highest priority on the needs of church members and attempted to ensure that recipients followed the moral dictates set forth by the Reformed Church.

Given the social dislocation of the late sixteenth century, magistrates in Holland were not necessarily hostile to a new charitable agency in their cities. Nevertheless, many local officials were less than enthusiastic about an ecclesiastical office over which they had little control and a poor relief program that favored church members over ordinary residents.[66] From their point of view, an independent diaconate would undermine the long tradition of magisterial intervention in social welfare and shatter the solidarity of the municipal corporation.

The underlying conceptual problem for civic and church leaders was their vision of the Christian community. On the social and economic fringes of society, the poor defined the borders of both the municipal corporation and ecclesiastical bodies in the late sixteenth and early seventeenth centuries. The institutional guidelines set forth by civic and ecclesiastical authorities to permit or deny charity to the poor defined who belonged to their respective community, and who had a claim to its resources. To receive regular relief from a civil agency, a recipient of poor relief was required to belong to the corporate civic body in order to obtain benefits from its charitable institutions. The decision to offer or deny charity to a poor person was essentially a judgement of status in relation to the community. The "deserving

---

[65] See Dorothy M. Brown and Elizabeth McKeown, *The Poor Belong To Us: Catholic Charities in American Welfare* (Cambridge, Mass., 1997); Anthony Brundage, "Private charity and the 1834 Poor Law," and Donald T. Critchlow, "Philanthropic foundations and the modern welfare state," papers presented at the conference "From Poor Laws to the Modern Welfare State: Private Charity and Public Assistance in Historical Perspective," Saint Louis University (St. Louis, Mo.), August 16, 1996.

[66] Van Deursen, *Bavianen*, pp. 102–27.

poor" belonged to the civic community and complied with its communal norms. Magistrates across Holland established requirements for residency and regulations for proper conduct to separate these "deserving poor" from outsiders and deviants.

Magistrates in Holland had managed the fragmented parish relief institutions in their cities for centuries by virtue of their status as the local "Christian authority" (*Christelijke overheid*). From the fourteenth through the sixteenth centuries, the cities of Holland had gained a great measure of autonomy from their Burgundian and subsequent Hapsburg overlords. These city officials used their authority to fight for economic advantage in the province, to promote the collective welfare of their urban communities, and to order social life in the municipality. The governing urban elites envisioned the civic corporation to be an organic Christian hierarchy under their paternal authority.

Reformed church officers also understood charity to be a communal function, although their community of reference was universal and eucharistic. According to Dutch Calvinists, the church was a gathered community of the elect obligated to carry out Christ's work in a fallen world. To ensure that the religious community lived up to this high standard, ministers preached the gospel and administered the sacraments, elders helped discipline the congregation, and deacons assisted the poor. Discipline protected the integrity of the community from the moral failings of its own membership and poor relief ensured that needy members were not neglected. Immigrants who appealed to the deacons for assistance had to present an *attestatie* (a certification of membership in good standing) to the consistory from their previous church before they could receive consideration. For the poor who were already resident in the city, the ecclesiastical officers attempted to make the diaconate the exclusive poor relief agency for those members who complied with the moral demands of the church officers.

Calvinists in Holland derived their communal notion of discipline and charity from John Calvin in Geneva and from Johannes a'Lasco, superintendent of the Dutch exile churches in London and Emden.[67] After 1572, Calvinist ministers returned to Holland and attempted to implement their confessional goals in local congregations. For many magistrates, however, these ideals were a pronounced departure from the homogenous blend of religious and civic custom that had overlain municipal life in past times. As such, the community-forming ambitions of Dutch Calvinism threatened the traditional idea of the municipal society as a single corporate body, served by a church for all citizens. In turn, the corporate nature of civic life also blunted the confessional impulses of the Reformed

---

[67] For Calvin's writings on the diaconate and its implementation in Geneva, see McKee, *Diaconate and Liturgical Almsgiving*; Robert M. Kingdon, "The deacons of the Reformed Church in Calvin's Geneva," in *Mélanges d'histoire du XVIe siècle offerts a Henri Meylan* (Geneva, 1970), pp. 81–90; Kingdon, "Social welfare in Calvin's Geneva," *American Historical Review* 76 (1971), pp. 50–69. For the connections between the exile communities and Holland, see Andrew Pettegree, *Foreign Protestant Communities in Sixteenth-Century London* (Oxford, 1986); Pettegree, *Emden and the Dutch Revolt: Exile and the Development of Reformed Protestantism* (Oxford, 1992).

Church in the Netherlands over the course of the sixteenth and early seventeenth centuries.

The development of charitable institutions in these six cities can inform our understanding of European poor relief in three fundamental ways. First, it reveals the enduring corporate civic and religious values that shaped urban charity well into the seventeenth century. Secondly, it shows the specific conditions that compelled a Reformed body to establish an independent poor relief agency in contrast to all other mainstream Protestant confessions. Finally, it shows how political and religious authorities in Holland resolved competing conceptions over what the Christian community was during a period of confessional strife in Europe.

In order to accomplish these goals, chapters 2 and 3 focus on the bases of municipal charity from the fourteenth to the seventeenth centuries. Chapter 4 discusses the Dutch Calvinist conception of the diaconate in relation to the other Protestant movements on the continent, while chapter 5 treats the implementation of poor relief in relation to social discipline. Chapter 6 traces the negotiations between Calvinist leaders and city leaders over the function of the diaconate within the new centralized programs of poor relief during the early years of the Dutch Reformation. Finally, chapter 7 suggests how these struggles left a lasting impression on social organization in early modern Holland.

2

The municipal community and parish charity in late medieval Holland

The harmonious alliance of civic culture and religious life ordered the motivations and institutional forms of charity in Holland's cities during the late middle ages. From the fourteenth to the sixteenth centuries, lay magistrates and parish priests worked together to relieve the most pressing manifestations of poverty in their cities. Churches offered a sacred incentive for charitable giving, contributed revenues for relief purposes, and furnished workers to care for the poor. For their part, city governments allocated funds for parish foundations, appointed the regents who managed them, and established the criteria to determine who might receive their services. By the early fifteenth century, magistrates governed most aspects of parish poor relief in their cities.

Urban patricians venerated tradition and scorned novelty. Convention legitimized a way of doing things; conversely, innovation threatened all that was right and good in civil society. And as we shall see in chapter 3, the poor relief policies of urban magistrates in the sixteenth century were not really all that new. Rather, they grew out of centuries of tradition. Therefore, the positions taken by magistrates with respect to economic hardship and the demands of Calvinist charity in the sixteenth century make little sense without reference to the civic customs and religious culture that encased poor relief in the middle ages. This chapter, then, examines charitable foundations in the six great cities before the sixteenth century within the context of their economic, political, and cultural development.

CITY AND PROVINCE IN MEDIEVAL HOLLAND

Growing commercial activity throughout Europe in the high middle ages fueled a revival of urban life that slowly manifested itself in the swampy lowlands of Holland. As the Dutch proceeded heroically in their quest to make dry land out of the sea, a number of small agricultural communities began to evolve into lively commercial and industrial towns in the fourteenth century. Among these growing towns, Dordrecht, Haarlem, Delft, Leiden, Amsterdam, and Gouda emerged as the most significant local centers of commerce and industry. Their economic vitality, combined with protracted power struggles among noble dynasties, enabled these six towns to acquire a large measure of municipal autonomy over the course of the late middle ages.

The starting point for urban expansion actually goes back to the thirteenth century, when counts of Holland began granting formal municipal charters (*stads-rechten*) to provincial towns.[1] As the counts were consolidating their authority over the province, they awarded charters to the most viable towns in exchange for an annual duty and for their political allegiance. In 1220, for example, the city of Dordrecht agreed to pay the count an annual sum of sixty Holland pounds; Rotterdam assented to one hundred pounds in 1340.[2] It is likely that these charters stemmed from earlier oral agreements between the count and local elites. Jaap Kruisheer has even shown that local elites in Haarlem, Delft, and Alkmaar initiated the process. Inhabitants in these towns, and perhaps in others, pressured the counts to grant them legal and fiscal privileges similar to those of the cities of Brabant.[3] In short, these charters were formal expressions of customary accords made by counts and elite townsfolk, which stipulated the mutual obligations incumbent upon both parties.

Yet the charters also marked a significant turning point in the development of urban life. Filled with terms such as *libertas* and *stadsvrijheid* (municipal freedom), city charters freed burghers from territorial courts and exempted them from a host of feudal duties. The charters empowered local elites to make laws, to establish criteria for citizenship, and to exercise their political authority over the municipality. In addition, these cities received an assortment of economic privileges, such as the right to hold markets, to work lands outside the municipality, and to collect duties on river traffic.[4] While municipal charters did not sever townsfolk from the larger agrarian world, these communities did take on a much more urban quality in the latter part of the thirteenth century.[5]

Dordrecht, one of the oldest cities in Holland, received its municipal charter early in the thirteenth century.[6] This early grant was an implicit recognition of the

---

[1] Most cities of the southern Low Countries had received charters in the twelfth century. The charters granted in the middle of the thirteenth century in Holland were modeled after the one in 's-Hertogenbosch: H. van Werveke, "De steden: rechten, instellingen en maatschappelijke toestanden," in *AGN*, vol. II, pp. 387, 394; Audrey Lambert, *The Making of the Dutch Landscape: An Historical Geography of the Netherlands*, 2nd edn. (London, 1985), pp. 155–8, 169.

[2] P. H. D. Leupen, "Heer en stad, stad en heer in de dertiende eeuw," in *De Hollandse stad in de dertiende eeuw*, J. M. Baart, D. H. de Boer, G. van Herwijnen, et al., eds. (Zutphen, 1988), p. 12; T. S. Jansma, "De oudste geschiedenis van Rotterdam," in his *Tekst en uitleg: historische opstellen aangeboden aan de schrijver bij zijn aftreden als hoogleraar aan de Universiteit van Amsterdam* ('s-Gravenhage, 1974), p. 26.

[3] Jaap Kruisheer, "Stadsrechtbeoorkonding en stedelijke ontwikkeling," in Baart, et al., *De Hollandse stad*, pp. 44–8; Kruisheer, *Het ontstaan van de stadsrechtoorkonden van Haarlem, Delft, Alkmaar* (Amsterdam, 1985), pp. 47, 54, 59; see also Leupen, "Heer en stad," p. 11.

[4] G. van Herwijnen, "Stad en land in het graafschap Holland en Zeeland in de dertiende eeuw," in Baart, et al., *De Hollandse stad*, pp. 18–19; D. H. de Boer, "Op weg naar volwassenheid," in Baart, et al., *De Hollandse stad*, p. 34; Jansma, "Rotterdam," pp. 22–6.

[5] De Boer, "Volwassenheid," p. 40.

[6] Leupen, "Heer en stad," p. 10. Since these charters arose from oral agreements, it is difficult to date their origins with precision. Furthermore, the original charters for Dordrecht, Leiden, and Amsterdam have not survived. The oldest charter for Dordrecht is from 1200, a grant that provided for a

city's commercial potential and of the favor it enjoyed with the counts of Holland. Strategically located on the waterways of the Maas, Waal, and Lek Rivers, Dordrecht was the most important port for the inland river traffic along the Lower Maas region. As a result, Dordrecht became the centerpiece of Holland's toll system. Originally granted in 1299 and expanded between 1344 and 1352, the "Right of Staple" was an extensive set of privileges that required all merchandise moving along these rivers to be offloaded and warehoused at Dordrecht until further shipment.⁷ The staple allowed the city to monopolize the commodity traffic along the Rhineland–Flanders–Brabant–Holland routes until Amsterdam and Rotterdam began to chip away at Dordrecht's earlier commercial supremacy.⁸

Despite Dordrecht's auspicious early history, it was another city in the northeastern corner of Holland that would become the most vital commercial center in the province and the chief marketplace in Europe during the Dutch Golden Age. Amsterdam acquired its city charter sometime around 1300 and rapidly became the most important link in the north–south trade along the Zuider Zee ports to the IJ River.⁹ Its deep harbor on the IJ and its easy access to inland regions would enable the city to become the premier port of call in the transfer of merchandise between Holland and northeastern Europe in the late sixteenth century. Amsterdam merchants were also beginning to make trading connections with the Baltic, which would place the city in a position to become the entrepot of northern Europe in the seventeenth century.

Receiving their charters in the middle of the thirteenth century, Haarlem, Delft, Leiden, and Gouda were also growing communities that exploited their positions on inland rivers.¹⁰ The official route (*binnenvaart*) designated by the count for ships traveling through the province extended from the IJ River to the Spaarne and from there to Haarlem and on to Gouda by way of the Haarlemmermeer to the Gouwe River.¹¹ In 1272, Gouda became an obligatory port of call for ships on the waterway

college of *schepenen*. It was twenty years later, in a subsequent charter, that Dordrecht received the privileges and rights that constitute a self-governing city: Jan van Herwaarden, Dick de Boer, Fred van Kan, and Gerrit Verhoeven, *Geschiedenis van Dordrecht tot 1572* (Hilversum, 1996), pp. 22–4; van Werveke, "De steden," p. 394; D. H. de Boer, M. H. Boone, and W. A. M. Hessing, *Nederlands verleden in vogelvlucht. Delta I de middeleeuwen: 300 tot 1500* (Leiden, 1992), p. 86.
⁷ Matthys Janszoon Balen, *Beschryvinge der stad Dordrecht* (Dordrecht, 1677), pp. 441–3. This privilege enabled the counts to collect duties on merchandise more effectively and placed Dordrecht at the hub of the river trade: H. van Werveke, "De opbloei van handel en nijverheid," in *AGN*, vol. II, p. 437.
⁸ Elliott, "The classis of Dordrecht," pp. 141–3.
⁹ Ph. J. van der Laan, ed., *Oorkondenboek van Amsterdam tot 1400* (Amsterdam, 1975), p. 23.
¹⁰ Haarlem received its charter in 1245, Delft in 1246, and Gouda in 1272: G. H. Kurtz, *Haarlemsche stadsrecht van 1245: tekst der oorkonden* (Haarlem, 1945), pp. 5–6; van Werveke, "De steden," pp. 395–6; Lambert, *Dutch Landscape*, pp. 155–6, 169; L. M. Rollin Couquerque and A. Meerkamp van Embden, eds., *Rechtsbronnen der stad Gouda*, 2nd series, nr. 18 ('s-Gravenhage, 1917), p. iii. It is possible that Leiden had obtained a charter earlier, but the oldest extant charter dates from 1266: F. J. W. van Kan, *Sleutels tot de macht: de ontwikkeling van het Leidse patriciaat to 1420* (Hilversum, 1988), p. 21.
¹¹ C. C. Hibben, *Gouda in Revolt: Particularism and Pacificism in the Revolt of the Netherlands, 1572–1588* (Utrecht, 1983), p. 21.

so that shippers could pay tolls levied by the count.[12] While Leiden and Delft were not on the official route, the former profited from river traffic on the Oude Rhijn and the latter gained an entree to the Schie and Maas Rivers in the late fourteenth century.[13]

Though river traffic was important to the economies of Haarlem, Delft, Leiden, and Gouda, they were much more dependent upon domestic production. Haarlem and Delft established themselves in the fourteenth century as centers for brewing hop-flavored beer, which had been available previously only through import from Germany. Locally grown hops and imported grain that could be easily transported along the rivers furnished brewers with the resources that enabled them to produce their distinctive beer and sell it in regional markets. Later in the fifteenth century, brewing also became the most important industry in Gouda, as brewers sought to export their famous lighter brew, the *Goudse kuitbier*. By 1450, Delft surpassed Haarlem and Gouda in brewing capacity, as beer flowed from two hundred Delft breweries.[14] Leiden became the heart of the woolen drapery industry in four-teenth-century Holland. A finishing point for imported English wool, Leiden reaped benefits from the large number of immigrants from the southern Low Countries who introduced new manufacturing methods. At its peak in the middle of the fifteenth century, Leiden boasted one hundred draperies.[15]

In concert with their rising commercial and industrial power, the chief cities of Holland also became important players in provincial politics. During the fifteenth century, the "States of Holland" evolved from an *ad hoc* consultative body into the institution that represented the province in negotiations with the Burgundian court. The States of Holland counted on the political clout of the six cities to make their case before the duke. Consequently, their votes shaped the resolutions in the States of Holland. By 1500, there were only seven corporate votes on matters that came before the States, one for the nobility as a single entity and one each for the six cities.[16] According to the "Great Privilege of 1477," each of the six cities was to be responsible for taxes that its own delegates approved. Although this provision lasted officially only until 1494, the prevailing practice was that all decisions within the States required unanimous approval by the six municipal and lone noble delegations. By the sixteenth century, the adoption of this principle had given the cities considerable leverage in negotiating their ordinary tax subsidies (*ordinaris beden*). Although Philip of Hapsburg nullified the cities' self-taxing prerogatives in

[12] Ignatius Walvis, *Beschryving der stad Gouda*, 2 vols. (Gouda, 1713), vol. I, pp. 2–6.
[13] Van Kan, *Sleutels*, p. 17; G. Verhoeven, *Devotie en negotie: Delft als bedevaartplaats in de late middeleeuwen* (Amsterdam, 1992), p. 15.
[14] Jacques van Loenen, *De Haarlemse brouwindustrie vóór 1600* (Amsterdam, 1950), pp. 9–10, 31, 61; V. C. C. J. Pinkse, "Het Goudse kuitbier: Gouda's welvaren in de late middeleeuwen," in *Gouda zeven eeuwen stad* (Gouda, 1972), pp. 91–5; D. Wijbenga, *Delft: een verhaal van de stad en haar bewoners*, 2 vols. (Elmar, 1984), vol. I, p. 61.
[15] Lambert, *Dutch Landscape*, p. 158. The city also contained twenty-eight beer and wine manufacturers before 1386: van Kan, *Sleutels*, p. 81.
[16] De Schepper, "Burgerlijke overheden," p. 324.

2.1 Rivers and towns in late medieval Holland

1494, these six cities continued to wield considerable political leverage in provincial politics.[17]

Within these growing urban economies, a distinct form of municipal authority emerged as patricians obtained increasing governmental power in the late middle ages. A dynastic conflict in the fourteenth and fifteenth centuries gave urban elites opportunities to acquire more direct control over legal and administrative offices in their cities. Dissension within the Wittelsbach family (of the counts of Holland) escalated into a protracted, albeit sporadic, civil war, known as the *Hoekse–Kabeljauwse* (Hooks and Codfish) conflict. All of the six cities except Dordrecht allied officially with the *Kabeljauwse* party, led by Willem V. Dordrecht supported Willem's mother, Margaret of Bavaria, to protect its staple privilege. The relevance of this struggle for the chief cities of Holland was that patriciates were in a favorable position to negotiate for expanded privileges and increased autonomy within their jurisdictions. In return, these cities supported the broader political aims of Holland's counts.[18]

The cities' earliest charters had recognized the legal authority of a college of municipal *schepenen* (aldermen) to adjudicate local disputes and, along with a small council (*raad*), to formulate policy in the city. Appointed by the counts, *schepenen*, council members, and *schouts* (sheriffs) drafted, administered, and enforced laws.[19] To ensure the political loyalty of the cities, the counts of Holland and dukes of Burgundy conferred more extensive authority on these officials and clarified their governmental duties over the course of the fourteenth century.

By this time, the *schepenen* made up a formal judicial college (*schepenbank*) that dispensed justice in civil and criminal cases. The small council eventually became a college of burgomasters (*burgermeesters*), which ranged in number from two to four. Before the emergence of burgomasters, the specific duties of the municipal council are not clear. In many city ordinances, a *raad* is often mentioned along with the *schepenen* and the *schout* as the law-making body. Consequently, these councils seem to have possessed a degree of legislative authority in conjunction with the *schepenen* and *schout*, although their precise function remains a mystery. Over the course of the fourteenth century, however, the burgomasters took over the routine

[17] James D. Tracy, *Holland Under Hapsburg Rule, 1506–1566: The Formation of a Body Politic* (Berkeley, 1990), pp. 19, 41; Tracy, *A Financial Revolution in the Hapsburg Netherlands: Renten and Renteniers in the County of Holland, 1515–1565* (Berkeley, 1985), pp. 52–4.

[18] See H. M. Brokken, *Het ontstaan van de Hoekse en Kabeljauwse twisten* (Zutphen, 1982), pp. 45–81, 260–70; J. F. Niermeyer, "Henegouwen, Holland, en Zeeland onder het huis Wittelsbach," in *AGN*, vol. III, pp. 104–7.

[19] Walvis, *Gouda*, vol. I, pp. 4–5; Kurtz, *Haarlemsche stadsrecht*, pp. 5–6; Wijbenga, *Delft*, vol. I, pp. 26–8; van Kan, *Sleutels*, pp. 22, 24; J. C. Breen, ed., *Rechtsbronnen der stad Amsterdam*, 2nd series, nr. 4 ('s-Gravenhage, 1902), pp. iii–iv; van Herwijnen, "Stad en land," p. 19.

administrative tasks of the city government and enacted ordinances for the municipality in consultation with the *schepenen* and the *schout*.[20] As a whole, these officers constituted the city government, sometimes known as the *gerecht*.[21] The major municipal offices responsible for governing the six cities of Holland were firmly established by the end of the fourteenth century.

Certainly the creation of municipal offices held by local citizens was a vital part of the formation of these self-governing cities. But the most pivotal development occurred during the middle of the fifteenth century when the elites in Holland's cities began to consolidate their grip on municipal authority through the establishment of a city council, known as the *vroedschap* or *vertigraad* (council of forty). During the late fourteenth and early fifteenth centuries, the *vroedschap* was an informal body of prosperous citizens who met in each city to advise magistrates in times of crisis. Thanks to expanded privileges granted by the counts of Holland and dukes of Burgundy between 1415 and 1450, the *vroedschap* became an official municipal council in these six cities.[22]

Despite local peculiarities, the *vroedschap* functioned much the same way in each city. This council, which usually numbered forty members, nominated all candidates for municipal offices.[23] The count would then select the new city government from this list of suitable candidates. The *vroedschap* chose its own new members through cooptation, a prerogative that enabled a small number of patricians to perpetuate their power over municipal governance.[24] By virtue of the *vroedschap*'s electoral function, patricians now had the constitutional means at their disposal to concentrate power within the leading families of the city.

[20] Dordrecht's city government was constituted a bit differently from the other cities. It had two different types of burgomasters, the city burgomaster (*van gemeente*) and the lord burgomaster (*van's Heeren weg*). The former served as an advocate for citizens before the city government and the latter administered the municipal courts. By the late fourteenth century, Dordrecht also created an eight-member council (*goede luiden van den achten*) chosen by the guilds to advise the city government: Balen, *Dordrecht*, pp. 241, 350–1.

[21] Other minor offices, such as a treasurer (*tresauris*), a secretary, and a city lawyer (*pensionaris*) were created to alleviate the burdens of the burgomasters: H. W. van Leeuwen, "Bestuurlijke en rechterlijke organisatie," in *De stad Delft: cultuur en maatschappij*, 2 vols. (Delft, 1981), vol. I, pp. 25–7; W. P. Blockmans, "Mobiliteit in stadsbesturen 1400–1550," in de Boer and Marsijle, *De Nederlanden in de late middeleeuwen*, p. 243.

[22] Amsterdam acquired a *vroedschap* by 1417, Haarlem by 1419, Delft by 1445, Leiden by 1449, Gouda by 1450, and Dordrecht by 1456: Renee Kistemaker and Roelof van Gelder, *Amsterdam: The Golden Age 1275–1795* (New York, 1983), p. 3; J. W. Marsijle, "De geografische, institutionele en politieke ontwikkelingen," in *Deugd boven geweld: een geschiedenis van Haarlem, 1245–1995*, G. F. van der Ree-Scholtens, ed. (Hilversum, 1995), p. 43; Couquerque and van Emden, *Gouda rechtsbronnen*, p. viii; Balen, *Dordrecht*, p. 359; Dirk Jaap Noordham, *Geringde buffels en heren van stand: het patriciaat van Leiden, 1574–1700* (Hilversum, 1994), p. 10; van Leeuwen, "Organisatie," p. 26.

[23] There were only thirty-six members of Amsterdam's *vroedschap*. Provided for by the "Great Privilege of 1477," this number reflected an increase of twelve over the composition of previous *vroedschappen*: Johan E. Elias, *Geschiedenis van het Amsterdamsche regentenpatriciaat* ('s-Gravenhage, 1923), p. 5.

[24] Jansma, "Holland en Zeeland onder de Bourgondische hertogen, 1433–1477," in *AGN*, vol. II, pp. 326–7.

26

Table 2.1 *Earliest mention (approximate) of municipal offices in the six cities*

	Schepenen	Schout	Raad	Burgomasters
Dordrecht	1200	1220	1220	1296
Haarlem	1245	1245	1280	?
Delft	1246	1246	1282	1409
Leiden	1260	1266	1299	1385
Amsterdam	1300	1300	–	1300
Gouda	1272	1272	?	1361

Note: Please note that the order of the six cities listed in this and all other tables or appendices is chronological based on municipal charter. This sequence also follows the rank by which the cities cast their votes in the States of Holland. In cities where there was an unconfirmed possibility that an office existed prior to a municipal charter, I have used the charter to date the office.

Source: G. van Herwijnen, "Stad en land in het graafschap Holland en Zeeland in de dertiende eeuw," in J. M. Baart, D. H. de Boer, G. van Herwijnen, et al., eds., *De Hollandse stad in de dertiende eeuw* (Zutphen, 1988), p. 19; Ph. J. van der Laan, ed., *Oorkondenboek van Amsterdam tot 1400* (Amsterdam, 1975), pp. 23–5; C. C. Hibben, *Gouda in Revolt: Particularism and Pacificism in the Revolt of the Netherlands, 1572–1588* (Utrecht, 1983), p. 27, n. 15; Ignatius Walvis, *Beschryving der stad Gouda*, 2 vols. (Gouda, 1713), vol. 1, pp. 3–5; F. J. W. van Kan, *Sleutels tot de macht: de ontwikkeling van het Leidse patriciaat tot 1420* (Hilversum, 1988), pp. 22–6; H. W. van Leeuwen, "Bestuurlijke en rechterlijke organisatie," in *De stad Delft: cultuur en maatschappij*, 2 vols. (Delft, 1981), vol. 1, pp. 24–7; Jan van Herwaarden, Dick de Boer, Fred van Kan, and Gerrit Verhoeven, *Geschiedenis van Dordrecht tot 1572* (Hilversum, 1996), pp. 110–11.

The patricians in these cities used this authority to set forth guidelines that would enable the most notable families to control the reins of local power and to exclude non-elites from municipal posts. In 1467 Dordrecht was the last of the six cities to adopt a policy that only members of the *vroedschap* could be considered for the offices of *schepenen* and burgomasters. Leiden had done so in 1385, as did Amsterdam in 1400, and Delft, Haarlem, and Gouda in the middle of the fifteenth century.[25]

Urban patricians in Holland also added residency and property requirements to

[25] J. A. Fruin, ed., *De oudste rechten der stad Dordrecht en van het baluwschap van Zuid Holland*, series 1, nr. 4, 2 vols. ('s-Gravenhage, 1892), vol. 1, p. 130; van Kan, *Sleutels*, pp. 25–6; Jan Wagenaar, *Amsterdam in zyne opkomst, aanwas geschiedenissen*, 3 vols. (Amsterdam, 1760), vol. 1, p. 144; Couquerque and van Embden, *Gouda rechtsbronnen*, p. viii; Walvis, *Gouda*, vol. 1, p. 58; Verhoeven, *Devotie en negotie*, p. 16. Dordrecht was the only city in which the guilds exercised a significant degree of influence in selecting the *vroedschap* or any municipal offices. In the fifteenth century, the guilds chose the forty members from a list of one hundred candidates. Even in Dordrecht, patricians were able to negate the influence of the guilds by establishing substantial property requirements for public office: Elliott, "The classis of Dordrecht," pp. 143–4.

prevent newcomers and ordinary folk from taking public office. For example, in 1351 the city government in Leiden specified that any candidate for the *schepen-bank* had to be a citizen for seven years, and in 1387 the city established a four-year requirement for the office of *schout*. By 1394, aspirants for any municipal position in Amsterdam had to prove citizenship of seven years. Dordrecht demanded in 1494 that all candidates for burgomasters and *schepenen* were to have a fortune of 1,000 Flemish guilders to be considered for these posts. Members of the *vroedschap* were required to demonstrate a worth of 800 Flemish guilders. By the middle of the sixteenth century, the minimum property standard rose to 1,000 Flemish guilders. Although it is not clear what residency and property qualifications were attached to public office in all of the cities, patricians throughout Holland culti-vated the expectation that municipal posts were reserved for the most prosperous men.[26]

The result of all of these regulations was that urban elites retained virtually all political power in Holland's cities at the end of the fifteenth century.[27] The patriciates of Dordrecht and Leiden are perhaps the most well-studied of Holland's cities in this period. W. P. Blockmans has demonstrated the oligarchical nature of Dordrecht's city government between 1400 to 1550. During this period, one-third of all municipal officials in Dordrecht belonged to families in which five other family members had previously served in the city government. Twenty-five per-cent of these magistrates held terms that were longer than fifteen years. Likewise, F. J. W. van Kan has shown that the top elite in Leiden served between eleven and twenty-three years in this same period.[28] While the elites of Delft, Haarlem, Gouda, and Amsterdam await similar analysis, it is beyond doubt that municipal authority in these cities were also synonymous with patrician rule.

The urban elites also gave form to the social structure of the medieval corpor-ation. Beneath the small number of patricians, there were two categories of urban residents in Holland, citizens (*poorters*) and common inhabitants (*inwoonders*). Citizens were fairly well-to-do folk who had been able to afford to purchase the right of citizenship (*poorterrecht*), and they enjoyed a variety of commensurate privileges.[29] While the specific rights of citizenship varied from city to city, citizens enjoyed certain basic liberties not available to simple inhabitants. These privileges included exemption from tolls in the countryside, freedom from arbitrary arrest, and immunity from imprisonment outside the city for debts. Only citizens could

---

[26] Van Kan, *Sleutels*, p. 24; van der Laan, *Amsterdam oorkondenboek*, p. 49; Blockmans, "Mobiliteit in stadsbesturen," pp. 242–3; Elliott, "The classis of Dordrecht," p. 143. For Delft and Gouda, see Verhoeven, *Devotie en negotie*, p. 16, and Walvis, *Gouda*, vol. I, p. 58.

[27] W. P. Blockmans has theorized that political power in smaller towns, such as those in Holland, was much more limited to a handful of elite families than the larger cities in Flanders: Blockmans, "Mobiliteit in stadsbesturen," pp. 237, 247, 256.

[28] *Ibid.*, pp. 244–7; van Kan, *Sleutels*, pp. 99, 111.

[29] In Amsterdam the price of citizenship averaged around five Holland pounds in the early fifteenth century: Breen, *Amsterdam rechtsbronnen*, p. 17.

run for municipal office, apply for guild membership, establish a business, and place their children in an orphanage. In return, new citizens had to abide by the city's customs and take an oath of loyalty. If citizens were found guilty of criminal conduct, left the city without permission, or appealed to a legal authority outside the city, they could forfeit their citizenship temporarily or permanently. Those who either were not able or chose not to purchase citizenship, but who had established residency, usually for one year, were classified as common inhabitants. They received a few privileges, such as the right to fish and travel on waterways close to the city, farm nearby land, and request parish poor relief. Only municipal officials could confiscate the property of inhabitants.[30]

Economic wherewithal certainly established one's social rank in the urban hierarchy, but it was the patriciate who determined, regulated, and enforced the financial criteria for social privilege. The earliest city charters gave municipal officials, normally the *schepenen* and the *schout*, the authority to determine who could become a citizen, or an inhabitant, and who could not.[31] The authority to decide who could become a part of the municipal corporation at these two levels meant that urban patricians shaped the social hierarchy of urban society. Not only did magistrates perpetuate the power of a small group of elite families, but they shaped the social contours of the civic community.

The goal of municipal governance, according to the Dordrecht magistrates, was "that all good cities and their people should live securely in good peace, prosperity, and great honor."[32] City governments throughout the province tenaciously pursued this end in the larger agrarian society that enveloped urban life in the late middle ages. The rural world offered both safeguards and risks to "good peace, prosperity, and great honor" for urban patricians, burghers, and residents. Magistrates attempted simultaneously to use the adjacent countryside for their own benefit and to protect the municipality from external threats.

One primary menace was the territorial nobility. Bernard Chevalier has argued that French burghers, due in part to the physical presence of walled fortifications, looked inward and conceived of the municipality as an island within a larger, hostile domain.[33] While Chevalier's view of the French *bonnes villes* does not readily lend itself to the complex interactions between the city and the hinterland in Holland, urban leaders were often wary of the intentions of the non-urban nobility. As discussed earlier, the original charters of Holland's cities established the principle

[30] Couquerque and van Embden, *Gouda rechtsbronnen*, pp. 119, 510, 662; Walvis, *Gouda*, vol. I, pp. 52–6; Wagenaar, *Amsterdam*, vol. III, pp. 142–51; van der Laan, *Amsterdam oorkondenboek*, pp. 23–5, 52, 117; Fruin, *Oudste rechten Dordrecht*, vol. I, pp. 5–7, 54–6; A. J. Enschedé and C. J. Gonnet, eds., *Kuerboeck der stadt Haerlem* ('s-Gravenhage, 1887), pp. 19–25, 64–76; van Herwijnen, "Stad en land," pp. 18–19; Theodorus Schreveli, ed., *Haarlemias of eerts stichting der stad Haarlem*, 3 vols. (Haarlem, 1754), vol. I, pp. 1–22.
[31] In 1411 Amsterdam burgomasters took over this task from the *schepenen*: Wagenaar, *Amsterdam*, vol. III, p. 156.
[32] Fruin, *Oudste rechten Dordrecht*, vol. I, p. 1.
[33] Bernard Chevalier, *Les Bonnes Villes de France du XIV au XVI siècle* (Paris, 1982), pp. 176–80.

of municipal freedom from noble jurisdiction. And, in Amsterdam and Dordrecht, citizens who appealed to any court outside the city would be fined ten Holland pounds and lose their citizenship for ten years. Thus, the early municipal charters marked an important separation between city and territory, a distinction that magistrates attempted to defend and to enlarge over the course of the fourteenth and fifteenth centuries.[34]

During this period, magistrates consistently complained about "robber barons" (*roofridders*) in the countryside who threatened the security and economic well-being of burghers. To counteract noble encroachments, cities procured from the counts prohibitions against the construction of "strong houses" close to the city walls. A Dordrecht ordinance of 1352 limited the walled thickness of houses adjacent to the municipality to one and one-half feet. In 1351 Leiden secured the territory immediately adjacent to the city by forbidding construction of all castles or stone structures within a specified distance from the city. Haarlem gained this provision in 1389, as did Delft in 1448–49, and Amsterdam in 1489. A privilege in 1484 allowed Gouda to extend municipal jurisdiction to one-quarter of a mile around the city wall. Concerned about attempts to avoid excise duties on the production of beer, Delft and Haarlem obtained resolutions prohibiting any construction within a distance of 600 meters of the city walls, except for the purposes of storing grain or cattle. Similarly, Leiden and Delft in 1351 forbade textile production within a three-mile range.[35]

Urban magistrates also recognized that the privileges of other provincial cities could impair their own livelihood. From the fourteenth to the seventeenth centuries, magistrates engaged in endless wrangling over commercial privileges, illegal tolls, ship fees, dike construction, and waterway regulation to protect local industries and to secure an advantage on the rivers. To protect local markets, magistrates imposed tariffs on imported beer and textiles, yet complained vigorously about duties on their exported goods. From the fourteenth to the middle of the sixteenth century, Haarlem, Delft, Rotterdam, Leiden, Gouda, and Amsterdam waged a relentless campaign to abolish or reduce Dordrecht's Right of Staple. Similarly Delft, Schoonhoven, Gorkum, and Rotterdam attempted to avoid tolls at Gouda by seeking alternative routes on the *binnenvaart*. Dordrecht and Amsterdam levied ship fees at their ports, but their merchants balked at paying fees elsewhere.[36]

Although the territories and communities outside the municipality posed all sorts of threats, city governments also realized that the countryside offered a

---

[34] Van Herwijnen, "Stad en land," p. 19; Wagenaar, *Amsterdam*, vol. III, p. 151; Fruin, *Oudste rechten Dordrecht*, vol. I, p. 63.

[35] T. S. Jansma, "Het economische overwicht van de laat-middeleeuwse stad t.a.v. haar agrarische ommeland, in het bijzonder toegelicht met de verhouding tussen Leiden en Rijnland," in Jansma, *Tekst en uitleg*, pp. 38–9, 43; Walvis, *Gouda*, vol. I, p. 40.

[36] Jansma, "Economische overwicht," p. 44. On at least three occasions in 1394, Amsterdam led a coalition of cities that made a formal protest of Dordrecht's staple right: van der Laan, *Amsterdam oorkondenboek*, pp. 430, 454–5.

resource necessary for economic expansion: labor. To recover from the demographic decline of the fourteenth century, magistrates used the countryside to repopulate an urban work force. By offering economic incentives to rural folk, municipal leaders tried to attract able-bodied laborers to their cities. As a result, thousands of Hollanders moved from outlying areas and fueled the rapid urban expansion of the fifteenth century.[37]

And for these rural dwellers economic prosperity was alluring. Consequently the favorable labor markets in these cities served as demographic magnets that attracted immigrants from the province and from other areas in northwestern Europe. Scholars of the Netherlands in the late middle ages have estimated that 60,000 out of a total population in Holland of 260,000 lived in cities by 1350. This trend accelerated throughout the fifteenth century, for, by 1514, 60 percent of all Hollanders were urban-dwellers.[38] This demographic profile made Holland one of the most urbanized provinces in Europe at the beginning of the sixteenth century.

The chief towns of Holland had come a long way from their humble beginnings in the thirteenth century. Over a 300-year period, the province of Holland had acquired a distinctly urban character. Governed by their most notable men, the cities had steered a course that provided them with a large measure of political autonomy. By virtue of economic expansion, the normative community structure in the Netherlands' most vital province was the civic corporation. Although seeds of economic contraction began to take root in the late fifteenth century, they did not mature into a fully fledged crisis until the sixteenth century. Until then, these well-populated cities developed as prosperous manufacturing and trading centers that provided magistrates with extensive municipal authority. These city officials used their authority to fight for economic advantage in the province and to promote the collective welfare of these urban communities.

THE RELIGIOUS BASES OF THE CIVIC COMMUNITY

The spiritual ideals and ceremonial forms of the Catholic church gave shape to urban culture in medieval Holland. While each city had its own particular traditions, the general characteristics of religious culture throughout Holland's cities were remarkably parallel. These cities were economic entities under patrician rule, and elites promoted the ideal that the municipality was an organic Christian community bound together by mutual concerns for salvation and prosperity. That is, religious piety undergirded civic culture.

---

[37] Jansma, "Economische overwicht," p. 40; de Boer, Boone, and Hessing, *Nederlands verleden*, pp. 177–8.

[38] De Boer, "Volwassenheid," p. 32. Of this 60,000, 40,000 lived in the seven leading cities: H. P. H. Jansen, "Holland's Advance," *Acta Historica Neerlandica* 10 (1978), pp. 1–20; W. P. Blockmans, G. Pieters, W. Prevenier, and R. W. M. van Schaik, "Tussen crisis en welvaart: sociale veranderingen 1300–1500," in *NAGN*, vol. IV, p. 44.

Table 2.2 *Population levels in the six cities*

	1300	1400	1500
Dordrecht	5,000	7,500	11,500
Leiden	5,000	5,000–6,000	14,000
Delft	2,000	6,500	10,000
Haarlem	2,000	8,000–10,000	12,000
Amsterdam	1,000	3,000	12,000
Gouda	1,000	5,000	8,500–10,000

Source: G. Verhoeven, *Devotie en negotie: Delft als bedevaartplaats in de late middeleeuwen* (Amsterdam, 1992), p. 8; J. W. Marsijle, "Het Haarlemse klerkambt in de 15e eeuw," in D. E. H. de Boer and Marsijle, eds., *De Nederlanden in de late middeleeuwen* (Utrecht, 1987), p. 182; de Boer, "Op weg naar volwassenheid," in J. M. Baart, de Boer, G. van Herwijnen, et al., eds., *De Hollandse stad in de dertiende eeuw* (Zutphen, 1988), p. 32; Baart, "De materiële stadscultuur," in Baart, et al., *De Hollandse stad*, p. 95; F. J. W. van Kan, *Sleutels tot de macht: de ontwikkeling van het Leidse patriciaat tot 1420* (Hilversum, 1988), p. 22; Ignatius Walvis, *Beschryving der stad Gouda*, 2 vols. (Gouda, 1713), vol. I, p. 32; Jonathan I. Israel, *The Dutch Republic: Its Rise, Greatness, and Fall 1477–1806* (Oxford, 1995), p. 114.

In this regard, cities in Holland bore a marked correspondence to urban communities throughout Europe. Scholars have devoted a great deal of attention to delineating the corporate religious nature of European cities.[39] Over the past twenty years, historians of the *Quattrocento* have harmonized the humanist quest for the ideal *civitas* with the medieval pursuit of salvation. North Italian cities are no longer seen as signaling the rise of a modern era bolstered by individualism and secularism. Rather, the shift toward a more extensive understanding of civic responsibility was rooted in the medieval ideal of a Christian community.[40]

Perhaps the most well-defined model of this ideal comes out of scholarship on the Free Imperial Cities, which Bernd has Moeller has described as "sacred communities." According to Moeller, "Each burgher understood that he was part of the whole, sharing responsibility for his part in the welfare of the great organic community, the collective individual,' to which he was tightly bound by laws and duties . . . Material welfare and eternal salvation were not differentiated and thus the borders between the secular and spiritual areas of life disappeared. We can

[39] A few of the most important works that have not been cited elsewhere: Natalie Zemon Davis, "The rites of violence," in Davis, *Society and Culture*, pp. 152–88; Barbara Diefendorf, *Beneath the Cross: Catholics and Huguenots in Sixteenth-Century Paris* (New York, 1991); A. N. Galpern, *The Religions of the People in Sixteenth-Century Champagne* (Cambridge, 1976); Robert W. Scribner, "Cosmic order and daily life: sacred and secular in pre-industrial German society," in *Religion and Society in Early Modern Europe*, Kaspar van Greyerz, ed. (London, 1984), pp. 17–35.

[40] For example, see Marvin B. Becker, "Aspects of lay piety in early renaissance Florence," in *The Pursuit of Holiness in Late Medieval and Renaissance Religion*, Charles Trinkhaus and Heiko A. Oberman, eds. (Leiden, 1974), pp. 181–90, and Edward Muir, *Civic Ritual in Renaissance Venice* (Princeton, 1981).

grasp an essential trait of the late medieval urban community if we characterize it as a sacred society.' "[41]

Moeller's model has come under criticism from Thomas Brady, not because it misrepresented an urban ethos, but because Brady believes that Moeller failed to address the social roots of this corporate consciousness. Brady argued that it is unlikely that each burgher understood that he was part of any great organic community. Rather, Brady stressed that the notion of a sacral community was an "urban corporate ideology" advanced by municipal leaders. The promotion of this corporate ideal, according to Brady, was most important during the late middle ages in areas that experienced "the rise and flourishing of self-governing towns."[42]

For the six self-governing towns of Holland, elites used the mythic legends of the past, the patterns of parish life, and the city-wide religious festivals of the liturgical calendar to try to foster a sense of spiritual unity for those within the municipal corporation. Burghers passed on their religious traditions and retold the most celebrated episodes of their history to succeeding generations. Connecting the past to the present, these traditions became a means by which an urban community recounted its history. This oral tradition became enshrined in massive municipal chronicles written in the seventeenth and eighteenth centuries. In Dordrecht, Haarlem, Delft, Leiden, Amsterdam, and Gouda, as well as other cities, local writers celebrated the rich legacy of civic culture and religious life in their cities over the previous three hundred years.[43]

These writers described in detail the miraculous power of icons and the uncommon spirituality of local mystics. While each chronicler heralded the distinctive features of his own city's religious heritage, their narratives tell a similar story. Their ancestors were pious folk committed to the collective welfare of their city. These chroniclers also shared the conviction that Hollanders were of a heroic Batavian stock that had thrown off Roman oppression in the ancient past and Spanish and papal tyranny in more recent times.[44]

---

[41] Moeller, *The Imperial Cities*, pp. 44–6. For late medieval Holland, Adriaan Bredero has also made the case that inhabitants made no distinction between social and religious matters: Bredero, *Christenheid en christendom*, p. 276.

[42] Brady has cautioned against isolating municipal cultural and economic life from its broader geographical locus, which only recall anachronistic "romantic glorifications" of the medieval city: Brady, *Ruling Class*, pp. 13–18.

[43] For example, see Dirck van Bleyswijck, *Beschryvinge der stadt Delft*, 2 vols. (Delft, 1667); Samuel Ampzing, *Bescryvinge ende lof der stad Haerlem in Holland* (Haarlem, 1628; republished edn., 1974); Balen, *Dordrecht*; Caspar Commelin, *Beschryvinge van Amsterdam*, 2 vols. (Amsterdam, 1691); Walvis, *Gouda*; Henrick Haestens, Jan Oorlers, and Jan Marie, *Beschrijvinge der stad Leyden* (Leiden, 1614).

[44] See E. O. G. Haitsma Mulier, "Grotius, Hooft and the writing of history in the Dutch Republic," in *Clio's Mirror: Historiography in Britain and the Netherlands*, A. C. Duke and C. A. Tamse, eds. (Zutphen, 1985), pp. 55–72; I. Schöffer, "The Batavian myth during the sixteenth and seventeenth centuries," in *Geschiedschrijving in Nederland: studies over de historiographie van de nieuwe tijd*, vol. II, P. A. M. Geurts and A. E. M. Janssen, eds. ('s-Gravenhage, 1981), pp. 85–109.

In Delft, Dirck van Bleyswijck was the author of a chronicle first published in 1667. He came from a regent family who had joined the Protestant party in the late sixteenth century.[45] In no way sympathetic to the Roman faith, van Bleyswijck nonetheless described in laborious detail the outward manifestations of Catholic piety throughout the middle ages. While he occasionally reminded readers that the observances were "popish superstitions," his chronicle exhibited a profound sense of civic pride in the city's rich religious legacy.[46] That a later Protestant writer could look back glowingly at a mythic spiritual past, antithetical to his own views, points to the corporate religious nature inherent within civic communities. That van Bleyswijck came from an old regent family suggests that the confluence of the spiritual and the civic was a social ideal promoted by urban leaders.

Likewise, in Haarlem, a Reformed minister, Samuel Ampzing, described the origins and development of Haarlem from its murky past to the seventeenth century. Ampzing provided readers a mental image of pious Haarlemmers by describing the massive parish church of St. Bavo, the miracle stories of St. Gangolf, the numerous charitable foundations, religious cloisters, and the sacramental processions in the city.[47] Similar descriptions of medieval civic piety appeared in all the chief cities of Holland. Casparus Commelin provided historical descriptions of Amsterdam, as did Matthijs Balen for Dordrecht, Ignatius Walvis (a Catholic priest) for Gouda, and Jan Janszoon Oorlers for Leiden. The chronicles testify not only to the time-honored ideals of the municipal community, but they also indicate the civic nature of late medieval piety in these cities.

One dominant theme in the chronicles was the spectacular instances of local piety which had been a part of oral tradition for hundreds of years. The conspicuous piety of individuals, most of whom were women, made them a part of a city's religious folklore. One of the most renowned accounts in Delft was the story of Gertruid van Oosten. Born in nearby Voorburg, she left her simple farming family and traveled to Delft in the 1330s. After arriving in the city, she initially stayed as an overnight guest in "modest" homes and inns. One day she had some sort of an encounter with a young man, though the exact nature of the experience remains unclear. Nevertheless, after this incident she was so overcome with guilt about her carnal desires that she fled to a *begijnhof* (a lay female religious community) in Delft. She spent the rest of her life in spiritual refuge there, as she attempted to embrace Christ as her bridegroom. She wrote mystical poetry and gained quite a following; she experienced stigmata around 1350. When she died, she was buried next to the tower on the south side of the Oude Kerk (Old Church).[48] Even today, a statue marks the approximate location of her grave.

[45] Boitet, *Delft*, pp. 131–2.   [46] See van Bleyswijck, *Delft*, vol. I, pp. 142–53, 161–7, 227–51.
[47] Ampzing, *Haerlem*, pp. 428–42.
[48] Wijbenga, *Delft*, vol. I, p. 87; van Bleyswijck, *Delft*, vol. I, pp. 308–11; A. H. Bredero, "De Delftse begijn Gertrui van Oosten (ca. 1320–1358) en haar niet-erkende heiligheid," in de Boer and Marsijle, *De Nederlanden in de late middeleeuwen*, pp. 83–4.

In Dordrecht, the origins of the Grote Kerk (Great Church) were shrouded in the renowned piety of a young maiden. According to the story, Sieuwertje (also Sura), who was from Dordrecht, became inspired to endow the building of a parish church in honor of the Virgin. Since the young woman was of inadequate means, however, the project was impossible. God honored her piety, however, by miraculously increasing her purse to meet construction costs. When the workers discovered she possessed such a large sum of money, they murdered pious Sieuwertje. She returned from the dead to forgive and free the imprisoned murderers, which motivated Dordrechters to complete the building of the Onze Lieve Vrouwe Kerk (the church of the Blessed Virgin, more commonly known as the Grote Kerk). Later, a fountain of healing waters issued forth at the spot of her murder.[49] The legends of Gertruid and Sieuwertje are but two examples of the stories of pious folk circulating throughout Holland in the late middle ages.[50] Local stories like these were passed down to give contemporaries an appreciation for the distinctive forms of piety in their city.

A second theme in the municipal chronicles was the intervention of saints in the lives of ordinary burghers. According to legend, the Virgin appeared in Delft on eleven different occasions between 1382 and 1387 to inspire people to build a church for her.[51] After construction began on the Nieuwe Kerk (New Church) in 1381, the Virgin's presence continued to make itself known in Delft. According to the *Chronicle of the New Church*, she performed at least ninety miracles for faithful parishioners and pilgrims who venerated her icon, Our Lady of Sorrows, in the Nieuwe Kerk from 1381 to 1516. This image, along with those of Maria van Jesse, the Lady of Seven Wounds, which were in the Oude Kerk, made Delft an important pilgrimage site in the late middle ages. From 1381 to 1516, the church wardens recorded 339 miracles associated with the icons in the Oude and Nieuwe Churches.[52]

Municipal leaders in these other five cities also cultivated cult followings of holy objects in their parishes. The parish of the Blessed Virgin in Dordrecht boasted a relic of the cross in the early fifteenth century. The "Holy Cross" was miraculously preserved during a fire in the parish church in 1457, which convinced parishioners of its authenticity. Afterwards, church wardens publicized this event and established strong support for the cult of the Holy Cross. The relic attracted a number of pilgrims from elsewhere in Holland who came to Dordrecht to experience its

---

[49] Theunis Watzes Jensma, *De Grote- of Onze Lieve Vrouwekerk van Dordrecht* (Dordrecht, 1987), p. 11.
[50] For other examples, see Ampzing, *Haerlem*, pp. 307–21, 440–2, and Walvis, *Gouda*, vol. I, p. 190. The stories about women appear to be related to a broad movement of female piety in late medieval Holland inspired by the *devotio moderna*: Pauline Hagemeijer, "Devote vrouwen in Holland omstreeks 1400," in T. S. Jansma, *In de schaduw van de eeuwigheid: tien studies over religie en samenleving in laatmiddeleeuws Nederland aangeboden aan prof. dr. A. H. Bredero* (Utrecht, 1986), pp. 224–32.
[51] D. P. Oosterbaan, "Kroniek van de Nieuwe Kerk te Delft," *Bijdragen voor de geschiedenis van het Bisdom Haarlem* 65 (1958), p. 17; van Bleyswijck, *Delft*, vol. I, pp. 227–38.
[52] Verhoeven, *Devotie en negotie*, pp. 5, 28–9.

2.2 *The miracle of Amsterdam.* Museum Catharijneconvent, Utrecht

miraculous powers. Between 1475 and 1509, church wardens attributed 175 miracles to the Holy Cross.[53]

In Amsterdam, a dying man's illness in 1345 subsided after he received Holy Communion. A woman who was caring for him noticed that the digested Host was still intact in his vomit. As she removed it, the Host produced a fire that burned throughout the evening, even though the Host itself was never consumed. After hearing of this miracle, Amsterdammers constructed the chapel of the Heilige Stede (Holy Place), on the site where it took place. The "miracle of Amsterdam" inspired writers and artists whose works publicized the story throughout the Netherlands. The Heilige Stede became a major pilgrimage site in Holland; its visitors included Charles the Bold, Maximilian I, and Charles V. Later Amsterdammers cultivated the belief that the city's prosperity was related to the miracle.[54]

Although Delft, Dordrecht, and Amsterdam contained the most well-publicized icons and relics, Haarlem, Leiden, and Gouda also advertised the powers of their own religious artefacts. Haarlemmers touted the healing powers of the icon of St. Gangolf in the Oude Almshouse and the relics of St. Bavo in the parish church. The St. Katherine Almshouse in Leiden contained relics of its patron saint, which, according to locals, were brought from the sea by travelers in 1204. Meanwhile, the icon of St. Jan was the source of local devotion in Gouda.[55] City magistrates in all of the six cities sought to obtain indulgence privileges, and in 1451–52 Amsterdam, Leiden, Dordrecht, Haarlem, and Delft won the right to have jubilee indulgences sold in their cities.[56]

While local folklore bears witness to the mythical spiritual heritage of the past, for Hollanders in the late middle ages, it was the parish that provided continuity for city folk through time. The parish church marked the pivotal points in the passage of an individual's life by way of the sacramental rituals of baptism, confirmation, marriage, and burial. In addition, clergy celebrated Masses on a daily basis, which provided divine grace needed for salvation. These rituals bound one into the corporate parish community and brought people together in a collective pursuit of salvation.[57]

Although the dates of the earliest parishes in these six cities are rather imprecise at best, in every case the parish predated the municipal charter by a very long

---

[53] G. Verhoeven, "De cultus van het heilig hout te Dordrecht: het onstaan van een bedevaart in de late middeleeuwen," in Jansma, *Schaduw van de eeuwigheid*, pp. 212–20. See also Verhoeven, *Devotie en negotie*, p. 5.

[54] J. F. M. Sterck, *De Heilige Stede in de geschiedenis van Amsterdam* (Hilversum, 1938), pp. 5–6, 36–8; P. J. Margry, *Amsterdam and het mirakel van het heilig sacrament: van middeleeuwsche devotie tot 20-eeuwse stille omgang* (Amsterdam, 1988), pp. 13–18.

[55] Ampzing, *Haerlem*, pp. 440–2; Schreveli, *Haarlemias*, p. 23; Ligtenberg, *Armezorg te Leiden*, pp. 21–2; van Kan, *Sleutels*, p. 204; Walvis, *Gouda*, vol. II, p. 237.

[56] J. van Herwaarden, "Middeleeuwse aflaten en Nederlandse devotie," in de Boer and Marsilje, *De Nederlanden in de late middeleeuwen*, p. 48.

[57] For an extensive analysis of how these rituals instilled a certain religious self-consciousness, see Roodenburg, *Onder censuur*, pp. 54–71.

period of time (see table 2.3). In a very literal sense, these cities were built around their first parishes and the historical evolution of the parish and the city were inextricably intertwined. By the late fifteenth century, Leiden was divided into three parishes, and Amsterdam, Delft, and Dordrecht each had two parishes, whereas Haarlem and Gouda each had only one parish.

The parish churches and their contiguous churchyards in all of these cities stood in the central square, usually facing the town hall. The architectural arrangement symbolized the dual pillars of a Christian society that converged in the center of the municipal community. Parishioners carried out all their life's activities in the midst of their spiritual past. Parish churches and their adjacent churchyards were the final resting place for deceased members of the community. Depending upon their ability to pay, citizens could opt for a choice burial plot inside the church, or otherwise be buried outside in the churchyard. Accordingly, these burial locations preserved the city's social hierarchy in perpetuity. Burial at the nucleus of social and religious life also kept departed souls at the forefront of a collective memory, binding the living and the dead into an inseparable corporate association. Reinforcing this remembrance, priests celebrated Masses for the salvation of the dead who had provided for the arrangements in their testaments.[58]

The parish church and its churchyard were also the nucleus of social life, where townsfolk came to loiter, chat, gossip, fight, and buy and sell at the market.[59] No doubt this square was a bustling, noisy place. To preserve a semblance of order, magistrates periodically issued ordinances regulating activity around the parish church. The Delft city government stipulated that "no wives, young women, or animals may sleep, eat, or drink in the churchyards, churches, almshouses in the city of Delft."[60] Haarlem magistrates mandated in 1390 that anyone found hunting with weapons in the churchyard would be banished from the city for one year. Later in 1462, they issued an ordinance that struck down the use of churches and churchyards for asylum.[61] Municipal ordinances continued to be issued throughout the sixteenth century, suggesting that old habits die hard. At least as late as 1590, Calvinist clergy in Delft were still complaining that activities around the parish churches distracted parishioners during worship services.[62]

Two of the most remarkable things about these parish churches, at least to this

[58] Spaans, *Haarlem*, p. 23; Natalie Zemon Davis, "Ghosts, kin, and progeny," *Daedalus* 16 (1977), pp. 92–6; R. R. Post, *Kerkelijke verhouding in Nederland vóór de Reformatie van 1500 tot 1580* (Utrecht, 1954), p. 369; Jensma, *Onze Lieve Vrouwekerk*, p. 30. In this regard, A. N. Galpern has observed that "Catholicism at the end of the Middle Ages was in large part a cult of the living in service of the dead": A. N. Galpern, "The legacy of late medieval religion in sixteenth-century Champagne," in Trinkhaus and Oberman, *Pursuit of Holiness*, p. 149.

[59] Spaans, *Haarlem*, p. 26; Jensma, *Onze Lieve Vrouwekerk*, p. 30.

[60] J. G. C. Joosting and S. Muller, eds., *Bronnen voor de geschiedenis der kerkelijke rechtspraak in het Bisdom Utrecht in de middeleeuwen*, vol. III ('s-Gravenhage, 1912), p. 2.

[61] *Ibid.*, pp. 117–18, 241. The city governments of Dordrecht and Amsterdam issued similar ordinances. See Breen, *Amsterdam rechtsbronnen*, p. 30; Fruin, *Oudste rechten Dordrecht*, vol. I, p. 84.

[62] *GAD. Kerkeraad* (May 14, 1590).

modern observer, were their sheer physical enormity and the large number of pious foundations in relation to the small size of the cities. The massive churches were a visual expression of piety that would not have been lost on either travelers or residents. The enormous energy and resources required to build such immense edifices also reveal the vitality of spiritual ideals in civic life. The sounds of construction on sacred foundations could be heard throughout the cities of Holland in the fourteenth and fifteenth centuries.

On the east side of the Amstel River, the Oude Zijde (Old Side) parish of Amsterdam boasted the sizable Oude Kerk, whereas parishioners on the Nieuwe Zijde began construction of its parish church, the Nieuwe Kerk, in 1408. The Oude Kerk possessed thirty-three ancillary altars and a high altar by the sixteenth century, including a statue of St. Nicholas, patron saint of the church. Each parish had its own ornate religious rituals and institutions that symbolized parish pride. The Nieuwe Zijde contained the chapel of the Heilige Stede, located on the spot of the "miracle of Amsterdam." On the Oude Zijde, parishioners erected the chapel of St. Olof and the chapel of Jerusalem, which contained a highly revered image of the Virgin.[63]

By the end of the fourteenth century, two parish churches, the Oude and Nieuwe Kerk, were the lifeblood of spiritual devotion in Delft. Under the patronage of St. Hippolytus, the Oude Kerk was founded at a date that is not certain, but the oldest extant document dates from 1242.[64] About 150 years later, builders laid the foundation for a second parish church (the Nieuwe Kerk). The construction of the Nieuwe Kerk, with one of the largest towers in the northern Netherlands, was completed in 1396. Separated only by a stone's throw, these two enormous parish churches, along with various ancillary religious institutions and thirteen cloisters, punctuated the city's skyline.[65]

In Dordrecht, somewhere between nine and thirteen cloisters, four churches, and twelve chapels were constructed during the thirteenth and fourteenth centuries. Like Amsterdam and Delft, Dordrecht had two parishes, the Grote and Nieuwe, although the Grote (also the Blessed Virgin) was by far the largest and most dominant parish in the city.[66] The center of religious life in Dordrecht, the

---

[63] Sterck, *Heilige Stede*, p. 15; Commelin, *Amsterdam*, vol. I, pp. 421–39; Johannes ter Gouw, *Geschiedenis van Amsterdam*, 8 vols. (Amsterdam, 1879–93), vol. V, pp. 146–60, 165–72.

[64] The foremost student of religious institutions in medieval Delft, D. P. Oosterbaan, has speculated that the origins of the Oude parish and its church date from 1240: Oosterbaan, *Oude Kerk*, pp. 10–11.

[65] *Ibid.*, pp. 10–11, 297; Wijbenga, *Delft*, vol. I, p. 81; M. A. Kok, "Het geestelijk leven te Delft," in *De stad Delft*, vol. I, pp. 106–7; van Bleyswijck, *Delft*, vol. I, pp. 317–58; B. W. F. van Riemsdijk, *Historische beschrijving van het klooster van Sinte Agatha met het Prinsenhof te Delft* ('s-Gravenhage, 1894), pp. 10–14.

[66] The Nieuwe parish and its church had lain within the domain of the lords of Merwede in the thirteenth century. By the early fourteenth century, however, the city had acquired this land and the parish became incorporated within the city limits of Dordrecht. It remained an independent parish and it also remained very small. According to the 1514 *Informatie*, the Grote parish contained 7,000 communicants, whereas the Nieuwe only had 750: Herwaarden, et al., *Dordrecht*, pp. 308–9; J. L. van Dalen, *Geschiedenis van Dordrecht*, 2 vols. (Dordrecht, 1931–33), vol. I, pp. 511–12.

Table 2.3 *Founding dates (approximate) of parish churches
in the six cities of Holland*

City	Parish church	Likely date
Dordrecht	Grote (Blessed Virgin)	1064?
	Nieuw	1307
Haarlem	(Bakenes)	(1250)
	(St. Gangolf)	(1256)
	St. Bavo	1472
Delft	Oude	1240
	Nieuwe	1381
Leiden	St. Pieter	1121
	St. Pankras	1315
	Blessed Virgin	1365
Amsterdam	Oude	1334
	Nieuwe	1408
Gouda	St. Jan	1335

Note: St. Bavo Kerk in Haarlem was not the oldest parish church in the city. The Bakenes Kerk (1250) and St. Gangolf Kerk (1256) held that distinction: Theodorus Schreveli, ed., *Haarlemias of eerts stichting der stad Haarlem*, 3 vols. (Haarlem, 1754), vol. I, pp. 15–19; W. P. J. Overmeer, *De hervorming te Haarlem* (Haarlem, 1904), p. 112.
Source: Theunis Watzes Jensma, *De Grote- of Onze Lieve Vrouwekerk van Dordrecht* (Dordrecht, 1987), p. 12; Jan van Herwaarden, Dick de Boer, Fred van Kan, and Gerrit Verhoeven, *Geschiedenis van Dordrecht tot 1572* (Hilversum, 1996), pp. 301–9; D. P. Oosterbaan, *De Oude Kerk te Delft gedurende middeleeuwen* ('s-Gravenhage, 1973), pp. 10–11, 17; F. J. W. van Kan, *Sleutels tot de macht: de ontwikkeling van het Leidse patriciaat tot 1420* (Hilversum, 1988), p. 17; Christina Ligtenberg, *Armezorg te Leiden tot het einde van de 16e eeuw* ('s-Gravenhage, 1908), p. 106; Ignatius Walvis, *Beschryving der stad Gouda*, 2 vols. (Gouda, 1713), vol. II, p. 9; Jan Wagenaar, *Amsterdam in zyne opkomst, aanwas geschiedenissen*, 3 vols. (Amsterdam, 1760), vol. II, pp. 90–1, 108.

Grote Kerk housed the city's most famous relic, the Holy Cross.[67] The parish church of Gouda, St. Jan's Kerk, was built sometime after 1335 but before 1375 when a fire destroyed large portions of the building. It featured silver and copper images of John the Baptist, patron saint of Gouda. By the late fifteenth century, St. Jan contained twenty-five chapels and vicaries and there were twelve monastic cloisters in and around the city.[68] By the late fifteenth century, a large single parish in Haarlem, served by St. Bavo Church, encompassed the entire city, as well as the neighboring villages of Heemstede, Zandvoort, Schoten, and Spaarendam. By the

[67] Verhoeven, "Het heilig hout," pp. 212–17. The chapels were usually attached to almshouses. See J. Sels, *Beschrijving der stad Dordrecht* (Dordrecht, 1853), pp. 27–50.
[68] Walvis, *Gouda*, vol. II, pp. 9, 15–35, 112–77.

fifteenth century Haarlem claimed three other churches, two chapels, and nineteen cloisters.[69] Leiden had more parishes than any of these six cities. St. Pieter's parish was the oldest: its church was constructed before 1276. St. Pankras' parish was added in 1313, and the Blessed Virgin in 1365.[70] Although one cannot measure piety by the number of religious buildings in a city, the increasing construction of sacred institutions in the late middle ages corresponded to the high-water mark for religiosity in the cities of Holland. For contemporary folk, the construction of churches, cloisters, and chapels was a tangible manifestation of the supernatural in the life of the city.

The religious heritage of a parish could engender a strong sense of loyalty that produced rivalry in cities with more than one parish. Such antagonism between parishes troubled Delft and Amsterdam in the fourteenth and fifteenth centuries. The construction of the Nieuwe Kerk in Delft from 1383 to 1396 grated on, and perhaps even goaded, parishioners in the Oude parish. According to the *Chronicle of the New Church*, the Oude Kerk contained only a handful of altars and its parishioners were put to shame. Such chiding stemmed from parish chauvinism that attempted to distinguish piety in the Nieuwe Kerk from the older parish. Impelled by growth in the Nieuwe parish, the Oude Kerk also underwent a prolonged revival of piety that made it the wealthiest parish in the city at the end of the fifteenth century.[71] Despite their growth, there was continued animosity between the two parishes during the late middle ages. Leaders in the two parishes vied for prominence in religious processions, forcing the city government to issue ordinances to regulate them.[72]

Due in part to social topography, the fiercest degree of rivalry occurred between the Oude and Nieuwe parishes in Amsterdam. Straddling the Amstel River, Amsterdam consisted of two distinct neighborhoods, the Oude and Nieuwe Zijden, on opposite sides of the river. By the early fifteenth century, each neighborhood embodied a parish that went by the same name. The oldest families in Amsterdam lived in the Oude Zijde, to the east of the river, and newcomers to the city moved to the western side of the Amstel, to the Nieuwe Zijde. This particular social topography fostered an intense loyalty to the respective parish, generating a fierce rivalry between the two neighborhoods. At a prearranged time, usually during the last week of July, boys from each parish would clash with one another on the bridges over the Amstel River. This annual ritual, known as the *hoopvechten*, was a staple of parish life, despite the efforts of the city government to prevent it. As in Delft, parish rivalries in Amsterdam also surfaced in planning city-wide religious

---

[69] Spaans, *Haarlem*, p. 23; W. P. J. Overmeer, *De hervorming te Haarlem* (Haarlem, 1904), pp. 111–23.
[70] Ligtenberg, *Armezorg te Leiden*, p. 106.
[71] Oosterbaan, *Oude Kerk*, pp. 297–300.
[72] In even years the procession would begin in the Nieuwe Kerk and feature its icons, while in odd years the Oude Kerk would be featured: Verhoeven, *Devotie en negotie*, p. 37. A. H. Bredero has argued that one reason the Catholic Church never canonized Gertruid van Oosten was because the parish leaders in the Nieuwe Kerk played down her influence: Bredero, "Gertrui van Oosten," p. 94.

celebrations. In 1498, for example, city authorities established that the annual Palm Sunday procession would be hosted in each parish in alternate years.[73]

Processions during the high points of the liturgical year afforded magistrates periodic opportunities to diminish inter-parish strife. Processions also functioned to foster a sense of civic unity among all townsfolk. With this objective in mind, magistrates called for and regulated city-wide celebrations and religious processions in times of crisis and during the course of the liturgical year. In 1480, the city government of Leiden organized a procession of the Holy Sacrament during a flare up of the *Hoekse–Kabeljauwse* conflict in order to appeal to God "that we may come to quiet, peace, and unity."[74] Gouda magistrates ordered processions on nine occasions between 1507 and 1521 to appeal for good weather, peace, and prosperity.[75] Beyond periods of crisis, these processions, held on the most important religious feast days and in conjunction with a city's own particular history, symbolized the visual definition of community advanced by urban elites.

The processions expressed the ideal that the municipal corporation was an indivisible sacred community. One of the most important religious celebrations in Haarlem and Amsterdam was the procession of the Holy Sacrament, held every Wednesday after March 12 and on the second Thursday after Pentecost.[76] City governments superintended the elaborate preparations for these events. Before the procession in Amsterdam, workers made sure the parade route, *Heerstraat*, was in good condition, a course that was designated "via sacra" because it led to the Heilige Stede.[77] Magistrates in Delft mandated that everyone had to clean the outside of their houses for their most significant procession on St. Odolf's Day.[78] In the procession of the Holy Sacrament in Amsterdam, the elevated host led the course, followed by the *schepenen*, *vroedschap*, guilds, militia, various relics, numerous people dressed as angels and devils, singers, and priests.[79] Incorporating municipal figures alongside religious ones, these rituals professed civic and religious unanimity in Amsterdam that was present in other cities of Holland during the late middle ages.

If harmony was one goal of religious processions, these occasions also reinforced

---

[73] Roodenburg, *Onder censuur*, pp. 47–8, 58. Natalie Davis has argued that a primary goal behind the sacramental processions in Lyons was to instill a sense of unity in the city's two parishes, which were separated by the Saône River: Davis, "The body social," p. 56.

[74] Quoted from Roodenburg, *Onder censuur*, p. 66.

[75] Couquerque and van Embden, *Gouda rechtsbronnen*, pp. 267, 285, 288, 291, 299, 313, 328, 342–3, 365. The Amsterdam city government called for a procession in the late fifteenth century for the same reasons: Breen, *Amsterdam rechtsbronnen*, p. 212. In 1458, the Dordrecht magistrates ordered an annual procession to preserve the memory of the miraculous preservation of the Holy Cross in the 1457 fire: Fruin, *Oudste rechten Dordrecht*, vol. I, p. 312.

[76] Roodenburg, *Onder censuur*, p. 62.

[77] O. F. ter Reegen, *De sacramentsprocessie: onderzoek naar de bronnen van het processie-ceremonieel in het ceremoniale episcoporum* (Brussels, 1965), p. 198.

[78] Verhoeven, *Devotie en negotie*, p. 36. The city government of Dordrecht made similar provisions in 1497: Fruin, *Oudste rechten Dordrecht*, vol. II, p. 191.

[79] Roodenburg, *Onder censuur*, pp. 63–4.

social distinctions. In a comparative study of several English cities in this period, Mervyn James has contended that processions reveal a city's social hierarchy. The degree of social rank, according to James, was determined by one's relative proximity to the Holy Sacrament.[80] This conclusion corresponded to the social distinctions of burial locations in the churches and churchyards of these cities. The highest civic orders in Delft and Amsterdam, the burgomasters and the guilds, marched closest to the Sacrament. Herman Roodenburg has placed emphasis on the representation of "reconciliation and consensus," as the social body centered itself around the body of Christ present in the consecrated Sacrament. Thus, Roodenburg concluded that the processions functioned to demonstrate that the city was "a great harmonious community in which not only the fraternal parishes were united, but also – and apparently in complete acceptance of the existing power relations – all members of society."[81]

Two of the major developments in late medieval Holland which had a major bearing on charitable institutions were the ascending political power of urban patriciates and the growing importance of lay piety. Patriciates fought for the particular economic interests of their cities in the province and ordered social life in the municipality. These efforts led to an intense identification with the local municipal community. The varied expressions of lay piety occurred within this political and social arrangement, yielding forms of piety that cannot be distinguished from the traditions of civic life. In promoting these ideals, magistrates conceived their cities to be sacred and civic communities under their governance. It was this tacit understanding of the community that had shaped charitable giving in Holland's chief cities during the late middle ages.

THE COMMUNAL CHARACTER OF LATE MEDIEVAL POOR RELIEF

Enveloped within this cultural ethos, poor relief in the cities of Holland conformed to the ideal that all inhabitants of the city were bound together within a sacred and civic community under the authority of the magistracy. The communal character of poor relief in Holland grew out of the medieval church's understanding of poverty and charity. Yet the administration of poor relief was not the primary prerogative of ecclesiastical leaders. For, as early as the fourteenth century, magistrates in these cities assumed fundamental control over parish poor relief and even exercised some influence in monastic charity. Concerned with the economic welfare of the city, magistrates regarded charity as both a civic responsibility and a religious duty within the cultural framework of medieval Christianity.[82]

The church taught that charity was a sacred task incumbent upon all Christians.

---

[80] Mervyn E. James, "Ritual drama and the social body in the late medieval English town," *Past and Present* 98 (1983), pp. 3–29. Edward Muir had made a similar point from Venetian processions: Muir, *Renaissance Venice*, p. 203.

[81] Roodenburg, *Onder censuur*, p. 68.   [82] Bredero, *Christenheid en christendom*, p. 277.

2.3 J. C. Droochsloot, *The seven works of mercy*. Centraal Museum, Utrecht

Based on Christ's sermon in the twenty-fifth chapter of St. Matthew, theologians identified "seven works of mercy" that became central to the relationship between a Christian society and its poor. In this account, Jesus identified the righteous to be those who fed the hungry, gave drink to the thirsty, clothed the naked, sheltered the stranger, comforted the sick, and visited the prisoner.[83] The church added a seventh duty: burying the dead. These benevolent actions brought rich and poor into a mutually beneficial personal relationship. The advantages accorded to the needy are clear, yet the well-off gained as well, because the poor were believed to be mediators between God and donors. The poor possessed a special relationship to God because they were understood to be sacred. As stated by the Spanish writer, Mateo Aleman, "to the rich are given temporal goods and to the poor are given spiritual goods, so that in return for distributing earthly possessions among the poor, grace is bought."[84] The church, therefore, reserved a dignity and a useful place for both those who were born into poverty and those clerics who swore to live a life of poverty.

Within the Catholic sacramental order, the poor offered the opportunity for the rest of society to participate in charitable giving, which was credited as penance. It was not uncommon for church authorities to assign monetary figures earmarked for poor relief as recompense for moral lapses. Canonists did distinguish between "sturdy beggars" and the "deserving poor," yet they cautioned that charity was not to be regulated with the intent of excluding the non-deserving, but only to help those who needed assistance.[85] The city's poor were essential to the sacramentalized social order of late medieval society. Or, as Natalie Davis has argued for sixteenth-century France, the poor, as part of the sacred in a city, were one way in which religion manifested itself in municipal values.[86] These religious assumptions shaped the theoretical bases that underlay pre-Reformation charity in Holland's cities.

CITY GOVERNMENTS AND MONASTERIES

Although the primary function of monasteries was corporate liturgical worship, they were also the oldest charitable institutions in Latin Christendom. Since the early middle ages, monks and nuns provided food to the poor who came to their gates, lodged travelers of all sorts, and worked in a variety of capacities to care for those in wretched circumstances. In a continent largely bereft of cities, monastic institutions became not only of agents charitable giving, but they were also the centers of intellectual creativity and agricultural production in medieval Europe. Unfortunately, the lack of extant source material makes it impossible to assess the extent of charity offered by monastic institutions in Holland. According to Brian Tierney, monastic benevolence in late medieval Europe was probably more indiscriminate

[83] See Matthew 25:31–46. [84] Quoted in Flynn, *Sacred Charity*, p. 76.
[85] Galpern, *Religions*, p. 43. [86] Davis, "The body social," pp. 40–1.

45

and less regulated than parish charity.[87] What is significant for this study, however, is how Holland's magistrates attempted to protect parish foundations from monastic encroachment and to utilize monastic revenues for parish relief.

In most areas of Europe, the establishment of cloisters preceded the formation of towns and cities. In Holland, however, urban growth took place before the peak period of monastic development. Certainly there were a number of monastic institutions in Holland before the fourteenth century, but they were not established on a large scale, at least in the vicinity of the six great cities, until the fifteenth century.[88] In fact, of the ninety-two monasteries that I have identified in and around the cities in 1500, fifty-nine had been established in the fifteenth century (see appendix 2.1). By that time, Dordrecht, Haarlem, Delft, Leiden, Amsterdam, and Gouda had already established a tradition of strong municipal governance.

Urban patricians and even city governments could play an active part in founding monasteries. In Leiden, for example, elite families took a strong leadership role in the establishment of several monastic foundations. Pieter uten Pol and his father Daniel collaborated with Claas van Ruven Dirkszoon van Tetrode to establish the Engelendael monastery in 1410. Both families donated land and involved themselves in the affairs of Engelendael. Simon Janszoon van Hilleghom, also from a patrician family, became prior of the cloister in 1422.[89]

The Gouda magistrates requested in 1418 that the Provincial of Cologne recognize formally a community of Observant Franciscans that would operate a hospital for the sick and poor. After all parties gave permission, the magistrates participated in working out the mutual responsibilities and obligations of the cloister and the pastor of St. Jan's Kerk. The monastery received donations from the city government, and in return the Franciscans alleviated the burden of the parish pastor by preaching in St. Jan. In 1453, Haarlem burghers also sent a petition to Philip of Burgundy and Pope Nicholas V asking them to permit the Franciscans to build a convent in the city.[90]

Although patricians could be favorably inclined toward religious orders, city governments also tried to prevent monasteries from draining the resources of the parish. Throughout Europe it was not uncommon for parishes to have an uneasy relationship with monastic institutions, especially if a monastery had the right of patronage over the parish. In this case, a monastery appropriated a portion of parish revenue for the upkeep of the cloister and for its charitable services. Thus, the

[87] Tierney, *Medieval Poor Law*, pp. 79–82. For some useful, albeit brief, information on monastic charity in Holland, see A. Querido, *Godshuizen en gasthuizen* (Amsterdam, 1960), pp. 10–12.

[88] A. G. Jongkees, "Holland in Erasmus' tijd," in de Boer and Marsijle, *De Nederlanden in de late middeleeuwen*, p. 381, has claimed that the number of monastic institutions in Holland reached a high point in 1475 at 180 monasteries.

[89] Other elite families in Leiden took similar initiatives in the Mariënpoel convent, the convent of St. Agatha, and the cloister of St. Jerome during the early fifteenth century: van Kan, *Sleutels*, pp. 203–5.

[90] J. Taal, *De archieven vande Goudse kloosters* ('s-Gravenhage, 1957), pp. 9–10; Overmeer, *Haarlem*, p. 117.

possibility existed that parish income devoted to charity could be diverted for monastic purposes.[91]

In 1262 the Delft city government intervened in a protracted dispute between the provost of Koningsveld abbey and the pastor of the Oude Kerk over patronage of the Oude Almshouse and its chapel.[92] Both the provost and the pastor regarded them to be within their own patronage. In an attempt to solve the conflict, the Delft government obtained a decision from the count of Holland in 1282 that granted the *schepenen* the authority to oversee the financial management of the Oude Almshouse.[93] The provost continued to have appointment powers over the chaplaincy of the almshouse, but the magistrates appointed two of the three regents (*gasthuismeesters*) who governed it.[94] So not only did the Delft magistrates defend what they believed were parish institutions from the abbey's control, but they also used this opportunity to assert municipal authority over them.

The city government of Amsterdam attempted to utilize monastic revenues for parish poor relief and to prevent religious orders from laying further claims to city property. In early fifteenth-century Amsterdam, lay poor relief officers in the Nieuwe parish distributed food to parish poor from the St. Margaret cloister. An edict of Count Willem VI of Holland in 1411 limited the ecclesiastical purchase of estates that lay within municipal jurisdiction to parish churches and almshouses. The decree aimed at preventing cloisters from accumulating large portions of property within the city limits of Amsterdam. In 1524, Emperor Charles V placed all monastic property on a par with all other ecclesiastical property in the city. Twelve years later, another imperial edict gave the Amsterdam *vroedschap* the power to administer all ecclesiastical properties within the city limits in order to maintain their services to the citizens of Amsterdam.[95] During the same period, all the cities resisted a decree by the Bishop of Utrecht to place many lay female communities (*begijnhofjes*) across Holland under a formal religious order. No doubt municipal opposition stemmed from property ramifications. As lay communities, beguine property was subject to temporal jurisdiction, but the lands of convents went into the dead hand of the church.[96]

Magistrates in Gouda, Dordrecht, and Leiden also attempted to make sure that the parish benefited from religious cloisters not under their control. In 1418, the Gouda magistrates began to appoint three regents to collect and administer the

---

[91] Tierney, *Medieval Poor Law*, p. 79.
[92] Lying just outside the city, Koningsveld Abbey was the first foundation of St. Norbert in Holland. The order placed a strong emphasis on charity: D. P. Oosterbaan, *Het Oude en Nieuwe Gasthuis te Delft* (Delft, 1954), p. 70.
[93] The count had the patronage right over the Oude Kerk. The count appointed the pastor in consultation with the Bishop of Utrecht: Verhoeven, *Devotie en negotie*, p. 21.
[94] Later in 1351, during the *Hoekse–Kabeljouwse* dispute, the count of Holland authorized the magistracy to appoint all the almshouse regents: Oosterbaan, *Gasthuis*, pp. 93–111.
[95] Commelin, *Amsterdam*, vol. I, pp. 196, 520–2.
[96] Hagemeijer, "Devote vrouwen," p. 231. The church's dead hand (*mortmain*) refers to the permanent inalienability of properties left to the Catholic Church.

rents for the sisters of St. Margaret. Later, when the *Collatiehuis* of the Brothers of St. Jerome fell on hard times from 1443 to 1447, and again from 1454 to 1455, the city government allocated the building and its revenues for parish poor relief.[97] A municipal ordinance in Dordrecht in 1442 stated that "the city government will have no more dealings with the jurisdiction of monastic government."[98] While it is not altogether clear to what matter this obscure ordinance refers, it does suggest that the Dordrecht city government had previously attempted to exercise its authority over monastic institutions.

In Leiden, the Engelendael cloister, which was affiliated with the local Windersheimer community, attained a distinguished reputation for care of the poor.[99] Not so coincidentally, the patron, Pieter uten Pol was a poor relief officer in the Blessed Virgin parish.[100] Though there is no direct evidence linking the charitable activities of Engelendael to parish relief, it would not seem unlikely that these three men could have worked to organize the efforts of these two foundations.

There is also some fragmented evidence indicating that cities inserted themselves in the affairs of monastic life. In 1445, because of complaints from the "good people of the magistracy of Leiden," the Bishop of Utrecht authorized the city fathers and the prior of the Franciscan monastery to expel monks who violated their orders. Any property vacated by the expelled friars was to be allocated for parish poor relief.[101] The Observant cloister that the Gouda city government helped establish in 1418 did not meet the expectations of the magistrates. So, in 1439, they sent a letter to the Council of Basel asking that the monastery be placed under the authority of the Observants of St. Omer instead of the Cologne Provincial. In this dispatch, the government complained about the "bad regiment" of brothers who failed to carry out their duties to the parish.[102] Scattered evidence from the six great cities shows that magistrates took a great deal of interest in the activities of these religious foundations. Magistrates often cooperated with abbots and priors in the realm of poor relief. At the same time, city governments kept a watchful eye on the lives of the regular clergy and guarded parish foundations from monastic control.

CITY GOVERNMENTS AND PARISH CHARITY

It was parish foundations that took on the most important role in urban poor relief in medieval Holland. By 1400 there were a multitude of endowments in each parish each with its own eleemosynary purpose. Despite all of their peculiarities, the two primary agencies for parish charity in all of the six cities were almshouses and

---

[97] Couquerque and van Embden, *Gouda rechtsbronnen*, p. 70. The Gouda magistrates also exercised a significant influence over the convents of St. Agnes and St. Bridget: Taal, *Goudse kloosters*, pp. 13–15, 34, 58, 63.
[98] Fruin, *Oudste rechten Dordrecht*, vol. II, p. 90.　　[99] Ligtenberg, *Armezorg te Leiden*, p. 11.
[100] Van Kan, *Sleutels*, pp. 203–5.
[101] Joosting and Muller, *Kerkelijke rechtspraak*, vol. IV, pp. 213–24.
[102] Taal, *Goudse kloosters*, p. 10.

outside relief agencies, known either as *Heilige Geestmeesters* (Holy Ghost Masters) or as *huiszittende meesters* (masters of the residing poor). Almshouses provided inside relief to the disabled, the sick, the orphaned, and the aged, and also gave temporary shelter to travelers. With the exception of travelers, inmates came from the ranks of the destitute who, for various reasons, could not reside anywhere else. Alongside, and sometimes in conjunction with, almshouses, *Heilige Geestmeesters* managed the distribution of food and clothing to the poor who had some sort of residence (*huiszittende armen*). These folk lived on their own and probably had little or no family to count on for support, but were not so sick or destitute that they needed to enter an almshouse.

In spite of the idiosyncratic nature of these institutions, as a whole they constituted a fragmented network of parish poor relief. For the purposes of this study, they reveal the communal nature of urban charity in late medieval Holland. Parish poor relief reflected the confluence of sacred obligations and civic responsibilities for the poor. Charity was the highest expression of Christian piety, and, at the same time, the parish institutions that carried out this obligation came under increasing magisterial control during the fourteenth and fifteenth centuries.

ALMSHOUSES

The almshouse was the oldest and one of the most important parish poor relief institutions in medieval Holland. Almshouses were first established in Dordrecht, Haarlem, Delft, Leiden, Amsterdam, and Gouda in the middle ages as their parishes underwent significant expansion. The earliest parish almshouses appeared in Delft (Oude Almshouse, 1252), Leiden (St. Katherine Almshouse, 1276), and Haarlem (Oude Almshouse, 1284).[103] Seven fairly small almshouses were created in Dordrecht between 1300 and 1363, four of which were founded by guilds.[104] Two guilds in Amsterdam, the almshouse guild and a fisher's guild, founded the Oude (also St. Elizabeth and Heilige Geest) Almshouse and the St. Pieter Almshouse in 1363 and 1382, respectively.[105] The first almshouses in Gouda was dedicated to St. Katherine sometime in the fourteenth century.[106]

Though they came in all shapes and sizes, almshouses in these six cities shared three basic characteristics. They constituted a well-organized system of relief; they embodied the sacral attributes of medieval charity; and they owed their origins to

[103] Oosterbaan, *Gasthuis*, pp. 3–6; Ligtenberg, *Armezorg te Leiden*, pp. 19–21; F. Allan, *Geschiedenissen beschrijving van Haarlem van de vroegste tijden tot onze dagen*, 4 vols. (Haarlem, 1883; reprint edn., 1973), vol. IV, pp. 2–4.
[104] The parish almshouses in Dordrecht were St. Nicholas (1300), Holy Cross (1306), and St. Jacob (1348). The guild almshouses were St. Pieter and St. Paul (1300), St. John (1300), the Blessed Virgin (1306), and Great Shipper (1363). In addition, there is mention of a Small Shipper's almshouse in 1064: Sels, *Dordrecht*, pp. 47–9.
[105] Wagenaar, *Amsterdam*, vol. I, pp. 27–8.
[106] The first official record relating to the almshouse is dated 1391, but it is very likely that it existed long before this date: Walvis, *Gouda*, vol. I, p. 154.

the benefactions of the lay urban patriciate. With the exception of Dordrecht, each city maintained a general-purpose almshouse, often the first of the oldest parish (see appendix 2.2). As benefactors founded new almshouses, they were usually smaller institutions endowed for a specific type of indigence (e.g., plague victims, old age) or a particular clientele (e.g., men, women, orphans). These secondary almshouses supplemented the charitable services of older parish-wide almshouses.

The oldest foundations were multi-functional: they housed the sick, the aged, and the orphaned of the parish, while the almshouse regents distributed outside relief to the residential poor. As new parishes were formed in Leiden, Delft, and Amsterdam, city governments worked with benefactors and religious authorities to organize almshouses for the new parish. In Leiden and Delft, the new parish almshouses were designated for a specific clientele, whereas the St. Elizabeth Almshouse in Amsterdam was also a general-purpose institution for the Nieuwe Zijde parish.[107] Thus, new almshouses were created with some forethought about how they might fit into the needs of the parish. Almshouses were part of a fairly well-organized relief network at a very early date in Holland.

A second characteristic of almshouses was that they embodied a collective pursuit of salvation through service to the poor. One of the most well-studied charitable institutions in Holland, Delft's Oude Almshouse, gives some indication of the spiritual ideals inherent in medieval poor relief. As the inscription over the entrance declared, the poor were "Christus in pauperibus." The brothers and sisters of St. Norbert (in the Koningsveld abbey) served in the almshouse, providing shelter to travelers, caring for the sick, and distributing food to the needy. Travelers requesting lodging had to present themselves between 7 and 8 p.m. in the winters and an hour later in the summers. They could not stay longer than two nights, although, with special permission, they could remain an extra night. Held to relatively rigid standards, the Norbertines underwent stringent fasting periods and went to confession at least once a month. Their clothing prescriptions reflected their sacred conception of charity. Designating servitude, a scapular was the prominent symbolic piece of their habit. The brothers wore a light gray scapular over an undertunic and gray caps, while the sisters attired themselves in a large-sleeved white robe with a narrow collar over which also hung a gray scapular.[108]

Service to the poor coalesced with religious worship in the Oude Almshouse. In 1265, the Bishop of Utrecht, Hendrik van Vianen, granted the almshouse the right to create a churchyard next to the chapel, where the clergy and poor of the almshouse

---

[107] For Leiden there were St. Elisabeth Almshouse in St. Pankras parish (c. 1315) and the Blessed Virgin Almshouse in the Blessed Virgin parish (c. 1365). Both of these almshouses were devoted to the care of poor women. For Delft there was St. Joris Almshouse in Nieuwe parish (1407). St. Joris was designated for the insane. For Amsterdam there was the Blessed Virgin Almshouse in Nieuwe Zijde parish (Ligtenberg, *Armezorg te Leiden*, p. 106; Oosterbaan, *Gasthuis*, pp. 36–8; Wagenaar, *Amsterdam*, vol. I, p. 27). In addition, the St. Nicholas Almshouse appeared in the Nieuwe Parish of Dordrecht–Merwede around 1300: Sels, *Dordrecht*, p. 48.

[108] Oosterbaan, *Gasthuis*, pp. 51–7, 63–8.

might be buried. Burial in the churchyard was limited to the brothers, sisters, and inhabitants of the almshouse, uniting the dead within its spiritual community.[109] The poor and the ministering clergy were understood to exist as community centered around the Christian understanding of poverty, charity, and piety.

The Oude Almshouse in Delft functioned much like other almshouses in Holland's urban parishes. The oldest document from the St. Katherine Almshouse in Leiden (1276) explicitly stated that the almshouse was dedicated to the ideal of performing the seven works of mercy.[110] Almost all almshouses contained chapels for the spiritual care of inmates and for the salvation of their patrons. In 1391, Frank Dirck Frankenszoon readied himself for his death by bequeathing a portion of his estate to erect a chapel at the Blessed Virgin Almshouse in the Nieuwe Zijde parish of Amsterdam. He stated to the burgomasters that he was doing this for "the salvation of my soul, my parents, my wives, my children, my brothers, and my sisters and in the honor of God."[111]

The charitable work within the Oude Almshouse of Haarlem was closely intertwined with worship within the church of St. Gangolf, where the resident priest celebrated Mass every Monday. The church wardens of St. Gangolf also maintained a churchyard where almshouse chaplains were buried alongside the poor inhabitants to whom they ministered.[112] Accordingly, this arrangement, like that of the Oude Almshouse in Delft, signified a community of indigent residents and spiritual caretakers bound together by a sacral relationship. In Gouda, nuns cared for the sick in the St. Katherine Almshouse and priests celebrated Mass there twice a week.[113]

A third feature of parish almshouses was that their greatest benefactors were urban patricians. In Leiden, the St. Elizabeth Almshouse located in the parish of St. Pankras was originally founded specifically for poor, sick, and traveling women. The original benefactors were Jan Dirck Coenenszoon and Katrijn Tedendochter who established St. Elizabeth between 1428 and 1432. He had served in numerous municipal and parish posts associated with poor relief in Leiden, including *Heilige Geestmeester* in 1413, church warden of St. Pieter Church in 1423, *huiszitten meester* in the parish of the Blessed Virgin in 1427, regent of the St. Katherine Almshouse in 1431, *schepen* in 1439, and burgomaster in 1450. In 1395, Claes Rengher, a former *schepen*, and his wife Machtelt van den Zijl, founded the almshouse of the Blessed Virgin. Motivated by religious sentiments, they created it "in the honor of God, the pure mother, and the Virgin Mary."[114]

In Haarlem, a local patrician, Coen Cusar, consigned his house to the Heilige Geest foundation in 1394. It became the almshouse of the Heilige Geest (also known as Coen Cuser Almshouse). Over the course of the fifteenth century, wealthy patrons endowed eight new almshouses, three of which were donated to

---

[109] *Ibid.*, pp. 86–8. [110] Ligtenberg, *Armezorg te Leiden*, p. 64.
[111] Van der Laan, *Amsterdam oorkondenboek*, p. 371. [112] Allan, *Haarlem*, vol. IV, pp. 2–3.
[113] Walvis, *Gouda*, vol. II, pp. 157–8. [114] Ligtenberg, *Armezorg te Leiden*, pp. 85 (quote), 106–7.

guilds.[115] In Gouda, Wilhelm Wilhelmszoon Vroesen bequeathed his estate to create an almshouse for old men (*Oudmannenhuis*) in Gouda in the sixteenth century. The municipal ordinance sanctioning the transfer of property noted that Vroesen acted "purely, according to God's will."[116] In Dordrecht, Tielman de Rode and Herman Haec Jacopszoon, a canon of the Grote Kerk, founded the Heilige Geesthuis of the Nieuw Kerk in 1436.[117] While the original patrons of all the almshouses in the six cities are not known, it is clear that urban elites, acting out of religious motives, were a significant element in the establishment of parish foundations.

OUTSIDE RELIEF

Over the course of the fourteenth and fifteenth centuries, there were several important developments that altered the structure of parish poor relief. These included the advent of a separate agency which administered outside relief to the residential poor, and the increased influence of lay magistrates in all areas of parish charity. As a result, almshouses became much more specialized, serving either as hospitals, orphanages, or as residences for the aged. By the sixteenth century, city governments had consolidated their authority over a parish relief network for those within the municipal community.

Appearing in these cities in the fourteenth century, the parish agency that eventually took over the responsibility for the residential poor was the Heilige Geest.[118] The terminology originated out of a fraternity led by Guy de Montpelier in twelfth-century France. The brotherhood committed itself to emulating Christ's teachings in the sixth chapter of St. Luke's gospel, which equated care for others with service to God. De Montpelier adopted "Holy Ghost" from St. Bernard of Clairvaux, who wrote, "Love is always the gift of the Holy Ghost."[119] Formally recognized by Innocent III, the fraternity spawned similar organizations throughout cities in France and the Low Countries in the late middle ages.[120]

[115] John Nicolaas Diertszoon founded the St. Anthony Almshouse in 1440 and donated it to the guild of the Holy Cross. Simon Gerritszoon Kooman endowed the St. Jacob Almshouse and bestowed it upon the guild of St. Jacob. Claes Brensoenszoon inaugurated the Blessed Virgin Almshouse in 1440; Huygen Roepers and his sister Catharine established the St. Martin Almshouse in 1472 and conferred it upon the brewers' guild: Allan, *Haarlem*, vol. IV, pp. 43, 140, 142.

[116] Walvis, *Gouda*, vol. I, p. 168. For similar measures in Amsterdam, see van der Laan, *Amsterdam oorkondenboek*, pp. 146–7.

[117] Balen, *Dordrecht*, p. 162.

[118] Another traditional responsibility of the Heilige Geest in Holland's cities was to care for orphans and foundlings: Wijbenga, *Delft*, vol. I, pp. 139, 141; Walvis, *Gouda*, vol. I, p. 192; Ligtenberg, *Leiden*, p. 177; Balen, *Dordrecht*, pp. 162, 170, 176; Schreveli, *Haarlemias*, p. 27. The only possible exception is Amsterdam, where I have not been able to determine if the Heilige Geest there performed this service.

[119] Quoted from M. C. C. Slotemaker de Bruine, *Het ideaal van de navolging van Christus ten tijde van Bernard van Clairvaux* (Wageningen, 1926), p. 34.

[120] The first mention of the Heilige Geest in the Low Countries was in Brabant in the first half of the thirteenth century: van Werveke, "De steden," p. 415.

While the precise origins and spread of the foundation into Holland is not clear, over the course of the fourteenth century the Heilige Geest became the parochial instrument of outside charity in all six cities. At that time, it was not a private confraternity, but it functioned as the parish poor relief agency for the residential poor. By 1300, the *Heilige Geestmeesters* of Haarlem were the primary relief agency for the residential poor in the city's only parish.[121] In 1316, Leiden's two *Heilige Geestmeesters* distributed food to the residential poor, yet also cared for the sick, and assisted travelers out of the St. Katherine Almshouse and later out of the church of St. Pieter.[122] *Heilige Geestmeesters* also served the residential poor in Delft by 1342; by the fifteenth century, the city had six *Heilige Geestmeesters*, three for each parish.[123] The earliest mention of the Heilige Geest in Gouda was in 1391, though it appears to have been already well organized at that time. In that year, Willem Sonderkanck announced to the city government that he wanted to leave a significant portion of his estate to the Heilige Geest. The six *Heilige Geestmeesters* took collections in the churches of the parish and dispensed food to residents of the almshouses and the residential poor nine times a month.[124] In Amsterdam, the Heilige Geest provided outside relief through the Oude Almshouse (also called the Heilige Geest Alms-house). The exact origins of the Heilige Geest in Amsterdam are also not clear. The earliest reference I have found is in 1363, when the *schepenen* approved the transfer of a house and its property to the Heilige Geest Almshouse.[125] By the early fifteenth century, Dordrecht maintained two Heilige Geest foundations, one for the Grote parish and one for the neighborhood around the Nieuw Kerk. The former dated from sometime in the fourteenth century, whereas the latter was first mentioned in 1436. Like their counterparts in the other six cities, they administered revenues and gave assistance to the residential poor of the city.[126]

The only evidence that I have found about the amount of charity that the Heilige Geest provided to the residential poor comes from fifteenth-century Leiden. In 1425 the Leiden *Heilige Geestmeesters* distributed shoes to 495 people out of a population of 6,000, and 1,500 received bread on a regular basis. At the end of the fifteenth century, they offered a food subsidy, consisting largely of bread, to 1,600 people during Christmas.[127]

While the sacred duties of Christian charity shaped the motivations of Heilige Geest foundations, they were lay parish organizations supervised by an urban magistracy. In rural parishes, it was not uncommon for a priest to serve as a *Heilige*

[121] Allan, *Haarlem*, vol. IV, p. 43.
[122] Van Kan, *Sleutels*, p. 206. In 1390, the ministry of the Heilige Geest took on the additional responsibility for the care of lepers: Ligtenberg, *Armezorg te Leiden*, p. 125.
[123] Verhoeven, *Devotie en negotie*, p. 26.
[124] Walvis, *Gouda*, vol. I, pp. 192–6; J. E. J. Geselschap, "Het verenigde Wees- en Aalmoezeniershuis te Gouda 1495–1948," in *Gouda zeven eeuwen stad*, p. 241.
[125] Van der Laan, *Amsterdam oorkondenboek*, p. 155.
[126] Both agencies maintained a hospital for plague victims and an orphanage: Balen, *Dordrecht*, pp. 162, 170; Jensma, *Onze Lieve Vrouwekerk*, p. 59.
[127] Ligtenberg, *Armezorg te Leiden*, pp. 13–14.

Geestmeester, but in the municipal parishes, clergy, as a general rule, did not serve in this capacity.[128] In Dordrecht, Haarlem, Delft, Leiden, Amsterdam, and Gouda, magistrates appointed its regents and oversaw the administration of its activities. Furthermore, in all of the six cities, the *Heilige Geestmeesters* came from the ranks of the urban patriciate.[129] Thus, as early as the fourteenth century, city governments in Holland had instituted a parish poor relief agency for the residential poor. Magistrates oversaw the work of the Heilige Geest and selected regents from their own social circles.

COORDINATION OF PARISH CHARITY

Civil control over outside relief paralleled governmental authority over all alms-houses. The magistrates in Amsterdam and Leiden undertook the most extensive programs to coordinate outside relief efforts and charity in almshouses. Since the early 1300s, the Amsterdam *vroedschap* had appointed all officers who administered the affairs of all almshouses, orphanages, and hospitals.[130] Sometime between 1370 and 1380, the Amsterdam government implemented a new outside agency in the Oude Zijde parish, known as the *huiszitten meesters*. Appointed by the magistrates, four *huiszitten meesters* became responsible for collecting revenues and distributing food to the residential poor in the city's only parish. After the creation of the Nieuwe Zijde parish in 1408, the magistrates formed a separate body of *huiszitten meesters* for each parish. Each college also took possession of a number of residences in the city that lodged a few aged men and women.[131]

With respect to the almshouses, the city government merged the Oude (Heilige Geest) Almshouse with the St. Pieter Almshouse in 1493. The expanded St. Pieter Almshouse served as the primary inside relief institution for old men in both parishes. The magistrates established the Blessed Virgin almshouse for old women in the city. In addition, the almshouses of St. Nicholas (also referred to as St. Anthony) and of St. Joris were converted into leper hospitals (*leprooshuizen*).[132]

A short time later, the city government of Leiden gradually began to streamline parish poor relief. In 1427, the Leiden magistrates established an entirely new

[128] G. J. Mentink, "Armenzorg en armoede in de archivische bronnen in de Noordelijke Nederlanden, 1531–1854," *Tijdschrift voor Geschiedenis* 88 (1975), p. 552.

[129] Allan, *Haarlem*, vol. IV, p. 140; Verhoeven, *Devotie en negotie*, p. 26; van Kan, *Sleutels*, pp. 206–7; Balen, *Dordrecht*, p. 162; Walvis, *Gouda*, vol. I, p. 192; Wagenaar, *Amsterdam*, vol. I, p. 27. The Leiden magistrates also selected a financial administrator (*rentmeester*) to manage the assets of the Heilige Geest. The administrator and the *Heilige Geestmeesters* were required to give an annual accounting to the magistrates: Ligtenberg, *Armezorg te Leiden*, pp. 166–7.

[130] Wagenaar, *Amsterdam*, vol. II, pp. 241–2.

[131] Evenhuis, *Ook dat was Amsterdam*, vol. II, p. 73; Wagenaar, *Amsterdam*, vol. I, p. 31, vol. II, pp. 262–3.

[132] The Heilige Stede Almshouse, established by the burgomaster Dirck Holland in 1422, housed both old men and women. Orphans were also cared for in St. Pieter and the Blessed Virgin Almshouses until 1524, when a new orphanage was built: Wagenaar, *Amsterdam*, vol. I, pp. 27–9, vol. II, pp. 242–3, 276, 301, 311.

organization, directed by lay almoners, who oversaw a wide range of relief activities. These almoners collected alms, purchased grain, distributed bread, and administered finances. Since they dispensed aid to the *huiszittende armen*, these officials, as in Amsterdam, were known as the *huiszitten meesters*. Eventually, the new municipal organization took over most of the responsibilities of the *Heilige Geestmeesters*, who after 1427 devoted their attention exclusively to the care of orphans and foundlings.[133]

After 1427, Leiden's *huiszitten meesters* worked in conjunction with the officers of the major parish almshouses: the St. Katherine Almshouse (of St. Pieter), and the St. Elizabeth Almshouse and the Blessed Virgin Almshouse (both of St. Pankras). Governed by lay regents who were appointed by the city government, the almshouses continued to house the infirm, while the almoners distributed outside relief from these institutions. The responsibility for raising funds for the St. Katherine Almshouse lay largely with the clergy of St. Pieter's parish. They appealed to prospective benefactors by offering Masses in their memory, in return for donations. Voluntary donations and testaments were the primary source of the almshouse's revenues, which furnished the almshouse with a sizable amount of capital by the late fifteenth century.[134]

The magistrates also selected the regents for the St. Elizabeth Almshouse, who were accountable to the city for the institution's financial affairs. In the middle of the fifteenth century, the almshouse had three regents; another was added by the sixteenth century. Spiritual care in the almshouse came under the authority of the rector of the St. Margaret monastery. He selected women to care for female denizens and clergy to administer the Holy Sacrament once a year and offer religious services on major feast days. The parish almoners for St. Pankras also tended to the needs of the residential poor out of the St. Elizabeth Almshouse.[135]

The Blessed Virgin Almshouse came under municipal authority in the early fifteenth century. Its benefactors (Claes Rengher and Machtelt van den Zijl) retained all authority over the almshouse from 1395 until their deaths in 1416. After their death, it came under the legal jurisdiction of the church wardens of St. Pankras parish. Several years later, the city government began to appoint regents to govern the Blessed Virgin, just as they had done for other parish almshouses.[136]

Consequently, by the early fifteenth century, parish poor relief in Leiden was fairly well defined. City magistrates appointed regents who took charge of financial affairs in the almshouses and lay almoners who administered charity to the residential poor. Clergy also participated by celebrating masses and caring for the inhabitants. Magistrates did not, however, abandon the religious bases of late medieval poor relief. The institutional reorganization does show that the magistracy, which

---

[133] Ligtenberg, *Armezorg te Leiden*, pp. 212–14, 220.   [134] *Ibid.*, p. 41.
[135] The St. Elizabeth Almshouse was devoted exclusively to caring for poor women: Ligtenberg, *Armezorg te Leiden*, pp. 106, 108, 114, 116, 118.
[136] *Ibid.*, pp. 85–8, 212.

understood itself to be the "Christian authority" (*Christelijke overheid*), assumed responsibility for social welfare measures for the municipal corporation.[137]

Parish poor relief in Amsterdam and Leiden appears to have been much more regulated than in Haarlem, Delft, Gouda, and Dordrecht. The former two cities, however, were not alone in establishing their authority over parish foundations and agencies. As eight new almshouses were founded in fifteenth-century Haarlem, the burgomasters selected the regents who administered the financial affairs of the almshouses.[138] Delft magistrates obtained ultimate oversight of the five smaller almshouses that were established in Delft between 1410 and 1500 that complemented the primary almshouse (Oude), and the relief network of the *Heilige Geestmeesters*.[139]

In Gouda, the magistrates transferred the management of a lepers' hospital to the *Heilige Geestmeesters* in 1408. This charge came in addition to their responsibilities for orphans and for the residential poor. The only other new almshouses in fifteenth-century Gouda were a hospital for the sick (Noodgodszieken Gasthuis) and an institution for indigent women (St. Elizabeth). These later almshouses simply supplemented the St. Katherine Almshouse. By the end of the fifteenth century, the *Heilige Geestmeesters* regulated all the parish foundations in Gouda. And by the end of the fifteenth century they also supervised care for orphans. At that time, the Heilige Geest in Gouda had extensive responsibilities within the various aspects of parish charity.[140]

In Dordrecht, only three additional almshouses were established in the fifteenth century, a hospital for old men (*Oudemannenhuis*), the Heilige Geesthuis of the Nieuw Kerk, and the Blessed Virgin in 1400. The lack of new almshouses in Dordrecht was perhaps due to the presence of twelve almshouses that had been formed in the 1300s. Even so, the Dordrecht patriciate retained just as much control over parish charity as the other cities.[141]

THE LIMITATIONS OF PARISH CHARITY

The magistrates of late medieval Holland not only held ultimate authority over parish charitable institutions, but they also set forth the rules to govern who qualified for any form of charity. A primary requisite for assistance was one's relationship to the municipal community. The municipal governments in all of these cities referred to recipients of outside relief as *huisarmen* or *huiszittende armen*. This terminology was an inherent classification. For those seeking alms, it meant

---

[137] *Ibid.*, p. 13.   [138] Allan, *Haarlem*, vol. IV, p. 25.

[139] The St. Joris Almshouse (also called Nieuwe) housed the mentally ill in 1407. And, in 1410, the city established almshouses for aged men (St. Christopher) and women (the Blessed Virgin). There were two other almshouses, St. Cornelius and St. Elizabeth, though we know almost nothing about them: van Bleyswijck, *Delft*, vol. II, pp. 494, 498, 526; Boitet, *Delft*, p. 481.

[140] Walvis, *Gouda*, vol. I, pp. 166–92, 196; Geselschap, "Aalmoezeniershuis te Gouda," p. 242.

[141] Balen, *Dordrecht*, pp. 157–75; Sels, *Dordrecht*, pp. 47–51.

that only those who had established residency status, usually for one year, could qualify.

City governments also issued restrictions on admissions for extensive stays in almshouses, hospitals, and orphanages that would have all but eliminated citizens and residents.[142] The city government of Gouda stipulated in 1408 that only sick residents could be admitted to the leper hospital; Amsterdam and Haarlem also issued residency requirements for orphanages. In addition, the magistrates in all six cities mandated that the denizens of all almshouses must bequeath what little, if any, personal property they owned to the almshouse.[143] Such a requirement would have narrowed the pool of prospective inmates to local residents who had no other means of support.

With respect to the economic threshold of poverty, there are no parish poor relief registers for this period, so we cannot analyze this issue nor the amount of parish charity provided in the six cities. What is clear, however, is that city governments empowered *Heilige Geestmeesters* (or *huiszitten meesters*) and almshouse regents to decide whether one's material conditions warranted benevolence. These officers appear to have had a great deal of discretion in judging the economic threshold for charitable assistance. I have not been able to find any written guidelines followed by almoners before the sixteenth century to determine the financial conditions that merited charitable assistance. The Gouda magistrates, for example, simply declared that alms would be given to those whom the *Heilige Geestmeesters* consented to give.

Almoners may have had some degree of latitude in deciding the degree of petitioners' needs, but they could give alms only to parish residents. Parish charity in late medieval Holland, therefore, was not indiscriminate, for city governments made a distinction between those who belonged to the municipal corporation and those who did not. Poor relief, then, marked the borders of the civic community. And it was the urban patriciate, which governed the city and oversaw the entire range of parish poor relief, who staked out those borders.

The city governments also drew up a host of regulations designed to protect parish institutions from beggars, particularly non-resident beggars. Begging could siphon off personal donations that might otherwise be given to parish poor relief. And, in all of the cities except Delft, magistrates passed ordinances designed to prohibit begging by foreign beggars.[144] In Haarlem (1390), Leiden (1397),

---

[142] In the fifteenth century, city governments began to limit the number of days that travelers could spend in almshouses: Querido, *Godshuizen*, p. 14.

[143] Walvis, *Gouda*, vol. I, pp. 161–2; Wagenaar, *Amsterdam*, vol. III, p. 150; J. Huizinga, *Rechtsbronnen der stad Haarlem in werken der vereeniging tot uitgraaf der bronnen van het Oud-Vaderlandsche Recht*, 2nd series, nr. 13 ('s-Gravenhage, 1911), p. 113; Ligtenberg, *Armezorg te Leiden*, p. 170.

[144] It is possible, and even likely, that the Delft city government issued similar anti-begging laws, but only fragments of Delft's medieval ordinances remain due to the fire of 1536. The extant ordinances do show that the magistrates, like regents in the other cities, restricted begging in the city. See J. Soutendam, ed., "Het oudste keurboek van Delft," *Nieuwe Bijdragen van Regtsgeleerheid en Wetgeving*, new series, 2 (1876), pp. 499–500.

Amsterdam (1413), and Gouda (1488), magistrates ruled that beggars must first obtain authorization from parish poor relief officials before they could beg in the city.[145] Even if someone received permission, he or she still could not beg in certain areas, such as in front of houses, inside churches, or around taverns.[146] Even though the Dordrecht city government did not begin to crack down on begging until the late sixteenth century, it did issue two ordinances in the second half of the fifteenth century that prohibited begging in churches, cloisters, and almshouses.[147]

Haarlem, Amsterdam, Gouda, and Dordrecht passed anti-begging legislation, but it was Leiden that took the strongest statutory measures against paupers. In 1459, the magistrates issued stronger ordinances that prohibited foreign beggars from staying in the tavern for more than one night in the summer and two nights in the winter. Furthermore, the only non-residents who could beg in the winters were women who had recently given birth (*kraamvrouwen*). No males between the ages of eighteen and fifty, resident or foreign, could beg in Leiden. Religious pilgrims were permitted to receive a meager stipend from the church wardens, but they had to promise to pay back the stipend on their return trip.[148]

If Leiden's government took the most resolute stance against foreign beggars, Amsterdam, Gouda, and Haarlem also attempted to restrict the movement of poor non-residents in the municipality. In 1413, Amsterdam magistrates admonished all innkeepers to inquire into the character and property of all "foreign guests" who came into their establishment. In the early sixteenth century, Gouda required that non-residents must obtain permission to lodge at an inn. As early as 1392, the Haarlem city government decreed that non-residents could not carry weapons, wear armor, or peddle goods near houses in the city.[149]

In a variety of ways, city magistrates displayed a certain mistrust about non-natives. They were outsiders who could threaten the peace of the civic community and deplete parish resources for the residential poor. An ardent concern for the collective welfare of citizens and residents prompted magistrates to draw a line between those within the municipal community and those outside its domain.

---

[145] In Leiden, beggars had to present themselves before a member of the city government, not the *Heilige Geestmeesters*: Huizinga, *Haarlem rechtsbronnen*, p. 54; Ligtenberg, *Armezorg te Leiden*, p. 285; Breen, *Amsterdam rechtsbronnen*, pp. 29–30; Couquerque and van Emden, *Gouda rechtsbronnen*, p. 94; Walvis, *Gouda*, vol. I, p. 196.

[146] Those who begged illicitly were subject to fines and deportation: Breen, *Amsterdam rechtsbronnen*, p. 30; Ligtenberg, *Armezorg te Leiden*, p. 286. Haarlem reissued proscriptions on begging at least twice more before the sixteenth century: Huizinga, *Haarlem rechtsbronnen*, pp. 54, 522; Couquerque and van Embden, *Gouda rechtsbronnen*, p. 94.

[147] Fruin, *Oudste rechten Dordrecht*, vol. I. p. 323; van Dalen, *Dordrecht*, vol. I, p. 302.

[148] Ligtenberg, *Armezorg te Leiden*, pp. 285–9.

[149] Breen, *Amsterdam rechtsbronnen*, p. 21; Couquerque and van Embden, *Gouda rechtsbronnen*, p. 311; Enschedé and Gonnet, *Kuerboeck Haerlem*, pp. 28, 39, 46.

CIVIC AUTHORITY AND RELIGIOUS CHARITY

One of the most important developments in the province of Holland in the late middle ages was the emergence of the urban community. As these six cities gained increasing autonomy, patricians consolidated their grip on political power within the municipal corporation. They advanced the economic interests of their cities in the province and promoted social stability in their communities. The latter entailed perpetuating communal ideals that bound all social levels into a cohesive corporate community. While each city developed its own unique traditions, the rituals and ceremonial forms of parish life within the Roman Catholic Church formed the theoretical basis for the routine cadence of everyday life. The centrality of parish religious life, in concert with magisterial paternalism, fostered the ideal of a cohesive urban community. Fusing sacred and civic values, this self-understanding shaped the cultural pattern of daily life in the late middle ages.

The alloy of civic and religious culture provided the cultural context for charitable institutions within the community. Church teaching equated piety with charity and legitimized poverty and the institutional forms for its alleviation. Yet, poverty was also a practical social concern that attracted the attention of urban magistrates, who had a stake in the social welfare of their citizenry. According, charitable institutions exhibited the hallmarks of the medieval community. In other words, magistrates considered poor relief to be a function of a corporate Christian community under their authority. It would be this vision of Christian community that would shape city governments' response to economic hardship and in the sixteenth century.

Appendix 2.1 *Monastic houses in the six great cities of Holland*

Dordrecht	
Observant Franciscans	1250
Augustinian Hermits	1300
Carmelites	1300s
Sisters of St. Mary Magdalen	1300s
Convent of Mariënborn	1302
Dominicans	1303
Priorienne Slotklooster	1326
Sisters of St. Clara in Jerusalem	1332
Convent of Black Sisters	1337
Huijs van het H. Zaligmakers	1382
Sisters of St. Agnes	1387
Alexian Brothers	1400s
Sisters of St. Barbara	1422
Regular Cloister at Heemsdonck	1443
Haarlem	
Carmelites	1249
Dominicans	1287
Order of Templars	1311
Sisters of St. Mary	1400s
Cloister of Regular Canons	1406
Cloister of White Friars	1414
Cloister of St. Michael	1416
Sisters of St. Ursula	1445
Sisters of St. Catherine	1446
Sisters of St. Margaret	1446
Sisters of St. Clara	1450s
Observant Franciscans	1453
Cloister of Barefoot Sisters	1465
Sisters of St. Mary Magdalen	1474
Sisters of St. Anne	1485
Augustinian Hermits	1490
Alexian Brothers	1496
Order of Lazarists	??
Sisters of St. Cecilia	??
Delft	
Koningsveld Abbey	1252
Sisters of St. Agatha	1380
Sisters of St. Barbara	1400s
Sisters of St. Ursula	1400
Cloister of Hieronymusdal	1403

Sisters of St. Clara	1415
Sisters of St. Agnes	1421
Carthusians	1430
Cloister of Zion	1432
Sisters of St. Anna	1441
Franciscans	1449
Sisters of St. Mary Magdalen	1450
Alexian Brothers	??

Leiden
Abbey of Rijnsburch	1133
Sisters of St. Margaret	1398
Cloister of St. Michael	1400s
Cloister of St. Ursula	1400s
Sisters of Abcoude	1400s
Sisters of Mary Magdalen	1400s
Sisters of Nazareth	1400s
Sisters of St. Catherine	1400s
Sisters of St. Cecilia	1400s
Sisters of Rome	1400s
Engelendael Cloister	1410
Cloister of St. Jerome	1420
Alexian Brothers	1421
Mariënpoel	1428
Aagten Cloister	1432
Franciscans	1445
Sisters of St. Agnes	1456
Leeuwenhorst Abbey	??
Schagen Cloister	??
White Nuns	??

Amsterdam
Observant Franciscans	1304
Carthusians	1392
Cloister of New Nuns	1395
Sisters of St. Clara	1395
Cloister of St. Lucas	1400s
Sisters of St. Mary	1400s
Sisters of St. Agnes	1406
Brothers of St. Paul	1409
Sisters of St. Margaret	1414
Sisters of St. Ursula	1419
Alexian Brothers	1440
Sisters of St. Mary Magdalen (Bethany)	1450s
Sisters of St. Clarissa	1475

Appendix 2.1 *(cont.)*

Cloister of Old Nuns	??
Sisters of St. Barbara	??
Sisters of St. Mary Magdalen	??
Gouda	
Cloister of St. Margaret	1386
Alexian Brothers	1395
Cloister of St. Mary	1400s
Observant Franciscans	1418
Brothers of St. Jerome	1419
Cloister of St. Catherine	1426?
Cloister of St. Mary Magdalen	1451
Cloister of St. Agnes	1455
Cloister of St. Bridget	1476
Cloister of St. Clarissa	1486

Note: Dates are approximations.

Source: Jansz. Matthys Balen, *Beschryvinge der stad Dordrecht* (Dordrecht, 1677), pp. 94, 117–52; J. Sels, *Beschrijving der stad Dordrecht* (Dordrecht, 1853), pp. 15, 27–32; J. L. van Dalen, *Geschiedenis van Dordrecht*, 2 vols. (Dordrecht, 1931–33), vol. II, pp. 739–72; W. P. J. Overmeer, *De hervorming te Haarlem* (Haarlem, 1904), pp. 115–23; Dirck van Bleyswijck, *Beschryvinge der stadt Delft*, 2 vols. (Delft, 1667), vol. I, pp. 317–58; F. J. W. van Kan, *Sleutels tot de macht: de ontwikkeling van het Leidse patriciaat tot 1420* (Hilversum, 1988), p. 205; Christina Ligtenberg, *Armezorg te Leiden tot het einde van de 16e eeuw* ('s-Gravenhage, 1908), p. 11; Henrick Haestens, Jan Oorlers, and Jan Marie, *Beschrijvinge der stad Leyden* (Leiden, 1614), pp. 83–91; Jan Wagenaar, *Amsterdam in zyne opkomst, aanwas geschiedenissen*, 3 vols. (Amsterdam, 1760), vol. I, pp. 19–25, 29–30; A. E. D'Ailly, ed., *Zeven eeuwen Amsterdam*, 9 vols. (Amsterdam, n.d.), vol. I, p. 134; J. Taal, *De archieven vande Goudse kloosters* ('s-Gravenhage, 1957), pp. 7–69; Ignatius Walvis, *Beschryving der stad Gouda*, 2 vols. (Gouda, 1713), vol. II, pp. 112–77.

Appendix 2.2 *Almshouses in the six cities of Holland*

Dordrecht	
Heilige Geest (Grote Kerk)	1300s
St. Jan	1300s
St. Nicolas	1300s
St. Pieter and Paul	1300s
Lazarus House	1300
Holy Sacrament	1301
Holy Cross	1306
The Blessed Virgin	1306
St. Jacob Orphanage	1348
Great Shippers	1363
The Blessed Virgin	1400s
Old Man House	1400s
Heilige Geest (Nieuw Kerk)	1436
Haarlem	
Oude	1284
St. Elizabeth	1300s
Heilige Geest	1300
Bakenesser Kamers	1395
Lazarus	1395
St. Barbara	1435
St. Jacob	1436
The Blessed Virgin	1440
St. Anthony	1440
St. Martin	1472
Delft	
Oude	1252
St. Joris (Nieuw)	1407
The Blessed Virgin	1410
St. Christopher	1410
St. Elizabeth	??
St. Cornelius	??
Leiden	
St. Katherine	1276
The Blessed Virgin	1395
St. Elizabeth	1428
St. Barbara	1431
St. Jacob	1477
Amsterdam	
The Blessed Virgin	1300s
Oude	1363

St. Pieter	1383
St. Catherine	1410
Heilige Stede	1422

Gouda

Lazarus	1300s
Heilige Geest	1391
St. Katherine	1391
St. Elizabeth	1410

Source: Jansz. Matthys Balen, *Beschryvinge der stad Dordrecht* (Dordrecht, 1677), pp. 157–75; J. Sels, *Beschrijving der stad Dordrecht* (Dordrecht, 1853), pp. 47–51; F. Allan, *Geschiedenissen beschrijving van Haarlem van de vroegste tijden tot onze dagen*, 4 vols. (Haarlem, 1883; reprint edn., 1973), vol. IV, pp. 1–4, 20–1, 42–4, 49–52, 61, 68, 77–8, 81, 87–9, 113–14; D. P. Oosterbaan, *Het Oude en Nieuwe Gasthuis te Delft* (Delft, 1954), pp. 3–6, 36–8; Dirck van Bleyswijck, *Beschryvinge der stadt Delft*, 2 vols. (Delft, 1667), vol. II, pp. 494, 498, 526; Reinier Boitet, *Beschryving der stadt Delft* (Delft, 1729), p. 481; Christina Ligtenberg, *Armezorg te Leiden tot het einde van de 16e eeuw* ('s-Gravenhage, 1908), pp. 19, 85, 106; Jan Wagenaar, *Amsterdam in zyne opkomst, aanwas geschiedenissen*, 3 vols. (Amsterdam, 1760), vol. I, pp. 11, 27–8; J. F. M. Sterck, *De Heilige Stede in de geschiedenis van Amsterdam* (Hilversum, 1938), p. 45; Jacobus Kok, *Amsteldamsche Jaarboeken*, 3 vols. (Amsterdam, 1781), vol. I, pp. 96, 145; Ignatius Walvis, *Beschryving der stad Gouda*, 2 vols. (Gouda, 1713), vol. I, pp. 154, 186, 192.

3

The civic community and poor relief, 1500–1614

Widespread changes in the structure of the European economy along with the failure of charitable institutions to meet new demands necessitated a different approach to poverty in the sixteenth century. Population growth throughout the continent had begun to surpass pre-plague levels without an attendant increase in agricultural production. By the middle of the sixteenth century, the influx of gold and silver from the Americas, the expansion of merchant capitalism, and the almost constant state of war between European rulers contributed to an acute period of inflation, often known as the "Price Revolution." As food prices rose, marginal folk, such as unskilled workers, widows with children, and dispossessed farmers, faced the prospect of destitution.[1] The patchwork of charitable foundations that had alleviated poverty for centuries was no longer able to handle the swelling ranks of paupers in sixteenth-century Europe.

The rationale for poor relief reform, however, came out of a stinging critique of contemporary Catholic piety. Christian humanists, such as Juan Luis Vivès, Thomas More, Thomas Starkey, and Cornelius Agrippa argued that indiscriminate giving produced begging, and begging in return promoted fraud, idleness, and disorderliness.[2] Humanists brought attention to abuses that needed reform, whereas Lutherans, and later Protestants, attacked the fundamental theological bases of traditional charity. The implications of *sola fide* undermined the spiritual merit of charitable giving that assisted in a donor's salvation. Protestants affirmed that

[1] Despite disputes over the level of inflation in various parts of Europe, economic historians agree that an exceptional increase in food prices occurred by the middle of the sixteenth century. For the best economic overviews of this period and the major lines of interpretation see T. H. Aston and C. H. E. Pilpin, eds., *The Brenner Debate: Agrarian Class Structure and Economic Development in Pre-Industrial Europe* (Cambridge, 1984); Braudel, *Civilization and Capitalism*; Carlo Cipolla, *Before the Industrial Revolution: European Society and Economy, 1000–1700*, 2nd edn. (New York, 1980); V. G. Kiernan, *State and Society in Europe, 1550–1650* (New York, 1980); Peter Kriedte, *Peasants, Landlords, and Merchant Capitalists: Europe and the World Economy, 1500–1800* (New York, 1980); Geoffrey Parker, *Europe in Crisis, 1598–1648* (Brighton, 1980); E. E. Rich and C. H. Wilson, *The Cambridge Economic History of Europe*, vol. IV, *The Economy of Expanding Europe in the Sixteenth and Seventeenth Centuries* (Cambridge, 1967); Wallerstein, *Modern World-System*.

[2] Marcel Bataillon, "J. L. Vivès: réformateur de la bienfaisance," *Bibliothèque d'humanisme et Renaissance* 14 (1952), pp. 141–59; Davis, "Poor relief," pp. 59–64; Alice Tobriner, *A Sixteenth-Century Urban Report* (Chicago, 1971), pp. 36–57; Pirenne, *Histoire de Belgique*, vol. III, pp. 288–90; Juan Luis Vivès, *De Subventione Pauperum*, in Salter, *Early Tracts*, pp. 6–22; Elton, "An early Tudor poor law," pp. 55–7.

charity was a Christian responsibility, but they believed it had no salvific benefits whatsoever.[3] Thus, for their own theological reasons, Protestants, like reform-minded Catholics, advocated different methods to deal with poverty. They called upon urban magistrates to eliminate begging, to consolidate parish foundations, to make charity a civil responsibility, and to create work for the poor.

Holland's cities also experienced serious economic difficulty and widespread discontent with the Catholic Church during the sixteenth century. Urban magistrates did not, however, begin to centralize parish foundations until the 1570s, a remarkably later time than most other cities in western Europe. One reason that the sixteenth-century reform program came so late to Holland was that parish foundations were already well organized. In fact, most of the components of the sixteenth-century program were already well in place by the fifteenth century.

Although the city governments of Dordrecht, Haarlem, Delft, Leiden, Amsterdam, and Gouda did make significant alterations in parish relief before the 1570s, they simply built upon the organization that had been established centuries earlier. Under the supervision of the magistrates, almshouses continued to house orphans, and sick, old, and disabled people, and the Heilige Geest continued to distribute alms to the domiciled poor. Before the 1570s, city governments made two primary adjustments in parish relief. They drew a sharper distinction between residents and foreigners, and they resorted to a variety of *ad hoc* financial and administrative strategies to deal with short-term crises. Between 1572 and 1614, all of the six cities reorganized parish foundations to varying degrees along the lines of the centralized programs in other areas of Europe. This chapter will examine the development of municipal poor relief in the six cities of Holland from 1500 to 1614 in the context of the changing structure of the Dutch economy. Although it will be necessary to make reference to Calvinist diaconates from time to time, the relationship between municipal and Reformed poor relief is discussed fully in chapter 6.

URBAN SOCIETIES IN TRANSITION

The disquiet with the Catholic Church in many parts of Europe settled into the cities of Holland in the early sixteenth century. The vigorous outpouring of lay piety in the fifteenth century eventually gave way to considerable dissatisfaction with conventional church life. Anti-clerical opinions ran strong in sixteenth-century Holland, as lay folk complained about absentee pastors, idle monks, and worldly prelates. Although these criticisms had not been uncommon in earlier times, it seems that, at the very least, Hollanders in the sixteenth century believed that the church and its clergy were failing to meet their spiritual needs as never before.[4]

L. J. Rogier, in his monumental study of Dutch Catholicism, has confirmed that contemporary folk had plenty to complain about. His survey of parish and diocesan

---

[3] Lindberg, *Beyond Charity*, pp. 95–118.   [4] R. R. Post, *Kerkelijke verhouding*, pp. 39–41, 124–51.

ministries in the northern Netherlands has demonstrated that pastoral work had deteriorated extensively due to corruption and neglect.[5] The problem was acute in Holland, a province that fell under the jurisdiction of a single bishop whose see was located outside the province in Utrecht. And, George van Egmond, the bishop from 1535 to 1559, showed little concern for even residing in his diocese. Membership in religious orders also began to dwindle, and traditional lay piety, as expressed in pilgrimages to local religious shrines, reached a low point in the early sixteenth century.[6]

If concern about heterodoxy is indicative of decline, then traditional religious practices in Holland were clearly in trouble. Christian humanism and late medieval dissent combined with evangelical theology to produce a forceful, albeit diffuse, critique of the Catholic sacramental system.[7] Protestant ideas made their initial appearance in Holland in the 1520s and attracted the attention of authorities throughout the Low Countries. In 1525 Margaret of Austria, the governess of the Low Countries, complained that Delft was a center for heresy. A year later, a critic in the States of Holland complained that Delft and Amsterdam were famous for their heretics.[8] Likewise, various strains of Anabaptism claimed a significant following in Haarlem, Dordrecht, and Leiden from the 1530s throughout the sixteenth century. Even though heterodox views gained only a handful of followers in Gouda, periodically its city government also was compelled to deal with heretics. In 1559, Philip II expressed concern that the Catholic Church would lose the Low Countries forever.[9]

Although Hapsburg rulers and local authorities took severe measures against heresy, Anabaptism in particular made strong advances in Holland and left a lasting imprint on sixteenth-century religious life.[10] By 1559, when Philip II inaugurated his plan to bring the Netherlands in line with Tridentine Catholicism, heterodoxy had been firmly implanted in Holland. No doubt the popularity of Anabaptism

---

[5] Rogier argued that Protestantism succeeded only in areas of the Low Countries where Catholic parish ministries were weak and where the Catholic missionary organization, the Holland Mission, was not operative: Rogier, *Katholicisme*, vol. I, pp. 21–39, 439, 486–7.

[6] R. R. Post, *Kerkelijke verhouding*, pp. 12, 151; Alastair Duke, "The origins of evangelical dissent in the Low Countries," in Duke, *Reformation and Revolt in the Low Countries* (London, 1990), pp. 8–11. Church wardens in Dordrecht registered no more miracles associated with the cult of the Holy Cross after 1509, nor did wardens in Amersfoort (cult of the Blessed Virgin) after 1545. In Delft, there were no additional miracles attributed to any of the four images in the Oude and Nieuwe Churches after 1519: Verhoeven, *Devotie en negotie*, pp. 4–5.

[7] Duke, "Evangelical dissent," pp. 24–8.

[8] M. A. Kok, "Opkomst van het protestantisme," in *De stad Delft*, vol. I, p. 108. For the development of Anabaptistic traditions in Holland during the early sixteenth century, see Gary K. Waite, *David Joris and Dutch Anabaptism, 1524–1543* (Waterloo, Pa., 1990).

[9] Spaans, *Haarlem*, pp. 29–30; Hibben, *Gouda in Revolt*, pp. 31–2; Elliott, "The classis of Dordrecht," p. 254; Christine Jane Kooi, "The Reformed Community of Leiden, 1572–1620," Ph.D. thesis, Yale University (1993), p. 257; Israel, *The Dutch Republic*, p. 74.

[10] Alastair Duke, "The face of popular dissent in the Low Countries, 1520–1530," in *Reformation and Revolt*, pp. 29–59; Duke, "Noncomformity among the kleyne luyden in the Low Countries before the Revolt," in *Reformation and Revolt*, pp. 101–24.

derived in part from the decline of Catholic piety in the early sixteenth century and the failure of reform before 1559.

All governments in the six cities consistently pursued a conservative religious policy before the Calvinist Reformation came to Holland in the 1560s. While most municipal governments were reluctant to execute any but the most obstinate heretics, city fathers realized that silencing heresy would keep provincial authorities from prying too closely into local affairs. Even after the cities joined the Revolt in 1572, only in Dordrecht and Amsterdam did magistrates give the Reformed Church a fairly wide degree of latitude in operating its ministries.[11] Patricians in Holland did not like public religious change, whether it was Lutheran, Anabaptist, Tridentine-Catholic, or Calvinist. This conservatism meant that city magistrates persisted in using traditional religious values to promote the unity of the municipal community throughout the sixteenth century. As a result, the religious basis of the civic community would continue to have a decisive influence on the social welfare policies of urban magistrates during this period.

Problems in the church may have obliged city governments to expand their influence over charitable institutions; nevertheless, it was predominantly the changing economic conditions that compelled magistrates in all six cities to make alterations in parish poor relief. After a long cycle of expansion, Holland's cities began to suffer serious reversals late in the fifteenth century. The economic downturn affected many regions and all industries well into the late sixteenth and (in some areas) the early seventeenth centuries when the urban economies began to show signs of recovery. According to Jan Luiten van Zanden, there were two intervals of recovery in Holland's textile industry. From 1580 to 1630, the introduction of lighter-weight woolens by Flemish immigrants led to the revitalization of textiles in Leiden, Haarlem, Delft, and Gouda. The second phase occurred between 1630 and 1670, a period characterized by steady growth and the renewed dominance of Leiden in textile production.[12] Beer, the primary staple in Delft, Haarlem, and Gouda, never again (at least in the seventeenth century) reached the high-water

---

[11] Dordrecht and Amsterdam experienced the most dramatic changes in their city governments. In both cases, Calvinists and Protestant sympathizers came to dominate the magistracy. Before the cities joined the Revolt, however, their magistrates displayed little enthusiasm for public religious dissent: Boogman, "De overgang," pp. 94–5; James D. Tracy, "A premature counter-reformation: the Dirkist government of Amsterdam, 1538–1578," *Journal of Religious History* 13 (1984), pp. 150–4.

[12] Jan Luiten van Zanden, "Economic growth in the golden age: the development of the economy of Holland, 1500–1560," in *The Dutch Economy in the Golden Age*, K. Davids and L. Noordegraaf, eds. (Amsterdam, 1993), pp. 9–11. There is disagreement over when economic recovery took place and how quickly the Netherlands made the transition to a commercial economy. Jan de Vries and Ad van der Woude argue that between 1585 and 1590 the textile industry made a spectacular comeback and that Holland's cities made a quick and very profitable transition to a commercial economy. Other economic historians such as van Zanden and Noordegraaf maintain that the transition occurred more gradually and that economic conditions were still rather precarious in the late sixteenth and early seventeenth centuries. While this is a very broad debate over many different types of evidence, my findings tend to support the latter view. See Jan de Vries and Ad van der Woude, *Nederland 1500–1815: de eerste ronde van moderne economische groei*, 2nd edn. (Amsterdam, 1995), pp. 420–42.

mark of the fifteenth century. Recovery in these cities came from increasing economic diversity. By the early seventeenth century, Holland's cities were producing a greater assortment of goods, such as paper, silk, cut diamonds, earthenware, refined sugar, lightweight linens, and printed materials, along with beer and woolen draperies. In addition, all of the cities began to participate in maritime commerce, which would make the Dutch the envy of Europe in the 1600s.[13]

Still, throughout most of the sixteenth century, the cities of Holland suffered through structural changes in the export markets for domestic goods. In addition to this long downward trend, periodic crises, such as wars, outbreaks of the plague, disastrous fires, and crop failures, exacerbated the social problems caused by economic contraction. These conditions placed a great deal of pressure on municipal authorities to relieve the needs of those people caught in the changing structure of the economy. Magistrates attempted to restore local industries and to cope with rising unemployment. Although poor relief was basically intended for those disabled by health or age, the underemployed laborer became an increasing burden for city leaders.

Dependent upon textile exports, Leiden suffered the most from these hardships. Leiden relied heavily on high-quality raw English wool for its cloth, but after 1480 the city's textile manufacturers found themselves mired in debt and could not satisfy their creditors at the English wool staple in Calais. By 1505 Leiden had rectified its credit profile only to encounter trade restrictions imposed by Henry VII in order to stimulate English production.[14] These difficulties became even more entrenched from the 1520s through the 1570s; production fell from 26,000 pieces in 1514 to only 3,800 pieces in 1570. Production in the entire province fell from 51,500 pieces in 1514 to fewer than 10,000 pieces in 1570.[15] Declining textile production affected Delft and Haarlem as well; Delft's draperies declined from seventy-five shops to twelve between 1504 and 1514. Nevertheless, Leiden, completely reliant upon domestic manufacturing, became the poorest of the six great cities in the early sixteenth century, even though it supported the largest population. In 1514, one-third of Leiden's population (15,000) received some form of parish assistance.[16]

While falling textile production posed difficulties for other provincial cities, it was the changes in export markets for beer that really hurt Delft, Haarlem, and

---

[13] Leo Noordegraaf, "Dutch industry in the golden age," in Davids and Noordegraaf, *Dutch Economy*, pp. 132–3.

[14] Over one-third of the population was employed in wool draperies in 1498: N. W. Posthumus, *De geschiedenis van de Leidsche lakenindustrie*, 2 vols. ('s-Gravenhage, 1939), vol. I, pp. 195–203, vol. II, p. 36.

[15] Van Zanden, "Economic growth," p. 9.

[16] Verhoeven, *Devotie en negotie*, pp. 12–14; Boogman, "De overgang," p. 104; Spaans, *Haarlem*, p. 175; Ligtenberg, *Armezorg te Leiden*, p. 14. N. W. Posthumus has shown that in 1597 the city government distributed bread to 14,064 people, a figure that may have risen to 20,000 as late as 1634: Posthumus, *Leidsche lakenindustrie*, vol. II, p. 135. For conditions, see also P. J. Blok, *Geschiedenis eener Hollandsche stad: een Hollandsche stad onder de Republiek* ('s-Gravenhage, 1916), p. 7.

Gouda. Holland's brewers faced higher tariffs from export markets in the southern Netherlands as cities in Flanders and Brabant were trying to protect their own fledgling breweries. As a result, production throughout the province decreased from 1,100,000 vats in 1500 to 650,000 in 1590. Gouda's output fell off from a height of 370,000 vats in 1480, to 122,000 vats in 1557, and to a low of 24,000 vats in 1572. Production in Haarlem dwindled from 26,800 vats in 1472/73 to 13,856 vats in 1500 and down to 11,684 vats in 1530/31.[17]

Delft's industry survived better than those of Haarlem and Gouda, although it did so through a trend of consolidation that drove smaller brewers out of business. Fifty of Delft's 200 breweries closed between 1450 and 1475, thirty more by 1495, and over a hundred by 1515. Consolidation also affected Haarlem, for the number of brewers declined from 114 in 1490/91 to 80 in 1520/21 to 18 in 1562.[18] The total volume of Delft beer remained constant until the middle of the sixteenth century, but consolidation within the industry created social tension as smaller brewers pitted themselves against the wealthy ones who had greater influence in the city government. According to the 1514 *Informatie* (survey of taxable wealth to the central government), 250 of the 2,600 residential houses in Delft were empty. The pastor of Delft's Oude Kerk claimed that 40 percent of his 5,000 communicants were receiving poor relief in 1514.[19]

More than half of the houses in Haarlem either were vacant or the inhabitants therein were exempt from taxes because of their poverty. Despite the real decline that had affected the textile and brewing industry, scholars have cautioned against the extremely pessimistic view of depression emanating from the *Informatie*. James Tracy has pointed out that it was in a city's interest to embellish evidence of difficulty in order to reduce its share of the provincial tax burden. In fact, city municipal treasury records often indicated that these cities were able to meet their obligations assessed in the 1514 *Informatie*. Nevertheless, Tracy concludes that all of the six great cities had to accept a "fiscal tutelage" from provincial tax commissioners during the 1490s, an affront that continued in Leiden until the Revolt.[20]

The two most important trading centers in Holland, Dordrecht and Amsterdam, were able to avoid the economic troubles that plagued the industrial cities. The primary reason these two cities avoided the problems of the other four derived from their participation in maritime commerce.[21] Owing to its "Right of Staple," Dordrecht had been the most important trading town in southern Holland since the fourteenth century. The city's reliance on the river trade had changed little over the course of 200 years. In 1555, 32 percent of those employed in Dordrecht made their

[17] Van Zanden, "Economic growth," p. 10; Hibben, *Gouda in Revolt*, pp. 21, 140; van Loenen, *Haarlemse brouwindustrie*, p. 53.
[18] Wijbenga, *Delft*, vol. 1, p. 61; Loenen, *Haarlemse brouwindustrie*, pp. 20, 87.
[19] Wijbenga, *Delft*, vol. 1, pp. 80, 95–6, 137. For the political history of the struggle among the Delft brewers, see J. J. Woltjer, "Een Hollands stadsbestuur in het midden van de 16e eeuw: brouwers en bestuurders te Delft," in de Boer and Marsijle, *De Nederlanden in de late middeleeuwen*, pp. 261–79.
[20] Tracy, *Holland Under Hapsburg Rule*, pp. 26–8.   [21] *Ibid.*, p. 30.

livelihood in businesses directly connected to trade, 12 percent were engaged in crafts subsidiary to shipping (e.g., carpentry and barrelmaking), and only 4 percent worked in textiles.[22] Compared to Leiden, Delft, Haarlem, and Gouda, Dordrecht retained a large degree of its prosperity until the 1630s, when Rotterdam became the most important trading center in southern Holland.

Despite Dordrecht's prosperity, its merchants had to contend with increasing competition from Amsterdam, Rotterdam, and southern cities in the Rhineland. In 1514, Dordrecht magistrates complained that the city's wine trade had been marginalized by competition from southern merchants who now traded directly with Antwerp. In addition, Dordrecht's ocean-going bulk fleet had dwindled from around twenty ships to two ships in the early sixteenth century.[23] Dordrecht's elites also saw the city's staple privilege severely restricted by the middle of the sixteenth century. In 1505, a number of cities joined together to mount another protest to limit Dordrecht's monopoly. Persistent agitation eventually paid off, as Charles V issued an edict in 1541 to restrict the privilege to goods traveling down the Rhijn and Maas Rivers.[24] After 1541, cities in Holland began to find water routes that bypassed Dordrecht more attractive. The preferred route from Amsterdam into Germany proceeded from the Amstel to the Haarlemmermeer, to the Gouwe, along the Hollandse IJssel, to Noord and then Merwede, into the Waal. Goods on their way from north Holland to Antwerp went from Gouda, to the Hollandse IJssel, along the Spui and on to Antwerp.[25]

While Dordrecht fared relatively well in the sixteenth century, Amsterdam represented a completely different economic profile. By the middle of the sixteenth century, Amsterdam had emerged as the most important point of exchange for goods between northern and northeastern Europe. Its merchants also aggressively pursued the Baltic trade that by the 1540s made Amsterdam one of the leading ports of entry for grain on the northern part of the European continent. The revenues for the town crane jumped 400 percent from 1496 to 1514, and the city boasted the largest taxable wealth in the entire province. Although declining textile production made its presence felt in Amsterdam in the middle of the sixteenth century, the city's commercial activity enabled it to grow at a dramatic pace.[26]

Yet Amsterdam's prosperity also brought great poverty into the city, as thousands of immigrants from northern Europe sought refuge there. Wouter Jacob-

---

[22] W. S. Unger, "De economische en sociale structuur van Dordrecht in 1555," *De Economist* 64 (1915), p. 958.

[23] Tracy, *Holland Under Hapsburg Rule*, p. 26.

[24] While Dordrecht continued to hold this modified privilege formally until 1795, it became a dead letter later in the seventeenth century: Unger, "Dordrecht," pp. 966–7; Clé Lesger, "Intraregional trade and the port system in Holland, 1400–1700," in Davids and Noordegraaf, *Dutch Economy*, p. 196.

[25] Hubert Nusteling, *Welvaart en werkgelegenheid in Amsterdam, 1540–1860* (Amsterdam, 1985), p. 78.

[26] Lesger, "Intraregional trade," p. 189; Nusteling, *Welvaart*, p. 80; L. Noordegraaf, *Hollands welvaren? Levensstandaard in Holland 1450–1650* (Bergen, 1985), pp. 80–1; van Zanden, "Economic growth," p. 9.

szoon, a priest who had fled Gouda in 1572, repeatedly complained about high food prices and widespread poverty in Amsterdam. In 1574, Jacobszoon claimed that two people had been found lying in the street, dead from starvation.[27]

Even though the cities began to recover at the century's end, their fragile economies were still vulnerable to abrupt calamities. A. Th. van Deursen has told the story of how a single storm in 1597 brought bankruptcy for three prosperous Delft brewers.[28] On a broader level, Leo Noordegraaf has shown that the Netherlands experienced the same economic crisis at the end of the sixteenth century that most other European lands did. For provincial cities in the sixteenth century which had weak maritime trading enterprises, bad harvests, plagues, and the insecurities brought about by the war with Spain magnified their dire economic straits.[29] The troubles in Holland brought hard times for urban folk, as rising food costs and stagnant wages became features of sixteenth-century life. While Hollanders were probably better off than people in other areas of Europe, these conditions brought a significant number of unskilled laborers closer to destitution.[30]

An important index of the susceptibility of urban laborers is the relationship between wage levels and food prices. The labor market in the northern Netherlands was large and urban, making wage labor a much more significant economic index than in other European lands.[31] Between 1460 and 1480, laborers in Holland received the highest wages in the Netherlands. Artisans earned on average three to five stuivers per work day, a rate that changed very little between 1460 and 1550. The wages of skilled artisans, however, rose from 50 percent to 67 percent between 1460 and 1480 and over 80 percent from 1525 to 1550. Jan de Vries has suggested that the increasing wages for skilled labor points to an abundant unskilled labor market.[32]

Yet, due to rising food prices, real wages for both unskilled and skilled laborers fell from 1500 to 1560. Poor weather conditions, along with political unrest, produced meager harvests between 1477 and 1494. The worst years were between 1480 and 1482, when grain prices doubled throughout Holland.[33] While more land came under cultivation and agricultural production showed a steady increase

[27] I. H. van Eeghen, ed., *Dagboek van broeder Wouter Jacobsz. (Gualtherus Jacobi Masius) prior van Stein. Amsterdam 1572–1578, en Montfoort 1578–1579*, 2 vols. (Groningen, 1959), vol. I, p. 299. Jacobszoon periodically noted dearth and rising food costs in Amsterdam and Gouda. See *ibid.*, vol. I, pp. 171, 179 (February 1574), 298 (September 1574), 355 (December 1574); vol. II, p. 666 (May 1577).
[28] Van Deursen, *Plain Lives*, p. 3.
[29] Leo Noordegraaf, "Dearth, famine, and social policy in the Dutch Republic at the end of the sixteenth century," in *The European Crisis of the 1590s: Essays in Comparative History*, Peter Clark, ed. (London, 1985), pp. 67–76.
[30] A. Th. van Deursen, *Dagelijks brood*, vol. I of *Het kopergeld van de gouden eeuw*, 4 vols. (Assen and Amsterdam, 1978–80), p. 91.
[31] Jan de Vries has argued that labor in the Netherlands was not as constrained by guild regulations or "feudal restraints" as in the rest of Europe: Jan de Vries, "The labour market," in Davids and Noordegraaf, *Dutch Economy*, p. 56.
[32] De Vries, "Labour market," pp. 58–68; Nusteling, *Welvaart*, pp. 122–3.
[33] Noordegraaf, *Hollands welvaren?*, pp. 20, 41–3.

Table 3.1 *Population levels in the sixteenth and seventeenth centuries*

Dordrecht	11,500 (1500)	10,000 (1550)	14,500 (1632)
Haarlem	11,500 (1500)	15,000 (1564)	40,000 (1622)
Delft	10,000 (1514)	14,000 (1560)	21,000 (1635)
Leiden	15,000 (1514)	12,660 (1574)	44,745 (1622)
Amsterdam	11,000 (1500)	30,000 (1578)	54,000 (1600)
Gouda	8,500–10,000 (1514)	10,000 (1570)	14,600 (1622)

Note: The seventeenth-century figure for Dordrecht is a rough approximation based on a 1632 survey that listed hearths. See J. L. van Dalen, *Geschiedenis van Dordrecht*, 2 vols. (Dordrecht, 1931–33), vol. I, pp. 511–12.

Source: Joke Spaans, *Haarlem na de reformatie: stedelijke cultuur en kerkelijk leven, 1577–1620* ('s-Gravenhage, 1989), p. 19; T. S. Jansma, "De betekenis van Dordrecht en Rotterdam omstreeks het midden der 16e eeuw," in Jansma, *Tekst en uitleg: historische opstellen aangeboden aan de schrijver bij zijn aftreden als hoogleraar aan de Universiteit van Amsterdam* ('s-Gravenhage, 1974), p. 147; Audrey Lambert, *The Making of the Dutch Landscape: An Historical Geography of the Netherlands*, 2nd edn. (London, 1985), p. 158; Hubert Nusteling, *Welvaart en werkgelegenheid in Amsterdam, 1540–1860* (Amsterdam, 1985), p. 72; N. W. Posthumus, *De geschiedenis van de Leidsche lakenindustrie*, 2 vols. ('s-Gravenhage, 1939), vol. I, p. 135, vol. II, pp. 40–7, 156; Jonathan I. Israel, *The Dutch Republic: Its Rise, Greatness, and Fall 1477–1806* (Oxford, 1995), p. 114.

throughout the sixteenth century, these gains lagged behind rising population levels in the cities.[34]

As wages remained stagnant until 1540, substantial price increases occurred from 1480 to 1490, 1520 to 1530, 1545 to 1546, 1556 to 1557, 1565 to 1566, 1570, 1587 to 1588, and 1590 to 1600.[35] According to Noordegraaf, the price of rye, the most important staple in a worker's diet, rose 300 percent, alongside healthy increases for peas and dairy products as well, between the late 1580s and 1599. Consequently, food costs outpaced wages in Alkmaar in 1586–88, 1590–91, 1594–99, and purchasing power in Nijmegan, Zutphen, and Venlo reached all-time lows in 1586.[36]

In Leiden, the price index for grain rose 100 percent from 1500 to 1600. And Hubert Nusteling has calculated that the index for subsistence expenses quadrupled in Amsterdam from 1500 to 1620.[37] As the urban economies began to improve in the later sixteenth century, there was a large demand for labor, met by an equally large work force (through migration and birth).[38] Around 1600 the demand for labor began to outpace supply, and real wages began to revert to their high mark in the late fifteenth century.

[34] Van Zanden, "Economic growth," pp. 6–7.
[35] Noordegraaf, *Hollands welvaren?*, pp. 15–27, 52–61.   [36] Noordegraaf, "Dearth," p. 69.
[37] Nusteling, *Welvaart*, pp. 126, 130.   [38] De Vries, "Labour market," pp. 58–68.

During the incipient phase of this recovery (1580 to 1630), however, inflated food prices made life precarious for common laborers, particularly in times of personal or family crisis. For example, the daily wage of a skilled artisan in 1600, as a general rule, averaged around fourteen stuivers per day, or eighty-four stuivers per week. Unskilled laborers drew around ten stuivers per day, or sixty stuivers per week. Even this figure optimistically assumes stable conditions and regular employment in a period of instability and underemployment. In many cases, particularly in Leiden at the time, workers earned considerably less. It has been calculated that a married couple with two children required at least thirty-five pounds of bread per week. If this family's food expenditure exceeded 44 percent of their household budget, they would fall below the subsistence level. Consequently, low-paid workers in Leiden could devote only 26.4 stuivers per week for food (i.e., 44 percent of 60 stuivers). Prices for twelve-pound loaves of rye bread in Leiden wavered between 6.4 and 9.4 stuivers from 1596 to 1620. So, when the price of rye hovered between 9.2 and 9.4 stuivers per twelve-pound loaf, as it did in 1597–99 and 1617, the families of low-wage earners faced a crisis. That is, it would have required 27.6 stuivers (9.2 x three twelve-pound loaves), or 46 percent of this family's income, to purchase thirty-five pounds of rye bread to sustain four family members. Therefore, most families could not always subsist on the labor of a single unskilled breadwinner, but they needed wives and children to contribute to the household income.[39]

Fluctuations in the economy, incapacitation of a breadwinner, or increase in family size could potentially make those families without financial reserves paupers. As a result, the economic distress of the healthy common laborer became an increasing burden on charitable foundations. When the city government of Amsterdam consolidated its poor relief institutions in 1598, the city council placed emphasis on assisting those laborers who "because of the bad times have been pushed out and are not able to meet their expenses and maintain their households."[40]

Political leaders throughout Holland could ill afford to neglect these pressing needs. Accordingly, governmental authorities exerted enormous efforts to obtain an adequate supply of grain for their inhabitants. The Provincial States of Holland established price controls and restricted exports during periods of acute shortages. Magistrates in Delft, Gouda, Leiden, Haarlem and Dordrecht purchased grain for the poor in times of severe shortage.[41] In 1596, Leiden issued a series of detailed

---

[39] Van Deursen, *Plain Lives*, pp. 5–7; W. P. Blockmans and W. Prevenier, "Armoede in de Nederlanden van de 14e tot het midden van de 16e eeuw: bronnen en problemen," *Tijdschrift voor Geschiedenis* 88 (1975), p. 502.

[40] Johannes Isaac Pontanus, *Historische beschrijvinghe der seer wijt beroemde coop-stadt Amsterdam* (Amsterdam, 1614), p. 128.

[41] *GAD. Keurboek*, vol. v, fols. 50r (1597), 70r (December 13, 1598), 319v (November 20, 1611); Wijbenga, *Delft*, vol. I, p. 144; Couquerque and van Embden, *Gouda rechtsbronnen*, p. 605; Ligtenberg, *Armezorg te Leiden*, p. 296.

regulations for the baking and selling of bread, so "that the good people, especially the poor, will receive their full weight and . . . that the poor might buy their bread at a certain established price."[42] In the prosperous city of Amsterdam, the magistrates made provisions for extraordinary grain purchases on nine occasions between November 1578 and January 1601.[43]

Even though it is unlikely that many people died of starvation in Holland,[44] it is important to call attention to the devastating effects of a poor diet over an extended time period. According to Peter Laslett, starvation occurred as an immediate and necessary result of deficient caloric intake, a phenomenon which is extremely difficult to document in sixteenth-century records. Chronic malnourishment, though, made people much more prone to sickness and disease. Stated in a sixteenth-century adage, "first dearth then plague."[45] Laslett has theorized that chronic malnourishment among the English peasantry in the seventeenth century led to a higher incidence of pestilence.[46] For Holland, Leo Noordegraaf and Gerrit Valk have argued that there was no direct correlation between periods of dearth and outbreaks of the plague. Nevertheless, they have shown that the lowest social groups were much more vulnerable to the plague than elites, because of mal-nourishment, crowded living conditions, and lack of bodily care. For the poor, then, rising food prices and an unfavorable labor market could have perilous consequences.[47]

The seventeenth century ushered in a time of prosperity that has become known as the Netherlands' Golden Age. If economic fortunes were beginning to turn gold for the cities of Holland as the sixteenth century drew to a close, they were but a pale shade of gray at the beginning of the 1500s. A rising population, constricted export markets, and sluggish real wages made underemployment a serious concern in Holland. It was these conditions that forced urban magistrates in the six cities to define the social boundaries of the municipal corporation more precisely.

INTERDICTION AS SOCIAL POLICY

Until city governments began to consolidate parish foundations at the end of the sixteenth century, the dominant initiative in social welfare policy was a host of exclusionary measures taken against poor non-residents. Most poor relief ordinances for most of the sixteenth century aimed at excluding poor non-residents,

---

[42] *Keuren ende ordonnantien opt backen van broot binnen deser stadt Leyden: opgelezen den negenden Decembris vijftien-hondert zes ende tnegentich* (Leiden, 1596), fol. 1r.

[43] *GAA. Vroedschapresoluties*, vol. IV, fols. 33r (November 21, 1578), 94r (December 12, 1579); vol. VIII, p. 75 (December 29, 1594), p. 85 (February 15, 1595), p. 185 (November 13, 1595), p. 197 (November 30, 1595), p. 528 (March 30, 1599), p. 654 (December 30, 1600), p. 658 (January 24, 1601).

[44] Van Deursen, *Dagelijks brood*, p. 91.

[45] Quoted from Andrew B. Appleby, *Famine in Tudor and Stuart England* (Stanford, 1978), p. 131.

[46] Peter Laslett, *The World We Have Lost, Further Explored*, 3rd edn. (New York, 1984), pp. 122–8.

[47] Leo Noordegraaf and Gerrit Valk, *De gave Gods: de pest in Holland vanaf de late middeleeuwen* (Bergen, 1988), pp. 43, 65–81.

usually referred to as foreigners, from parish charity. In so doing, magistrates delineated the poor who belonged to the municipal community and had a claim on its resources by defining the poor who were "outsiders." The policy of interdiction became more intense over the course of the sixteenth century.

The campaign to ban poor non-residents from cities in the sixteenth century was rooted in the traditional authority of patricians to control the social order in the municipal corporation. Since the thirteenth century, urban patricians had determined the criteria for citizenship and residency, specified their respective privileges, and enlisted labor from the surrounding countryside. During the troubles of the sixteenth century, they continued to recruit skilled artisans, to refuse charity for non-residents, and to restrict begging.

There is a fairly large body of scholarship that has identified poor relief reform in sixteenth-century Europe as a new rational mechanism to regulate the labor market.[48] Many of these studies ignore the cultural framework that shaped the range of alternatives civic leaders could take. Although poor relief could have functioned inadvertently to influence the market for unskilled labor, that was not its primary purpose. In Holland, social welfare throughout the sixteenth century was rooted in an age-old understanding of the Christian community, which did not disappear in a period of economic difficulty. And magistrates had established a long tradition of defining the social order in the civic corporation. In the face of rising levels of poverty and disease in the 1500s, city magistrates built on this tradition by distinguishing between insiders and outsiders. In other words, magistrates were defining the borders of the civic community with more precision and with greater rigidity. Furthermore, with the exception of Leiden, city governments in Holland did not begin to eliminate all begging until the 1590s. This is important because those who argue that poor relief regulated the labor market often use the elimination of begging as a marker for rationalized social welfare.

The criteria used to define insiders and outsiders were social level and place of birth. Non-natives who were not considered to be a drain on parish foundations were suitable additions to the municipal community; poor non-residents, on the other hand, were not welcome. The Amsterdam *vroedschap*, for example, welcomed skilled craftsmen into the city, endowing them with citizenship and paying 50 guilders to anyone who brought a loom with them and 200 guilders for every weaver.[49] The poor who had not established a period of residency, however, were considered outside the scope of municipal charity. Residency requirements for poor relief in Holland's cities were not new. Since the fourteenth century, parish agencies had directed their efforts to those who had resided in the city for at least

[48] Lis and Soly, *Poverty and Capitalism*, pp. 220–1; Braudel, *Civilization and Capitalism*, vol. II, pp. 506–11; Wallerstein, *Modern World-System*, pp. 254–5; Tawney, *Rise of Capitalism*, pp. 262–4.

[49] J. G. C. A. Briels, *Zuidnederlandse immigratie in Amsterdam en Haarlem omstreeks 1572–1630* (Utrecht, 1976), p. 6.

one year. As municipal parishes became overburdened in the second half of the sixteenth century, magistrates in Haarlem, Gouda, Amsterdam, and Delft lengthened residency requirements to either two or three years.

In 1552, Haarlem magistrates expelled all the "foreign poor" (*vreemde armen*) from the city. The city government defined foreigners as those who had not lived in the city for the previous two years.[50] At the end of the sixteenth century, the Haarlem *vroedschap* specified that those born outside Holland must have resided in the city for five years to receive aid; it was still two years for native Hollanders.[51] The city government of Gouda stipulated in 1556 that the Heilige Geest would deny alms to those who had not been residents of the city for a period of three years.[52] In order to qualify for relief, recipients in Amsterdam were required to prove a residency of two years, a prerequisite that was extended to three years later in the seventeenth century.[53] In 1579, the Delft magistrates specified that those who could not prove two-year residence must leave within three days.[54]

As for Leiden and Dordrecht, I have found no explicit evidence that either city lengthened residency requirements, though each took harsher measures against poor non-residents. In 1555 Leiden reissued earlier ordinances that stipulated that only residents were permitted to receive assistance from the *huiszitten meesters* and the almshouses. It was not until the outbreak of the Revolt in 1572 that the Dordrecht city government took similar measures against non-residents. At that time, the magistrates forbade anyone from coming into the city without first showing certification of previous residence and occupation. Although the ordinance was aimed primarily at quelling disorder during wartime, the city fathers also stipulated that no foreign poor would be allowed to enter the city.[55]

The movement to expel and ban poor non-residents was part of a renewed campaign to combat vagrancy and begging. As we know, anti-begging legislation was one of the central features of poor relief reform in sixteenth-century Europe. The assumption that underlay proscriptions against beggars was that each community was responsible for the care of its own residents only. Magistrates across Europe harbored suspicions against outsiders and banned vagrants from the city. Begging even by residents became either highly regulated or forbidden outright. Within the Empire, Charles V officially approved this policy in 1531. By contrast,

---

[50] Huizinga, *Haarlem rechtsbronnen*, p. 524. Thirty years earlier, the Haarlem *vroedschap* stipulated that clergy outside the city were not entitled to the funds collected for Masses for the dead. The *vroedschap* reasoned that since this income came from the burghers of the city, it should go to pay the celebrating clergy in Haarlem "who are themselves the poor children of the city" and not to "foreign" priests: *GAH. Vroedschapresolutien*, vol. II, fol. 66r (May 14, 1522).

[51] *GAH. Vroedschapresolutien*, vol. VII, fols. 50v–51v (June 26, 1597).

[52] Furthermore, they ordered that "no foreigners will receive alms here unless they can show a proper certification from their last place of residence": Couquerque and van Embden, *Gouda rechtsbronnen*, p. 604.

[53] Reference to this requirement is found in *GAA. Kerkeraad*, vol. IV, p. 124 (November 6, 1614).

[54] *GAD. Keurboek*, vol. III, fol. 316r (July 15, 1579).

[55] Ligtenberg, *Armezorg te Leiden*, p. 297; Fruin, *Oudste rechten Dordrecht*, vol. I, pp. 177–8.

city officials either cared for the "deserving" poor in municipal institutions for the destitute or provided outside relief to those who had a place to live.[56]

City governments in Holland labored mightily to discourage vagrancy and to restrict begging throughout the entire century. This effort was not a sudden break with past practice, but an outgrowth of the anti-begging legislation of the fifteenth century. Even though the cities' policies differed in details and in the timing of implementation, statutory actions against beggars and vagrants occurred in two general phases. Until the middle part of the century, magistrates in all of the six cities except Dordrecht reissued fifteenth-century laws with increasing frequency, established greater restrictions on begging (particularly by non-residents), and set forth more stringent punishments for beggars. From the second half of the sixteenth to the early seventeenth century, all six city governments began to proscribe all begging and to banish all poor non-residents from their cities.

During the first phase, Leiden, Haarlem, and Gouda took the earliest and most stringent measures against begging, particularly against non-resident beggars. It had become a truism for contemporaries that "Leiden alone produced more beggars than the rest of the entire county of Holland."[57] For their part, magistrates in Leiden battled vagrancy by issuing nine ordinances against begging and vagrancy between 1450 and 1550. The city government prescribed where non-resident beggars could lodge and limited their stay to one or two nights. In addition, people between the ages of eighteen and fifty were prohibited from begging, upon pain of imprisonment or deportation. In 1544 and 1555, the city drafted laws that restated the restrictions on parish relief and begging to the poor of the municipal community.[58]

Haarlem's city government either reissued or passed new ordinances on twenty-five occasions between 1501 and 1564. Before 1526, the primary restriction was a prohibition against begging in parish churches. In 1526, the magistrates required that all beggars must receive permission to beg from the *Heilige Geestmeesters*, a condition that was reiterated again in 1532 and 1546. The *Heilige Geestmeesters* shouldered the thankless task of sifting out professional beggars from residents who had little recourse except to solicit alms. The 1546 ordinance was titled "ordinances against the beggars," and it specified that only the "deserving poor should be properly maintained and no one may beg without the knowledge of the *Heilige Geestmeesters* and receiving a mark from them." Six years later, the government required that all poor non-residents leave the city.[59]

On at least six occasions between 1507 and 1521, the Gouda magistrates re-

[56] Gutton, *La Société et les pauvres en Europe*, pp. 94, 105; Braudel, *Civilization and Capitalism*, vol. II, p. 508; Salter, *Early Tracts*, p. 34.
[57] Quoted from Kooi, "Leiden," pp. 19–20.
[58] Ligtenberg, *Armezorg te Leiden*, pp. 285, 288–9, 290–1.
[59] A calendar of these ordinances is located in Huizinga, *Haarlem rechtsbronnen*, pp. 523–4. For the 1546 ordinance, see p. 524.

enacted ordinances that were originally passed in 1488. The law required beggars to register with the *Heilige Geestmeesters* and outlawed begging at various places (such as at inns, houses, and churches). Anyone receiving alms in Gouda had to will all their possessions to the Heilige Geest. They further declared that all vagrants seeking lodging in an almshouse would be punished. These restrictions led to a 1556 law that required all non-residents to present a certificate declaring their previous residence before they could stay in the city.[60] The cumulative effect of this body of legislation was not only to restrict begging, but also to keep poor non-residents out of Gouda.

Despite the relative infrequency of anti-begging legislation in Amsterdam and Delft, their city governments did take punitive actions against vagrancy. Amsterdam proscribed begging by foreigners in 1527 and 1529, and Delft established a similar statute in 1537. The Delft magistrates charged the *schout* with the responsibility of deporting foreign beggars. Almost twenty years later, the Delft burgomasters decreed that anyone who begged must first obtain written permission from a committee comprising the *schout* and several members of the magistracy. Between 1538 and 1571, 138 people were expelled from Delft; unfortunately, it is not clear how many of the deportees were actually beggars.[61]

According to municipal records, Dordrecht did not seem to be so inundated with non-resident beggars. In 1438, the municipal government had stipulated that any possessions of almshouse residents would be consigned to the foundation. And in 1463, begging had been prohibited in churches and cloisters.[62] If these laws were reissued, they were not recorded again in the city statute book. According to these sources, Dordrecht did not really begin to restrict begging by residents and non-residents until 1566.

The second wave of anti-begging legislation took place during a period of political turmoil and military conflict with Spain. The Revolt led to a growing fear of outsiders at both the provincial and municipal levels. The States of Holland, consisting largely of municipal delegates, passed resolutions designed to protect the province from political enemies and the cities from vagrants. In 1579 the States required that all refugees from the southern territories obtain certification from the city into which they immigrated within three days of their entry. Two years later, the States stipulated that all new immigrants must take an oath of loyalty to the Republic. In 1583, they ordered that new immigrants must be centrally registered, and they proposed that healthy beggars should be placed in the army to fight against Spain. In 1586 the States denied permission to remain in Holland to those who practiced various forms of quackery, such as feigning sickness and telling fortunes. And, in 1589 all non-Hollanders who could not find work after one month were to

---

[60] Couquerque and van Embden, *Gouda rechtsbronnen*, pp. 94, 125, 167, 202, 233, 264, 305, 604.

[61] Nusteling, *Welvaart*, p. 162; Wijbenga, *Delft*, vol. 1, p. 138; *GAD. Burgermeesteren*, fol. 195r (February 10, 1556).

[62] Fruin, *Oudste rechten Dordrecht*, vol. 1, pp. 274, 323.

be punished and deported.[63] Given the turbulence of the times, delegates to the States of Holland were making a clear distinction between insiders and outsiders.

These provincial resolutions simply gave legislative sanction for the stringent policies that city governments were already taking against non-residents in the later sixteenth century. By this time, Gouda had already put in place fairly severe guidelines to ward off vagrants. Building upon earlier statutes, the magistrates in 1555 formulated a set of procedures for the *Heilige Geestmeesters*. With respect to vagrants, the policy placed the *Heilige Geestmeesters* in charge of policing beggars. Only residents who obtained the approval of the officers could beg in Gouda. Anyone who was admitted to an almshouse was required to remit their possessions to the Heilige Geest at his or her death.[64] The 1555 policy was not a pronounced departure from the flurry of ordinances that the city government passed from 1507 to 1521. But the 1555 plan did establish a more centralized bureaucracy (discussed in a later context) to protect the city from foreign beggars and it expanded the responsibilities of the *Heilige Geestmeesters*.

Eleven years later, Dordrecht magistrates took several steps to shield the city from the *beeldenstorm* that swept Flanders, Brabant, and Holland. They disallowed all non-residents in the city without the consent of the burgomasters. If citizens and residents lodged a guest, they had to submit the name to Claes Corneliszoon Muys, a burgomaster. Six years later, in September 1572, immediately after the *overgang* in Dordrecht, the reconstituted city government ordered that all "vagrants, beggars, and whores" must leave the city within twenty-four hours or they would be sent to the galley ships. They also stated that anyone who boarded vagrants and beggars would be deported.[65]

The most dramatic programs of attempting to eliminate begging and vagrancy, however, occurred later in the sixteenth century. Leiden, which took the initial steps to centralize parish poor relief in 1577, provided the model that other cities would eventually emulate. The 1577 proposal banned all foreign and domestic begging and set aside 2,000 to 3,000 guilders to provide work for able-bodied resident beggars.[66] Going beyond mere restrictions and outright bans, the work project in Leiden represented the first positive attempt in Holland to eliminate begging. As such it marked a shift from proscribing begging to providing a means by which poor residents could sustain themselves. Centralization in Leiden, however, offered no new proposals for vagrancy.

Compared to Leiden, the city governments of Haarlem, Delft, and Amsterdam took a somewhat more incremental approach to vagrancy and begging during the

[63] *Resolutiën van de Staten van Holland*, 278 vols. (n.p., 1524/43–1793), vol. VI, pp. 324, 456; Briels, *Zuidnederlandse immigratie*, pp. 2–3; Noordegraaf and Valk, *De gave Gods*, p. 100; van Deursen, *Plain Lives*, p. 51.
[64] Walvis, *Gouda*, vol. I, pp. 194–7. This did not apply to people who had surviving children: Geselschap, "Aalmoezeniershuis te Gouda," p. 245.
[65] Fruin, *Oudste rechten Dordrecht*, pp. 164–71, 177–9.
[66] Van Deursen, *Dagelijks brood*, p. 81; Ligtenberg, *Armezorg te Leiden*, pp. 298–305.

1570s and 1580s. But, by the end of the sixteenth century, their policies bore a marked resemblance to Leiden's. The most serious efforts to combat begging and vagrancy in Haarlem got underway in the 1590s.[67] In March 1591, when the city council initiated a public works project employing the poor to repair the city walls, a number of non-residents came into the city to find employment. In order to regulate the increasing number entering the city, the burgomasters ordered the *Heilige Geestmeesters* in the following October to register all beggars receiving bread distributions during the winter months.[68]

Six years later, the Haarlem magistracy attempted to eliminate foreign begging as it augmented the endowments of charitable institutions in the city. In April 1597, the city government once again outlawed the solicitation of alms by foreigners. The following year, the magistrates extended this measure, banning all begging in Haarlem. This measure distinguished between foreign and resident beggars: the former were to be deported and the latter were to receive charity from city almoners. Furthermore, no vagrant could not enter a tavern and all non-residents had to receive permission from the *schout* to remain in the city. Poor travelers could lodge for one night only in the St. Jacob Almshouse for men or the Blessed Virgin Almshouse for women. All transgressors were subject to imprisonment on bread and water.[69]

The actions taken against non-resident beggars in the 1590s were not, however, carried out consistently. Observing an increase in vagrants, the Haarlem city council in 1605 called for incarceration of foreign beggars. Four years later, the magistrates took a more radical approach that was gaining some popularity in Holland: the creation of a workhouse. Established with city monies and private donations, a steward administered the resources of the workhouse, while three city officials went through their assigned districts and brought non-resident beggars into the institution. This institution quickly took on the character of the infamous House of Discipline (*Tuchthuis*) in Amsterdam, which functioned to teach incorrigible beggars the virtues of manual labor. Unable to eliminate vagrancy through deportation, the Haarlem workhouse consigned outsiders to discipline and punishment.[70]

In the summer of 1570 magistrates in Delft allowed vagrants to beg in the city for two days, after which time they had to leave or face punishment at the discretion of the *schepenen*. Complaining of the number of vagrants, the magistrates also

---

[67] During the political crisis of the 1560s and 1570s, the Haarlem *vroedschap* did crack down on non-residents. From August 1566 to 1578, the *vroedschap* required that all travelers register themselves with city hall before boarding overnight and that all "foreign" beggars were deported. Poor foreigners were allowed shelter for one evening in an almshouse: *GAH. Vroedschapresolutien*, vol. IV, fols. 94r–94v (August 23, 1566); Spaans, *Haarlem*, p. 168.

[68] *GAH. Vroedschapresolutien*, vol. VII, fol. 103r (March 1, 1591); Spaans, *Haarlem*, p. 175.

[69] *GAH. Vroedschapresolutien*, vol. VIII, fols. 36 (April 4, 1597), 39 (April 10, 1597); Spaans, *Haarlem*, pp. 176–9.

[70] *GAH. Vroedschapresolutien*, vol. IX, fols. 159v (October 10, 1605), 301r (April 25, 1609).

threatened those who begged at the port of Schiedam with deportation to the galleys in November 1570. The turbulence and insecurity brought on by the war with Spain led the burgomasters to appoint several officials to patrol the city in order to apprehend all vagabonds and take them to the *schout*.[71] In November 1584, they ordered all outsiders (*vreemde personen*), who planned to lodge at an inn to present themselves before the burgomasters and attest to their "quality, trade, and business."[72] Although later ordinances modified procedures, the laws of 1579 and 1584 formed the basis of Delft's policy toward outsiders until 1610.[73]

When the Delft magistrates consolidated parish relief within the *Kamer van Charitate* (House of Charity) in 1597, they also attempted to exercise greater control over resident beggars by prohibiting begging at inns. In the previous year, the magistrates had declared that no one was to seek alms during funeral or marriage services.[74] Resident beggars were required to seek permission to beg from the regents of the *Kamer van Charitate*. According to the statute, the regents would entertain such requests and decide whether a person should beg and, if so, where and for how long.[75] When the regents permitted someone to beg, it was most commonly for a three-month period, at the end of which the beggar might seek permission for another three-month allowance. There seems to be no limit to the number of times a person might seek permission.[76] On January 14, 1610, the city fathers issued an ordinance banning all begging in Delft. The law gave all beggars until May 1 to leave the city or face deportation.[77]

Amsterdam had been the fastest-growing city in Holland since the middle of the sixteenth century. The city's prosperity and reputation for religious toleration attracted thousands of immigrants from economically depressed and war-torn lands. Municipal authorities welcomed skilled workers into the municipal corporation. The government undertook reclamation projects to ease crowded conditions caused by the influx of immigrants. Developed for this purpose in the late sixteenth century, the Jordaan neighborhood was inhabited for the most part (60 percent) by new-

---

[71] *GAD. Keurboek*, vol. III, fols. 65r (1570), 73r–74r (November 6, 1570); *GAD. Memorialboek*, fol. 200r (April 14, 1572).

[72] *GAD. Keurboek*, vol. IV, fols. 61v–62r (November 18, 1584).

[73] When Delft established the *Kamer van Charitate* (discussed pp. 179–85) in 1597, the principles in the 1579 and 1584 regulations formed the basis of the city government's policies toward begging. See *ibid.*, vol. IV, 273r (January 4, 1596), 46v–47r (November 24, 1596); vol. V, fols. 53r–53v (December 16, 1597). In 1600, the magistrates reiterated their stricture against lodging for foreigners and in 1601 forbade leprous beggars from entering the city: *ibid.*, vol. V, fols. 108v (December 31, 1600), 114v (June 16, 1601). The magistrates repeated the anti-lodging injunction on October 22, 1613; and, in May and August of the same year, they prohibited foreigners from selling glass, cheese, and butter in Delft: *ibid.*, vol. V, fols. 360r (May 5, 1613), 364v (August 28, 1613).

[74] *Ibid.*, vol. IV, fol. 269v (August 1595); vol. V, fols. 18r (November 3, 1596), 19r (November 10, 1596).

[75] *Ibid.*, vol. V, fols. 52v–53r (December 16, 1597).

[76] The numerical pattern of initial requests indicate that the peak period was between 1598 and 1599, dropping off sharply (to 55 percent) in 1600, and gradually tapering off to a small number by 1610. See *GAD. Archief Kamer*, inv. nr. 50, *Bedelaer boek, 1597–1610*.

[77] Initially, the ordinance stipulated that the deadline for emigration was April, although at that time the magistrates extended the deadline to May 1: *GAD. Keurboek*, vol. V, fol. 280v (April 25, 1610).

comers.[78] During this period, poor relief officials in Amsterdam also provided temporary assistance to skilled artisans and religious refugees. The *huiszitten meesters* on the Nieuwe Zijde supported 6,000 people or 1,611 families. Of this number only 200 were Hollanders; others were from France, Brabant, Flanders, Friesland, Emden, England, and Westphalia.[79] Within the city, the Amsterdam *vroedschap* promoted religious peace and tolerated a wide array of dissidents as diverse as Roman Catholics and Jews, despite official legislation against them.[80] In the seventeenth century, the burgomaster C. P. Hooft summed up the duty of these Amsterdam regents as "we should do justly for the widows, orphans, poor and rich, foreigners and familiar, without distinction because we are the fathers of the burghers."[81]

Yet a high rate of immigration also brought with it a high level of vagrancy. Between 1580 and 1699, the *schout* apprehended 30,100 foreign beggars in Amsterdam. The pattern of these arrests indicate that vagrancy continued to rise in Amsterdam throughout the seventeenth century.

While the Amsterdam *vroedschap* welcomed skilled artisans, the city fathers did not look as kindly upon the dispossessed who flooded into the city to "steal alms from the deserving poor."[82] To combat these outsiders, the Amsterdam burgomasters stipulated in 1581 and 1586 that vagrants could stay within the city for only two or three days and then had to leave. In 1596, the magistrates required all beggars to seek written permission from city authorities before they could beg in the city.[83]

Two years later in March 1598, the city government centralized the almshouses in Amsterdam. As part of that program, they unleashed a seventeen-point program designed to regulate begging more extensively. In this statute, the burgomasters intended to show their stern commitment to driving out intractable beggars, a determination symbolized by the erection of a pillory for vagrants to which they attached the city's coat of arms. Under the direction of the *schout*, inspectors (*opsienders*) were charged to monitor begging and vagrancy. The mandate included patrolling the streets: to record the names and movements of all beggars, to bring all incoming vagrants to city hall for registration, to cast out vagrants who had been denied permission to beg, to ensure that beggars did not squander alms, to prevent beggars from practicing deception in order to elicit charity, to clear the church doors of beggars during worship services, and to prohibit begging on Sundays and specified days of prayer (*biddagen*). According to the act, only those with written permission from city authorities could beg; others who caused no trouble were to be deported, while recalcitrants could be whipped and placed in stocks.[84]

[78] Briels, *Zuidnederlandse immigratie*, pp. 7–8.   [79] Pontanus, *Amsterdam*, p. 129.
[80] Briels, *Zuidnederlandse immigratie*, p. 7; Elias, *Amsterdamsche regentenpatriciaat*, pp. 29–32.
[81] Cornelis Pieterszoon Hooft, *Memoriën en adviesen* (Utrecht, 1871), p. 163.
[82] Quoted from Roodenburg, *Onder censuur*, p. 345.
[83] GAA. Keurboek, vol. F, fols. 230v–231r (April 1581), 284r (July 19, 1586); vol. H, fol. 61 (January 25, 1596).
[84] GAA. Memorialboek, fol. 179 (April 27, 1597). The magistrates renewed this legislation in 1613, replacing the *opsienders* with a college of almoners: Roodenburg, *Onder censuur*, p. 345.

Table 3.2 *Beggars arrested in Amsterdam, 1580–1699*

Period	Number	Percentage of all arrests
1580–1599	1,100	12
1600–1619	2,200	15
1620–1639	6,400	25
1640–1659	9,200	36
1660–1679	10,400	26
1680–1699	10,600	27

Source: Hubert Nusteling, *Welvaart en werkgelegenheid in Amsterdam, 1540–1860* (Amsterdam, 1985), p. 163.

Following the ideas of the Dutch humanist, Dirck Volckertszoon Coornhert, the 1597 reform program in Amsterdam centered around the creation of the House of Discipline (*Tuchthuis*). In 1567, Coornhert had put forward the notion in his *Boeventucht* that the poor could be taught the skills they needed to function in society through coerced labor. According to Coornhert, criminals and beggars should lose their freedom and be compelled to learn industriousness and piety through the discipline of manual labor. These ideas found a favorable reception among several influential Amsterdam magistrates, namely Hendrick Laurenszoon Spiegel and Sebastian Egbertszoon. In 1595, they persuaded their colleagues to implement these ideas, and the Amsterdam magistrates ordered a House of Discipline for men and a Spinning House (*Spinhuis*) for women. The foremost concern was to segregate criminals and beggars from the municipal community and to return them as useful members of civil society.[85]

Despite all of the punitive measures and centralizing schemes that magistrates implemented over the course of the sixteenth and early seventeenth centuries, they never eliminated begging and vagrancy. Proscriptions and punishments could not keep vagrants out of a city permanently. In fact, at least until the creation of various types of workhouses, city magistrates do not appear to have even conceived of eliminating vagrancy on a long-term basis. Most measures political authorities in Holland took against vagrants were intensive campaigns of short duration that cleared the landscape temporarily, only to have beggars reappear later.[86]

What magistrates did try to do was to protect the civic community from outsiders. Within the large body of legislation, magistrates used the word "foreign"

[85] Lis and Soly, *Poverty and Capitalism*, pp. 118–20; A. W. Weismann, "Het tuchthuis en spinhuis te Amsterdam," *Oud Holland* 26 (1908), p. 335; van Deursen, *Plain Lives*, pp. 53–5. The House of Discipline also became known as the *rasphuis* because inmates rasped Brazil wood. The House received much adulation from other cities and subsequently spawned cognate institutions throughout Holland, the Low Countries, and the rest of Europe.

[86] Van Deursen, *Plain Lives*, p. 50.

3.1 Cornelis van der Voort, *Regents of the House of Discipline*.
Amsterdam Historical Museum, Amsterdam

(*vreemde*) as a universal adjective to describe a begging non-resident.[87] Certainly, "foreign" denoted non-native status, but it also had a moral connotation. Begging non-residents symbolized the antithesis of a municipal community's values. They were lazy thieves who preferred begging and pilfering to working. More important- ly, they had no community, a crime that made them suspect in the eyes of the urban patriciate. Municipal ordinances also accused these outsiders of damaging or being a burden to the "honorable poor."[88] Undoubtedly, magistrates feared that hand- outs to foreign beggars would divert pennies that should be given to poor residents. But more importantly, elites harbored a notion that the presence of vagrants imputed a dissolute reputation onto poor residents who were forced to beg out of genuine need.

[87] For a few examples, see *GAD. Keurboek*, vol. III, fol. 65r (1570); vol. IV, fol. 61v (November 18, 1584); Fruin, *Oudste rechten Dordrecht*, vol. I, pp. 83, 101, 178–9, 192, 324; Breen, *Amsterdam rechtsbronnen*, pp. 21, 270; Huizinga, *Haarlem rechtsbronnen*, p. 524; Couquerque and van Embden, *Gouda rechtsbronnen*, pp. 128, 311, 604. For an excellent analysis of linguistic images of the poor in the language of relief legislation in Reformation Zurich, see Wandel, *Always Among Us*, pp. 124–69.
[88] *GAD. Keurboek*, vol. III, fol. 316r (July 15, 1579).

Several studies of poverty in other parts of Europe have called attention to literary and visual depictions of begging transients in the sixteenth and seventeenth centuries. Rogue literature of the sixteenth century portrayed vagrants as crafty, lawless, able-bodied drifters. According to Gamini Salgado and Frank Aydelotte, popular literature characterized vagrants as cunning sharks who feigned sickness, injury, misfortune, or even piety to trick people out of their money around taverns.[89] Likewise, artistic depictions reinforced the contemporary view that vagrants were sordid miscreants who preyed upon the good folk of the city.[90]

These pamphlets say more about popular perceptions than they do about a culture of vagrancy itself.[91] A. L. Beier has argued that authorities regarded vagrants as a threat to public order because they had no master. Given the corporate nature of sixteenth-century society where everyone functioned in a prescribed social role, vagrancy was a "crime of status."[92] While the same could be said for sixteenth-century Holland, the stereotype that emerges in poor relief legislation in the six cities is that vagrancy was a crime against community. Vagrants were outsiders who had no community; consequently, they deserved expulsion from the civic corporation.

One of the dominant social welfare policies pursued by Holland's magistrates in the sixteenth century was to exclude outsiders from municipal resources. Residency requirements, ordinances against foreign beggars, and workhouses distinguished the resident poor from non-residents. Virtually autonomous since the fourteenth century, the civic community walled itself off from the outside world. Inside the city walls, urban leaders promoted the collective ideals that underlay parish charity. These were exclusive communities for citizens, residents, and skilled immigrants.

MODIFICATIONS IN PARISH POOR RELIEF, 1500–1572

City governments in Holland did make some changes in the structure of parish poor relief before the Revolt. Nevertheless, it was not until the States of Holland altered the legal status of ecclesiastical property in the 1570s that magistrates began to recast the fundamental character of parish-based charity. Even then, municipal poor relief retained the same basic purpose of parish charity: to sustain indigents of the civic and Christian community. Furthermore, magistrates still considered

---

[89] Gamini Salgado, *The Elizabethan Underworld* (London, 1977), pp. 24–48, 97–134; Frank Aydelotte, *Elizabethan Rogues and Vagabonds* (New York, 1913), pp. 76–101. A. L. Beier has argued, through plot and language analysis of these pamphlets, that the rogue genre in the latter sixteenth century was an embellished imitation of pamphlets written in the 1530s: A. L. Beier, *Masterless Men: Vagrants and Vagrancy in England, 1580–1640* (Cambridge, 1987), pp. 123–4.

[90] Jütte, *Poverty and Deviance*, pp. 14–15. For several useful studies of artistic depictions of the poor, see Wandel, *Always Among Us*; Muller, *Charity in the Dutch Republic*; Elisabeth Sudeck, *Bettlerdarstellungen am Ende des XV. Jahrhunderts bis zu Rembrandt* (Strasbourg, 1931).

[91] Vagrants in Holland primarily came from the ranks of dismissed soldiers, unemployed clients, rural victims of war, and dispossessed farmers: van Deursen, *Dagelijks brood*, p. 72.

[92] Beier, *Masterless Men*, pp. 122–4.

86

themselves to be the collective "Christian authority" (*Christelijke overheid*) within the municipality.

Economic conditions in the cities of sixteenth-century Holland provided a ripe opportunity for assimilating the decentralized charitable institutions into a municipal poor relief system. Taking its cue from the 1531 edict of Charles V, the central government in Brussels ordered this program to be established within all cities in the Netherlands. Before 1531, discussions had taken place in the States of Holland over the implementation of the reforms. At a meeting in 1529, the advocate of the States urged the cities to adopt such a plan. After delegates consulted with their fellow magistrates back home, a later meeting was scheduled for March 16. At that meeting, Delft, Haarlem, Amsterdam, and Dordrecht were favorably disposed, but Gouda and Leiden were hesitant.[93] Thus, nothing tangible emerged from these collective discussions with regard to poor relief and it remained an individual city government's prerogative to determine the structure of its charitable institutions.

The non-action of the cities in the States of Holland during such a critical time raises the question: why did they not adopt these policies as other towns and territories were doing? England formulated a reorganizational plan along such lines in 1530.[94] On the continent, Charles V gave them sanction throughout the Empire in 1531. Culminating in the Edict of Moulins in 1566, the French government had begun issuing moderate Parlementary *arrêts* and royal edicts in 1532 that restricted begging, established centralized municipal organizations, and provided for public works projects. These reforms took hold in Lyons, Dijon, Troyes, Amiens, Poitiers, Orléans, and Paris by middle of the century.[95]

The most likely reason that the six cities voted down the proposal was because parish poor relief was already well organized by the early sixteenth century. Amsterdam and Leiden had established *huiszitten meesters* to govern outside relief in 1408 and 1427, respectively. And in all the cities magistrates placed restrictions on begging, appointed *Heilige Geestmeesters* and almshouse regents, and oversaw the range of parish poor relief. If the cities did not consider it necessary to adopt the new poor relief program, it is also likely that they were reluctant to mandate reform of parish foundations through a provincial assembly. Throughout this entire period, urban patricians in Holland consistently resisted any attempts by outside political authorities which might limit their own authority over their cities. It is not apparent how the proposal would have undercut municipal authority, but it is clear that urban elites believed that the internal affairs of their cities were best left up to municipal governments.

[93] J. A. van Houtte, "Hervorming van de armenzorg," in *AGN*, vol. IV, p. 248; Ligtenberg, *Armezorg te Leiden*, p. 16.

[94] Jordan, *Philanthropy in England*, pp. 84–5.

[95] Camille Bloch, *L'Assistance et l'état en France à la vielle de la Révolution* (Geneva, 1909), pp. 41–4; Leon Cahen, *Le Grand Bureau des pauvres des Paris au milieu du XVIIIe siècle* (Paris, 1904), pp. 3–4, 28–9; Gutton, *La Société et les pauvres*, pp. 105–9.

Although the States of Holland rejected the proposal, certain components of humanist poor relief did exert an influence on local magistrates. Joke Spaans has suggested that the spirit of the reforms took hold in Haarlem without official regulation. For Delft, D. P. Oosterbaan contended that the increased influence of city authorities over the Oude Almshouse was a product of the reforms in the cities of the southern Netherlands.[96] In Leiden, Gouda, Amsterdam, and Dordrecht, municipal authorities continued to expand their authority over parish relief in the sixteenth century. So it is possible that the European reform program had influenced parish poor relief in the six cities before the end of the sixteenth century.

Even if this connection can be made, magisterial involvement in charitable foundations grew out of developments in the late middle ages. The growing authority of magistrates in poor relief in Holland derived from long-held conceptions of the municipal community. Despite the expanded role of city governments in sixteenth-century Holland, the institutional structure of poor relief retained the fundamental parish-based character that it had inherited from the late middle ages.

Until centralization took place, almshouses and Heilige Geest foundations continued to shoulder the weight of parish charity in the cities of Holland. Underemployment and disease brought increased pressure on these institutions to relieve the needs of the poor. In order to meet these challenges, city governments attempted to shore up sagging revenues and impose greater controls over parish foundations.

Leiden already had the most well-organized parish relief network. Until 1577, Leiden's magistrates made no significant administrative changes, but concentrated on raising revenue for outside relief and almshouses. In 1551 and 1555, the city government levied a tax on all householders and authorized a special city-wide collection for the residential poor. Another collection in 1557 yielded 700 guilders. This amount was far from sufficient, so the *vroedschap* decided to sell a portion of the lands of the Heilige Geest. After 1557, the city fathers also began to redirect municipal excises for poor relief purposes.[97]

The actions of the Delft city government were also primarily intended to help the Oude Almshouse and the Heilige Geest remain solvent. After a disastrous fire in 1536, the city government permitted the *Heilige Geestmeesters* to sell off 200 acres (100 *morgens*) of their lands in order to meet their obligations to the residential poor. This short-term expedient diminished their endowment and placed them under increasing hardship during a prolonged period of financial shortage.[98] In 1531, 1543, and 1559 they issued food vouchers (*armen geld*) worth one-quarter of a stuiver, which would enable recipients to purchase food and shoes from local merchants, but could not be redeemed in taverns.[99] In 1545 the government of Delft appealed to Charles V to hold a lottery to support the Oude Almshouse in

[96] Spaans, *Haarlem*, p. 171; Oosterbaan, *Gasthuis*, p. 116.
[97] Ligtenberg, *Armezorg te Leiden*, pp. 203, 226.
[98] Van Bleyswijck, *Delft*, vol. II, pp. 489–90; Boitet, *Delft*, p. 45.   [99] Wijbenga, *Delft*, vol. I, p. 140.

1545, but was denied. Philip II did grant a similar request in 1563.[100] An outbreak of the plague, lasting from May 1557 to November 1558, sent the city reeling as, reportedly, anywhere between 5,000 and 6,500 people died during this seventeen-month period. A significant portion of the population were left without a source of income, thereby putting increased pressure on relief institutions.[101]

The *Heilige Geestmeesters* had attempted to economize even before the 1550s by differentiating more clearly between the residential poor who genuinely needed aid and those who misused their subsidy. Later in the century, the magistrates relieved some of the *Heilige Geestmeesters*' burden with regard to their care for orphans, by converting the Heilige Geest Zuster cloister (Sisters of the Holy Ghost) into a house for orphaned girls in 1577.[102]

In 1541, Haarlem's city government established a more efficient bureaucracy to manage the assets of the Heilige Geest and parish almshouses. They appointed a regent, Boudewijn de Weendt, as the chief financial officer for all parish foundations. Almshouse regents and *Heilige Geestmeesters* could continue to receive donations and testaments from parishioners, but they had to provide a financial report to de Weendt every Sunday. Furthermore, no parish poor relief officer could make any land transactions, enter into contracts with merchants, undertake expensive repairs, or sell or purchase *renten* without the consent of the burgomasters. In the ordinance, the burgomasters reaffirmed their authority as the ultimate poor relief officials (*oppergoodtshuysmeesters*) over parish institutions.[103]

Fourteen years later, the city government of Gouda adopted a similar policy for the Heilige Geest. In 1555, the magistrates authorized the *Heilige Geestmeesters* to manage all parish almshouses. Chosen by the city government, *Heilige Geestmeesters* were to draw up a register of all the poor, determine who might beg, and take charge of the property of almshouse inhabitants. Almshouses were also granted a few privileges during the middle of the sixteenth century. In 1557, the magistrates declared that all almshouses were exempt from excise taxes on grain. And, in 1566, they demanded that anyone who went to live in an almshouse would have to pay three *Karolus gulden*.[104] In addition to tightening controls, the Gouda *vroedschap* frequently tried to raise money for poor relief agencies or for extraordinary bread distributions through city-wide collections.[105]

Beginning in the early fifteenth century, Amsterdam magistrates had created *huiszitten meesters* for both the Oude and Nieuwe Zijde parishes to supervise the distribution of outside relief. In 1505, the city government discussed a proposal to

[100] Oosterbaan, *Gasthuis*, p. 124.   [101] Wijbenga, *Delft*, vol. I, p. 149.
[102] Van Bleyswijck, *Delft*, vol. I, p. 331; Boitet, *Delft*, pp. 488–90.
[103] Huizinga, *Haarlem rechtsbronnen*, pp. 260–1.
[104] Walvis, *Gouda*, vol. I, pp. 194–7. It is possible that the requirement referred to *proveniers*, inhabitants who paid rent to live in the almshouse, but the ordinance did not refer specifically to them: Couquerque and van Embden, *Gouda rechtsbronnen*, pp. 605–6, 615, 618.
[105] *GAG. Vroedschapboeken*, vol. XLIV, fols. 12v (January 27, 1564), 18–19v (August 14, 1565), 27v (July 3, 1566), 38–9 (October 8, 14, and 24, 1567), 43v (May 10, 1570).

unite the *huiszitten meesters* under one administration in order to prevent recipients from obtaining alms from both parishes. It does not appear, however, that the magistrates actually implemented the plan.[106] Although the basic organizational structure of the *huiszitten meesters* remained intact for most of the sixteenth century, the magistrates did make some administrative alterations in 1547. At that time, Amsterdam was divided into seven districts (*wijkjes*), four on the Nieuwe Zijde and three on the Oude. This number was expanded to eleven districts in 1579.[107] Appointed by the *huiszitten meesters*, two *wijck meesters* (district masters) were to keep a register of all the residential poor in each district.[108] The resolutions of the *vroedschap* are filled with extraordinary measures which this municipal body enacted to ensure the financial solvency and an adequate store of grain for the *huiszitten meesters*.[109]

THE CENTRALIZATION OF MUNICIPAL CHARITY, 1572–1614

Though economic factors compelled Holland's cities to centralize relief, it was the legal transformation of church property that enabled all magistrates in Holland to convert parish charity into a municipal relief structure. Before the Reformation all church property and revenues in Holland had attained the legal designation *bona ecclesiastica*, and was under the domain of canon law. This property also included the church fabric (*kerkfabriek*) and charitable foundations established by private benefactors.

With the advent of the Reformation, the States changed the legal jurisdiction of these properties from canon to civil law, and they were to be administered by temporal authorities rather than ecclesiastical ones. In July 1572, the States of Holland decided to appropriate the incomes of cloisters and churches. Chosen officials were to inventory moveable goods (*roerende goederen*), such as altars, images, and candles, as well as church property (*onroerende goederen*), and file a statement of all assets, rents, and debts. Holding to the principle that these revenues would still be reserved "for pious uses" (*ad pios usus*), the States ultimately allocated this income for the parish under the complete control of the magistracy.

---

[106] P. D. J. van Iterson and P. H. J. van der Laan, eds., *Resoluties van de vroedschap van Amsterdam, 1490–1550* (Amsterdam, 1986), p. 27. A statement of the interest on the property (*rente brieven*) of the *huiszitten meesters* in 1613 lists the Oude and Nieuwe Zijden separately: Commelin, *Amsterdam*, vol. I, p. 524.

[107] *GAA. Keurboek*, vol. F, fol. 202v (October 23, 1579).   [108] Wagenaar, *Amsterdam*, vol. II, p. 274.

[109] The *vroedschap* exempted them from taxes, purchased grain, sold *renten*, and provided subsidies. For their purchasing grain, see: *GAA. Keurboek*, vol. H, fols. 45v (March 30, 1595), 60r (December 15, 1595); *GAA. Vroedschapresoluties*, vol. IV, fols. 33r (November 21, 1578), 94r (December 12, 1579); vol. VIII, p. 75 (December 29, 1594), p. 85 (February 15, 1595), p. 95 (March 16, 1595), p. 185 (November 13, 1595), p. 528 (March 30, 1599), p. 654 (December 13, 1600), p. 658 (January 24, 1601). For their providing subsidies, see: *GAA. Memorialboek*, fol. 163v (October 6, 1588); *GAA. Vroedschapresoluties*, vol. IV, 205v (May 8, 1582); vol. V, p. 66 (July 15, 1584), p. 287 (April 19, 1586); vol. VI, p. 217 (July 15, 1589); vol. VIII, p. 450 (March 11, 1598). For their providing exemptions from taxes, see: *GAA. Vroedschapresoluties*, vol. IV, fol. 19r (September 1, 1578).

The States did not necessarily believe they were creating a novel structure, but intended to maintain the old framework, albeit without any clerical control. At no time did the Reformed Church ever administer any of this property.[110]

On March 2, 1575, the States of Holland also eliminated the legal obstacles to centralization of poor relief. The States' resolution authorized the cities to consolidate these revenues at their discretion. Revenues for the upkeep of the church fabric and poor relief were to retain their previous functions. Managed by the college of church wardens, the revenue continued to pay for the upkeep of the parish, provide for the expenses of religious services, and support parish poor relief under the authority of city magistrates.[111] Although magistrates had controlled almost every aspect of parish charity for a very long time, they did not possess the legal authority to centralize parochial institutions until after the Reformation.

Magistrates in Gouda wasted no time in converting ecclesiastical revenues and church property to civic use. After haggling with the local military governor (Adriaen van Swieten) and the States of Holland, the city government was able to secure the appointment of Johan Dirkszoon as the local receiver in April 1574. The selection of Dirkszoon was a coup for local patricians, for he was a member of the *vroedschap*.[112] Between 1574 and 1576, the magistrates sold the buildings of the Franciscans, the Sisters of St. Clarissa; they converted the cloister of the Alexian Brothers into a Latin school; they diverted the revenues of the *Collatiehuis* to the Heilige Geest; and they redirected the income from the convent of St. Mary Magdalen to the almshouses.[113] In administrative terms, the city government expanded the role of the Heilige Geest, so that the wardens cared not only for the *huiszitten* poor and orphans, but they also became regents of the St. Katherine Almshouse.[114] By 1576, the city government had built upon earlier adjustments to provide additional support for parish foundations in a time of financial difficulty and social unrest. The final step in the trend of consolidation in Gouda occurred in 1586, when the magistrates established a new college of almoners. Six almoners, appointed by the *vroedschap* for two-year terms, managed relief mechanisms for the *huiszitten* poor and the duties of the Heilige Geest were restricted to the care of orphans.[115]

[110] Jan Frederick van Beeck Calkoen, *Onderzoek naar den rechtstoestand der geestelijke en kerkelijke goederen in Holland na de reformatie* (Amsterdam, 1910), pp. 37–8, 50, 280; Eeghen, *Dagboek*, vol. I, p. xvii.

[111] B. van Beuningen, *Het geestelijk kantoor van Delft* (Arnheim, 1870), p. 13; van Beeck Calkoen, *Rechtstoestand*, pp. 47–8.

[112] Eeghen, *Dagboek*, vol. I, p. xvii.

[113] In addition, the convents of St. Mary and St. Catherine were sold in 1582 and 1593, respectively: Taal, *Goudse kloosters*, pp. 7, 11, 15, 40, 45, 49, 66.

[114] Couquerque and van Embden, *Gouda rechtsbronnen*, p. 624; Eeghen, *Dagboek*, vol. I, p. xvii. Later, in 1587, the city established a centralized orphanage, which was called the *Almoessenier*'s House: Walvis, *Gouda*, vol. I, pp. 206–7. It is not clear what happened to the St. Elizabeth Almshouse. I have found no mention of it in late sixteenth-century sources.

[115] The almoners also cared for those orphans who were over ten years of age and whose parents were not *poorters*: Geselschap, "Aalmoezeniershuis te Gouda," pp. 258–61.

Because of particularly acute economic conditions, Leiden also took advantage of the new legal arrangements. On February 20, 1577, a commission of burgomasters, assigned to study the problems of poverty and poor relief in Leiden, presented their findings to the *vroedschap*. The report, probably authored by Jan van Hout,[116] underscored the responsibility of the magistracy, as the Christian authority, to support the needy of the community and to banish the unworthy. The commissioners placed the poor of Leiden into three categories: those without skills who actually enjoyed begging, those with skills who still preferred to beg, and those who worked but "immediately consumed and squandered everything." According to the report, many languished in poverty because cloisters had distributed alms indiscriminately, farmers gave to beggars out of fear, and greedy textile manufacturers paid workers such low wages that they had to beg on Sundays.[117]

The commission's report issued a number of recommendations to consolidate charity in Leiden. All incomes and properties devoted to poor relief in the city were to be directed into a central fund. There were four groups of residents who merited some form of assistance: old people, the *huiszitten* poor, orphans, and lepers. The provisions for each were characterized by institutional consolidation and by stronger magisterial control. Supervised by six regents, a municipal almshouse for the aged would replace the St. Katherine Almshouse, the Blessed Virgin Almshouse, and the St. Elizabeth Almshouse. Orphans and lepers would receive care in a single orphanage and leper's hospital. Finally, the *schout* would apprehend and punish all beggars. Foreign beggars could stay in the city for one day and one night, but they could not beg.[118]

After deliberating, the *vroedschap* voted not to merge the almshouses, but it did delegate all provisions for the *huiszitten* poor to the burgomasters. Later, on August 8, 1577, the burgomasters approved a centralized treasury. Although the centralization of almshouses occurred at a more gradual pace, they were eventually united as well.[119] The magistrates also stipulated that poor relief recipients were not to gamble, nor were they to frequent taverns or brothels upon pain of banishment. Furthermore, all beggars were subject to deportation. Finally, in 1582 the Leiden magistracy merged the Reformed diaconate with the college of municipal almoners.

Haarlem also began to reorganize the charitable foundations of its single parish, St. Bavo, in 1577. The process in Haarlem, however, occurred in gradual steps over a twenty-year period. Five years of war in the province and two sieges had taken

---

[116] J. Prinsen, "Armenzorg te Leiden in 1577," *Bijdragen en Mededeelingen van het Historische Genootschap te Utrecht* 26 (1905), p. 113.

[117] Ligtenberg, *Armezorg te Leiden*, pp. 299–300.

[118] *Ibid.*, pp. 301–4.

[119] In 1577, the St. Barbara Almshouse became the *huiszitten huis* (a general-purpose almshouse maintained by the municipal almoners) for the city. In 1583, the magistrates united the Blessed Virgin Almshouse and the St. Elizabeth Almshouse, and in 1593 they added the Leper's Hospital into the expanded almshouse. The St. Katherine Almshouse remained a separate hospital until 1596. At this time it became connected to a plague hospital and an insane asylum: Ligtenberg, *Armezorg te Leiden*, pp. 229–30, 305.

their toll on local industries and the city treasury. Under these conditions, the city government took initial steps to reform poor relief. It placed religious houses under a municipal commission and established a new college of municipal almoners to superintend distributions to the *huiszitten* poor. Administered by a financial administrator, a portion of the incomes from the cloisters was diverted to several poor relief agencies, namely the city almoners, the Reformed diaconate, and the almshouses. The almoners took over most of the responsibilities of the *Heilige Geestmeesters*, who were now assigned to care specifically for orphans and the aged. With respect to the *huiszitten* poor, church deacons provided assistance to church members, whereas almoners distributed alms to all non-members. A few years later, the magistrates established a separate college of almoners for poor southern refugees.[120]

These measures did not, however, completely centralize poor relief in Haarlem. Throughout the 1580s, there was no central poor relief fund in the city; rather, municipal almoners, the Heilige Geest, the Reformed diaconate, and almoners for southern refugees served the poor from their own constituencies and administered charity through separate chests. The burgomasters apportioned revenues from various sources to fund these organizations. The almshouses also retained their incomes and proceeded to care for the sick and disabled in the traditional manner. During the 1590s, the city continued to struggle with large numbers of destitute people; in 1595 a committee reported to the *vroedschap* that 6,000 people in the city would gladly take bread if an extraordinary distribution were undertaken.[121] In order to cope with this situation, the city government steadily moved toward tighter consolidation. The *vroedschap* eliminated the separate college of almoners for southern refugees, adopted more stringent residency requirements for municipal relief recipients, and eliminated all begging in Haarlem. Immigrants from Flanders and Brabant were served either by the municipal almoners or, if they were members of the Reformed Church, by the Dutch deacons. In 1597, the *vroedschap* required a residency of five years for non-Hollanders and two years for native Hollanders. In 1598, the magistrates issued a prohibition against all begging.[122]

Centralization in Amsterdam occurred in 1598, but it entailed no administrative changes in relief for the *huiszitten* poor. In 1408, the city government had undertaken a major reorganization, when it established *huiszitten* meesters for both Oude and Nieuwe parishes. Apparently, outside relief was well organized in Amsterdam, for it remained intact throughout the entire period under examination. The only change came as a result of the Reformation. When the Reformed Church organized itself in Amsterdam, the diaconate became the charitable agency for poor church members. Thus, like the situation in Haarlem, outside relief in Amsterdam was

[120] Spaans, *Haarlem*, pp. 172–3.
[121] *GAH. Vroedschapresolutien*, vol. VII, fols. 224–225 (December 23, 1595).
[122] *Ibid.*, fol. 36 (April 4, 1597), 52r (June 26, 1597); Spaans, *Haarlem*, pp. 172–8.

3.2 Werner van den Walckert, *Registration of the poor and orphans in the Almoners House in Amsterdam* (1626).
Amsterdam Historical Museum, Amsterdam

divided along civic and confessional lines, *huiszitten meesters* gave assistance to the city poor and deacons offered charity to the church poor.[123]

The transformation of church property brought minor alterations to the network of almshouses that housed sick folk, old people, orphans, and lepers. Shortly after the *alteratie*, the city government converted the convent of St. Margaret into a leper hospital and turned the Old Nuns Cloister into an almshouse for old men.[124] In 1584, the St. Pieter Almshouse became living quarters for immigrants. In March 1598, the Amsterdam *vroedschap* took the next logical step, merging their revenues and providing for a college of regents to manage the financial affairs of the almshouses.[125] Finally, in 1613, the municipal government employed revenues from former church property to consolidate city's orphanages into the large Municipal Orphanage (*Burger Weeshuis*).[126] So, by the early seventeenth century, there were four primary relief agencies in Amsterdam: *huiszitten meesters*, deacons, almshouses, and orphanages. All but the deacons were under the authority of the city government.

Delft combined its parish institutions at roughly the same time that Amsterdam did, but the organization of the charitable agencies in the two cities was quite different. Delft took an initial step in December 1597, when the *vroedschap* established a new relief institution, the *Kamer van Charitate*. The *Kamer* did not replace the *Heilige Geestmeesters*, nor the almshouses, nor church deacons, but it existed alongside these agencies. The city government created the *Kamer* to combat begging and to provide for the poor of the city. Aside from its anti-begging function, the *Kamer* was to help apprentice young boys, provide spinning work for young girls, offer schooling for children, and extend charity to the *huiszitten* poor. While the *Heilige Geestmeesters* also distributed alms, their role within the municipal structure became more confined to the care of orphans.[127] It was the Reformed diaconate that took on most of the obligations for outside relief in the city.[128]

This arrangement lasted until 1614, when the city government forced the Reformed Church to incorporate the diaconate within the *Kamer van Charitate*.[129] While the negotiations between the consistory and the magistracy are discussed at some length in chapter 6, the pertinent point here is that, by 1614, Delft had a fully integrated municipal poor relief system. The regents of the *Kamer* in concert with church deacons distributed alms to the *huiszitten* poor three days per week: Mondays, Wednesdays, and Saturdays. The reconstituted *Kamer* continued to provide work and a modicum of education to children. The Heilige Geest foundation took charge over orphans, the Oude Almshouse served as a hospital for old and

[123] Van Manen, *Armenpflege in Amsterdam*, pp. 8, 46, 49–52.
[124] Wagenaar, *Amsterdam*, vol. I, pp. 20, 22.
[125] *GAA. Vroedschapresoluties*, vol. VIII, p. 450 (March 11, 1598).
[126] Wagenaar, *Amsterdam*, vol. I, p. 286.
[127] *GAD. Keurboek*, vol. V, folio 52r (December 16, 1597).
[128] Wouters and Abels, *Nieuw en ongezien*, vol. II, pp. 229–37.   [129] Boitet, *Delft*, p. 462.

sick people, and the Nieuwe Almshouse (St. Joris) was designated for plague victims.[130]

Institutional poor relief arrangements in each city had their own peculiarities, but charitable organization in Dordrecht was the most atypical. The general pattern of consolidation that occurred in the other five cities also emerged in Dordrecht, yet poor relief agencies in this city retained a certain degree of decentralization well into the seventeenth century. Heilige Geest foundations in both the Grote Kerk and the Nieuw Kerk proceeded to operate out of separate incomes through this period. Like the functions of the Heilige Geest in Haarlem, Gouda, and Delft, however, the foundations in Dordrecht concentrated on care for orphans and plague victims. In addition, the *Heilige Geestmeesters* of the Grote Kerk distributed vouchers for meat and bread to 350 people six times a year.[131]

Even though traditional institutions persisted in Dordrecht, it was the Reformed diaconate that became the most important charitable agency, especially for the *huiszitten* poor. Church deacons not only relieved the needs of church members, but they also took over almost the entire realm of outside charity. Given the rather confined activity of the *Heilige Geestmeesters*, the Reformed diaconate functioned as both a civic and an ecclesiastic agency that served two different categories of the poor. As such, church deacons in Dordrecht served as the primary element of poor relief consolidation that emerged in the other cities of Holland at the end of the sixteenth century.[132]

POOR RELIEF REFORM AND THE MUNICIPAL COMMUNITY

The economic decline that affected the cities of Holland during most of the sixteenth century generated significant alterations in the forms of poor relief. Hardship, however, did not substantially alter the fundamental character of charitable institutions nor erase the union of the sacred and social. The poor relief policies of the sixteenth century were not an abrupt change, but the continuation of a tradition rooted in 200 years of history. The collective welfare of the municipal community had been a joint concern of civil and ecclesiastical leaders in Dordrecht, Haarlem, Delft, Leiden, Amsterdam, and Gouda since the thirteenth century. Magistrates oversaw the governance and financial administration of almshouses and parish agencies devoted to the care of the residential poor, while clergy attempted to meet the spiritual and physical needs of the poor. Despite all the

---

[130] Willem van der Lely, *Beschryving van de Kamer van Charitaten, de diakonie en het leprooshuis* (1732), pp. 5–10; Oosterbaan, *Gasthuis*, p. 38.

[131] The Heilige Geest of the Nieuw Kerk also cared for orphans, the sick, and distributed alms. At the end of the sixteenth century, however, the Heilige Geest of the Nieuw Kerk went into decline. In 1604, there were no orphans under its care; there were only thirty in 1679. At the end of the seventeenth century, this foundation became defunct and the Heilige Geest of the Grote Kerk took over care of its orphans: Elliott, "The classis of Dordrecht," pp. 359–60.

[132] *Ibid.*, p. 364.

changes, the religious bases that sixteenth-century poor relief inherited from the middle ages remained a guiding principle of municipal charity. And the magistrates who superintended this network continued to refer to themselves collectively as the "Christian authority."[133]

The communal basis of municipal charity came into direct conflict with Calvinist Reformers who grounded their understanding of poor relief in a very different vision of Christian community. The Reformed presence would alter civic culture, church life, and charity as much as these forces would compel Reformers to recast their confessional understanding of community. In fact, as the foregoing discussion has implied, one of the primary variables that resulted in the disparate arrangements by the seventeenth century was the role of the Reformed diaconate within the poor relief network of each city. Chapter 6 will account for those distinctions, but first we must turn our attention to the Dutch Calvinist concept of community and poor relief.

[133] For example, see Ligtenberg, *Armezorg te Leiden*, p. 299; *GAD. Keurboek*, vol. I, fols. 306r (September 19, 1577), 311v (April 27, 1578).

4

Poor relief in a confessional community: the creation of the Dutch Reformed diaconate, 1566–1578

The Calvinist Reformation introduced a new poor relief agency in Holland, the Reformed diaconate. Firmly grounded in an emerging Reformed tradition in Europe, the diaconate of the Calvinist Church of the Netherlands was an ecclesiastical office based upon the model of the New Testament Church. At the same time, the diaconate also possessed a uniquely Dutch character, as it developed in the exiled refugee churches from 1566 to 1572. The exile experience fostered an understanding that the church was an exclusive religious community which enjoined church officers to assist poor members without civil interference. As Dutch Reformers set about the task of organizing the church and defining its offices, they inscribed the responsibilities of deacons in resolutions from synods that met between 1571 and 1586.

This chapter will explore the theoretical foundations of the Reformed diaconate and trace the historical circumstances that shaped Calvinist poor relief in Holland. It will do so by surveying the body of Reformed thought on poor relief in Europe, examining the exile experience of Dutch refugee churches in Emden and London, analyzing the resolutions of Reformed synods from 1571 to 1586, and discussing the early implementation of the diaconate in the six cities of Holland. But, first, it is necessary to describe the events that led to the peculiar nature of the Calvinist Church of the Netherlands.

A PUBLIC YET CONFESSIONAL CHURCH

After 1572, when the States of Holland and Zeeland proclaimed the Dutch Reformed Church to be the "privileged" ecclesiastical institution in the rebellious provinces, it bore the earmarks of both a public church for all people and a voluntary confessional church for members. By 1581, the Reformed Church gained the sole legal right to exercise public worship as the States officially proscribed open Catholic services. Reformed clergy married and baptized anyone, except the most vocal heretics, without discrimination.[1] Church services were open to all who

---

[1] F. L. Rutgers, ed., *Acta van de Nederlandse synoden der zestiende eeuw* ('s-Gravenhage, 1889), p. 74; J. Reitsma and S. D. van Veen, *Acta der provincial en particuliere synoden, gehouden in de Noordelijke Nederlanden gedurende de jaren 1572–1620*, 8 vols. (Groningen, 1892–98), vol. II, pp. 42–4, 145–6; van Deursen, *Bavianen*, pp. 132, 144.

wished to attend. Managed by the church wardens, parish endowments not specifically designated for the purposes of Catholic worship continued to support their former purposes.[2] Holding to the ideal that the municipal corporation was a sacred and civic community, magistrates considered this public church to be a reformed version of its Roman Catholic predecessor.

For all its public character, the Reformed Church was also a eucharistic community closed to non-members and members under disciplinary sanction. The Calvinist Church of the Dutch Republic never became a formal state church in the normal European mold. Membership was strictly voluntary and the administration of parish properties came under civil jurisdiction.[3] While everyone was welcome to attend services, the Lord's Table was reserved for members who met the moral demands of the religious community.

To become members, individuals had to submit themselves to the discipline of the church, subscribe to the Dutch Confession of Faith, undergo at least rudimentary instruction in the Heidelberg Catechism, and give evidence of good moral character. If joining the church was more than perfunctory, remaining in good standing could be downright difficult. Calvinist consistories, comprising ministers and lay elders, went to extraordinary efforts to protect the purity of the communion table by excluding unworthy sinners. Calvinists believed any compromise of their religious and moral standards would besmirch the community and invite the wrath of God.[4] It was this eucharistic conception of Christian community that framed the motivation and direction of Calvinist poor relief in Holland.

The circumstances that led to the ambivalent character of the Dutch Reformed Church came out of the political turbulence of the 1560s. Calvinism had made strong inroads in the southern provinces in the 1550s, but did not gain a significant following in Holland until the early 1560s. The first public Calvinist service did not take place in Holland until July 1562.[5] Over the course of the next four years, outdoor services (hedge-preaching) became much more conspicuous. Since most of these services took place outside municipal jurisdictions, there was little that local authorities could do to suppress the illicit activity. Inside most cities, municipal authorities also demonstrated a reticence to enforce the anti-heresy edicts of the central government rigorously. Most magistrates hoped simply to preserve a semblance of social stability by steering a middle course between the heresy laws of Charles V and the demands of radical Calvinists.[6]

From 1564 to 1566, the nobility of the Netherlands was putting strong pressure on the government in Brussels to relax the anti-heresy edicts. Faced with the

---

[2] Van Beeck Calkoen, *Rechtstoestand*, pp. 37–68.   [3] Van Deursen, "Kerk of parochie?" pp. 531–5.
[4] Van Deursen, *Hel en hemel*, vol. IV of *Het kopergeld*, p. 48.   [5] Geoffrey Parker, *Dutch Revolt*, p. 72.
[6] A. J. Roelink, "Het calvinisme," in *AGN*, vol. IV, p. 285; Alastair Duke and D. H. A. Kolff, "The time of troubles in the county of Holland," in Duke, *Reformation and Revolt*, p. 129; Overmeer, *Haarlem*, pp. 19–21; J. H. van Dijk, "Bedreigd Delft," *Bijdragen voor Vaderlandsche Gescheidenis en Oudheidkunde*, 6th series, 6 (1928), p. 179; Boogman, "De overgang," p. 105; Elias, *Amsterdamsche regentenpatriciaat*, pp. 6–9.

prospect of rebellion in the spring of 1566, Margaret of Parma signed a decree in April that allowed local authorities leniency in enforcing the laws.[7] In this "miracle year," Calvinists seized the opportunity to come out into the open. As a result, armed Calvinists assembled in outdoor preaching services in and around Haarlem, Delft, Leiden, and Amsterdam. Local Calvinists had also begun to organize consistories in these four cities throughout the summer and autumn of 1566. Reformed Protestantism made small gains in Dordrecht but almost none whatsoever in Gouda prior to 1572.[8]

In the summer of 1566, the conflict between the central government, the Dutch nobility, and Calvinist confederates came to a head. The open services of the Calvinists alarmed Margaret of Parma and the Council of State in Brussels, while Calvinists demanded complete toleration for themselves and for Lutherans. The nobility, led by William of Orange, continued to press the central government for leniency and tried to control militant Calvinists. The center did not hold, however, as mobs began to ransack churches and monasteries throughout Flanders in August. This sparked the *beeldenstorm* throughout the southern and northern provinces which lasted from August through October 1566.[9]

In the wake of this widespread iconoclasm, Calvinists in Holland lost the recent measure of freedom they had gained.[10] The central government could not overlook the destruction nor its revolutionary implications. Philip II himself authorized the suppression of religious dissent, sending the Duke of Alva to the Netherlands. Through the infamous "Council of Troubles," Alva imposed a rather harsh regime in the Low Countries. Between 1567 and 1572, Alva's tribunal sentenced more than one thousand people to death.[11]

After Beggar forces invaded and subdued most of the cities of Holland in 1572, the States of Holland rewarded their Calvinist allies by granting the Reformed faith its privileged status. The States, however, stopped short of making it a compulsory state church. This limitation was an attempt to placate magistrates, who harbored no love for the uncompromising and militant stance of Calvinists in the 1560s. As the success of the Revolt in Holland became clear by 1579, urban patricians gained almost complete control over the cities as the distribution of power became even more decentralized. In fact, the province of Holland at the end of the sixteenth

---

[7] Geoffrey Parker, *Dutch Revolt*, p. 71.
[8] Consistories also emerged in Alkmaar, Den Briel, The Hague (Den Haag), Naaldwijk, and Gorcum during this time: Jaanus, *Hervormd Delft*, pp. 16, 19; Duke and Kolff, "Time of troubles," pp. 126–32, 139–40; Alastair Duke and Rosemary Jones, "Towards a reformed polity in Holland, 1572–1578," in *Reformation and Revolt*, p. 375; Overmeer, *Haarlem*, pp. 20, 30–1; Spaans, *Haarlem*, p. 35; Evenhuis, *Ook dat was Amsterdam*, vol. I, pp. 59–60; Elliott, "The classis of Dordrecht," p. 146; Hibben, *Gouda in Revolt*, p. 32.
[9] Phyllis Mack Crew, *Calvinist Preaching and Iconoclasm in the Netherlands, 1544–1569* (Cambridge, 1978), pp. 10–38.
[10] Geoffrey Parker, *Dutch Revolt*, p. 70.
[11] William S. Maltby, *Alba: A Biography of Fernando Alverez de Toledo Third Duke of Alba, 1507–1582* (Berkeley, 1983), p. 140.

century bore a closer resemblance to a confederation of urban republics than a united Dutch Republic.

The ambiguities of this new church produced intense conflicts among both clergy and laity until the conclusion of the National Synod of Dordrecht in 1619. The strongest opponents of Calvinism formerly came from the urban magistracies (along with a handful of Reformed clergy) who clung to the legacy of the Christian community that had arisen in the late middle ages. Libertine ministers, such as Caspar Coolhaes, Hubert Duifhuis, and Herman Herbertszoon, Cornelis Wiggertszoon, and Tako Sybrants, promoted a non-dogmatic evangelical piety. From their viewpoint, the magistracy, as the Christian authority, had preeminent authority to define the social order and to superintend religious affairs in the municipal corporation.[12] Accordingly, the political authorities, with the best interests of the Christian community in mind, were responsible for selecting ministers, elders, and deacons, as well as for poor relief and social discipline.

Orthodox Calvinists, on the other hand, operated from a confessional vision of church community. Calvinists believed that the appointment and training of ministers were best left to ecclesiastical governance, represented by the consistories, classes, and synods of the Reformed church. Protecting the community through discipline and providing relief for the poor via an independent diaconate were central to a biblically based Christian church.

POOR RELIEF AND CHRISTIAN COMMUNITY IN REFORMATION THOUGHT

Throughout the sixteenth century, *diakonia* lacked a universally accepted definition in the Christian churches of Europe. In the Catholic Church, the diaconate had undergone a long and gradual transformation since the early days of Christianity.[13] Holding permanent office in imperial Rome, deacons helped provide charity to the needy and assisted priests in liturgical tasks. Over the course of the middle ages, the liturgical aspects of the office became more dominant as the diaconate developed into a transitional stepping stone to the priesthood. The diaconate retained its clerical designation up to the sixteenth century. Deacons performed a variety of liturgical duties, sometimes in lieu of a priest. Within the Roman episcopacy, deacons were, for the most part, attendant clerical servants with an eye to potential elevation to a priest.[14]

---

[12] See Kaplan, *Calvinists and Libertines*, pp. 68–110.
[13] For a historical survey of the diaconate, see Jeannine E. Olson, *One Ministry, Many Roles: Deacons and Deaconesses Through the Centuries* (St. Louis, 1992).
[14] G. W. H. Lampe, "Diakonia in the early church," in *Service in Christ: Essays Presented to Karl Barth on His 80th Birthday*, James I. McCord and T. H. L. Parker, eds. (London, 1966), pp. 49–59; G. Barrois, "On medieval charities," in McCord and Parker, *Service in Christ*, pp. 65–6; Glenn S. Sunshine, "Geneva meets Rome: the development of the French reformed diaconate," *Sixteenth-Century Journal* 26, 2 (1995), p. 330; McKee, *Diaconate and Liturgical Almsgiving*, p. 129.

As Martin Luther severed the ties between spiritual welfare and a mediatorial clergy, he called attention to the work of the seven deacons in the New Testament. According to Luther, deacons' responsibilities consisted solely of "distributing the Church's aid to the poor, in order that the priests might be relieved of the burden of temporal concerns and give themselves more freely to prayer and the Word. For this was the purpose of the institution of the diaconate, as we read in Acts 5 [6:1–6]."[15] Yet Luther regarded the creation of deacons in Acts 6 as only a historical development meeting a temporary need in the primitive church. Perhaps for this reason the German Reformer recommended in 1523 to the city of Leisnig in Electoral Saxony that poor relief should be administered centrally from a common municipal chest.[16] Subsequently, within the state-sponsored Lutheran churches, all forms of poor relief came under the jurisdiction of the civil magistrate.

In terms of civil control over poor relief, the situation in the city of Zurich paralleled arrangements in Lutheran cities. Owing to the influence of Ulrich Zwingli, Zurich magistrates opted for a public Protestant faith that eventually bore the reformer's name over the course of the 1520s and 1530s. As Zwingli's evangelical ideas acquired legal status in Zurich, the city council reconstituted charitable institutions in keeping with its vision of a Protestant community. Due in part to Zwingli's sermons and writings on Christian charity, the town council enacted a poor law in January 1525 that consolidated all charitable institutions in the city under the direct administration of the city government. The settlement replicated many aspects of the centralizing reforms adopted by municipalities in southwestern Germany and Flanders. The Zurich poor law called for a diverse array of services and regulations, including civil control over relief, restrictions on begging, and schools for poor children. By virtue of the civic body's identification as the Christian community, there was no distinct institutional form of Protestant charity.[17] Given this social and political configuration, Zwingli did not offer an operative definition of the diaconate and the Reformed Church in Zurich did not have any deacons.

The poor relief arrangements in Lutheran and Zwinglian territories reflected a reaffirmation of the traditional ideal of the sacral community. Both Luther and Zwingli, despite their theological differences, continued to regard all of society as the *corpus christianum*, which needed to be purged of corruptions caused by clerical pretensions to independent temporal jurisdiction. For Zwingli, the religious community was coterminous with civil society; consequently, he accorded magistrates unrestricted authority in carrying out his reform program. Zurich magistrates supported ecclesiastical discipline with civil punishments and oversaw the entire

---

[15] Martin Luther, *The Babylonian Captivity of the Church* (1520), in vol. XXXVI of *Luther's Works*, Abdel Ross Wentz, ed. (Philadelphia, 1959), p. 116.

[16] Grimm, "Luther's contributions," pp. 226–7; Johannes Everts, *De verhouding van kerk en staat in bijzonder ten aanzien der armverzorging* (Utrecht, 1908), pp. 36–7.

[17] Wandel, *Always Among Us*, pp. 145–62.

range of poor relief. Luther distinguished the true invisible *Gemeinschaft* from the external visible church. The latter, however, was part of the "Kingdom of the World" under the administration of temporal authorities.[18] For that reason, Luther wedded the routine administration of poor relief to the civil supervision of the municipal community.

Just as Luther and Zwingli granted complete authority to the civil magistrate in regulating poor relief, their notions of Christian community also emerged under favorable political conditions. Reformers in Zurich (and in the southern German cities) and Lutherans in northern German territories enjoyed the sponsorship and protection of state governments. Such arrangements, whether organized at a territorial or a municipal level, forged a unitary political community centered around a particular confession. Civil and religious officers acted interchangeably as stewards of a unified political and confessional society. It is no coincidence that scholars of the Lutheran Reformation have devoted so much attention to the relationship between Lutheranism and state-building in early modern Germany, while historians of Zwinglianism have delineated the theocratic bases of polity that took hold in Zurich and the south German cities.[19]

In Reformed Protestantism, Martin Bucer was one of the most significant early figures in articulating a theory for a permanent diaconate.[20] Under Bucer's influence, from 1523 to 1549, Strasbourg became one of the leading centers of the Reformation on the continent, alongside Wittenberg and Geneva. Bucer was influential in the theological development of several Protestant leaders throughout sixteenth-century Europe, not the least of whom was John Calvin, who lived in Strasbourg from 1538 to 1541.[21] It was in *De Regno Christi*, his chief theological work, that Bucer gave full expression to his understanding of the diaconate and poor relief.[22]

Bucer took as his starting point Christ's universal command to love thy neighbor. Accordingly, the hallmark of the Christian community was loving service to others. "For those whom the Lord has given to us in special close relationships fall particularly under the second great commandment, in which the whole law is contained and fulfilled: 'Thou shalt love thy neighbor as thyself' (Matt. 22:39)."[23] From the principle of Christian love, he called upon congregations to organize a

---

[18] See Robert C. Walton, *Zwingli's Theocracy* (Toronto, 1967), pp. 17–29; Thomas A. Brady, Jr., "Luther and the state: the reformer's teaching in its social setting," in *Luther and the Modern State in Germany*, James D. Tracy, ed. (Kirksville, Mo., 1986), pp. 31–44.

[19] For an introduction to these issues, see the essays in Tracy, *Luther and the Modern State* and Walton, *Zwingli's Theocracy*.

[20] F. R. J. Knetsch, "Diakonaat als ambtelijke armenzorg I," *Nederlands Archief voor Kerkgeschiedenis* NS 64 (1984), p. 158.

[21] Miriam U. Chrisman, *Strasbourg and the Reform: A Study in the Process of Change* (New Haven, 1967), pp. x, 226–8.

[22] Martin Bucer, *De Regno Christi*, in *Melanchthon and Bucer*, Wilhelm Pauck, ed. (Philadelphia, 1969), pp. 157–9. Although *De Regno Christi* was not published until 1557, it was largely an expanded synthesis of his earlier writings.

[23] *Ibid.*, p. 307.

comprehensive program for relief and comfort administered by lay deacons. For Bucer, discipline and charity were not separate from one another; both grew out of a Christian community committed to brotherly love and moral piety.[24] As he stated, "For such should be compelled by the churches to take care of their own; toward this end the deacons ought to be at hand and of service to the bishop and the elders, as for the entire discipline of Christ."[25]

Laying stress on ministry, Bucer was not so much concerned with demonstrating apostolic precedent as he was trying to expand the office of the diaconate. Its duties consisted of identifying those who genuinely merited aid, dismissing the poor who lived dishonorably, and keeping accurate accounts of the congregation's resources. Because some of the needy might be too ashamed of their poverty to present themselves before the deacons, members acquainted with their needs should report them to the deacons.[26]

Although Bucer strongly advocated these tasks for the diaconate, he believed the office could function in a variety of circumstances. He never specified, therefore, how many deacons should serve nor how the congregation should choose them, nor did he give a precise explanation of the relationship between the diaconate and other church offices. While he devoted more attention to other ministerial offices, Bucer believed that there could be no true communion without relieving the needs of the poor. As a consequence, voluntary almsgiving through a collection box became a distinct symbol of social obligation in Reformed churches.[27]

Influenced by Bucer, John Calvin made the diaconate one of the four offices in the church. Because of his stature in Reformed Protestantism, he exercised considerable influence over the formation of the diaconate within Reformed practice. Calvin rooted his teachings on the diaconate in the belief that the restoration of social and spiritual life was part of Christ's redemptive work and the mission of the church. According to Calvin, human greed came with the Fall and corrupted the natural economic order. Moral pollution manifested itself, among other ways, in the unequal distribution of wealth within the natural world. Consequently, Calvin preached against conspicuous consumption and argued that the wealthy were the stewards of God's riches and should voluntarily redistribute them to the poor. The benefaction of the wealthy was obligatory, yet without merit. As recipients of this patronage, the poor were vicars of Christ, although Calvin in no way equated poverty with holiness.[28] On one occasion Calvin wrote, "God adorned his Son more

[24] Willem van 'T Spiker, *De ambten bij Martin Bucer* (Kampen, 1970), pp. 255–6.
[25] Bucer, *De Regno Christi*, p. 308.
[26] *Ibid.*, pp. 308–9, 313. Borrowing from the early and medieval church, Bucer also assigned deacons a vast array of liturgical responsibilities: Sunshine, "Geneva meets Rome," p. 331.
[27] Basil Hall, "Diakonia in Martin Butzer," in McCord and Parker, *Service in Christ*, pp. 94, 98–100; Knetsch, "Diakonaat," pp. 149, 158; McKee, *Diaconate and Liturgical Almsgiving*, pp. 48, 59. Despite his efforts, Bucer was unable to establish an independent diaconate in Strasbourg, where magistrates had already centralized charitable institutions: Chrisman, *Strasbourg*, pp. 275–85.
[28] André Biéler, *La Pensée economique et sociale de Calvin* (Geneva, 1959), pp. 159, 322–33, 363.

with the wretched appearance of a beggar than if he had glistened with all the regalia of kings."[29] Furthermore, the poor were not to beg, but were to improve their lot through industry and to content themselves with the situation in which God had placed them.[30]

To facilitate the church's redemptive work in the material world, Calvin turned to the model of the diaconate in New Testament practice.[31] Unlike Luther, Calvin held that the apostolic precedent of the diaconate was the norm for all Christian communities and was necessary for a thorough application of Scripture to social life. Calvin envisioned poor relief as a religious duty via a lay diaconate, which distributed alms to the poor as a form of worship.[32]

In actual practice in Geneva, however, he exhibited a considerable degree of flexibility on the ways in which contemporary requirements might shape the diaconate's tasks.[33] Operating out of a state church, Calvin expected the diaconate to oversee the entire range of poor relief in the city. Since Geneva had already centralized its poor relief structure around the *Hôpital général* before Calvin's arrival, he simply gave ecclesiastical expression to the existing institution. In the 1541 Ecclesiastical Ordinances Calvin offered no significant innovations in the administration of the *Hôpital* and church records devote little attention to the selection or the work of deacons.[34] One of Calvin's primary struggles with regard to poor relief was to endow it with an ecclesiastical nature in the closely intertwined civil and religious domains in Geneva.[35] Perhaps that was why Calvin consistently alluded to the regents of the *Hôpital* as deacons, whereas the registers of this institutions referred to them as civil administrators. In essence, he endowed city regents who were already working in the *Hôpital* with this apostolic office.[36]

The Geneva deacons were charged with caring for the sick, repressing begging,

---

[29] Quoted from William Bouwsma, *John Calvin: A Sixteenth-Century Portrait* (Oxford, 1988), p. 196.

[30] Max Weber's controversial thesis regarding Calvinism's influence on attitudes about work and poverty (see *The Protestant Ethic and the Spirit of Capitalism*, 2nd edn., Talcott Parsons, trans. [London, 1930]) has not found much support from scholars who study Calvin. For criticisms of Weber or parts of his thesis, see McKee, *Diaconate and Liturgical Almsgiving*, pp. 123–4; Biéler, *Calvin*, ch. 6; Bouwsma, *Calvin*, pp. 202, 233; Michael Walzer, *The Revolution of the Saints: A Study in the Origins of Radical Politics* (Cambridge, Mass., 1965), pp. 307–16; Carter Lindberg, "Through a glass darkly: a history of the church's vision of the poor and poverty," *Ecumenical Review* 33 (1981), p. 46. In support of Weber, see Tawney, *Rise of Capitalism*; Lis and Soly, *Poverty and Capitalism*. For a recent discussion of Weber and Calvinist historiography, see Philip Benedict, "The historiography of continental Calvinism," in *Weber's Protestant Ethic: Origins, Evidence, Context*, Hartmut Lehman and Kenneth F. Ledford, eds. (Cambridge, 1993), pp. 305–26.

[31] Biéler, *Calvin*, p. 365.

[32] Everts, *Verhouding van kerk en staat*, pp. 52–7; McKee, *Diaconate and Liturgical Almsgiving*, pp. 136–7; Kingdon, "Deacons in Calvin's Geneva," p. 81.

[33] J. K. S. Reid, "Diakonia in the thought of John Calvin," in McCord and Parker, *Service in Christ*, pp. 104–5.

[34] Kingdon, "Deacons in Calvin's Geneva," pp. 82, 85–6; E. William Monter, *Calvin's Geneva* (New York, 1967), p. 139.

[35] McKee, *Diaconate and Liturgical Almsgiving*, pp. 132–3.

[36] Kingdon, "Deacons in Calvin's Geneva," pp. 82–4.

and providing for orphans and widows, activities already sanctioned by the *Hôpital*. The procurers and hospitallers carried out the work of the *Hôpital*; the former raised and administered financial resources and the latter appropriated funds for the poor on a daily basis. According to the Ecclesiastical Ordinances, five deacons (four procurers and one hospitaller) should be elected annually by the General Council of Geneva and they were to give an accounting of their finances every three months to the pastors of the church.[37] After Calvin came to Geneva, these city officials became the deacons of the church. Consequently, Robert Kingdon has suggested that the deacons in Geneva were actually regarded as officials of the state.[38] As such, the civil authority and the church in Geneva cooperated closely to relieve poverty.

Calvin's revival of the diaconate along New Testament lines corresponded to his understanding of the Christian community. In contrast to the pattern of church–state relations in the other Swiss Protestant cities, he rejected any magisterial supervision over the church. In the 1543 edition of the *Institutes*, Calvin asserted unconstrained clerical control over the visible church. This does not mean, however, that Calvin envisioned any sort of separation between church and state for Geneva. Rather, he supported the interaction of temporal and ecclesiastical to promote his idea of a godly society. Both church governance and civil authority were directed to the same ends, the edification of public and private life. Magistrates were to support the consistory's efforts to uphold orthodoxy and eliminate moral corruption, but civil authorities were not to obstruct the work of the clergy.[39] Although Calvin developed his ideas on polity and poor relief within the confines of a state-sponsored church in Geneva, he did so with a broader audience in mind. According to Harro Höpfl, "Calvin's Genevan Church was intended to be exemplary (Geneva for its own sake did not matter to Calvin) – his heart was in Strasbourg and with the Brethren in France."[40]

Calvin played an important role in the development of the Reformation in France, where the relationship between Protestant and municipal poor relief was highly complex. Natalie Davis has shown that Protestants and Catholics in Lyons collaborated in creating the municipal *aumône générale* in 1534.[41] The conciliatory atmosphere that reigned in Lyons, however, was not necessarily the norm throughout sixteenth-century France. In southern France, Nîmes offers an altogether different model of the relationship between diaconal and municipal poor relief. Raymond Mentzer has pointed out that, after Calvinists gained the upper hand there in the 1560s, they provided relief to needy members through the church

---

[37] *Ibid.*, p. 82.

[38] *Ibid.*; Monter, *Geneva*, p. 139. The deacons also cared for exiles fleeing religious persecution, using special funds. See Jeannine Olson, *Calvin and Social Welfare: Deacons and the Bourse Française* (London, 1989).

[39] Harro Höpfl, *The Christian Polity of John Calvin* (Cambridge, 1982), pp. 103–28; William G. Naphy, *Calvin and the Consolidation of the Genevan Reformation* (Manchester, 1994), pp. 222–32.

[40] Höpfl, *Christian Polity*, p. 121.   [41] Davis, "Poor relief," pp. 29–36, 56–9.

rather than through a municipal agency.[42] If these studies intimate the varied approaches to poor relief, Glenn Sunshine's study of the French diaconate has underscored the diverse sources that shaped this ecclesiastical office. Sunshine has recently argued that French congregations drew from both Catholic and Genevan models of the diaconate before the National Synod of Paris in 1559. Even after the synod, he concluded, Catholic practices continued to influence the formation of the French Reformed diaconate.[43]

Thus, the leading Protestant Reformers on the continent supported a fully integrated system of poor relief. Luther, Zwingli, and Calvin supported the civil administration of social welfare promoted by humanists and adopted in many cities throughout Europe. For Luther and Zwingli the reorganization of poor relief revealed a continuation of the medieval Christian corporation. Although Calvin made an important distinction between *ecclesia* and *civitas*, he endorsed municipal control over social welfare. The prevailing Protestant pattern in these state-sponsored churches was complete centralization of poor relief. Most Reformers in Holland would embrace Calvin's vision of Christian community, although it would have different implications for civic and religious charity. The differences stem from the exile experience of Dutch Calvinists.

THE GENESIS OF THE DUTCH REFORMED DIACONATE

While Calvin's thought wielded enormous doctrinal influence on Reformed Protestantism throughout Europe, it was the exile experience of Dutch Calvinists that shaped the diaconate in the northern Provinces after 1572. As the undisputed leader of Reformed refugee communities in Emden and London, Johannes a'Lasco exerted the most direct theological influence on the formation of the diaconate in the Dutch Reformed Church. A Polish nobleman and Archdeacon of Warsaw, a'Lasco broke with the Roman Church shortly after 1538. After traveling in Germany, he moved to Emden in 1540 and three years later became the superintendent of the Reformed churches there. Until his departure for England in 1548, he was instrumental in implementing a reformed polity in Emden. After settling in London, a'Lasco accepted the same superintendent post of the Dutch and French exiled churches which he had so forcefully executed in East Friesland. From 1548 until the accession of Queen Mary in 1553, a'Lasco worked vigorously to frame a reformed church order for the refugee communities. During his tenure in England, a range of reformers from Thomas Cranmer to John Hooper held him in high esteem. Hooper in particular followed his reform program closely and Cranmer sought a'Lasco's response to the 1549 prayerbook. After Mary's accession, a'Lasco moved back to Emden where he worked as a pastor until 1555. A'Lasco left Emden

---

[42] Raymond A. Mentzer, "Organizational endeavour and charitable impulse in sixteenth-century France: the case of Protestant Nîmes," *French History*, 5 (1991), p. 7.

[43] Sunshine, "Geneva meets Rome," pp. 333–46.

to serve as a pastor at Frankfurt-am-Main. He later returned to his native Poland, where he died in 1560.[44] Because of his close connection to the Dutch church and his influence on the development of ministerial offices in the Netherlands, a'Lasco has been called a "second Calvin."[45] That both Arminians and Calvinists claimed him as the spiritual predecessor of their own parties in the seventeenth century indicates a'Lasco's abiding influence on the Dutch Reformation.[46]

Following the ideas of Martin Bucer, Johannes a'Lasco understood the church as a community of believers grounded in Scripture and committed to serving one another for common edification. According to a'Lasco, the members of this cohesive body were mutually interdependent; they were responsible before God for edifying and supporting those within the community. Care for the poor within the "household of faith" was basic to the task of the church and a sacred duty for the deacons. A'Lasco wrote that prosperous members of the congregation, as stewards of their God-given bounty, were to give freely to meet the material needs of poor members. He also charged the poor to free themselves from bitterness, to be grateful, and to give to others. In holding on to this apostolic example, the community would honor God and serve as a witness to those outside the faith.[47]

In both London and Emden, a'Lasco instituted a diaconate that would care exclusively for poor church members. Tim Fehler, a historian of poor relief in Emden, believes that it is possible that a'Lasco attempted to establish this diaconate in the 1540s, but it is certain that the Emden consistory approved it in 1557. The consistory referred to the poor relief college as the *Becken* diaconate, after the alms dish (*becken*) they placed in the church. The *Becken* diaconate worked alongside deacons for the *Haussitzenden* (*huiszittende* in Dutch) poor. These were civil administrators of relief for the needy in the entire city.[48] The partitioning of poor relief according to one's standing in a specific community, either civic or confessional, would be the operative model for Calvinist leaders in Holland.

Under the supervision of the consistory, *Becken* deacons were to serve the community by collecting alms, maintaining alms dishes, keeping accurate accounts, inquiring into the needs of the congregation, visiting the sick, and distributing

[44] A. G. Dickens, *The English Reformation* (New York, 1964), pp. 187, 232; Timothy G. Fehler, "Social welfare in early modern Emden: the evolution of poor relief in the age of reformation and confessionalization," Ph.D. thesis, University of Wisconsin–Madison (1994), pp. 250–1.

[45] P. Biesterveld, J. van Lonkhuizen, and R. J. W. Rudolph, *Het diaconaat: handboek ten dienste der diaconieen* (Hilversum, 1907), p. 132. While his theology was certainly congenial to that of the Genevan Reformer, a'Lasco probably stood closer to Zwinglian thought than to Calvinist, by virtue of his close friendship with Henry Bullinger. The term "second Calvin," therefore, should not be understood as a description of a'Lasco's theology, but rather of his stature among leaders of the Dutch Reformed Church. On a'Lasco's relationship to Bullinger, see Pettegree, *Foreign Protestant Communities*, pp. 48–9.

[46] For the Calvinist claim, see Jacobus Trigland, *Kerckelycke geschiedenissen* (Leiden, 1650), pp. 131, 144. For the Arminian claim, see Johannes Uytenbogaert, *Kerckelijcke historie* (Rotterdam, 1647), p. 142.

[47] Wilhelm Bernoulli, *Das Diakonenamt bei J. a Lasco* (Grifense, 1951), pp. 12, 16.

[48] Fehler, "Social welfare in Emden," pp. 257–78.

funds to those in distress. A'Lasco regarded the diaconate as a religious calling and required deacons to meet together regularly for Bible study with elders and ministers. In affairs of church discipline, the deacons were responsible for ferreting out recipients who conducted themselves dishonorably and cast shame onto the congregation.[49] Heinz Schilling has argued that poor relief and discipline in Emden were a dual-pronged attempt to forge a self-sustaining and pure religious community.[50]

The growing number of religious refugees after 1566 required the daily attention of the diaconate, who listened to requests and decided who merited how much assistance.[51] The scale of this diaconal operation was considerable, as the size of the diaconate grew from twelve to twenty-eight by the late sixteenth century. Between 1569 and 1576, they served 2,000 needy people from the Netherlands.[52] The large number of poor refugees required a strong degree of organization. Deacons from each "nation" (Holland, Brabant, Friesland, and Groningen) administered charity to their respective congregations. Diaconal finances were supported largely from contributions from immigrants from the different provinces and from general collections. These sources of revenue fell far short of the needs of the diaconal chest by 1568. In 1569, the deacons were 500 guilders in arrears and requested that the Emden city council appropriate revenues from the former property of the Catholic Church to make up this deficiency. Unfortunately for the deacons, the magistrates refused. The revenues for the Holland community, however, received a major boost from wealthy Amsterdam merchants who fled to Emden during the late 1560s.[53]

The Dutch Reformed Church in London also experienced rapid growth during the 1560s. It grew from 700 members (429 men and 271 women) in 1561 to 2,000 at its peak in 1568. Like Emden, poor relief in the Dutch community in London also went hand in hand with spiritual discipline. The close association between the consistory's efforts to ensure doctrinal and moral conformity and the diaconate's attempts to alleviate distress has prompted Andrew Pettegree to characterize these dual activities as an endeavor in "social concern and social control."[54] The former agenda focused on the poor, sick, and dying as deacons distributed "outside relief" to the underemployed and oversaw a poor house for the infirm. These activities entailed broader responsibilities in the community than might be apparent.

In their assigned districts, each deacon was compelled to know the members personally and to acquaint himself with their material needs. This task alone

---

[49] Bernoulli, *A Lasco*, p. 15.

[50] Heinz Schilling, "Reformierte Kirchenzucht als Sozialdisziplinierung? Die Tätigkeit des Emder Presbyteriums in den Jahren 1557–1562," in *Niederlande und Nordwestdeutschland: Studien zur Regional- und Stadtgeschichte Nordwestkontinentaleuropas im Mittelalter und in der Neuzeit*, Wolfgang Ehbrecht and Heinz Schilling, eds. (Cologne and Vienna, 1983), pp. 263, 273–5, 321.

[51] *Ibid.*, p. 287.   [52] Evenhuis, *Ook dat was Amsterdam*, vol. II, p. 74.

[53] Pettegree, *Emden and the Dutch Revolt*, pp. 152–6, 167.

[54] Pettegree, *Foreign Protestant Communities*, pp. 182–214.

required extensive social interaction with members of the community. Pettegree
has portrayed the diaconate as wholly sympathetic to the plight of their compatriots
and he shows that they extended charity even to fellow citizens who were not
official church members. Given the church's concern for discipline, however, it
would seem likely that even attendees (*liefhebbers*) would be held to the general
moral and doctrinal strictures of the Confession of Faith. Deacons also paid for
medical treatment, served as executors of estates, helped set up businesses, kept
accounts of their purse, and helped to raise revenue. The financial restraints of the
rather meager collections in church services were offset by individual donations,
wills, and the periodic generosity of the Bishop of London. It seems likely that the
diaconate played no small role in the various enterprises designed to augment their
income.[55]

Through these activities, the diaconate in the Dutch refugee churches in Emden
and London activated the confessional poor relief principles laid down by a'Lasco,
and to a lesser extent, by Calvin and Bucer. More importantly for this study, these
practices also provided a working model of the diaconate for Reformers in Holland,
as they attempted to form confessional communities in the wake of the Revolt.

Not only did Dutch Reformers institute a formal ecclesiastical structure as
refugees, but the exile experience itself reinforced the strong confessional basis for
their ministries. Pettegree has identified an inherent "exile psychology" within
Calvinism that enabled its partisans to become an international movement.[56]
Similarly, Heiko Oberman has argued that Calvinists envisioned themselves as
perpetual refugees who were committed to "renovat[ing] and reform[ing] society to
visibly reflect the glory of God." This understanding led to an "organizational
self-government which gave congregations the flexibility to dominate cities when
winning a majority or to survive as persecuted underground communities."[57]

For Dutch Calvinists, the Christian community was a gathered community of
the elect carrying out its redemptive mission in a fallen world. Ben Kaplan has
shown that the Calvinist drive for "holy uniformity" motivated them "to craft a
religious unity that transcended the limits of parish, city, and province."[58] Thus, in
contrast to the local communal vision of magistrates, Calvinists regarded their
community to be an international body of like-minded believers. To that end,
Dutch Calvinist ministers would vigorously assert ecclesiastical control over
church offices.

The dynamic presence of Reformed church leaders in these communities formed
the connection between diaconal poor relief in exile and subsequent practice in

[55] *Ibid.*, pp. 198–214.
[56] Andrew Pettegree, "Exile and the development of Reformed Protestantism," paper presented to the
Sixteenth-Century Studies Conference (Toronto, Ontario, October 28, 1994).
[57] Heiko Oberman, "*Europa afflicta*: the reformation of the refugees," *Archiv für Reformationsgeschichte*
83 (1992), p. 99.
[58] Benjamin J. Kaplan, "Dutch particularism and the Calvinist quest for holy uniformity," *Archiv für
Reformationsgeschichte* 82 (1991), p. 249.

Holland. Throughout Holland in the years immediately after 1572, no fewer than twenty-six of the Reformed ministers resident in the province had actively participated in the Emden community, while others returned from refugee churches in the Palatinate.[59] The fact that the first generation of ministers in Holland either came from a refugee church or labored in congregations "under the cross" bolstered the strong confessional orientation for poor relief after the establishment of the Reformed faith. Of the seven ministers in Delft during the 1570s, at least three had served in Dutch exile congregations in the Palatinate and one had preached "under the cross."[60] In Amsterdam, at least two of the three ministers in 1578 had exile experience: Johannes Cuchlinus in Emden and Petrus Dathenus in Frankenthal in the Palatinate.[61] Likewise, the first two Reformed ministers in Haarlem came from similar backgrounds, as Johannes Damius had served in the Palatinate while Gerard Blockhoven worked in Mechelen.[62] Dordrecht's leading Calvinist pastor in the 1580s, Hendrik van der Corput, studied at the University of Heidelberg and worked in churches in the Palatinate during Alva's rule.[63]

The fact that the Reformed Church never enjoyed state sponsorship suggests that these ministers would perpetuate the constituent elements of their exclusive "household of faith" within a civic environment. During this period, a'Lasco's leadership in promoting confessional ideals provided them with a working model of the diaconate that church leaders would graft onto their congregations in Holland after 1572.

THE FORMALIZATION OF THE DUTCH REFORMED DIACONATE

As the Dutch Reformation gained momentum in the late 1560s and early 1570s, Reformers faced the task of imposing organization and uniformity onto their congregations. The structure that developed over the 1570s was a presbyterian form of church government. The consistory governed the local congregation and the classis (a regional body made up of consistorial delegates) oversaw the activities of consistories, examined ministerial candidates, and handled unresolved discipline cases. Within the province, Holland was divided into two provincial synods, one for the synod of north Holland and one for the synod of south Holland. The provincial synods usually met on an annual basis to clarify church polity and discuss problems within local classes. Finally, national synods were convened in 1571 (Emden), 1578 (Dordrecht), 1581 (Middelburg), 1586 (The Hague), and 1618 (Dordrecht) to forge a national church order and to deal with the most problematic theological issues.

The broadest Reformed guidelines for deacons and poor relief were spelled out in the provincial and national synods that met between 1571 and 1578. Until the

---

[59] Duke and Jones, "Reformed polity," p. 223.
[60] Van Bleyswijck, *Delft*, vol. I, pp. 450–1; Jaanus, *Hervormd Delft*, p. 100.
[61] See *GAA. Kerkeraad, Predikanten*.   [62] *Ibid*.   [63] Elliott, "The classis of Dordrecht," p. 151.

National Synod of Dordrecht in 1618–19, political authorities in Holland did not formally ratify the resolutions of any Reformed synod. The States of Holland did not approve them and city governments never committed themselves to upholding synodal decisions. In many instances they steadfastly opposed them. Even though church synods carried no official weight until 1619, they still set forth the basic positions on doctrine and church organization that consistories in five of the six cities (excepting Gouda) attempted to follow.[64] Consequently, the synodal resolutions reveal the theoretical aims and character of Calvinist poor relief.

Before the first formal synod in 1571, a handful of Reformed ministers met at Wesel in 1568. Although succeeding synods never recognized the "convent" of Wesel as an official policy-making body, this assembly laid out general principles that would be embraced by later synods.[65] With Petrus Dathenus as its presiding officer, the convent of Wesel identified the four ecclesiastical offices of the Reformed Church: doctors, ministers, elders, and deacons. These offices corresponded to the requisite elements in forming "true" Christian communities. Doctors interpreted Scripture to make sure that the teaching of God's Word was based on sound biblical exegesis. Ministers preached the Word and administered the sacraments to the faithful. In conjunction with ministers, lay elders governed local congregations and protected the integrity of the communion by disciplining members. Lay deacons relieved the needy and comforted the sick and dying.[66] Restricted to those within the "household of faith," poor relief was understood to be an important component in maintaining a cohesive and a confessional church.[67]

Corresponding to practices in Emden and London, the convent authorized deacons to collect and dispense alms. The assembly did not specify the process whereby they might be chosen. Perhaps this omission resulted from a conscious recognition of the disparate circumstances that Reformed communities might encounter, for the resolutions acknowledged this qualification when it specifically avoided prescribing how many deacons should serve. Though the convent proved flexible on quantity, it was insistent on the quality of deacons. Based on First Timothy 3, elders were to ensure that prospective deacons were faithful, industrious, and munificent.[68]

The 1571 National Synod of Emden affirmed the ecclesiastical office of the diaconate and the duties of deacons that were set forth at Wesel. In addition, the delegates adopted requirements for religious immigrants who requested assistance. In so doing, the synod sought to guard against the misuse of alms by indigents who did not live up to the moral and doctrinal standards of the Reformed faith. The Emden synod required that incoming travelers must present written documentation of good standing (*attestatie*) from their previous congregation before they could

---

[64] For Gouda's opposition to provincial and national synods, see Hibben, *Gouda in Revolt*, pp. 104–11.
[65] Biesterveld, et al., *Het diaconaat*, p. 154. The convent of Wesel was not a formal synod. J. J. Woltjer has called it a "pressure group" attended by only a few Calvinists: Woltjer, "De calvinisten," p. 13.
[66] Rutgers, *Acta*, pp. 12–13.   [67] Everts, *Verhouding van kerk en staat*, p. 61.   [68] *Ibid.*, p. 25.

qualify for poor relief.[69] The obligation remained incumbent upon immigrants requesting membership and poor relief throughout the Reformation period in the Netherlands. The only recipients the Emden synod provided for were members of the Reformed Church.[70]

Because of the pattern of military conquest in Holland, the Provincial Synod of South Holland took an initial and important leadership role in instituting the fundamental structure of the Dutch Reformed Church in Holland. All of the most important cities in the synod of south Holland were under the prince of Orange's command by the autumn of 1572. These cities included Dordrecht, Leiden, Delft, and Gouda. The rebel forces would not acquire control over Haarlem and Amsterdam until 1577 and 1578, respectively. The latter two cities fell under the jurisdiction of the synod of north Holland. It was the first meeting of the Provincial Synod of South Holland that met in Dordrecht in June 1574 that would have the most decisive influence on poor relief policy for local congregations.

The Dordrecht synod followed and expanded upon the provisions of Emden synod. It recognized the diaconate as an independent ecclesiastical office and it determined that the consistory consisted of clergy and elders; deacons were to conduct their meetings separately.[71] Deacons could participate in consistorial meetings only in the event that a congregation could not identify an adequate number of capable elders. The language in the synodal articles made it clear that this arrangement was not preferable and it existed only in areas where church organization was underdeveloped.[72]

According to the Dordrecht synod, the consistory possessed ultimate authority over the diaconate. Consistories were to draw up a list (containing twice as many names as there were vacancies) of qualified candidates for the diaconate and present these names to the congregation. After allowing the congregation a period of time to communicate either recommendations or misgivings about the candidates, the congregation would then select deacons from the list of candidates. As the church's poor relief officers, deacons bore the specific responsibilities for visiting the sick, collecting, administering, and distributing funds for the poor of the congregation. To ensure order and combat favoritism in the administration of charity, deacons were to meet together weekly to consider requests for assistance and the assembly at large decided who did and did not merit relief.[73] Under the charge of the consistory, deacons were to appear before them monthly to present a statement of their accounts and to report on the status of the church's poor relief efforts.

The synod designated the diaconate as the only ecclesiastical relief organ for members of the Dutch Reformed Church.[74] Three years later at the Provincial Synod of South Holland meeting in Rotterdam, someone raised the question of

---

[69] *Ibid.*, p. 81.   [70] Ibid., p. 62.   [71] Biesterveld, et al., *Het diaconaat*, p. 157.
[72] Reitsma and van Veen, *Acta*, vol. II, p. 130. Van Deursen has shown that church organization in general, and diaconates in particular, were very weak in rural areas: van Deursen, *Bavianen*, p. 103.
[73] Reitsma and van Veen, *Acta*, vol. II, p. 139.   [74] *Ibid.*, pp. 130, 135.

"whether the diaconate may serve those outside the congregation." The delegates answered: "no, but if no [formal] congregation has been established, the [political] authorities should serve pious men. Otherwise the deacons belong to the congregation."[75] These resolutions indicate that Calvinists intended to limit Reformed charity to poor church members.

The synodal representatives also addressed the important issue of the relationship between the diaconate and municipal poor relief agencies. The ideal was an independent diaconate that received a portion of its revenues from the income of parish poor relief agencies. *Heilige Geestmeesters*, or a cognate parish organization, should care for the "general" poor in the city and the church should limit its relief efforts to church members. That is, the deacons should receive financial assistance from the city without municipal interference.[76] Apparently the synod realized this model might be jeopardized by an insufficiently funded diaconate. In a situation in which the "Christian congregation" was meager, the synod permitted deacons to work in conjunction with *Heilige Geestmeesters*. In such a collaborative environment, the deacons, with consistorial representatives, were allowed to account for their revenues to the magistrates. Despite any such collaboration, the consistory retained its authority over the diaconate and individual churches were to defend their right to collect alms for the poor of the congregation. If the diaconate received its revenues only from ecclesiastical sources, namely church collections, the synod determined that they were to give their financial report only to the consistory.[77]

The Provincial Synod of Dordrecht laid the basis for the operation of the diaconate in the churches of south Holland. The diaconate was an ecclesiastical office responsible for poor relief under the ultimate authority of the consistory. The synod maintained the church's right to operate this office independently of municipal interference. Even in cases where the diaconate might cooperate with a civil agency, the church preserved its right to select deacons, take collections in worship services, and administer relief to its own members. If required to appear before the city council, the deacons did so with members of the consistory, signifying that the deacons were not under the authority of the magistrates. The policies of this body had a strong influence throughout Holland, as the Synod of North Holland adopted these guidelines a month later in Edam.[78] Four years later, the National Synod of Dordrecht utilized this protocol to institute the diaconate office for Reformed churches throughout Holland.

In 1578, the National Synod of Dordrecht gave local consistories control over all church affairs and an expansive influence in civil matters. The synod accorded the consistory the right to regulate the diaconate, to appoint all ministers, elders, and deacons, and to discipline the congregation, as well as to appoint school teachers, to restrict dancing, activities of local theatrical societies (chambers of rhetoric), and to censor printed material. The Dordrecht synod also stipulated that, in cases where

---

[75] *Ibid.*, p. 280. [76] Everts, *Verhouding van kerk en staat*, p. 62.
[77] Reitsma and van Veen, *Acta*, vol. II, pp. 138–9. [78] *Ibid.*, vol. I, p. 26.

the municipal authority impeded the work of the diaconate, the consistory was to defend the activity of the diaconate vigorously and to call upon the classis for support.[79] The explicit consideration of municipal interference by the synodal delegates is highly suggestive.

The question implied that the entry of the diaconate into the realm of poor relief, a matter traditionally regulated by civil authorities, had already created tension in some cities, and the delegates expected it to foster conflict in others. For example, Pieter Corneliszoon, a staunch Calvinist minister in Leiden, complained in 1576 that the city government was interfering with the deacons' work and that the magistrates considered the diaconate a civil office rather than an ecclesiastical one.[80] Given the historic civic ideal of an inseparable corporate community under the authority of a magistracy, the confessional demands of a members-only church posed a threat to urban leaders. Reformers understood that poor relief had the potential for becoming one point where these competing conceptions of society would come into conflict. The underlying concern from the Reformers' point of view was the independence of the church to carry out its spiritual mission. The synodal response indicates that the Reformers would cling tenaciously to their vision of the church in the face of municipal resistance. To a certain extent, this question was prophetic, for the issue of poor relief required intermittent negotiation between Reformed consistories and city magistrates until the early decades of the seventeenth century.

Regarding diaconal protocol, the delegates endorsed the procedure for selecting elders and deacons laid down four years earlier in the provincial synod. They further specified that, after presenting the list of candidates to the congregation, the consistory should wait eight days for discrete responses (*beproeving*) from members before choosing the actual officers. The term of office for both elders and deacons was two years, with half being selected in rotation each year. The deacons' responsibilities and relationship to the consistory remained largely the same. The synod did sanction a proviso that the diaconate should guard against the misuse of alms by recipients of poor relief. Informally, deacons already had exercised some supervisory oversight in reporting cases of moral and doctrinal breaches to the consistory. This regulation endowed them with formal authority over the poor within the congregation. Consequently, church leaders wedded discipline to poor relief as a means of achieving a tightly knit confessional community.[81]

Later synods really added nothing new to poor relief policies in the Dutch Reformed Church. The National Synods of Middelburg in 1581 and The Hague in 1586 sought to limit political encroachment in church affairs, including diaconal poor relief.[82] Thus, during the 1570s, the national and provincial synods of the

[79] *Ibid.*, vol. II, p. 267.   [80] Kooi, "Leiden," p. 63.
[81] The Provincial Synod of South Holland meeting in Rotterdam in 1575 established a precedent for this responsibility: Reitsma and van Veen, *Acta*, vol. II, pp. 164–5, 238–9.
[82] R. H. Bremmer, *Reformatie en rebellie: Willem van Oranje, de calvinisten en het recht van opstand tien onstuimige jaren, 1572–1581* (Franeker, 1984), pp. 88, 176.

Dutch Reformed Church labored to refine a church polity and ecclesiastical structure that would enable them to build strong confessional communities. The diaconate had an integral role in this redemptive mission as material mediators between rich and poor church members. The theoretical definition of the diaconate and the church's emphasis on poor relief owed a great deal to the teachings of Martin Bucer, John Calvin, and Johannes a'Lasco. Because of a'Lasco's influence in the Dutch exiled church, his community-oriented understanding of poor relief became a practical guide for Dutch Reformers who played a prominent role in the synodal assemblies. Following a'Lasco, they bonded relief to moral and doctrinal standards and authorized elders and deacons to regulate these affairs. Under the authority of the consistory, deacons were to interact with poor church members, identify needs, distribute alms where required, and keep an account of their fund. Above all, the diaconate was to serve the church's membership without municipal interference.

These synodal prescriptions were theoretical, formed abstractly by church leaders who intended to implement theory into practice in their respective locales. The conversion of theory into practice warranted some accommodation, especially since Calvinist poor relief was directly antithetical to traditional parish poor relief and the centralizing efforts undertaken by city governments at the end of the sixteenth century. The early implementation of diaconal poor relief in Holland is a study in this interactive process as church leaders attempted to recast their respective societies in ways that contrasted with the communal ideals of city magistrates.

THE IMPLEMENTATION OF THE REFORMED DIACONATE IN THE SIX CITIES OF HOLLAND

As the cities of Holland recognized, albeit sometimes grudgingly, the public establishment of the Reformed faith, church leaders attempted to form exclusive confessional communities, marked by preaching the gospel, administering the sacraments, disciplining the congregation, and providing charity to poor members. Due to the diverse local political circumstances, their fortunes varied considerably. Of the six cities, the weakest Calvinist organization occurred in Gouda. One of the most meager congregations in Holland, the Reformed community in Gouda numbered no more than fifty members by 1578. It took two years before a consistory and diaconate emerged, and an independent classis did not arise until 1578. Throughout most of the 1580s, no minister stayed in Gouda longer than two years and the church there had a difficult time arranging salaries for the clergy.[83]

What is more problematic for the modern historian is that there are no extant consistory or diaconal archives in Gouda before 1620. Supposedly, the reason for

---

[83] Hibben, *Gouda in Revolt*, pp. 111–15.

the lack of consistorial and diaconal source material was that the Remonstrant ministers took the church records with them when they were dismissed from their posts after the Synod of Dort.[84] Eventually, the church records became lost and so was much of Gouda's religious history. The only direct evidence of the diaconate in Gouda in the early years of the Reformation is in the records of the *vroedschap* in November 1574 and October 1576. In the former entry, the deacons requested freedom from the tax on rye bread so that they would be able to bake and distribute more bread to the poor. Two years later, several deacons joined the elders in asking the city council for a pastor.[85] The failure of the church to attract members and the underdeveloped church organization, however, would suggest that the diaconate in Gouda was not a very sizable operation.

The Reformed church in Leiden also started out with a small congregation and a fledgling ecclesiastical organization. The church had at least three ministers after July 1572 and there is mention of a consistory in 1573. On January 6, 1574, the magistrates authorized the election of six elders and five deacons.[86] Until 1579, the consistory nominated diaconal candidates, but the magistracy asserted its authority to approve all candidates before the congregation elected them.[87] If the city government kept an eye on the election of church officers before 1579, after that time the magistrates attempted to control all church elections. The Leiden magistracy rejected the expansive powers the 1578 synod of Dordrecht gave to local consistories. Throughout the 1580s, the Leiden city government and Calvinist members of the consistory engaged in a bitter struggle over the jurisdiction of church officers. The magistrates chose church officers, restricted church discipline, opposed strident Calvinist preachers such as Pieter Corneliszoon, and supported Libertine ministers like Caspar Coolhaes and Peter Hackius. Due to severe economic difficulties in the textile industry, the magistrates forced the church to merge the diaconate with municipal almoners in 1582. Thus, an independent diaconate for church members in Leiden lasted less than ten years.[88]

Dordrecht represented the opposite end of the spectrum from Gouda and Leiden. Close ties between the consistory and the magistracy in Dordrecht enabled the church to institute a consistory and diaconate in the summer of 1573. The classis of Dordrecht also ordered an investigation into the status of poor relief throughout the area in August 1573 so that the poor might attend to the Word of

---

[84] J. E. J. Geselschap, "De ontwikkeling van het kerkelijk leven in Gouda vanaf de hervorming," in *Gouda zeven eeuwen stad*, p. 307.

[85] *GAG. Vroedschapboeken*, vol. XLV, fols. 82v (November 4, 1574), 156v (October 5, 1576).

[86] J. J. Woltjer, "Een niew ende onghesien dingh: verkenningen naar de positie van de kerkeraad in twee Hollandse steden in de zestiende eeuw," Afschiedscollege, Rijksuniversiteit te Leiden (1985), p. 4.

[87] Kooi, "Leiden," p. 61.

[88] Ligtenberg, *Armezorg te Leiden*, p. 231. Unfortunately, there is no consistent record of the diaconate's operation in Leiden from 1574 to 1582. The consistory in Leiden did select their own deacons, but these church officers also stood under the authority of the magistrates.

God. The results of this inquiry confirmed the need for a diaconate and, shortly thereafter, one was established in each community.[89]

In the city of Dordrecht, ministers met with "some of the magistrates" in June 1573 to nominate twelve elders, six of whom were to be chosen by the consistory. A month later, the magistrates and ministers collaborated again to choose eight deacons from sixteen nominees.[90] There can be little doubt that the contingent of magistrates who met with the consistory were Calvinists. In fact, the case of Dordrecht represents the highest degree of cooperation in poor relief between a city government and a Reformed consistory in the six cities. The Dordrecht government helped finance the diaconate and it did not interfere in the selection of deacons.[91] The expansive character of Reformed poor relief in Dordrecht came by way of the dominating Calvinist presence on the magistracy that rose to power after the Revolt.

Although the deacons placed priority on assisting the poor of the "household of faith," the Dordrecht diaconate played the most important role in providing relief to all the poor in the city.[92] The deacons gave an accounting to the consistory and frequently pressed the ministers and elders to help raise more revenue to purchase bread.[93] The Dordrecht consistory relied on wealthy members of the congregation as well as the city government to support diaconal poor relief.[94] There is also some indication that the consistory expected the deacons to pitch in financially, for in December a nominated candidate wanted to withdraw because he would not be able to "advance pennies" for the comfort of the poor.[95]

It was the close association between the Reformed Church and the city government that enabled Dordrecht to conform more closely to a Calvinist state model than other cities in Holland. Consequently, the diaconate in Dordrecht bore a stronger resemblance to the Genevan structure than did its counterparts in other cities of Holland. As such, ecclesiastical poor relief possessed a universal character, even though it was rooted in the offices of the church.

Outside the city of Dordrecht, Reformed communities in the classis of Dordrecht often found it difficult to find capable deacons. C. A. Tukker has shown that none of the deacons in the village of Sliedrecht could write and in other areas bookkeeping suffered from neglect. In these rural areas, civil authorities had a say in the selection process and the deacons often reported to magistrates rather than to the consistory. This civil interference most assuredly did not

---

[89] Tukker, *Dordrecht*, p. 78.

[90] Th. W. Jansma, ed., *Uw rijk kome: acta van de kerkeraad van de Nederduits Gemeente te Dordrecht, 1573–1579* (Dordrecht, 1981), pp. 1, 3.

[91] Elliott, "The classis of Dordrecht," pp. 364–5.

[92] In November 1574, the consistory directed the deacons to "above all care for the members of our community," and to draw up a register of all recipients, designating which ones were members and which ones were not: Jansma, *Uw rijk kome*, pp. 24–5.

[93] *GADR. Kerkeraad* (September 6, 1580; November 3, 1580).   [94] *Ibid.* (November 17, 1580).

[95] *Ibid.* (December 9, 1610).

please the classis, which began to fight for the independence of the diaconate in the late 1570s.[96]

As part of the negotiations with the prince of Orange in 1577, city magistrates in Haarlem accepted a provision that would allow "the Reformed to collect and distribute their alms."[97] As a result, poor relief in Haarlem was split along confessional and communal lines. The Reformed diaconate cared for those poor numbered in the "household of faith," while municipal almoners oversaw the wide range of relief foundations that served the general poor of the city. The consistory selected the first deacons in the spring of 1577 and charged them with collecting, distributing, and keeping account of church alms. In principle, the deacons provided relief only to members in good standing, thereby imprinting the confessional nature of the Reformed church onto charity.[98]

Source materials from Amsterdam and Delft provide a much more detailed picture of the diaconate within Reformed communities at this early juncture. In the largest congregation in Holland's most populous city, the diaconate in Amsterdam originated publicly on May 24, 1578.[99] After a brief tug-of-war, the *vroedschap* consented to allow the consistory to select the deacons for the congregation.[100] Six elders and six deacons served a congregation whom the highest estimates have numbered around 3,000, 900 of whom received weekly relief.[101] Amsterdam Calvinists formed the largest group of Dutch refugees in the Emden community, suggesting that the exiles linked the operation in Emden to subsequent poor relief practices in the Amsterdam congregation.[102] Similar to diaconal activity in Emden, deacons in Amsterdam shouldered broad responsibilities. Initially, they met twice a week in the Nieuwe Kerk to hear requests, settle their accounts, examine the beliefs of the poor, and determine who merited assistance. They met on Thursday for those living on the Nieuwe Zijde and on Saturdays for the poor on the Oude Zijde.[103]

Designated inspectors (*opsienders*) assisted the deacons by identifying the poor, monitoring behavior, and reporting their observations to the deacons and the consistory. The deacons were to visit the recipients at home in order to exhort them to godliness, while *ziekenbezoekers* (visitors of the sick) ministered to the sick and dying.[104] By virtue of their responsibility for supervising the morals of the poor, the deacons participated with the consistory in devising a policy for excommunication of recalcitrant members in August 1579.[105] The diaconate also took extraordinary

[96] Tukker, *Dordrecht*, pp. 78–9.
[97] Article 14 stated: "de Hervormden zouden vrijelijk hunne aalmoezen mogen verzamelen en uitdeelen" (quoted from Overmeer, *Haarlem*, p. 94).
[98] Spaans, *Haarlem*, p. 181.   [99] *GAA. Kerkeraad* (May 24, 1578).
[100] *Ibid.* (July 7, 1579); Evenhuis, *Ook dat was Amsterdam*, vol. II, p. 74.
[101] Commelin, *Amsterdam*, vol. I, pp. 488–9. Arguing that the Amsterdam church did not take off until heavy immigration after 1585, Briels has cautioned against this inflated figure. Nevertheless, even if it was inflated by 100 percent, the Amsterdam church could still claim the largest membership in Holland: Briels, *Zuidnederlandse immigratie*, p. 9.
[102] Evenhuis, *Ook dat was Amsterdam*, vol. I, p. 71.   [103] *GAA. Kerkeraad* (November 14, 1579).
[104] *Ibid.* (April 7, 1579).   [105] *Ibid.* (August 15, 1579).

The reformation of community

collections for poorer congregations in Holland and churches "under the cross" in the south.[106]

The Reformed church in Amsterdam also employed female deacons (*deaconessen*) to meet the special needs of widows and single women within the congregation. While this office could have existed as early as 1566, the consistory did not record the names of these women until 1583.[107] The consistory selected *deaconessen* in the same manner that they chose deacons, but the former never participated in consistorial assemblies nor did they administer revenue.

Arent Cornelisz, the most prominent minister in Delft from 1573 to 1605, represented the most direct link between diaconal activity in exile and its organization in Delft.[108] Called by his critics "the pope of Delft," Corneliszoon was the driving force behind the Delft church, and one of the most notable ministers in Holland. He served as scribe to the Provincial Synod at Dordrecht (1574) and to the National Synod in Dordrecht (1578), president of the national synod at Middelburg (1581), and *assessor* of the National Synod at The Hague (1586).[109] Preserved in the municipal archives in Delft, his voluminous correspondence attests to his broad influence throughout the Low Countries.[110] Before his tenure in Delft, Corneliszoon had served as a minister for over two years to the Holland refugee congregation at Frankenthal in the Palatinate. Beyond his own experience in an exiled religious community, Corneliszoon maintained friendships with a number of colleagues who also worked in refugee churches, including Thomas Tilius, Petrus Dathenus, Menso Alting, and Jacobus Regius. Tilius and Dathenus worked alongside Corneliszoon at Frankenthal, and the former joined Corneliszoon in Delft from 1575 to 1590.[111] Heavily influenced by a'Lasco, Dathenus maintained a life-long friendship with Corneliszoon and their relationship was marked by a strong sense of mutual respect throughout their careers. Alting served at Emden, while Regius was active in London and Ghent.[112]

Not only did Corneliszoon gain exposure to diaconal poor relief in refugee

[106] The first collection mentioned in the consistory records was in 1578. The diaconate sent thirty guilders to a congregation in Schoonhouven. One year later the deacons sent 400 guilders to Antwerp: *ibid.* (October 9, 1578; October 13, 1579).
[107] While the consistory listed the names of the *deaconessen* for the first time in 1583, the language of the consistory indicated that they were replacing the *deaconessen* who had served the previous year. It seems likely, then, that the consistory had already recognized these female deacons in 1582: *ibid.* (March 17, 1583).
[108] The son of burgomaster M. Cornelis Huygenszoon van 's-Gravesande, Corneliszoon grew up in Delft. He was born in 1547 and remained with his family until he matriculated into the University of Heidelberg in 1565: Jaanus, *Hervormd Delft*, pp. 94–7.
[109] Woltjer, "Een niew ende onghesien dingh," p. 9; W. Nijenhuis, "Varianten binnen het Nederlandse Calvinisme in de zestiende eeuw," *Tijdschrift voor Geschiedenis* 89 (1976), p. 358 n. 6.
[110] His correspondence is located at *GAD. KrCor.*
[111] Bernoulli, *A Lasco*, p. 18; Jaanus, *Hervormd Delft*, p. 100. Dathenus headed a delegation to the Wesel convent (1568) and was partially responsible for the formulation of diaconal care in the Walloon churches: Biesterveld, et al., *Het diaconaat*, pp. 154, 156.
[112] Jaanus, *Hervormd Delft*, p. 98. Corneliszoon attempted to recruit Alting to Delft in 1575, but he elected to stay at Emden: *GAD. KrCor* (November 13, 1575).

communities, but, as an officer at the 1574 Dordrecht synod, he played a significant role in establishing diaconal protocol for the churches of south Holland. Selected and supervised by the consistory, the deacons in Delft collected alms, kept accounts of their fund, and distributed charity to those in need. Citing the Dordrecht synod, the Delft consistory adopted these guidelines for their diaconate on August 1, 1574.[113]

Until the diaconate merged with the *Kamer van Charitate* in 1614, the consistory selected the church's deacons with no interference from the city government. Until this time, the relationship between municipal and ecclesiastical poor relief in Delft paralleled the arrangement in Dordrecht. Delft deacons shouldered most of the responsibility for relieving the needs of the *huiszitten* poor.[114] As we shall see in chapter 6, the primary reason the consistory agreed to do this was so that the church would be able to maintain a diaconate for church members.

The deacons in Delft performed the same tasks as their counterparts in Dordrecht, Haarlem, and Amsterdam. They met weekly in the choir of the Nieuwe Kerk to entertain requests and to settle their accounts. In addition, each deacon assumed responsibility for members in one of the four districts (*wijkjes*) drawn up at least by 1575 for purposes of discipline and poor relief. The consistory chose inspectors to report the "geloofs ende wandelen" (belief and walk) of poor relief recipients.[115] The consistory did not confine their understanding of confessional community to Delft, for on fifteen occasions between 1575 and 1592 they made contributions to destitute congregations outside the city. The churches to which Delft contributed included Oudewater, Leiden, Gouda, Brussels, Ghent, Antwerp, and Delftshaven. Since many of the Delft clergy had lived "under the cross," they were particularly responsive to the requests from Reformers in the south.[116]

The deacons funded their efforts primarily through collections during worship services, with additional revenue coming from private donations and testaments.[117] The consistory specified that members were to give all contributions to deacons, and not to elders or ministers, in order to relieve the consistory from the suspicion of soliciting donations while carrying out their house visits.[118]

Emerging from its formative experience in exile, the Dutch Reformed churches

---

[113] *GAD. Kerkeraad* (March 8, 1573; August 1, 1574; August 2, 1574; September 3, 1574; October 26, 1574); *GAD. Regle*, nr. 313.

[114] Wouters and Abels, *Nieuw en ongezien*, vol. II, pp. 212–24.

[115] The first mention of the creation of districts for diaconal relief occurred on May 2, 1575: *GAD. Kerkeraad* (May 2, 1575). The 1602 visitation book of Arent Corneliszoon listed the diaconal districts at that time. See *GAD. ACC*, nr. 300, *Wijkboekje van Arent Cornelisz. Crusius*, pp. 26–7.

[116] *GAD. Kerkeraad* (September 12, 1575; October 14, 1577; December 24, 1578; May 13, 1578; December 28, 1582; December 12, 1583; February 13, 1584; August 20, 1584; September 10, 1584; April 1, 1585; June 17, 1585; February 3, 1586; November 11, 1586; December 30, 1591; January 13, 1592).

[117] *Ibid.* (August 1, 1574; August 2, 1574; September 13, 1574; September 10, 1582, September 24, 1582; August 28, 1583). See also *GAD. Memorialen*.

[118] *GAD. Kerkeraad* (March 8, 1574).

in Holland established the diaconate as the poor relief arm of an exclusive religious community. The limits and requirements of Reformed poor relief flowed from their understanding of a confessional community bound together by preaching, the sacraments, discipline, and poor relief. Yet this confessional community was also a public body yoked to magisterial expectations that the church would fulfill the functions of the Roman Catholic Church under the authority of the city government.[119] While magistrates consented to the establishment of a Calvinist church, many city governments began to limit the church's autonomy in the 1580s, a process that culminated in a new blend of political authority and religious life in the seventeenth century. Yet, even as early as 1573, when church leaders were organizing their communities, they had to work with civil authorities who, in most cases, regarded consistorial objectives warily. The periodic negotiations between city magistrates and consistories throughout Holland eventually defined the role of the church in municipal society by 1619. This process reveals, among other things, the clash between religious pluralism and confessional identity in a society bereft of centralized political authority. Before examining these negotiations, however, it is important to understand the relationship between moral discipline and poor relief in the Dutch Reformed Church.

[119] Van Deursen, *Bavianen*, p. 21.

5

The dynamics of the Reformed community: discipline and poor relief, 1572–1620

In his "Description of the Office of Elder in the Community of Christ," the Delft pastor Arent Corneliszoon summed up his vision of the church:

The end to which the gathering of a church, God's community on earth, chiefly exists is that the people will learn to know their shepherd and savior Jesus Christ and to serve his will obediently until they are united with him in complete holiness and salvation in heaven. Thus, the people have an undisputed need for his [Christ's] words and the administration of the sacraments so that they may diligently increase in God's riches and faithfully carry out his work.[1]

According to this Calvinist minister, the elect placed their hopes in a heavenly union with Christ. As they sojourned through their earthly existence, they were a gathered religious community called to carry out Christ's work in a fallen world. The community of Christ actualized the calling by following biblical teachings and by taking communion. As the authoritative guide for conduct and belief, Scripture provided the standards for life within the "household of faith." While Dutch Calvinists are famous for their emphatic biblicism, it was the communion service that took center stage in uniting the visible saintly community in corporate worship. Everyone in the city was encouraged to attend the exposition of scripture, but communion at the Lord's Table distinguished members of the spiritual community from everyone else.[2] Ben Kaplan has observed that the Calvinist understanding of community "transcended the limits of parish, city, and province." That is, members of local congregations were united in a translocal, even international, eucharistic community of like-minded believers.[3]

It was the officers of the church who protected the integrity of the community by enforcing its moral norms and executing its mission. At another place Corneliszoon elaborated on these duties:

Dear Christians, you know the desire of the Lord Christ that in his church there should be not only shepherds or preachers who provide the nourishment of God's Words and the Holy Sacrament, but there have also been others who labor not with words, but under the supervision of preachers to help rule the flock and establish good discipline and order. Also

---

[1] *GAD. ACC*, nr. 99, *Beschrijvinghe des Ampts der ouderlinghen inder Ghemeijnte J. Christi.*
[2] Van Deursen, *Plain Lives*, pp. 262–7.   [3] Kaplan, "Holy uniformity," pp. 249–51.

123

there are those who care for the poor, or deacons, through whom the alms of Christ are collected and distributed so that the poor member of our Lord Christ will not be neglected.[4]

According to Corneliszoon, the elect were to lead disciplined lives, follow God's Word, and attend to "the poor member of our Lord Christ." Charity in the Dutch Reformed Church was intertwined with moral discipline; poor relief was a function of a sacred confessional community.

These declarations were not arcane ecclesiological statements from an obscure Dutch Calvinist. Corneliszoon was the most respected authority in this local church and one of the most influential ministers in Holland. Given his position in the Delft church, Corneliszoon's concept of religious community played a vital role in the implementation of the Reformed ministry not only in Delft but throughout Holland during the early years of the Reformation. For Corneliszoon and like-minded Calvinists, these ministries constituted the redemptive mission of the church in the world.

The Dutch Calvinist model of poor relief compelled those with some financial means to use them for the glory of God, a requirement that entailed sharing their God-given bounty with the needy.[5] On the other hand, the "pious poor" were to display the qualities of godliness by showing gratefulness for all benevolence, by being content with meager resources, and by using their labor to feed themselves. In addition, the needy were to shun begging and incurring debts, actions which would perpetuate their poverty. More importantly, all church members were prohibited from activities that would dishonor God, damage the reputation of the faithful, and besmirch the communion table.[6]

To carry out these religious directives, synodal resolutions required the consistory to regulate the morals of members and the synod charged the diaconate, independently of municipal control, to serve the poor in the body of Christ. As we will see in chapter 6, political and economic conditions in the six cities often forced Reformed leaders to go to great lengths to maintain this ideal. While Calvinist leaders displayed a certain degree of flexibility in negotiating with magistrates, they nevertheless attempted to defend their ideal of a separate relief system for the poor within the "household of faith."

In order to appreciate the confessional dynamic of Calvinist poor relief, it is important to examine the relationship between discipline and charity in the Dutch Reformed Church. Just as city magistrates had circumscribed parish charity within the confines of the civic corporation by excluding outsiders, so also Calvinist church officials established the moral economy of their religious community through discipline. Although each congregation in each city faced its own unique set of circumstances, the confessional motivations and administrative procedures to discipline the congregation and relieve poverty remained largely uniform across

---

[4] *GAD. ACC*, nr. 100, *Gebeden ende Meditaties.*   [5] See Biéler, *Calvin*, ch. 5.
[6] Roodenburg, *Onder censuur*, p. 145; van Deursen, *Bavianen*, pp. 204–6; van Deursen, *Plain Lives*, pp. 266–7; Schilling, "Reformierte Kirchenzucht als Sozialdisziplinierung?"

Holland. This chapter, therefore, will explore the alliance between moral discipline and poor relief primarily in the Delft congregation whose archives are the richest among local Reformed congregations in Holland.[7]

The rigorous enforcement of religious discipline was a hallmark of Calvinist churches in Reformation-era Europe. Since Calvinists identified the eucharistic community as the pure assembly of saints, it was necessary for Reformed ministers to defend the Lord's Table from human corruption.[8] To that end, consistories labored to reconcile "sinners" with the community; if reconciliation failed, the sinner faced exclusion from the communion table. For John Calvin, the integrity of the community hinged upon discipline:

Accordingly, as the saving doctrine of Christ is the soul of the church, so does discipline serve as its sinews, through which the members of the body hold together, each in its own place. Therefore, all who desire to remove discipline or to hinder its restoration – whether they do this deliberately or out of ignorance – are surely contributing to the ultimate dissolution of the church.[9]

Followers of the Reformed tradition in the Netherlands, Scotland, and Hungary went a step beyond Calvin and made discipline one of the three marks of the true church.[10] Furthermore, the Reformed believed that failure to regulate morals would provoke the wrath of God. Martin Bucer, for example, concluded that Charles V's Interim was divine punishment for failing to institute discipline in the Protestant churches of the Empire.[11]

---

[7] The consistorial archives in Delft are not only consistent throughout this period but are also far more detailed about poor relief matters than those of Dordrecht, Haarlem, Leiden, Amsterdam, and Gouda.

[8] Studies on Calvinist churches in France and the Netherlands have emphasized the communal motivations that underlay ecclesiastical discipline. See Kaplan, "Holy uniformity," pp. 241, 249–51; van Deursen, *Bavianen*, pp. 193–217; Schilling, *Civic Calvinism*, p. 42; Roodenburg, *Onder censuur*, pp. 26–7; Raymond A. Mentzer, "Disciplina nervus ecclesiae: the Calvinist reform of morals at Nîmes," *Sixteenth-Century Journal* 18 (1987), pp. 89–115; Mentzer, "Ecclesiastical discipline and communal reorganization among the Protestants of southern France," *European History Quarterly* 21 (1991), pp. 163–83; Mentzer, "Marking the taboo: excommunication in the French Reformed churches," in *Sin and the Calvinists: Morals Control and the Consistory in the Reformed Tradition*, R. A. Mentzer, ed. (Kirksville, Mo., 1995), pp. 97–128.

[9] John Calvin, *Institutes of the Christian Religion*, 2 vols., John T. McNeill, ed., Ford Lewis Battles, trans. (Philadelphia, 1960), vol. II, p. 1230.

[10] According to James Spalding, discipline in the Reformed confessions of these lands derived from the influence of Martin Bucer, Theodore Beza, and Peter Martyr Vermigli: James Spalding, "Discipline as a mark of the true church in its sixteenth-century Lutheran context," in *Piety, Politics, and Ethics: Reformation Studies in Honor of George Wolfgang Forell*, Carter Lindberg, ed. (Kirksville, Mo., 1984), pp. 119–20.

[11] Van Deursen, *Bavianen*, pp. 200, 204; Amy Nelson Burnett, "Church discipline and moral reformation in the thought of Martin Bucer," *Sixteenth-Century Journal* 22 (1991), p. 439.

In the aftermath of the Revolt in Holland, Calvinist leaders worked to establish an independent religious community in conformity with the Dutch Confession of Faith and the Heidelberg Catechism. In order to fulfill the biblical mandates for moral purity and Christian charity, consistories subjected members to the discipline of the church, and diaconates distributed alms to the poor. Church officers applied discipline to all miscreant church members, from a high-ranking burgomaster to a lowly widow on poor relief.

The lay elders and deacons who helped ministers enforce discipline were, by and large, men with a significant degree of social standing and financial resources. Gerrit Groenhuis has observed that deacons throughout Holland were not generally *kleine mannen* or men of small means.[12] Furthermore, van Deursen has reminded us that in urban areas the ethos of rulership in sixteenth-century Holland upheld the notion that those in authority should be men of "quality." The implied characteristics of "quality" included a concern for the public interest, moral uprightness, social standing, and economic independence. In socio-economic terms, this understanding excluded the "simple artisan."[13] In early modern Europe, magistrates and regents were often expected to be able to contribute from their own personal income in times of financial shortage, at least in the form of loans.

In Delft, almost 80 percent of the lay elders who served in the consistory from 1573 to 1621 came from the highest social groups in the city, while just over 50 percent of the deacons came from the same social group during the same period.[14] In Dordrecht, almost one-third of elders and deacons were former or current magistrates from 1573 to 1639. From 1573 to 1579, four of fourteen city government positions were filled by elders or deacons.[15] And since the official inception of the Reformed church in Amsterdam and Haarlem, deacons and elders in these two cities also had strong ties to leading regent families.[16]

Elders and deacons assumed responsibility for members in one of the districts into which the cities were divided for purposes of administering discipline and regulating poor relief.[17] Before the communion service, which was held between four and six times a year, ministers and elders were to visit church members in their districts to discern their spiritual health. Reformed officers had help in identifying deviance and poverty in their districts from officially designated inspectors. The consistories appointed these church members to keep abreast of "the belief and

---

[12] Groenhuis, *De predikanten*, p. 25.   [13] Van Deursen, *Bavianen*, pp. 87–8.
[14] Wouters and Abels, *Nieuw en ongezien*, vol. I, pp. 384–5.
[15] Elliott, "The classis of Dordrecht," pp. 156–7.
[16] Evenhuis, *Ook dat was Amsterdam*, vol. I, pp. 100–1; Spaans, *Haarlem*, pp. 283–6. At least in the 1570s, Leiden was an exception to the common pattern: Woltjer, "Een niew ende onghesien dingh," p. 12. Unfortunately, we know almost nothing about the diaconate in Gouda.
[17] The 1574 Provincial Synod of Dordrecht encouraged churches to organize into districts and such districts were used in Dutch Reformed Churches: *GAD. Kerkeraad* (May 2, 1575); Jansma, *Uw rijk kome*, pp. 97–8 (March 2, 1578); *GAA. Kerkeraad* (November 14, 1579). In an attempt to separate the deacons from the *huiszitten meesters*, the Leiden consistory proposed this idea to the city government in May 1586. The city government rejected the proposal: Ligtenberg, *Armezorg te Leiden*, p. 231.

walk" of members in their neighborhoods.[18] Inspectors talked with members and non-members in these neighborhoods, took note of rumors, and reported their findings to the church officers.

Discipline procedure in the Reformed Churches of the Netherlands was a three-step process.[19] When information about an alleged moral infraction reached the consistory, its first step was to investigate the charges. If the accusations had any validity, the consistory suspended the individual from the Lord's Table until the matter could be resolved.[20] If the accused was not exonerated, the temporary suspension of a guilty member remained in effect until the offender had repented, shown remorse, rectified the consequences of the violation, and demonstrated improved conduct. The interaction between the accused and the consistory occurred either in the weekly meetings of this ecclesiastical body or in house visits carried out by assigned elders or ministers. Until the matter was settled to the satisfaction of the consistory, the accused could not take communion. In the event that a suspended member was on the deacons' poor relief register, the consistory would also determine whether or not the deacons should continue to extend charity to the recipient, and, if so, under what conditions.

If a member either resisted the consistory's admonitions or transgressed again, he or she entered the second step of discipline, which warranted a more permanent exclusion from communion.[21] In addition, a minister would admonish the recalcitrant or recidivist from the pulpit (known as a *voorstelling*) at first without naming the guilty party. If the transgression was particularly scandalous and if the transgressor was particularly obstinate, the minister would identify the person in subsequent admonitions. In order to be readmitted to the community, the transgressor was required to confess his or her sins (often publicly), endure another probationary period, and demonstrate improvement in conduct. Once these conditions were met, the member was usually permitted to take communion again. If a recipient consistently failed to comply with the consistory's reprimands throughout this process, he or she entered the final third step: expulsion from the church through formal excommunication.

Possessing ultimate authority in the local congregation, the consistory managed this disciplinary network and oversaw the relief work of the diaconate. In routine cases, the deacons, numbering anywhere from four to twelve in each congregation, handled matters pertaining to the poor: identifying the needy, investigating their

[18] Wouters and Abels, *Nieuw en ongezien*, vol. I, p. 209; Elliott, "The classis of Dordrecht," p. 465. For a list of inspectors in Delft, see *GAD. Regle*, nr. 312. The use of such inspectors was also common in French Reformed Churches: Janine Garrisson-Estèbe, *Protestants du Midi, 1559–1598* (Toulouse, 1980), p. 105.
[19] See Roodenburg, *Onder censuur*, pp. 115–45.
[20] At the 1571 Synod of Emden this procedure was adopted: Rutgers, *Acta*, pp. 68–72.
[21] Ray Mentzer has demonstrated in "Marking the taboo," pp. 102–4, that in the Languedoc region a similar distinction existed between those suspended from communion temporarily and those excluded on a permanent basis. He argued that this distinction corresponded to the medieval practice of minor and major excommunication.

situation, denying relief to some, granting alms to others, determining the amount of the subsidy, and specifying the length of time the grant would be allotted.[22] The deacons met weekly to deal with new requests and to determine whether extensions in alms should be provided for those whose period of relief had expired. The deacons, however, did not act independently of the consistory; the entire range of their responsibilities was subject to consistorial authority.[23] Consistories also intervened regularly in problematic poor relief cases, namely those that involved either moral offenses by recipients or disputes over a decision by the diaconate.

HORIZONTAL AND VERTICAL DISCIPLINE NETWORKS

Although the ministers and elders managed disciplinary procedure, it was the cooperative agency of the collective membership that made discipline possible. The Reformed Church was a community of believers, and at the same time it was subsumed within a highly interactive social network of families and neighbors. The heart of local life, neighborhoods in early modern cities brought residents into daily contact and thereby created a familiar social environment where everyone knew everyone else. The intensity of neighborhood life and the drive to maintain one's honor produced strong alliances and passionate animosities.[24] Thus, the ecclesiastical mechanisms for identifying moral transgressions and relieving poverty were enmeshed in the common interaction of neighborhood life.

Reformed efforts at discipline often profited from the cultural ethos of neighborhood life in which people kept an eye on their neighbors, gossiped about them, held grudges against some, and made friends with others. Numerous entries in the consistory records begin by stating that "it has been reported that . . ." or there are complaints that . . ." and even "there are rumors that . . ."[25] Members of the Reformed Church exercised no small influence in morals control by virtue of the everyday informal discursive matrix. The church council notes teem with cases introduced by members' complaints about injustice or maltreatment inflicted upon them by others.

Consider also that throughout most of this period Reformed churches had a

---

[22] Throughout most of this period Delft had four deacons, and Dordrecht and Amsterdam, eight. In 1577, Leiden had twelve deacons: Wouters and Abels, *Nieuw en ongezien*, vol. I, pp. 333–5; Elliott, "The classis of Dordrecht," p. 362; Commelin, *Amsterdam*, vol. I, p. 487; Kooi, "Leiden," p. 59.

[23] For example, a minister attended the Sunday meetings of the diaconate, and the deacons were required to give a monthly account of their finances to the consistory: *GAD. Regle*, nr. 314.

[24] James R. Farr, *Hands of Honor: Artisans and Their World in Dijon, 1550–1650* (Ithaca, 1988), pp. 156, 165.

[25] For example, in Delft there were "complaints" or "rumors" against Joachim Janssen in *GAD. Kerkeraad* (September 13, 1593); Aeltgen Hendricxzoon (April 24, 1573; June 10, 1587); Cornelis Arienssen (March 17, 1603); Jaspar Gerritszoon (August 29, 1605); Maritge Crijnen (August 31, 1592); Gerrit Claeszoon (June 11, 1607); Hans Tootman (December 28, 1607). In Dordrecht complaints were lodged against Vincen d'Krijne on August 22, 1574, Godfridus Vermason on December 16, 1574, and Jacob Willemszoon on December 23, 1576. See Jansma, *Uw rijk kome*, pp. 12, 31, 71.

fairly low ratio of church officers to members. The small number of officers relative to the size of the congregation would have compelled the consistory to rely on hearsay to gain information about alleged infractions. In April 1576, the consistory in Dordrecht decided not to hold any more house visitations, but instead to pursue disciplinary investigations only as people reported instances of misconduct to the church officers.[26] Herman Roodenburg has shown that the Amsterdam consistory depended upon neighbors reporting misdeeds in order to investigate suspicious activity.[27] Gossip, innuendo, rumor, and idle speculation among neighbors and townsfolk enabled consistories to identify deviance of church members.

Many of these allegations involved sexual impropriety or disputes among neighbors, offenses which were conducive to rumor. For example, the Delft consistory questioned Hendrick van Haspel about his relationship to a servant girl in September 1579 when neighbors became suspicious of adultery.[28] Likewise, neighbors complained about the dishonorable behavior of Belitghe de Witte between November 1599 and February 1600.[29] Since François van der Steen's dispute with Gerrit Claeszoon Wusten (an elder) was widely known, it warranted a consistorial investigation.[30] The consistory took stern measures by taking two women off the deacons' poor relief register in June 1586 because their dispute "gave offense to many people, especially the neighbors."[31] The consistory sought out neighbors "who profess the religion" to inquire into Barber Conner's heterodox associations in July 1581.[32] These instances were but a small number of the cases in which rumor and innuendo alerted the Delft consistory to possible misdeeds. People watched their neighbors and gossiped about dubious activity, which eventually brought discipline cases before the consistory.[33]

Allegations of misconduct were not always from vague sources, but occasionally came directly from identifiable third parties. Jan Andries accused Anna Gillis in January 1584 of going around slandering the consistory.[34] Francis Albertszoon protested in December 1609 that Gerrit Claeszoon said he (Albertszoon) was unworthy to go to communion and spoke ill of a minister.[35] In February 1593, Catelijne Clarissen reported to the consistory that her brother-in-law, a member of the Walloon congregation, should not be allowed to take communion because of

---

[26] Jansma, *Uw rijk kome*, p. 50.   [27] Roodenburg, *Onder censuur*, pp. 350–69.
[28] *GAD. Kerkeraad* (September 21, 1579; September 28, 1579).
[29] *Ibid.* (November 22, 1599; February 14, 1600).   [30] *Ibid.* (July 17, 1606).
[31] *Ibid.* (June 23, 1586).   [32] *Ibid.* (July 24, 1581).
[33] Citing the commotion among neighbors for similar offenses, the consistory took disciplinary measures against the following (all *ibid.*): Aeltgen Elias (December 4, 1589; January 1, 1590); Catelijne Jans (June 14, 1604; June 21, 1604); Maijken Hendricx (September 16, 1585); Neeltge Jans (May 13, 1579); Michiel de Wale (August 8, 1581); Tanneken van Bruijssel (January 29, 1590; March 18, 1591); Pieter van Stralen, Cornelis Janssen, and Ariaen Janssen (September 9, 1591); Commertghen Ariens (June 8, 1598); Belitghe de Witte (November 22, 1599).
[34] *Ibid.* (January 2, 1584; February 24, 1584).
[35] *Ibid.* (December 28, 1609). Embroiled in a dispute with Capiteijn de Witte in 1607, Adam Witfort became the subject of a consistorial investigation because de Witte thought Witfort unworthy of communion: *ibid.* (October 15, 1607).

their ongoing dispute.[36] Later in the same year Clarissen reported a woman swearing in the market.[37] In September 1611, the wife of Glaude de Backer complained that she could no longer live with her husband and that she was being taken for a whore.[38] These examples indicate that ordinary social discourse made ecclesiastical discipline possible. Furthermore, the willingness of some people to inform the consistory of misconduct suggests that morals regulation was, to a certain extent, a collaborative venture between clergy, lay leadership, and common folk.

Yet all this tattling is not necessarily indicative of a strong grass-roots commitment to confessional Calvinism. Common folk recognized that church discipline was a new way to settle old scores. That is, church folk attempted to manipulate the consistory for their own personal ends. A primary motivation that led common folk to participate in this process stemmed from an obsession to protect their sense of honor.

Aided by anthropological studies on honor and shame, historians have recently called attention to the extreme importance that common folk attached to honor in pre-industrial Europe. In his study of artisans in Dijon, James Farr has argued that honor was a "paramount social value" because it was a measurement of an individual's worth in relation to a recognized societal norm. As J. G. Peristiany has observed, "honor and shame were constant preoccupations of individuals in small-scale exclusive societies." In this "familiar public world," honor was a self-evaluation based on one's social standing and reputation for personal virtue.[39] The disputes among these church folk and neighbors in Delft resulted from indignities that they considered to be an assault on their innate value. Reporting these indignities to the consistory was a strategy to restore one's honor and to punish the offender.

Although many of these cases involved women, it does not appear that either the consistory or common folk harbored a greater concern for female behavior than for male behavior. For, throughout this period, men came under censure at a higher rate than women in every category of offense. Paul Abels and Anton Wouters have calculated that the Delft consistory disciplined a maximum number of 1,199 people from 1572 to 1621. Of the 1,157 for whom sex can be determined, 664 (57.4 percent) were men and 493 (42.6 percent) were women.[40] Whether or not the consistory or church folk operated under distinct notions of female and male honor awaits future study.

If ordinary members were instrumental to discipline, the consistory nevertheless exercised considerable leverage over morals. This influence derived from the consistory's authority to control access to the Lord's Table. The consistory's prerogative with respect to communion was an effective instrument because communion figured so prominently in the religious life of church folk in Delft.

[36] *Ibid.* (February 1, 1593).   [37] *Ibid.* (June 21, 1593).

[38] *Ibid.* (September 26, 1611). For earlier disputes, see *GAD. Kerkeraad* (March 21, 1611; March 28, 1611; August 22, 1611; August 26, 1611).

[39] Farr, *Hands of Honor*, p. 177; J. G. Peristiany, ed., "Introduction," to Peristiany, *Honor and Shame: The Values of a Mediterranean Society* (London, 1965), p. 1.

[40] Wouters and Abels, *Nieuw en ongezien*, vol. 1, p. 106.

Between 1580 and 1620, there were at least 127 requests by members to return to communion (see appendix 5.1). This number is not based on a systematic quantitative study of suspension and excommunication. The list of people pertains only to those instances when members asked to take or return to communion. It should also be noted that the line between a denied request and an investigation is very blurred, because an investigation often meant that the member was denied communion until the consistory gained more information or deliberated over the gravity of the charges. Admittedly, the percentage of petitions in relation to all those under discipline at specific intervals would give more precision to the importance of communion among members. Nevertheless, even this preliminary figure suggests that a significant number of members felt a strong need to take communion.

Often there was a prolonged interval (several months to years) from the point members had been suspended to the time they made their request for readmittance. Even after a disciplined member indicated that he or she desired to return, it could take an extensive period before the member actually "reconciled" to the satisfaction of the consistory. The reason that it took so long to resolve these cases derived from three interrelated factors: the individual's desire to return to communion, the strict demands of the consistory, and members' stubborn defense of their honor.

Why did members place such importance on taking communion in the Reformed Church? Administered six times per year in Delft, communion took center stage in uniting the visible religious community in corporate worship. Since the Lord's Table marked the community of saints in the Dutch Reformed Church, many submitted themselves to discipline in the first place out of a quest for moral purity. Suspension from communion, consequently, was a powerful tool in the hands of the consistory to compel conformity to the community's moral norms.

There are also hints here and there in the consistory records that call attention to the importance of communion in these people's lives. When appealing for readmission to communion, a number of the disciplined expressed anxieties about a troubled conscience, maintained their innocence, or defended their honor. These particular expressions suggest that church folk equated moral purity with moral honor and innocence. In his study on Calvinist discipline in Valangin, Jeffrey Watt remarked that members there desired admittance to communion, because it constituted a "certificate of morality."[41] This desire for moral affirmation was very similar to a number of those disciplined in Delft who regarded admittance to communion as a declaration of their honor. For example, Lieven van Vijven, who had been excommunicated in Amsterdam for adultery in 1594, reported to the Delft consistory in 1598 that "he could find no peace in his conscience as long as he was kept away from communion."[42]

[41] Jeffrey Watt, "The reception of the Reformation in Valangin, Switzerland, 1547–1588," *Sixteenth-Century Journal* 20 (1989), p. 99.
[42] Reitsma and van Veen, *Acta*, vol. II, p. 135.

With similar motivations, other members requested to return to communion, yet balked at admitting to any wrongdoing or refused to undergo any public penance. Tame de Naeijster (February 1597) and Maritghen Dannebier (June 1599) requested permission to return to communion because they claimed they were innocent of the charges against them.[43] The consistorial secretary noted in February 1603 that Griete Pauwells, who was alienated from her husband, "requested to take communion and made her husband responsible for the separation."[44] The tacit logic in Pauwells' complaint linked innocence with taking communion. The Lord's Table symbolized moral purity and taking communion imputed that purity to communicants. For these people, and perhaps for many others, the right to take communion established their innocence, and hence their moral honor.

Since members believed there was a connection between the communion table and purity, charges against them often produced intense conflicts with the consistory. In fact, members could be quite tenacious in negotiating with the consistory and defending their honor. Concerned about their daughter's reputation, Jacob van Godsenhove and his wife demanded in November 1608 to know who had made the accusations against her.[45] Embroiled in several bitter disputes with members and ministers alike, Jan Pauw not only refused to take communion, but he was also unwilling to attend church services between 1592 and 1594. In November 1594, he protested that the minister Arent Corneliszoon had labeled him as a troublemaker. After they reconciled, Pauw further requested that Corneliszoon go and make a statement of reconciliation to Pauw's wife, "who was not a little offended by him."[46]

Because of the importance of honor among ordinary members, consistorial charges often embroiled the church leadership and the disciplined in protracted haggling that could last for years. Gerrit Claeszoon Wusten, the wayward former elder, admitted to the consistory in May 1607 that he had committed adultery. Because the affair had become public knowledge, the consistory demanded in September 1607 that he make a public confession of guilt before the congregation. Wusten stated in August 1607 that he did not want to suffer a public confession. When faced with humiliation before his peers, Wusten refused to make a public confession, stating "that such censure is not found in God's Word."[47] The consistory threatened, admonished, and visited him at least until October 1612, but he never submitted to the demands of the church college.[48] Likewise in June 1587, Marinius Snijder "would not break bread with the community" because he

---

[43] *GAD. Kerkeraad* (February 21, 1597; June 7, 1599).   [44] *Ibid.* (February 21, 1603).

[45] *Ibid.* (November 10, 1608; December 15, 1608).

[46] *Ibid.* (November 21, 1594). The following week Corneliszoon reported to the consistory that he had complied with Pauw's request: *ibid.* (November 28, 1594).

[47] *Ibid.* (September 24, 1607).

[48] *Ibid.* (May 28, 1607; June 4, 1607; June 11, 1607; June 25, 1607; July 9, 1607; August 11, 1607; September 24, 1607; October 22, 1607; October 26, 1607; December 28, 1607; January 28, 1608; May 25, 1609; December 28, 1609; March 29, 1610; April 5, 1610; April 23, 1610; October 8, 1612).

believed the consistory was partisan in arbitrating his dispute with Jan Engelszoon, a former elder.[49]

The concern for one's honor, therefore, was a double-edged sword for the consistory. On the one hand, taking communion confirmed members' morality before their peers, which gave the consistory leverage over members. On the other hand, the defense of one's honor often embroiled the church council and the disciplined in protracted disputes over both the validity of the charges and public penance. This aspiration was inseparably linked to members' defense of their honor and their moral character within both the religious and neighborhood community.

While we should avoid imposing the concerns of these members onto all those who requested readmittance, these attitudes do point to a concern about moral honor among the rank-and-file membership in this religious community. The assertion of honor and moral purity was inseparably linked to one's standing among peers in the church and the neighborhood. Members often became incensed when other members or church officers called their honor into question and, therefore, they would refuse to undergo the penitence required for reincorporation. In a religious community identified visually by taking communion, it would seem that a combination of guilt, shame, jealousy, and anger animated those who could not partake of the elements.

While scholars have rightly called attention to the strong emphasis on social control in Calvinist discipline, the concern for respectability among one's contemporaries was a form of morals regulation that was energized by both the consistory and the lay membership. The degree to which the consistory was successful in disciplining the community depended upon members' desire to take communion and to maintain their honor among their peers. Despite the wide range of circumstances surrounding these members under discipline, these cases show that discipline involved a negotiation between the consistory, the accused, and other involved parties over moral purity. The ministers and elders certainly attempted to impose a Calvinist morality onto its congregation, but ordinary members also shared a strong concern for their own moral honor. It was the enforcement of these moral standards, however, that created rancorous disputes.

For a variety of reasons, then, members of the Reformed Church in Delft participated in the consistory's efforts to establish a pure religious community. Social discourse among peers in the church and in neighborhoods combined with popular notions of moral honor led members to report one another to the consistory. Rumors and public disturbances caused by flagrant violations compelled the church leadership to act quickly, decisively, and severely. Since so many people desired to return to communion, the Delft Church best resembled a eucharistic community whose members shared a concern for moral purity, honor, and innocence. Some of those who left this community did so, in part, out of a similar quest for purity.

---

[49] *Ibid.* (June 22, 1587). Jan Engelszoon served one term as elder from 1579 to 1581.

At the same time, members' defense of their honor and innocence thwarted the possibilities for reconciliation with the consistory. This concern for honor and morality was a part of everyday social intercourse and common notions of propriety. The extent to which the consistory was successful in disciplining owed a great deal to the coalescence between clerical and popular norms of behavior and belief. Those cases in which disciplining did not achieve its desired goal of reconciling "sinners" also point to the moral autonomy of common folk in post-Reformation Holland. Discipline in the Reformed Church at Delft, therefore, was an interactive process that was often obstructed by the moral autonomy of common folk, yet also relied heavily on their moral agency.

<h3 style="text-align:center">DISCIPLINING POOR RELIEF</h3>

There was an inherent tension between the consistory's efforts to safeguard the purity of communion and providing relief to the poor. This conflict resulted from the wayward conduct of poor relief recipients. What was the consistory to do if desperately poor people who depended upon church alms to sustain their household transgressed the moral borders of the religious community? Since their days in exile in London and Emden, discipline in the Dutch Reformed Church included not only spiritual banishment from the communion table, but also the threat of material exclusion from the diaconal register.[50] That is, members who received alms could count on a great deal of supervision over most aspects of their lives. Those recipients who violated the community's moral norms imperiled their place on the poor relief register.[51] Given the strong communal dynamic within Dutch Calvinism, it is not surprising that Reformed officers excluded recalcitrant sinners from church alms. Yet this process could be a rather complex matter. In some cases, consistories did direct the deacons to deny relief to the poor, yet the church officers also negotiated endlessly with other recipients over their moral offenses and the alms they received.

In Amsterdam, a city in which the Reformed deacons provided relief only to church members, the consistory proved to be somewhat reluctant to exclude them from alms altogether. Between 1582 and 1612, there were at least twenty-five cases (seventeen women and eight men) of poor members who fell under the suspicions of the diaconate (see appendix 5.2). In most cases, when a poor member was initially charged with a transgression, the deacons did not cut them off automatically. The deacons reported these cases to the consistory, which in turn would summon the member to give an account of their behavior. If these members appeared contrite before the consistory, the ministers and elders would normally admonish them and charge the deacons to pay careful attention to their subse-

---

[50] Fehler, "Social welfare in Emden," pp. 469–86.
[51] Pettegree, *Foreign Protestant Communities*, pp. 182–214; Spaans, *Haarlem*, p. 181; van Deursen, *Bavianen*, pp. 126–7; Wouters and Abels, *Nieuw en ongezien*, vol. II, pp. 50–1.

quent behavior. If the member lapsed into "ungodliness" again, he or she faced a sterner judgement, including censure and dismissal from the diaconate's relief roll.

For example, the consistory simply admonished Fem Harmensdochter in 1582 but decided to continue supporting her because she had two small children who would suffer if they denied her alms.[52] In fact, in thirteen of the twenty-five cases (nine women and three men, one man appearing twice on different charges), the members escaped with a warning and a forceful admonition to do better. The consistory instructed the deacons to discontinue aid to nine (four women and four men, one woman appearing twice on different charges) other poor members who came before the council during the same period (see appendix 5.2). In three cases (two women and one man) it is unclear what action the consistory took with regard to their poor relief status.[53]

Clearly the consistory and diaconate held poor members to the same doctrinal and behavioral guidelines as well-off members. The consistory in Amsterdam betrayed a certain patience with members receiving poor relief, but at the same time it would deny relief to members who failed to show improvement and to members who caused a public scandal. Poor members who either were not cooperative or whose infractions caused a scandal were the ones to whom the consistory denied alms.[54] The fact that most of the members (seventeen of twenty-five in the previous sample) were female is hardly surprising, since women probably made up a majority of those members on the diaconal register, given their economic vulnerability in early modern societies. Regardless of gender, this profile does suggest that discipline drew the moral borders of diaconal charity in the religious community.

In Delft, where the deacons also gave charity to non-members and where the consistory intervened in a large number of poor relief cases, the relationship between moral standards, membership, and Calvinist charity is much clearer. From 1579 to 1609,[55] the Delft consistory intervened in at least eighty-six cases of poor relief (involving ninety-one people). These cases ranged from simple petitions for assistance (or for specific grants) to complicated negotiations over the relief of disciplined members. The appendices provide a list of these people, as well as the length of the consistory's inquest, and the consistory's actions with respect to relief. The appendices also indicate if the consistory records verify that the recipient was a church member and if the member was under discipline. The poor relief cases that attracted the attention of the consistory represented a small fraction of those who received

---

[52] *GAA. Kerkeraad* (July 12, 1582).
[53] S. Michielszoon (adultery) in April 1587, Mary Pieters (unclear) in September 1599, and Franchois Gielis (misuse of alms) in October 1602: *ibid.* (April 30, 1587; September 16, 1599; October 17, 1602).
[54] Roodenburg, *Onder censuur*, pp. 111–14.
[55] While there were scattered poor relief cases discussed in the consistory meetings before 1579 and after 1609, the overwhelming majority of these instances occurred between 1579 and 1609. It is for this reason that I have concentrated on the cases within these years.

charity from the Delft deacons.[56] It is likely that many other recipients negotiated with church officers in the informal network outside the official actions of the consistory. Nevertheless, since these cases are recorded in the consistorial records, they give us a glimpse of the tension between the church's moral standards and the conduct of many poor relief recipients in an important Reformed congregation.

There were three categories of poor relief cases in which the consistory intervened. One type involved recipients who the records specifically indicate were members (thirty-five in thirty-two cases; see appendix 5.3) who either petitioned for assistance or were already receiving alms, yet came under disciplinary sanction for moral offenses. The consistory took a less charitable attitude toward these people whose offenses had warranted suspension from communion.[57] Their transgressions included public disputes (five), domestic disputes (five), adultery (four), indebtedness (two), absence from church services (two), "bad household" (one), beggary (one), drunkenness (one), and misuse of alms (one).[58] There were also nine members who committed multiple offenses.[59]

Not only did the consistory deny communion to these members, but it was also less likely to grant assistance, continue assistance, or permit extraordinary grants. Since negotiations between the consistory and the disciplined could drag on for an extended period of time, the ministers and elders made multiple decisions in each case. The consistory made fifty-nine such decisions in the cases of members under discipline (see appendix 5.2). The ministers and elders denied either regular assistance or specific requests twenty-four times and granted either assistance or requests twenty-two times, albeit with stringent conditions or strong threats. On seven more occasions the consistory dispatched an officer to investigate a charge or request, and in six instances no further decision was mentioned in the consistory records.

[56] In his *wijkboekje* (house visitation journal), Arent Corneliszoon noted in 1602 that 499 people received ordinary relief from the deacons: *GAD. ACC*, nr. 300, *Wijkboekje van Arent Cornelisz. Crusius*, p. 26. Five years later, the register of the deacons listed over 600 people who received ordinary relief: *GAD. Memorialen, Register vande personen die ordinarilijck bedient worden*, 1607. Anton Wouters and Paul Abels have placed the size of the Reformed congregation at 2,380 members in 1605, and 2,675 members in 1609: Wouters and Abels, *Nieuw en ongezien*, p. 232.

[57] The consistory records give some indication that at least forty-nine of the total ninety-one individuals were, or had been, members of the Reformed Church. It is likely that many more were members. I counted as members only those people whom the consistory made a decision about their competence to take communion or the individual requested an *attestatie*.

[58] One additional offense was not specified. A "bad household" (*quade huishouding*) was an offense that connoted financial and moral irresponsibility that impaired other family members. It often was used to describe the effects of indebtedness or drunkenness. The single charge of a "bad household" was applied to Jan Louriszoon in October 1599. The consistory admonished him before the congregation and advised the deacons to assist his family: *GAD. Kerkeraad* (March 15, 1599; October 18, 1599).

[59] These transgressions were a combination of the offenses listed above and sometimes included drunkenness as well. Perhaps because drunkenness leads to other social problems, no recipient whom the consistory records specifically indicate was a member was accused only of drunkenness. In five of the eight multiple offense cases, members were accused of drunkenness. The other charges in these five cases usually involved a dispute of some kind or indebtedness.

The second category comprised the twenty-five recipients or petitioners (in twenty-five cases) who were accused of a moral offense, but, according to the consistory records, had not been suspended from communion (see appendix 5.4). The consistory was more sympathetic toward those who were not under discipline. The offenses were: indebtedness (ten), disputes (four), not needy (three), beggary (two), going to the Mennonites (one), drunkenness (one), "bad household" (one), and bearing false witness (one). It should also be noted that there were only two multiple offenses in this category.[60] The consistory made thirty decisions in these cases, denying assistance or requests eight times, and granting assistance or requests thirteen times. In addition, there were nine occasions in which the consistory either simply investigated the matter or no further decision was recorded.

Finally, the third category included thirty-one people (in twenty-nine cases) who had not committed any moral infraction (see appendix 5.5). The consistory was slightly more open-handed with these poor who were not charged at all than with those in the second category. In thirty-four total decisions in these twenty-nine cases, the consistory granted benefits sixteen times, denied them seven times, and in two instances referred the petitioner to city authorities. On nine occasions the consistory investigated a request with no further record.

This overview suggests that the consistory tried to relieve the most pressing manifestations of poverty for those in desperate circumstances especially if they were not under discipline. The ratio of grants to denials was lowest for members under discipline (22:24) and much higher for those not under discipline (13:8), and even higher for those under no moral sanction (16:7). If individuals could convince the consistory that they needed alms to feed themselves and their family and they had not committed a flagrant offense, it was likely that the church officers would come to their aid. These numbers indicate that the moral standards upheld by the consistory established the limits for receiving alms.

Yet this overview does not indicate the expectations nor the demands the poor made upon the consistory. That is, while the consistory set moral guidelines for recipients, the poor themselves asserted their own prerogatives to the consistory. In order to understand the tensions in this interaction, it is necessary to examine consistorial standards and the poor who challenged them.

CONSISTORIAL GOALS AND THE DISCIPLINE OF POOR RELIEF

The consistory pursued two basic aims in its poor relief policy: to meet the most basic needs of the poor and to compel recipients to comply with the church's moral norms. Church officers went to great efforts to assist the poor, and, at the same

---

[60] In February of 1592 the consistory accused Jacob Hieronimuszoon of drunkenness and slander (dispute), and in September of 1592 the consistory denounced Janneken Jans for begging and going to Mennonite meetings. The consistory threatened Hieronimuszoon's assistance and denied alms to Jans: *GAD. Kerkeraad* (February 17, 1592; September 21, 1592).

time, they worked tenaciously to reconcile recipients with Reformed moral standards. Reconciliation with the community was also an attempt to protect the integrity of the Reformed congregation. Lee Wandel's study of poor relief in Reformation Zurich suggests why these goals were such a driving preoccupation in the administration of Protestant charity. The poor in Zurich, according to Wandel, helped define the basis of a new Protestant Christian community. The poor were visible images of Christ's mercy, and charitable giving dramatized how a Reformed society practiced brotherly love.[61] Likewise, the Delft ministers believed that relieving the poor was the work of Christ, which in turn brought honor to God among the inhabitants of Delft. The church officers' aim to provide charity to the poor, however, could run counter to their goal of protecting the sanctity of the community, particularly when the conduct of the needy breached Reformed moral standards. Christian charity, then, necessarily demanded vigorous stewards to guard it from defilement.[62]

The consistory sought to protect church relief from degradation by denying assistance or by deliberating endlessly with those whom the officers suspected were unworthy of alms. Morals assumed paramount importance in cases of members under discipline, yet to a certain extent the issue of wrong behavior was a factor in all of the disputes between church officers and recipients. There was a difference, however, in the consistory's actions toward those under suspicion for a moral infraction related to poverty and those who had committed a scandalous public offense. The former were poor people who, the consistory believed, had obtained alms fraudulently, begged, or incurred debts irresponsibly. The latter were those whose public offenses had caused a commotion (*ruchtbaerheid*) and thereby damaged the reputation of the church.

The consistory carefully investigated the claims of the poor rumored to be unworthy of alms for reasons related to poverty. One reason for these inquiries was the dire financial straits of the diaconal chest. The burden of diaconal poor relief placed an enormous strain on the church's resources, making the consistory extremely sensitive to speculations that a recipient could get by without help from the deacons. Because the deacons were heavily in arrears in 1600, the consistory instructed the deacons in April of that year to shorten their register for the summer.[63] Throughout this entire period, the consistory regularly dispatched ministers, elders, or deacons to investigate claims that recipients did not actually

---

[61] Wandel, *Always Among Us*, pp. 170–3. There is one important difference between Delft and Wandel's model of Zurich. Unlike Zurich, where Zwingli and a Reformed magistracy merged *civitas* and *ecclesia*, poor relief in the Delft church was independent from municipal authority until 1614.

[62] Natalie Davis has demonstrated in "The rites of violence," pp. 157–61, that both the Protestants and Catholics of Lyons were deeply concerned about public moral decay and would go to great efforts to purge the community of immorality.

[63] *GAD. Kerkeraad* (April 4, 1600). Shortly thereafter, the deacons complained about opposition from recipients and the consistory advised the deacons to investigate discreetly the needs of the poor: *ibid.* (April 17, 1600).

need relief. When Commertghen Ariens complained in June 1592 about her debts, the ministers and elders noted that she had a husband, she was not encumbered with children, and furthermore she could work. The consistory decreased Lijsbeth Boot's regular assistance because her only burden was a crippled daughter. Likewise, Janneken Lambrecht was denied further assistance because she was single and healthy, and she had sought assistance from both the Mennonites and the city almoners.[64]

Yet denying assistance to the "non-needy" went beyond an attempt to balance the diaconal accounts. That is, the church officers considered it morally inappropriate for people to receive assistance if they could win their own bread. There was grumbling in the consistory over Lieven de Hoemaecker's request for assistance in May of 1592. Although the consistory appears to have conceded to assist him, the secretary noted that the officers had learned from experience not to give him more than he could put in his mouth. One month later, he was judged "not worthy of the Religion."[65] Upholding labor as the means for the able-bodied to overcome poverty, the church officers believed that begging and borrowing money only perpetuated poverty for the poor and their families.

The consistory, therefore, worked to inhibit begging and indebtedness by negotiating with those guilty of these offenses. Like all Calvinist Reformers, the consistory at Delft was vehemently opposed to begging because the practice violated its interpretation of the scriptural mandate to "win one's bread" through labor. Deprived by the deacons of weekly relief for begging, Aeltgen Jans first came before the ministers and elders in November of 1585. The consistory noted that "the pious residential poor do not go from house to house in order to beg." Nevertheless, six weeks later it allotted her twelve stuivers per week.[66] In this and other cases of begging, the consistory sharply reprimanded people for soliciting, yet also realized that begging was a symptom of material need. In these cases, they often warned the recipient but usually continued to grant assistance.[67] One may argue, then, that the consistory usually granted assistance to those who begged and attached specific conditions on their relief in order to reconcile the needs of these poor people with Reformed morality.

The consistory followed the same policy with people who had contracted debts. On the most basic level, the consistory attempted to ensure that diaconal alms went only to assist the destitute in procuring food, clothing, and shelter. With that

---

[64] *Ibid.* (June 29, 1592). Later, in January of 1594, after it was found out that she had used false witnesses who had claimed she was innocent of drunkenness, the consistory denied communion and alms to Boot: *ibid.* (January 10, 1594; January 24, 1594).

[65] *Ibid.* (May 4, 1592; June 22, 1592).

[66] *Ibid.* (November 11, 1585; December 30, 1585). There is no indication that she had been suspended from communion for this offense. Given the public nature of the charge, it would not be unlikely. The consistory did suspend her in February of 1587 for a dispute with Annetge Simons: *ibid.* (February 2, 1587; February 20, 1587).

[67] For the three other cases of begging that came before the consistory during this period, see *ibid.* (September 21, 1592; February 26, 1593; March 10, 1604).

purpose in mind, the consistory rarely granted requests for loans or for help in repaying debts. In twenty-seven decisions relating to indebtedness or loans, the consistory granted assistance only in five cases (see appendices 5.2–5.4). In four of these instances, the consistory cited mitigating circumstances that justified the request.[68] While the consistory noted that it did not normally assist people with their debts, it granted six guilders to Jacques Haeckendoren in July 1592 because the ministers and elders judged that "elsewhere he had come into much blood and nakedness."[69] When Mensghen Ariens sought diaconal assistance for her debts in February 1593, the consistory denied her request. It informed her that "the deacons have enough to do with sustaining the mouths of the poor."[70]

There was a tacit understanding of the "humble and honorable poor" emerging in these cases that paralleled a designation often used by political and religious authorities in the Netherlands.[71] The "upright poor" (*oprechten armen*) was a term used in the late sixteenth century to discriminate between the poor who merited assistance and those who did not.[72] The central criterion that authorities used to classify the poor was whether or not the poor belonged to their community and if the poor were responsible for their poverty. In the cases of the able-bodied this meant that poverty was a temporary condition that would be reversed when the economy rebounded, they remarried, or they recovered from illness. Thus, the chronic poor who were able-bodied jeopardized the granting of ecclesiastical charity to the pious poor. As we have seen in chapter 3, city magistrates also operated under this notion. In Delft, they frequently prefaced municipal ordinances against beggary with a statement that "such beggars do damage to the upright poor."[73] This idea went beyond a concern that beggars would deplete resources available to poor residents; it suggests that beggars and debtors damaged the moral reputation of the upright poor. The consistory in Delft applied a similar standard to determine who had a claim to church alms. Above all, the honorable poor were to be content, grateful, and do their best to feed themselves.

At the same time, however, the consistory was aware that some poor people affiliated with the church in order to increase their chances of gaining material assistance. In October of 1578 Lenaert Pieterszoon had complained to the consistory

---

[68] For example, the consistory granted an undisclosed sum to a woman (listed only as "Pieters") in November of 1605 because someone had failed to pay an obligation to her: *ibid.* (November 7, 1605).

[69] *Ibid.* (July 27, 1592).   [70] *Ibid.* (February 1, 1593).

[71] The Delft ministers described the poor as "humble and honorable" in their charge to the lay inspectors: *GAD. Regle*, nr. 312.

[72] Delft magistrates used the following terms in various ordinances to describe the poor who were deserving of municipal charity: "the modest poor," "the needy poor," "the poor of the city," "the upright poor," "the true and upright poor," and "the *huisarmen*." Those who did not merit municipal assistance were designated *vreemdeling personen* (foreign people) or beggars: see *GAD. Resolutieboeck*, vol. II, fol. 52v; vol. III, fol. 94v; *GAD. Kamer*, nr. 43, fols. 3r, 7r; *GAD. Burgermeesteren*, nr. 1215; *GAD. Keurboek*, vol. III, fols. 65r, 77v, 316r.

[73] For a few examples, see *GAD. Kamer*, nr. 43, fol. 3r (May 25, 1586); *GAD. Keurboek*, vol. IV, fols. 17r (March 25, 1584), 52r (December 16, 1597).

about his meager allotment from the deacons.[74] Perhaps the complaint, combined with Pieterszoon's absence from church services, led the consistory to conclude that he had joined the church "only for alms."[75] It does not appear, however, that Pieterszoon was denied alms altogether, for in November 1580 he made a similar complaint.[76] On other occasions, the consistory made similar observations about Margeriete Brans (April 1584), Catelijne Clarissen (February 1592), and Ariens Cornelissen (September 1594), yet continued to support them nevertheless.[77]

Continuing assistance for members regarded as less than faithful would seem to indicate that church leaders in Delft used charity to retain church members. Building on the work of Pieter Geyl, L. J. Rogier argued that Calvinists applied social and economic pressures in order to compel a reluctant population to embrace the Reformed religion. In particular, he contended that Calvinists used poor relief to recruit members.[78] Scholarship over the past twenty years has largely undermined this thesis by concentrating on the church's limited resources and the "sectarian tendencies" in Dutch Calvinism. Van Deursen challenged Rogier's argument by pointing out the limited resources of Reformed congregations and the low membership of such congregations (with the congregation of Amsterdam being the only exception). And Alastair Duke and Willem Nijenhuis have argued that the slow growth of the Reformed Church in the Netherlands was the result of the Calvinists' emphasis on discipline and variant theological strains in Dutch Calvinism.[79] Nevertheless, Wouters and Abels, noting that forty-three poor relief recipients in Delft became church members from 1607 to 1618, have stated that "it is far from unthinkable that the deacons in many of these cases functioned as a side porch for entrance into the Reformed community."[80]

While it may not be inconceivable that diaconal charity encouraged some poor folk to join the church, Wouters and Abels also show that it is highly unlikely that the Delft deacons deliberately used poor relief as a recruitment mechanism.[81] In none of the six cities did poor people have to join the church to obtain relief. In Delft and Dordrecht, deacons provided just as much financial assistance to a non-member as they did to a member. In Amsterdam and Haarlem, non-church members could apply for aid from municipal almoners. And, in Gouda and Leiden, poor people had little choice, because municipal agencies were the only viable poor relief agencies in town.

At least in Delft the church records indicate that the consistory was far more interested in keeping unworthy people from communion than they were in using poor relief to attract potential church members. Furthermore, there was no "side porch" for becoming a member of the Reformed community; all who wanted to join

[74] *GAD. Kerkeraad* (October 29, 1578).   [75] *Ibid.* (April 25, 1579).
[76] *Ibid.* (July 1, 1579; January 18, 1580; February 15, 1580; November 21, 1580; December 5, 1580).
[77] *Ibid.* (April 9, 1584; February 21, 1592; September 21, 1594).
[78] L. J. Rogier, *Eenheid en scheiding: geschiedenis der Nederlanden* (Utrecht, 1968), p. 107.
[79] Van Deursen, *Bavianen*, pp. 102–7; Duke, "Ambivalent face," pp. 112–13; Nijenhuis, "Varianten."
[80] Wouters and Abels, *Nieuw en ongezien*, vol. II, p. 239.   [81] *Ibid.*, vol. I, p. 303.

the church had to shoulder the same moral and religious obligations. One of the fundamental theological principles of Dutch Calvinism was that God elected true church members, so there was no compelling reason for Reformed Churches to resort to recruitment through poor relief. Rather, the consistory's decisions in these cases point to the effort to reconcile the discrepancy between maintaining a pure religious community and trying to assist people who did not always affirm the same ideals as the church leadership did.

POOR RELIEF AND PUBLIC SINS

The Delft consistory took the most severe measures against those recipients guilty of flagrant public offenses. The consistory regarded conspicuous immorality as particularly scandalous; therefore it warranted harsh discipline. As the consistory informed Mechtelt Pietersdochter, who was accused of running a brothel in 1581, "since her sin has become public before the world, she must also earnestly prove her penitence."[82] The primary reason the consistory considered conspicuous violations to be so heinous was that public sins dishonored God and damaged the reputation of the religious community. The consistory operated under the ideal that members were to live a quiet and tranquil life in obedience to duly constituted authorities. In the summer of 1592, hardship had forced Margeriete Brans to consider leaving the Delft church for the Catholic-controlled city of Ghent. Brans had quarreled with the deacons over the years about her meager relief and now she decided to leave Delft. Her vigorous complaints and her threat to leave town caused rumors, and the consistory regarded this "an offense that is infamous among many." She responded that the deacons were unable to sustain her sufficiently and had accused her of exaggerating her illness. This situation with all its effrontery compelled her to seek better financial opportunities. The Delft consistory regarded Margeriete's decision as "forsaking Christ for a handful of goods"; therefore a minister publicly admonished her before the congregation.[83]

In one of the most notorious cases, Lieven van Vijven's adulterous affair had led to his excommunication in Amsterdam in 1594.[84] Van Vijven came before the Delft consistory in August 1598, asking that he be permitted to take communion and receive alms. The Delft consistory turned him down because it had been apprised of this transgression by the Amsterdam consistory.[85] Van Vijven defended himself by arguing that he had done all he could to comply with the community's standards

---

[82] *GAD. Kerkeraad* (August 21, 1581).

[83] *Ibid.* (April 4, 1584; April 30, 1584; July 25, 1584; June 22, 1587; July 27, 1592; August 10, 1592).

[84] Van Vijven was actually accused of polygamy; on the basis of the testimony of witnesses, the consistory could substantiate, however, only that he had committed adultery: Roodenburg, *Onder censuur*, p. 290.

[85] Van Vijven's request for poor relief did not make its way into the consistorial records until December 1598. Even though this request came a few months later, he was a poor (former) member guilty of a public sin: *GAD. Kerkeraad* (December 21, 1598).

and rectify his past sins; he had confessed publicly, so he argued, he had repented, and he had maintained that not taking communion troubled his conscience.[86] Furthermore, his first wife was now dead and he was married to the "other woman" with whom he had produced a child.

The Delft consistory found itself in a difficult position. The ministers and elders had a hard time imagining a known adulterer attending communion, yet van Vijven had proven himself obedient to all consistorial demands. Consequently, the consistory promised to have the matter clarified at the next meeting of the Synod of South Holland at The Hague. That decision came a couple of weeks later, when the synodal delegates stated that "for such a man to be permitted communion would have a very evil consequence . . . for, if such a marriage were well known by the church [i.e., the congregation], it could easily make a damaging breach [of morality] transgression, so that many would begin to commit such sins boldly. Thus for the scandals that would arise, he shall refrain from communion until a national synod can meet."[87]

The synod believed that some transgressions were so damaging that they threatened the fundamental dynamic of the community and no amount of rectification could undo the destruction. If other members knew that van Vijven had so grossly violated spiritual standards and yet was permitted to take communion, they would be tempted to encroach upon the moral standards of the congregation. The synod also believed it was best to try to keep transgressions hidden from the public. The assembly declared: "Regarding a member who has fallen into adultery whose sins are known only to the consistory, the synod judges that according to the rule of God's Word secret sins should not be made known, which would be the cause of much scandal."[88] Such public sins polluted the church and threatened the religious community with dishonor. The Delft consistory enforced this decision and denied Lieven van Vijven's requests until the matter could be resolved by a higher ecclesiastical body. Even though van Vijven subsequently appealed to the consistory several times, he never was allowed access to the Lord's Table. Notwithstanding this harsh decision, he did nevertheless receive a one-time grant in aid in July 1601.[89]

The synodal decision in the van Vijven case corresponds to a general pattern in the consistory's actions against recipients who committed public offenses. For example, the consistory denied communion and further alms to Aeltgen Elias, Catelijne Jans, a woman bearing only the name "Meinste," Catelijne Jans, and Neeltge Damen. Juffrouw van Vliet was granted assistance only after the ministers and elders decided she had purged herself from the evil she had caused.[90]

Even when the consistory became satisfied that recipients were innocent of a particular charge, it would often still threaten recipients for putting themselves into

---

[86] Reitsma and van Veen, *Acta*, vol. III, p. 135.   [87] *Ibid.*, p. 135.   [88] *Ibid.*

[89] *GAD. Kerkeraad* (December 21, 1598; July 26, 1599; September 20, 1600; November 13, 1600; July 2, 1601; July 9, 1601).

[90] *Ibid.*: (July 11, 1588), Meinste; (January 1, 1590), Elias; (May 30, 1605), Damen; (June 14, 1604; June 21, 1604), Jans; (October 25, 1591; November 11, 1591), van Vliet.

situations that would lead to rumors or accusations. Members were to be above reproach, which meant that even unsubstantiated accusations implied that the member was guilty of some impropriety. As James Tracy has observed, "the actual guilt or innocence of the individual was sometimes a secondary consideration."[91] This attitude was exemplified in the case of Janneken Ceels, who had been implicated in a dispute in 1604. When she appeared before the consistory in November, Ceels convinced the ministers and elders of her innocence. Nevertheless, the consistory admonished her to "avoid all appearance of evil and to labor that she might again win a good name," promising that they "would not neglect her in her need."[92] The promise also implied a threat: if circumstances permitted such accusations, the church officers would dismiss her requests.

The records show, then, that earning back one's reputation and restoring one's name was a central condition that the consistory placed on recipients. To accomplish this restoration, the consistory constantly monitored the behavior of recipients under discipline to determine if they were meeting the standards that would allow them to receive alms once again. The essential characteristics within this standard were humility and obedience. Becoming reincorporated always involved repentance, rectification, and remorse, and in public cases it meant displaying these attributes publicly before the congregation. On July 19, 1593, the consistory denied communion to Jan Michielssen for public drunkenness. A week later, he asked the ministers and elders for a sizable loan, presumably to repay a debt. The consistory responded that he should "work as a servant for a long time and apply himself to piety and making a good name."[93]

The aim to promote adherence to the church's moral norms was not really doctrinal in nature. Although some were denied assistance for frequenting other religious groups, the consistory did not eliminate any one from the poor relief rolls for heterodoxy. It even continued to support Willem Bronckhorst, who practiced sorcery of some sort for at least four years.[94] Rather, Reformed discipline promoted the normative social conventions of civil society.[95] Family life was one of the most important social institutions that the consistory attempted to safeguard. In the case of Neeltgen Jans, the consistory supported her mother in light of Neeltgen's irresponsible financial behavior.[96] The consistory helped a certain Barthelmeus who had confessed his adultery, so that he could travel to Amsterdam to reconcile with his wife.[97] On the other hand, the wife of Wessel Hendricx was denied assistance until she reconciled with her husband.[98]

[91] Tracy, "Calvinist church," p. 268.   [92] *GAD. Kerkeraad* (November 1, 1604).
[93] *Ibid.* (July 26, 1593).
[94] *Ibid.* (August 27, 1607; October 22, 1607; January 28, 1608; February 11, 1608; March 17, 1608; August 23, 1608; November 22, 1610; February 14, 1611; February 21, 1611).
[95] See van Deursen, *Hel en hemel*, p. 48; Schilling, "Reformierte Kirchenzucht als Sozialdisziplinierung?," p. 274.
[96] *GAD. Kerkeraad* (October 30, 1581).   [97] *Ibid.* (January 15, 1595).
[98] *Ibid.* (November 1, 1604).

The consistory certainly used poor relief as a leverage to compel compliance with its moral standards and with accepted social convention. Scholars from different disciplines have focused on a heightened concern over deviance and attempts to acculturate the poor to elite standards in the early modern period.[99] Influenced by this tradition, Janine Estèbe and Bernard Vogler have argued forcefully that consistories joined with their civil counterparts as new agents of social control: "the consistory easily shouldered the role of arbiter which was connected traditionally to the agent of seignier, notary, or curé."[100] On the other hand, more recent work on the consistories of Emden (Heinz Schilling) and Amsterdam (Herman Roodenburg) has uncoupled ecclesiastical discipline from criminalization by distinguishing the state's power to punish punitively from the church's authority to discipline sin.[101]

Yet the poor also asserted their own agency to secure continued assistance or to obtain specific requests. Poor relief petitioners and recipients appealed to the circumstances of their poverty, protested sanctions, and promised moral behavior to gain access to church alms. In an attempt to coax Anna Gillis to return to the Reformed fold, the consistory instructed the deacons to repay a debt she incurred from a Mennonite congregation. While there is no evidence of hard bargaining on Gillis's part, it does seem likely that her future religious affiliation was a strategy to advance her request.[102] In the autumn of 1583, Josijntgen and Pieter de Spinner had become embroiled with the consistory over charges they had slandered another member of the congregation. After a bitter dispute, the consistory declined to help them repay debts, but did grant them a small sum because of this couple's "great anger."[103] The widow of Hendrick van Lier complained about her needs to the consistory four times between April 1586 and February 1587. Her persistence paid off, for the consistory instructed the deacons to help pay her rent.[104] Aeltgen Jans successfully appealed for twelve stuivers per week in 1585 and 1588 by promising not to beg.[105] Charged with fraud and disputing, Catelijne Clarissen negotiated with the consistory intermittently for eleven years over her various needs. In July 1603, she threatened to separate from the church, so the consistory decided to support her for one more month.[106] Willem Bronckhorst had been charged by

---

[99] Two primary examples are Foucault, *Discipline and Punish*, and Spierenburg, *Spectacle of Suffering*.

[100] Estèbe and Vogler, "Une société protestante," p. 386.

[101] Schilling, "Reformierte Kirchenzucht als Sozialdisziplinierung?," p. 284; Roodenburg, *Onder censuur*, pp. 17–27; van Deursen, *Hel en hemel*, p. 48.

[102] *GAD. Kerkeraad* (January 21, 1579).

[103] *Ibid.* (August 15, 1583; September 5, 1583; September 19, 1583; October 3, 1583; October 10, 1583; November 7, 1583). Josijntgen appeared before the consistory again on November 27, 1583, requesting a regular subsidy of five stuivers. She promised to continue her moral improvement, and the consistory consented to her request: *ibid.* (November 27, 1583). Thus while the consistory compelled her to improve, at the same time, she used a promise of moral improvement to secure assistance.

[104] *Ibid.* (April 7, 1586; January 12, 1587; February 2, 1587; February 23, 1587).

[105] *Ibid.* (December 30, 1585; December 19, 1588).

[106] The consistory made it clear that this grant would extend only for a month and no longer: *ibid.* (July 21, 1603).

several officers and members of misusing his alms. But he retained his place on the diaconal register by protesting his innocence and by pointing out his wife's illness.[107]

Interaction over poor relief and morals in Delft, therefore, was a negotiated process in which both the consistory and poor relief recipients attempted to manipulate diaconal charity for their own ends. For Arent Corneliszoon and the consistory, poor relief of the Reformed congregation was intertwined with the moral norms that distinguished a Reformed Christian community. Given the small amounts of money the diaconate and consistory allotted to recipients, these officers wanted to demonstrate Christian charity in action and to make sure the poor were not altogether neglected.[108] Confronted with poor folk who violated these norms, the consistory labored to reconcile the sinner with the church and protect the reputation of the church. Without an ordered structure policing its ideals, such a community could not have existed. Nevertheless, the poor were not passive victims of acculturation in post-Reformation Delft, but they made forceful appeals to the consistory by promising good conduct and by asserting their needs. Such negotiations underscore the intense efforts by both church leaders and the poor to reconcile the community's moral standards with the circumstances of poverty in Holland during the late sixteenth and early seventeenth centuries.

Poor relief in the Dutch Reformed Church emanated out of a Calvinist vision of their religious community. Discipline protected the communion table and the collection box from moral corruption and dishonor. Ideally, a diaconate, independent of municipal control and under the authority of the consistory, was to devote church alms to the poor of the congregation. As we shall see in chapter 6, local consistories often had a difficult time maintaining these ideals against lay magistrates and some ministers, who embraced a very different conception of Christian community. Just as magistrates limited municipal charity to those within the municipal corporation, Calvinists also intended to offer relief to those within the "household of faith." When compelled to cooperate with municipal authorities, Calvinists still placed the highest priority on "the poor member of our Lord Christ."

[107] *Ibid.* (August 27, 1607; January 28, 1608; February 11, 1608).
[108] Most ordinary grants ranged from four to sixteen stuivers per week. Van Deursen has calculated that the average weekly wage in 1600 for unskilled laborers in Amsterdam was fourteen stuivers per day: van Deursen, *Plain Lives*, pp. 4–7.

Appendix 5.1 *Members who requested to return to communion in Delft*

	Date	Name(s)	Consistory's decision
1	11–16–79	Lijsbeth Jacobsz	Denied; granted 3–21–83
2	11–26–84	Jacob Willems and wife	Denied
3	4–11–86	Dirck Jacobszoon	Denied
	12–8–86	Dirck Jacobszoon	Denied
4	4–11–86	Jan Meyers	Denied
5	12–8–86	Anna Gillis	Denied
6	2–20–87	Coenraedt van Doerne	Denied
	4–27–98	Coenraedt van Doerne	Denied
7	12–14–87	Jan Musis and wife	Denied; granted 2–15–88
8	1–9–89	Herman Herckens and wife	Granted
9	6–12–89	Wife of Claes Felckertszoon	Denied
10	7–17–89	Jan Well Geeredtszoon	Investigated
11	10–27–89	Wife of Hans de Backer	Investigated
12	4–26–91	Mary Commers	Investigated
13	2–17–92	Barber Pieters	Denied; granted 4–20–92
14	2–21–92	Catelijne Clarissen	Denied
	4–10–95	Catelijne Clarissen	Investigated; granted 6–23–00
15	4–6–92	Grietghen Lenaerts	Granted
16	4–20–92	Adriaritghen Conners	Granted
17	2–26–93	Barber Gonaerts	Denied
18	4–12–93	Abraham Brulkmans	Denied
19	8–16–93	Magdalena de Weerdinne	Denied
20	2–13–94	Aeltghen Jans	Granted
	2–11–08	Aeltghen Jans	Denied
21	5–9–94	Willhem Cornelissen[a]	Denied
22	6–24–94	Adrian van Hecke	Granted
23	8–26–94	Magdaleencken Jans	Denied
24	10–24–94	Maertghen Heijndricks	Granted
25	1–23–95	Machtelt Robedens	Investigated
26	2–6–95	Elsghen Matthijs	Investigated
27	2–20–95	Adriaen Aelbrechtssen	Granted
28	4–24–95	Stellanus	Denied
29	4–8–96	Tanne Gerrits	Investigated
30	2–21–97	Tame de Naeijster	Denied
31	2–21–97	Janneken	Denied
32	6–23–97	Tame and Maeij Laps	Denied
33	2–20–98	Dirck Jacopssen	Denied
34	6–22–98	Christina Backer	Denied
35	12–21–98	Lienen van Vijven	Denied
36	2–15–99	Mantghen (gravedigger)	Denied
37	6–7–99	Maritghen Dannebier	Granted

	Date	Name(s)	Consistory's decision
38	2–14–00	Belitghe de Witte	Denied
39	6–23–00	Jacomijne	Denied
40	8–14–00	Arien Janssen	Denied
	5–7–01	Arien Janssen	Denied
41	12–26–00	Anneken Jans	Granted
42	2–19–01	Jacopghen Ariens	Denied
43	4–23–01	Teens Pauwelssen	Denied
44	4–30–01	Wouter Ottenssen	Investigated
45	8–6–01	Tanneken Frank	Denied; granted 8–24–01
46	8–6–01	Claes Pieterssen	Investigated; granted 8–13–01
47	8–6–01	Jan Vranckenssen	Investigated
48	8–6–01	Bartholomeus Heijndricks	Investigated; denied 8–20–01
	6–27–03	Bartholomeus Heijndricks	Denied
49	12–17–01	Cornelis Lambrechtssen	Denied
50	4–26–02	Danmas Cornelissen	Investigated
52	9–23–02	Grietghe Pauwells	Denied
	2–21–03	Grietghe Pauwells	Granted
53	10–21–02	Jan Vrancken	Granted
54	10–21–02	Claes Rijckewaert and wife	Investigated
55	10–25–02	Mariken Jacops	Denied; granted 12–9–02
56	12–16–02	Heijndrick ten Brincke	Investigated
57	12–16–02	Neeltghen Claes	Investigated
58	4–21–03	Heijndrick de Spinnewielmaecker	Granted
59	7–28–03	Willhem Cornelissen[a]	Investigated
60	8–4–03	Grietghen Jans?	
61	8–21–03	Claes Vrancken	Denied
62	10–20–03	Cent Pieterssen	Denied
	7–9–07	Cent Pieterssen	Investigated; denied 8–24–07
63	10–24–03	Beijken Faes	Granted
64	10–24–03	Mr. Barent	Investigated
65	10–24–03	Aechtghen Willems	Granted
66	2–23–04	Stijntghe Jans and Anthonij Graue	Investigated; granted 2–27–04
67	2–23–04	Wilhelm Houdtaen	Granted
68	6–25–04	Arianken Pieters	Investigated; denied 2–14–05
69	8–23–04	Wife of Claes de Scheemaecker	Investigated; granted 8–27–04
70	8–23–04	Willhem Joosten	Investigated; denied 8–27–04
71	10–29–04	Neeltghen Damen	Denied
	6–23–06	Neeltghen Damen	Denied
	12–18–06	Neeltghen Damen	Investigated
	2–11–08	Neeltghen Damen	Investigated; granted 2–22–08
72	12–20–04	Adriaen Cornelissen	Investigated

73	3–14–05	Willhem de Prins	Investigated
74	3–21–05	Joost Jacopssen	Investigated
75	8–15–05	Willhem Cornelissen[a]	Investigated; granted 8–26–05
76	10–17–05	Ariaenken Bomincx	Granted
77	10–24–05	Lijsbeth Jans	Granted
78	6–5–06	Willem Kijck	Denied
	10–23–06	Willem Kijck	Denied
79	6–19–06	Jan Claeszoon vander Mast	Denied
80	10–23–06	Engeltge in de Cromstraet	Granted
81	12–18–06	Aeltgen Andries	Granted
82	12–18–06	Cornelis Janssen	Granted
83	2–5–07	Frederick Henricxen	Investigated; denied 2–12–07
84	2–12–07	Maertgen Leenderts	Denied
85	2–23–07	Maillaert Looten	Granted
	10–29–12	Maillaert Looten	Granted
86	2–23–07	Wife of Moucheren	Denied
87	4–27–07	Hans Tootman	Investigated
	12–28–07	Hans Tootman	Denied
	4–21–08	Hans Tootman	Granted
88	6–18–07	Jan van Wellden	Denied
89	7–9–07	Jan Ide	Denied
90	7–9–07	Liebers, wife of Willem Slouwer	Investigated
91	10–26–07	Reijer Boot	Investigated
92	12–10–07	Widow of a Scotsman	Granted
93	12–10–07	Maillaert de Crauwe	Investigated
94	12–10–07	Mother of Blind Harmen	Investigated
95	2–11–08	Aeltgen Pieters	Denied
96	3–10–08	Egbert van Rechteren	Denied
	4–21–08	Egbert van Rechteren	Denied; granted 8–18–08
97	4–14–08	Ebert Heijndrickssen	?
98	4–14–08	Willem Corneliszoon Altena	Denied
	8–29–08	Willem Corneliszoon Altena	Granted
	6–24–11	Willem van Altena	Granted
99	5–26–08	Vincent Pieterszoon	Investigated
100	8–25–08	Jan Kerssel and wife	Granted
101	2–20–09	Wouter and wife Maeijken	Granted
102	3–9–09	Maertgen Crijnen	Denied; granted 4–24–09
103	6–22–09	Jacob Pieterszoon	Granted
104	6–26–09	Willem Dirckszoon	Granted
105	6–26–09	Anne Pieters	Granted
106	7–13–09	Arien Pieterszoon	Investigated; granted 7–20–09
107	7–20–09	Marij Wacchans	Granted
108	10–12–09	Unnamed woman	Denied
109	12–14–09	Pieter Janssen	Denied
110	12–21–09	Christina de Clopper	Investigated; granted 10–25–10

Appendix 5.1 (*cont.*)

	Date	Name(s)	Consistory's decision
111	2–8–10	Jan Jacobszoon	Denied/granted 2–22–10
112	2–25–10	Jan Janszoon (Lindewever)	Investigated; granted 6–25–10
113	6–25–10	Prins den Tuijnder	Granted
114	8–9–10	Huijch Cornelissen	Denied
115	8–27–10	Benjamin Claessen	Denied
	10–29–10	Benjamin Claessen	Denied
	11–1–10	Benjamin Claessen	Denied
116	1–24–11	Willem Bronckhorst	Investigated; denied 2–14–11
	2–13–12	Willem Bronckhorst	Denied
117	4–22–11	Gerrit Ysselsteijn	Investigated
118	8–15–11	Aeltgen Franssen	Investigated; granted 8–26–11
119	8–22–11	Wouter Pieterszoon	Granted
120	4–16–12	Aeltgen Jans	Denied
121	10–27–14	Jannecken Willems	Granted
122	12–29–14	Jacques van Sluijs	Granted
123	2–16–15	Lijsbet Aelbrechts	Granted
124	2–27–15	Wife of Lombard	Granted
125	3–28–16	Daughter of J. Godshoven	Granted
126	3–3–17	Marijtgen Allerts	Granted
127	6–24–19	Betgen Gillis	Investigated

Source: ᵃ Willhem Cornelissen was called Willhem Janssen on June 24, 1594. There are three references to a "Willhem Cornelissen" in the archive; it is unclear whether the references are to the same person.

Appendix 5.2 *Continued relief for disciplined members in Amsterdam*

Name	Gender	Charge	Date
Fem Harmensdochter	F	?	7/82
Unnamed	F	?	3/83
Neeltgen Nijs	F	Drunkenness	7/86
Naenken Rosiers	F	Begging	4/89
Wijntgen Frans	F	Singing	1/90
Fije Joris	F	Begging	8/90
Barbel Jans	F	Drunkenness	1/91
Claes Jacobszoon	M	Nonattendance	12/94
Aelbrecht de Grave	M	Adultery	4/96
Aelbrecht de Grave	M	Begging	9/96
Pieter van Suick	M	Misuse of alms	5/03
Z. Neremans	F	Adultery	9/06
Betteke de Witt	F	Dancing	11/12

Poor members denied diaconal relief in Amsterdam

Name	Gender	Charge	Date
Pieter Pieterszoon	M	Misuse of alms	8/91
Nicholas de Looper	M	Drunkenness	6/94
Rogier Janszoon	M	Misuse of alms	6/99
H. Hendricszoon	F	Begging	3/01
Wijbe Janszoon	F	Adultery	5/04
H. Hendricszoon	F	Adultery	5/04
E. Lenaertszoon	F	Adultery	9/06
Aeltgen Janszoon	F	Adultery	9/06
Merten Pieterszoon	M	?	5/14

Source: GAA. Kerkeraad (according to date).

Appendix 5.3 *The poor relief status of members under discipline in Delft*

	Name	Period	Charge	Consistory's decision
1	Gillis	1–79/4–87	Absent	GR, ?A
2	Pieterszoon	4–79/12–80	Absent, debts, drunk	GA, DR
3	Jans	10–81/2–82	Domestic dispute	GA (to his mother)
4	Spinner (2)	8–83/11–83	Dispute, drunk	GA, DA, GA
5	Brans	4–84/8–92	Absent, dispute	IA, GA, DA
6	Lier (2)	8–85/2–87	Debts	DR, GA
7	Jans	9–85/12–88	Beggary	DA, CA
8	Elsgen and Lijsbeth	6–23–86	Dispute	DA
9	Bruijssel	2–87/8–90	Adultery	GA, DA
10	Bosman	7–89/8–89	Misuse of alms	DA
11	Elias	12–89/4–92	Drunk, dispute	IA, DA
12	Dominic	3–90/12–98	Debts	GR, DR, ?A
13	De Backer	9–91/10–91	Domestic dispute	DA
14	Clarissen	1–92/7–03	Debts, dispute	DR, GA, DR, DA
15	Homaker	5–92/6–92	Dispute	GA, DA
16	Ariens	6–92/5–02	Debts, disputes, bad household	DR, CA, IA
17	Magdal.	8–92/1–93	Adultery	DA
18	Griets	8–93/11–93	Domestic dispute	DR
19	Cornelis.	5–93/4–95	Absent, debts	GA, DA
20	Coenssen	7–93/12–93	Absent	IA, ?A
21	Barthel.	1–15–95	Adultery	GR
22	Meerland	12–21–98	Drunk	?A
23	Vijven	2–98/7–01	Adultery	DA, GR
24	Louriszoon	3–99/10–99	Bad household	GA (to his family)
25	Dirckx.	5–99/6–99	Dispute	?A
26	Huijsman	2–02/4–02	Domestic dispute	CA, GA
27	Jans	2–04/6–04	Adultery, drunk, dispute	DA
28	Cleerne	8–23–04	?	DA
29	Wesel	11–1–04	Domestic dispute	DA
30	Damen	5–05/10–11	Dispute	DA, GA, TA
31	Steen	7–06/2–10	Dispute	IA, DA, GA
32	Bronck.	8–07/2–12	Misuse of alms, sorcery	GA, ?A

Note: 32 cases, 35 people

Appendix 5.4 *Recipients charged with moral offenses in Delft*

	Name	Period	Charge	Consistory's decision
1	Janssen*	1–84/5–84	Not needy	IA, GA
2	Pieters	6–9–86	Debts	?
3	Meinste	7–11–88	Dispute	DA
4	Mauringen	10–23–89	Bad household	DR, IA
5	Hieronimusz	7–91/2–92	Drunk, dispute	CA
6	Laureijs	9–16–91	Debts	GR
7	Van Vliet	10–91/11–91	Dispute	TA, CA
8	Valcke	5–18–92	Debts	?A
9	T. Valcke	1–25–93	Debts	GR
10	Boot	6–92/1–94	False witness	DA
11	Lambrecht	7–27–92	Mennonites, aid from city	DA
12	Haeckendoren	7–92/8–92	Debts	GR
13	Joosten	6–29–92	Not needy	IA
14	Jans	9–21–92	Beggary, Mennonite	DA
15	Michielssen*	7–26–93	Debts	DR
16	Erasmus	2–26–93	Beggary	IA
17	Breschildt	11–7–94	Drunkenness	TA
18	Matthijs*	5–5–97	Debts	DR, GA
19	Marijne	12–23–02	Dispute	IA
20	Themissen	3–02/4–02	Debts	DR, CR
21	Heijndrickx	4–29–02	Not needy	IA
22	Classen	3–1–04	Beggary	GR
23	Hermanssen	11–04/3–05	Debts	IR
24	Ceels*	11–1–04	Dispute	GA
25	Pieters	11–7–05	Debts	GR

Note: 25 cases, 25 people

Appendix 5.5 *Poor relief recipients under no charges in Delft*

Name	Period	Request	Consistory's decision	
1	Two widows	5–6–70	Travel request	IR
2	Gillis	10–1–82	Assistance	IA
3	Dierxz	12–24–82	Assistance	GA
4	Unnamed	6–18–84	Assistance	GA
5	Wieldtreijer	7–16–84	Travel request	GR
6	Meyers*	4–86/11–86	Assistance	DA, IA
7	Widow*	7–28–87	Assistance	IA
8	Unnamed man	5–88/6–88	Assistance	GA
9	Leijdts*	9–91/2–93	Assistance	GA, DA
10	Pieters	6–92	Assistance	RC
11	Hubrechts	8–10–92	Assistance	GA
12	Reenewas	9–21–92	Assistance	IA
13	Sara	10–23–92	Assistance	GA
14	Ariens	2–1–93	Loan	IR
15	Janssen	6–7–93	Assistance	GA
16	Unnamed woman	7–26–93	Assistance	GA
17	Centen	10–93/3–94	Assistance	IA, GA
18	Ariens	7–18–94	Travel request	DR
19	Matruijt	8–1–94	Assistance	GA
20	Corneliszoon	10–16–95	Loan	DR
21	Willemerts	7–1–96	*Attestatie* to receive relief	DR
22	Van Stavel	8–97/3–99	Loan, assistance	DR, GA
23	Unnamed	5–4–98	Travel request	GR
24	Janssen couple	7–27–98	Assistance	GR
25	Widow Jans	8–27–99	Property stolen	RC
26	Frederickx	7–22–05	Assistance	GA
27	Dijckhuijsz	10–07/10–08	Assistance	GA
28	De Putter	11–07	*Attestatie* due to poverty	DR, IA
29	Wachanssen	4–13–09	Assistance	IA

Note: 29 cases, 31 people

KEY TO APPENDICES 5.3–5.5:
* = Member
GA = granted assistance; GR = granted request; TA = threatened assistance;
CA =assistance on specific conditions; DA = denied assistance; DR = denied request; IA and IR = request investigated; RC =referred to city authorities; ?A = assistance presumed, but no explicit evidence

6

Municipal welfare and the Calvinist diaconate, 1572–1620

In 1616, Cornelis Pieterszoon Hooft, an Amsterdam burgomaster and an ardent opponent of orthodox Calvinism, claimed that an independent Reformed diaconate had subverted an equitable system of poor relief in his city:

> [Diaconal charity] has continued now for so many years, notwithstanding the great number of people driven into bankruptcy. On the other side are the people at the bottom who use the city's other charitable foundations that the lord Burgomasters (according to their responsibility) customarily administer for all. I do not know if I can recount the many mistakes that have been made over the past sixty years. And yet the church still remains on its old course in such practices, so that many of the poor have been improperly burdened. Some enjoy a double portion while there are other poor people who must make do with a meager portion.[1]

Not only did Hooft maintain that Reformed charity had created more problems than it had solved, but he also believed that a dual system of poor relief favored the church poor over those who had to make do with allotments from municipal institutions. Furthermore, he complained that the Amsterdam deacons had free rein over an annual purse of 70,000 guilders to distribute to the church poor, many of whom were foreigners from Flanders.[2]

For Hooft, an independent diaconate violated the magistracy's prerogative to guarantee the rights of native Amsterdammers to receive alms equitably and to worship freely without financial compulsion.[3] According to Hooft, this dual poor relief structure shattered the solidarity of the civil community, it undermined the long tradition of magisterial authority over social welfare, and it enabled deacons to use charity to promote the narrow confessional goals of the Reformed Church.

Hooft was not alone in his criticism of an independent Reformed diaconate. Writing thirty years later, Johannes Uytenbogaert, a prominent Remonstrant minister, contended that the diaconate in Delft had corrupted the civic unity that had been held together in past times by a Christian magistracy. Uytenbogaert argued that an independent diaconate "causes a partitioning of Christians into sects that try to enlarge themselves by attracting people through alms."[4] For

---

[1] Hooft, *Memoriën en adviesen*, p. 54.   [2] *Ibid.*, pp. 53–4.

[3] H. A. Enno van Gelder, *De levensbeschouwing van Cornelis Pieterszoon Hooft, burgemeester van Amsterdam, 1547–1626* (Amsterdam, 1918), p. 98.

[4] Uytenbogaert, *Historie*, p. 799.

Uytenbogaert and Hooft, the only remedy for these sectarian divisions was a single poor relief network under the auspices of the civil government.

The allegation that Calvinists in Holland used poor relief to attract members has also been a staple of modern Dutch historiography. L. J. Rogier, the renowned Catholic historian, argued that Calvinist poor relief was an integral part of a systematic campaign to "protestantize" the northern Netherlands.[5] Rogier built upon the protestantization thesis of Pieter Geyl to account for the slow but steady growth of the Reformed Church from the late sixteenth through the seventeenth centuries.[6] According to Rogier, protestantization developed in two phases. The first occurred during the late sixteenth and early seventeenth centuries and was directed at the poor; the second transpired over the course of the 1600s and was aimed at regents and well-to-do folk. In the first phase, Calvinists used charity to entice converts into church membership. Rogier claimed that, by the early seventeenth century, most converts were either paupers or people who depended upon charity.[7] While a number of studies have severely undermined Rogier's thesis, it still retains a certain amount of influence in modern Dutch historiography.[8]

To a large degree, the discussion over protestantization and poor relief is the Dutch version of the more widespread debate concerning the process of confessionalization in Europe. Recent scholarship on a wide variety of European territories has shown that authorities in Catholic, Lutheran, and Calvinist lands attempted to recast their territories into orderly Christian societies. Despite the differences in religious creeds, this was a broad effort driven by political anxieties about social order with ecclesiastical apprehensions over orthodoxy.[9] The development of charitable agencies during this time reflected the mutual concerns with order and orthodoxy. In most cases, poor relief institutions either came under civil jurisdiction or became a joint concern of political and ecclesiastical authorities.

---

[5] Rogier, *Katholicisme*, vol. i, pp. 422–33; Rogier, *Eenheid en scheiding*, p. 107.

[6] Geyl employed the term "protestantization" to depict how Calvinism succeeded in the northern Netherlands. According to Geyl, protestantization occurred through primary school education, political disenfranchisement (of non-Reformed church members), and poor relief. See John Elliott's excellent discussion of Geyl and Rogier in the context of the historiography of the Dutch Revolt, in Elliott, "The classis of Dordrecht," pp. 17–47.

[7] L. J. Rogier, "De protestantiseering van het Noorden," in *AGN*, vol. v, pp. 330–3.

[8] Most local studies of poor relief have either indicated or argued directly that Reformed church officers lacked the desire, the resources, and the opportunity to recruit members via poor relief. Van Deursen makes an exception with regard to the Amsterdam diaconate, although he believes that recruitment there cannot be proven or disproven. See Elliott, "The classis of Dordrecht," pp. 397–401; Ligtenberg, *Armezorg te Leiden*, pp. 231–3; Spaans, *Haarlem*, pp. 163–89; ten Boom, "De diaconie te Tiel"; Wouters and Abels, *Nieuw en ongezien*, vol. i, p. 303; van Deursen, *Bavianen*, pp. 102–27. Nevertheless, historians also recognize that the offering of church alms could have attracted poor people to church membership: Wouters and Abels, *Nieuw en ongezien*, vol. ii, p. 239; Roodenburg, *Onder censuur*, p. 112. As I stated in chapter 5, the poor did not have to join the Reformed Church to receive charity in the six cities. For those who have adopted Rogier's conclusion, see J. A. de Kok, *Nederland op de breuklijn*, p. 11; J. G. C. A. Briels, *Zuidnederlanders in de Republiek, 1572–1630: een demografische en cultuurhistorische studie* (St. Nicholas, 1985), p. 276; Nusteling, *Welvaart*, pp. 164–5.

[9] See Kaplan, *Calvinists and Libertines*, pp. 5–12.

Consequently, charity became a more effective instrument for ensuring social order and religious orthodoxy, as authorities demanded that poor relief recipients comply with the demands of the confessional state.[10]

The European pattern of confessionalization, however, does not readily lend itself to understanding the evolution of poor relief institutions in the six cities of Holland during the Dutch Reformation. The Dutch Reformed Church was not a state church. Furthermore, magistrates tolerated Catholics, Mennonites, Lutherans, and Jews, and they sought to check the confessional influence of Calvinism within their cities. City governments intended for municipal poor relief, whether augmented by diaconal charity or not, to assist the needy of the civic community, regardless of their religious beliefs. For their part, Calvinist church leaders, according to the synodal resolutions from 1571 to 1586, preferred for the deacons to assist only those needy people who were church members. Because of the expectations of local magistrates, consistories in Dordrecht and Delft were willing to offer charity to non-members, provided that the deacons could retain control over relief for the poor in their eucharistic community.

Thus, it seems best to explain the negotiations over poor relief in the cities of Holland as a conflict over competing conceptions of community. Poor relief was one of the most pressing local issues involved in the transition from a society with no real distinctions between civic and religious culture to one in which leaders clearly staked out confessional and political boundaries by 1620. This extended dialogue resulted in a reformulation of the old municipal corporation and the fragmentation of the traditional Christian community.

This chapter will examine this reorganization in the six great cities of Holland from the establishment of the Reformed Church in 1572 to the aftermath of the Synod of Dordrecht in 1620. The negotiations with regard to poor relief varied considerably in each city and three different trends emerged. The first was for the diaconate to be merged with or subjugated under a city poor relief agency controlled by the magistracy, as was the case in Leiden and Gouda, and eventually Delft (in 1614). The second arrangement, represented by Haarlem and Amsterdam, split poor relief along confessional and municipal lines. The last trend was for the diaconate to take over poor relief for the entire corporation, as exemplified in Dordrecht and Delft (before 1614).

MERGED/SUBJUGATED POOR RELIEF: LEIDEN AND GOUDA

Of the six cities of Holland, the magistrates in Leiden and Gouda exhibited the strongest animosity toward Reformed Calvinism. For these city governments, any religious reformation was a local affair under their jurisdiction; outside interference by synods, classes, or provincial authorities was not welcome. The Reformation in

---

[10] Jütte, *Poverty and Deviance*, pp. 100–5.

Leiden has become synonymous with conflict between a Libertine city government and a consistory itself racked with division between stalwart Calvinists and a moderate Reformed party. Throughout the 1580s, a strongly Erastian magistracy worked to subdue Calvinist influence in the city and to thwart a confessional church order. Although there was an interval of cooperation from 1590 until the Arminian controversy in 1605, it was during the rancorous 1580s that the function of the Reformed diaconate became established in the city.[11]

Capitulating to the side of the Revolt in June 1572, the city government of Gouda was probably the most reluctant to embrace a Reformed Church. Gouda's magistracy harbored sympathy neither for the Reformation nor for the Revolt against Spain. And throughout this period, Gouda resisted efforts to establish an independent Calvinist Church, refused to enforce heresy laws against Catholics, and protected the Libertine ministers of St. Jan's Church.[12] The strident anti-confessionalism among the city governments of Leiden and Gouda obstructed the establishment of an independent diaconate in these two cities.

When Leiden's magistrates began to centralize parish charity in 1577, the Reformed diaconate there was just over three years old. Since January 1574, deacons of the Reformed Church in Leiden endeavored to relieve the needs of poor church members from the proceeds of collections taken at weekly worship services. Although there are no extant diaconal records in Leiden during this period, the consistory did establish a diaconate along the lines specified at the National Synod at Emden. The consistory selected elders and deacons, subject to final approval from the city government.[13] Based on apostolic example, diaconal charity was the material means for maintaining a confessional community separate from the larger civic body.

From the point of view of the Leiden magistracy, however, poor relief was a function of the municipal community. The magistrates regarded a diaconate under the exclusive authority of an independent-minded consistory with a good deal of suspicion. As early as 1576, the minister Pieter Corneliszoon complained to Arent Corneliszoon in Delft that the city government was trying to prescribe how much and to whom church alms should be given. Pieter Corneliszoon further complained that the city government regarded the diaconate as a civic institution.[14]

When the municipal government began to centralize parish institutions in 1577, the magistrates originally intended to merge the deacons with the *huiszitten meesters*. The commission's report of 1577 also proposed eliminating collections during the church services entirely, because they interfered with the sermons and because many people, especially Catholics, refused to attend church.[15] Yet after deliberations with the consistory, the magistracy did allow the church to operate an independent diaconate that would serve only poor members. Christine Kooi has

---

[11] See Kooi, "Leiden," pp. 33–190.
[12] L. A. Kesper, "De Goudsche vroedschap en de religie," *Bijdragen voor Vaderlandsche Geschiedenis en Oudheidkunde*, series 4, 2 (1902), pp. 391–428; Hibben, *Gouda in Revolt*, pp. 103–12.
[13] Kooi, "Leiden," pp. 59–61.   [14] *Ibid.*, pp. 61–2.   [15] Prinsen, "Armenzorg," p. 154.

suggested that this decision was a result of the presence of large numbers of religious refugees who would have overstrained municipal resources.[16] The strident Calvinists on the consistory believed that charity was an integral part of the confessional community; but for the burgomasters it was a way to relieve the native Leideners of the burden of municipal charity for foreign religious refugees.

Five years later, however, the Leiden magistracy reversed itself. In 1582, the magistrates forced the consistory to merge the diaconate with city almoners. According to this new arrangement, six deacons served alongside six almoners, uniting ecclesiastical and municipal poor relief into one administrative unit. All revenues for poor relief, including church collections, city-wide collections, donations, propertied revenues, and testaments went into a central chest. The *vroedschap* limited the deacons' specific domain of service to the *huiszitten* poor. Both the *vroedschap* and consistory participated in the annual selection of deacons, who served for a term of two years.[17]

This decision came during fierce struggles between the magistracy and strongminded Calvinists in the consistory over the role of the new church in postReformation Leiden. Rallying around Pieter Corneliszoon, Calvinists on the consistory attempted in 1579 to implement provisions of the 1578 Synod of Dordrecht. The Leiden city government, as well as those of Gouda and Delft, had vigorously denounced the 1578 synod.[18] In an extensive rejoinder addressed to the States of Holland, Jan van Hout, the *pensionaris* of Leiden, likened the synod's provisions for discipline to a revival of the Spanish Inquisition.[19] Leiden's magistrates found allies in the consistory, the most notable of which was the Libertine minister Caspar Coolhaes, and later Pieter Hackius. These ministers supported the magistrates' drive for a broadly evangelical church under the control of the civil authority.

Although William of Orange and the States of Holland intervened in October to resolve the conflict, these issues continued to plague the Reformed Church in Leiden until 1590.[20] Throughout the 1580s, the Leiden magistracy attempted to keep a tight rein over the consistory and to moderate clerical discipline. The city government subsidized Coolhaes until 1586 and the magistrates offered political support to Peter Hackius in the last half of the 1580s.[21]

[16] Kooi, "Leiden," pp. 63–4, n. 82.   [17] Blok, *Hollandsche stad*, pp. 183, 327.
[18] Hibben, *Gouda in Revolt*, pp. 102, 108.
[19] For the full reply of the Leiden *vroedschap*, see J. C. Overvoorde, "Advies van burgermeesters en gerecht van Leiden aan de Staten van Holland over de acta van de 1578 te Dordt gehouden," *Nederlands Archief voor Kerkgeschiedenis* 9 (1912), pp. 117–49.
[20] The conflict manifested itself in disputes over the election of the consistory. The compromise provided that the consistory would choose its candidates unless the vacancies were more than half the total seats. In that situation, the magistrates would select the elders. No one could become an elder over the objection of the consistory. Since elders served two-year terms, this meant that the consistory would fill the regular vacancies of those who rotated off the church college every year. The magistracy would fill any additional irregular vacancies. This flawed "arbitral accord" left plenty of room for future disputes: Woltjer, "Een niew ende onghesien dingh," pp. 5–6.
[21] Kooi, "Leiden," p. 151; Duke, "Ambivalent face," p. 128; Woltjer, "Een niew ende onghesien dingh," pp. 4–8.

The bitter divisions in Leiden were largely the result of the composition of the magistracy and the consistory in the period immediately after the Revolt. The most decisive years in the alteration of the magistracy were between 1572 and 1576. In November 1572, five months after the city succumbed to Beggar troops, William of Orange modified the makeup of the *vroedschap* to purge it of potentially traitorous elements and to give representation to Protestant sympathizers. Following a failed Spanish siege in 1574, the *vroedschap* was once again reconstituted. In the summer and autumn of 1574, twelve members were ousted, six new members were added, and twenty-two retained their seats.[22] While several convinced Protestants sat in this new *vroedschap*, a number of Catholics who had been loyal to the rebel cause also held seats in the college. In fact, Sterling Lamet has identified only nine of the thirty-two members of the *vroedschap* chosen in this two-year period as Protestant.[23] In addition, Jan van Hout, a vigorous adversary of orthodox Calvinism, continued to hold the position of municipal secretary until his death in 1609.[24]

Thus, the Leiden magistracy after the Revolt pursued a consistent and cautious religious policy. As Robert Fruin has observed, the Leiden city government "respected rather than loved the new order."[25] With a memory of the 1566 *beeldenstorm* and the destructive plundering of Beggar troops in 1572, the *vroedschap* intended to keep a firm check on the Calvinist church. Leiden regents harbored a strong suspicion of Calvinism that made them infamous among the more strident Reformers in Holland.[26]

Calvinists in Leiden, though, considered the dramatic developments of 1572–74 as a vindication of the Reformation.[27] And they intended to make sure that confessional Calvinism would take its rightful place in the city. The stridently orthodox minister Pieter Corneliszoon gave voice to the uncompromising demands

---

[22] Of the entire magistracy, that is the colleges of the *vroedschap*, burgomasters, and *schepenen*, forty-one (60 percent) disappeared between 1572 and 1574. Of this number, seventeen (25 percent) were eliminated for religious and political reasons, while twenty-four (35 percent) left for reasons extraneous to the turmoil. Twenty-two of the new members selected between 1572 and 1574 were already holding minor municipal offices and thus came from the ruling elite: Sterling Lamet, "The *vroedschap* of Leiden 1550–1600: the impact of tradition and change on the governing elite of a Dutch city," *Sixteenth-Century Journal* 12 (1981), pp. 19, 25; Noordham, *Geringde buffels*, pp. 28–9.

[23] Lamet, "The *vroedschap* of Leiden," pp. 19–25. Lamet has argued that the pre-1572 ruling elite was able to retain political power after 1574 through the cooptation of younger family members. Recently, Dirk Noordham has cast doubt on the ability of these old families to retain their political influence after the 1572–74 period. He argues that, from 1574 to 1618, two-thirds of the *vroedschap* were recruited from families who had obtained power during 1572–74. In Noordham's view, the Leiden *vroedschap* in the late sixteenth century became dominated by up-and-coming local families who displaced an older patriciate: Noordham, *Geringde buffels*, pp. 28–9, 103. Regardless of these different views, the Leiden magistracy pursued a very consistent policy with respect to the Reformed Church.

[24] Kooi, "Leiden," p. 24.   [25] Quoted *ibid.*, p. 25.

[26] For a description of the destruction of Catholic church property in 1566 and 1572, see L. Knappert, *De opkomst van het protestantisme in eene Noord-Nederlandsche stad* (Leiden, 1908), pp. 220–60; Rosemary Jones, "De Nederduitse gereformeerde gemeente te Leiden in de jaren 1572–1576," *Leidse Jaarbook* 66 (1974), pp. 126–8.

[27] Kooi, "Leiden," pp. 47–8.

for ecclesiastical autonomy among local Calvinists. Corneliszoon and his followers received support from the large numbers of immigrants from Flanders who poured into Leiden. Many came as religious refugees fleeing persecution, and contemporaries regarded these refugees as the most stringent Calvinists in the Dutch Reformed Church. And J. J. Woltjer has pointed out that these emigres came from the ranks of artisans, making them of an inferior social status vis-à-vis the native urban patriciate in Leiden.[28]

Until the mid-1580s, the consistory and the diaconate contained a very high proportion of these refugees from Flanders and Brabant. In October 1577, six of eight nominees were Flemish. In 1585 Flemings and Brabanters composed a majority of the deacons and elders and in 1587 recent immigrants from the south held nine of the twelve church positions.[29] Thus, the consistent resistance in an urban magistracy wary of Calvinism combined with the high percentage of southern refugees in church offices created an atmosphere of suspicion and hostility. The period from the inauguration of centralized poor relief to the merger of the diaconate (1577–82) was fraught with tension between stringent Calvinists and moderates in the consistory and the magistracy.

After 1582, when the magistracy placed the diaconate under municipal control, the deacons and the city almoners did not work very well for several years. The basic problem for the consistory was municipal control. Following Reformed traditions, Calvinist ministers in Leiden rooted the diaconate in the ministerial office of the church under the authority of the consistory because providing for the material needs for those in the "household of faith" was a primary task of the Christian community. Even though the magistrates had deprived the consistory of any authority in matters of poor relief, the church officers betrayed a special concern for poor church members. In May 1586, the consistory considered visiting all needy church members to determine their burdens, and in March and April 1587 it discussed taking an "extraordinary" collection only for church members.[30] Apparently, the deacons did solicit on behalf of the church poor, for in November 1587 a committee of magistrates attended the consistory meeting and expressed displeasure that a collection had taken place without their approval.[31]

As a result of their very different views of Christian society, the consistory and magistracy clashed over the administration of poor relief in Leiden. In May 1586, the consistory proposed to divide the city into four districts so that deacons and elders could visit, help, and admonish the poor to live up to the doctrinal and behavioral guidelines set forth by the Dutch Reformed Church. The magistrates rejected the proposal because it would undermine the authority of the almoners. Later, in December 1586, the almoners protested to the city government that the consistory tried to pressure them to give more liberally to church members than to

[28] Woltjer, "Een niew ende onghesien dingh," p. 12.
[29] Kooi, "Leiden," p. 58; Woltjer, "Een niew ende onghesien dingh," p. 14.
[30] *GAL. Kerkeraad* (May 6, 1586; March 20, 1587; April 14, 1587).   [31] *Ibid.* (November 1, 1587).

the general poor. Subsequently, the magistrates informed the consistory that it had no authority in matters of poor relief.[32]

The following February, the church leaders submitted two complaints to the *vroedschap* about the joint poor relief operation. First, the consistory protested that the almoners slighted the pressing needs of the poor, because they regulated amounts of relief too strictly on the basis of prescribed formulae. Secondly, the consistory objected to assisting those outside the "household of faith" because the Christian community should not subsidize "barbarians."[33]

In response to these fundamental differences, the *vroedschap* decided to keep the revenues centralized, but to separate the deacons and almoners. This resolution, therefore, would enable the diaconate to operate its relief network along the confessional lines sanctioned by the Reformed Church. The deacons would still be responsible for contributing to the common poor relief chest and, if requested, to provide an account of their distribution. To the dismay of the consistory, this arrangement was shortlived due to logistical problems. The *vroedschap* feared that the overlapping districts of city almoners and church deacons would enable some recipients to obtain economic benefits from both communities. In April 1587, only two months after the division, the *vroedschap* united the deacons and almoners again. This settlement lasted until the middle of the seventeenth century.[34]

The relationship between ecclesiastical and municipal in Leiden was clear-cut. In the face of economic hardships in the city and religious struggles in the church, a fiercely Erastian magistracy forced the diaconate to become a part of the municipal poor relief structure. Although the consistory was not happy with this decision, there was little it could do short of an illegitimate rebellion against the God-ordained political authority. Just as the *vroedschap* kept a firm hand in other church matters, they subjugated Reformed poor relief to municipal control. The process in Leiden revealed the primary conditions that would compel a consistory to accommodate its confessional aims to municipal culture: a hostile magistracy committed to its vision of the municipal community and a consistory fragmented by doctrinal divisions.

The situation in Gouda was similar to that of Leiden, with one important exception. Like Leiden's, Gouda's economy had suffered through a chronic recession throughout most of the sixteenth century. Like Leiden's, Gouda's magistracy was openly antagonistic to Reformed Calvinism. Yet unlike the vigorous Calvinist voice on the consistory in Leiden, the Reformed community in Gouda took a long time to establish a significant presence in the city. When the congregation did begin to grow in the late 1580s, it did so under the leadership of Herman Herbertszoon, a Libertine minister who advocated civil control over almost all church affairs.[35]

[32] Ligtenberg, *Armezorg te Leiden*, pp. 232–3.   [33] *Ibid.*, p. 232.   [34] *Ibid.*, pp. 232–3.
[35] A. J. van den Berg, "Herman Herberts (ca. 1540–1607) in conflict met de gereformeerde kerk" in *Kerkhistorische opstellen aangeboden aan Prof. dr. A. J. van den Berg*, C. Augustijn, P. N. Holtrop, G. A. M. Postuhumus Meijes, and E. G. E. van der Wall, eds. (Kampen, 1987), pp. 22–7.

Given the weak organization of the early Calvinist church, it seems likely that the diaconate in Gouda was largely insignificant. Because of the unfortunate scarcity of direct evidence, however, we can only infer this from the general condition of church organization.

Gouda has earned the reputation of being the most conservative city that capitulated to the prince of Orange. The *vroedschap* resisted efforts to curb Catholic religious observances in June 1572, and two months later several members even involved themselves in a plot to restore Gouda to Philip II.[36] Due to lingering suspicions of the patricians' loyalty, the prince of Orange purged the magistracy in August 1573. In the *vroedschap*, he removed eighteen members and selected twenty-three new ones, while he displaced three of the four burgomasters and four of the seven schepenen. These changes were not as drastic as they might seem. For, in January 1574, the *vroedschap* began gradually filling magisterial vacancies with members whom Orange had displaced in 1573. By 1578, most of the pre-1573 members had returned to their former positions. C. C. Hibben has concluded that this magisterial constancy "does much to explain the extraordinary conservatism of the *vroedschap*'s policies after 1573."[37]

Throughout this period, the Gouda magistracy foiled every attempt to establish a Reformed Church independent of its authority. In June 1572, the city government capitulated to Adriaen van Swieten, a Beggar military commander, and consented to allow public Reformed services to be held in the Blessed Virgin Chapel. The agreement between van Swieten and the *vroedschap* guaranteed "freedom of religion" in Gouda. Unfortunately, religious freedom carried a different meaning for the city magistrates and van Swieten.[38]

For local regents, it meant that public Catholic worship would continue in St. Jan's Church, and on July 10 the *vroedschap* reopened the parish church for that purpose.[39] Freedom of religion also implied that the magistrates had final say in religious affairs in Gouda; an external religious settlement would not be imposed on the city. Even then, the city government regarded this provision as a temporary measure and did not accept the reality of a public Reformed Church until the Union of Utrecht in 1579. Even after the Union, Hibben has shown that Gouda's magistracy "vigorously pursued a policy of complete religious autonomy."[40] For van Swieten, religious liberty ultimately meant freedom only for the Reformed religion, and not for Catholic superstition. For two years, van Swieten and the *vroedschap* did battle over the rights of Catholics to worship openly and over the allocation of church property.[41]

The policy of religious autonomy allied Gouda with other cities in Holland, most

[36] Eeghen, *Dagboek*, pp. 371–2.   [37] Hibben, *Gouda in Revolt*, pp. 73–4, 76 (quote).
[38] Kesper, "Goudsche vroedschap," pp. 393–5.
[39] *Ibid.*, p. 396. After St. Jan's was reopened, soldiers plundered the church and the *vroedschap* had to close it again.
[40] Hibben, *Gouda in Revolt*, p. 102.   [41] Kesper, "Goudsche vroedschap."

The reformation of community

notably Leiden, against ongoing Calvinist efforts to organize a presbyterian form of church government separate from civil control. During the intermittent negotiations between the States of Holland, the stadholder, and church officials from 1572 to 1620, Gouda's *vroedschap* consistently refused to approve the calling of Reformed synods, to sanction a national church order, and even to recognize the authority of a supralocal ecclesiastical body. In March 1582, the *vroedschap* declared that the resolutions of the Synod of Middelburg were "against liberty," and in January 1586 the magistrates stated that "issues of religion and conscience are matters only for God to judge."[42] From 1582 to 1607, the city government sought to shield their Libertine minister, Herman Herbertszoon, from ecclesiastical proscriptions against him, and it would not even permit him to appear at synods to answer his critics.[43] In essence, the Gouda magistrates made the local Reformed Church into a municipal institution.[44] Given Gouda's hostility to an independent church, it would seem likely that the magistrates opposed the church's claim to appoint its clergy and church officers, to discipline its members, to reform popular culture, and to operate an independent diaconate.

Beyond a couple of short-lived disputes with several ministers in the 1570s, these issues really never came to a head in Gouda as they did in other cities. The reason that they generated so little conflict is because of the negligible size of the Reformed congregation until the early 1580s. Although sparse source material prevents a clear assessment of the size of the congregation, contemporary estimates suggest that it was very small. Hibben has also demonstrated the pastoral and organizational weakness of Gouda's Reformed ministry until the arrival of Herbertszoon in 1582. And, until 1579, no minister served for more than two years in Gouda.[45] Unfortunately, the lack of contemporary records leave most of the questions posed by this study unanswered. By 1574, the church in Gouda did have a consistory and a diaconate, although it is impossible to assess the scope of their activity.[46] Given the outlook of local magistrates on church matters, it would seem likely that the *vroedschap* played a large role in selecting elders and deacons and supervising their operations.

While it is not clear how deacons functioned in Gouda, a diaconate had no significant influence on municipal poor relief. In fact, Ignatius Walvis, the eighteenth-century city chronicler, asserted that "the public religious changes in no way changed care for the poor." According to Walvis, poor relief officers in Gouda continued to care for all of the poor.[47] On the other hand, Walvis was a Catholic

---

[42] *GAG. Vroedschapboeken*, vol. XLVI, fol. 196r (January 14, 1586).
[43] They refused to let Herbertszoon attend the synodal meeting in 1586 and would not allow him to debate Arent Corneliszoon in 1591: *ibid.*, fols. 206r (July 1, 1586), 207r (July 22, 1586), 307–8 (September 11, 1591).
[44] Van den Berg, "Herman Herberts," p. 25; Hibben, *Gouda in Revolt*, pp. 103–11.
[45] Hibben, *Gouda in Revolt*, p. 112.
[46] *GAG. Vroedschapboeken*, vol. XLV, fol. 81v (November 4, 1574).
[47] Walvis, *Gouda*, vol. I, pp. 203–4.

164

priest in Gouda and so his views about the contributions of Reformed poor relief might be somewhat tainted. Nevertheless, it seems not unlikely that the diaconate in Gouda operated under the watchful eye of the magistrates. Due to the hostility of the magistracy to an independent Reformed ministry, the organizational weakness of Gouda's church before 1582, and the leadership of Herbertszoon, it is likely that an independent diaconate became subjugated to municipal control in the early 1570s and continued to function as a component of municipal welfare throughout this period.

DUAL POOR RELIEF: HAARLEM AND AMSTERDAM

A very different outcome in poor relief arrangements took place in the cities of Haarlem and Amsterdam. Ironically, the factors that led to a merger in Leiden resulted in a dual poor relief system in Haarlem. The languishing beer and textile industries, combined with high levels of southern immigration, put great stress on Haarlem's poor relief institutions. The magistracy in Haarlem was also wary of Reformed Calvinism and pursued a vigorous pluralistic religious policy after the city came into the rebel camp permanently in 1577. Also similar to Leiden, the Haarlem consistory exhibited both strong Calvinist and Libertine sentiments.

Unlike in Leiden, however, Haarlem magistrates divided poor relief along confessional and civic lines. Yet, by doing so, the city fathers in Haarlem pursued the same goal as their counterparts in Leiden, albeit with a different strategy. That is, the Haarlem city government attempted to cordon off Calvinist charity and thereby limit Reformed influence in the civic community. This approach attests both to the various alternatives that were possible and to the strong degree of municipal autonomy during a period in which the role of the new church was highly ambiguous.

Joining the Revolt at roughly the same time as Haarlem, Amsterdam exhibited a profile more in common with Dordrecht than with Leiden and Haarlem. In the city on the Amstel, the consistory had close ties to a city government dominated by Calvinists. As a result, the Amsterdam magistrates gave a great deal of support to the Calvinist cause and permitted the consistory to establish a diaconate independent of, yet supported by, municipal regents. For very different reasons, therefore, Haarlem and Amsterdam permitted the Reformed Church in their cities to establish an independent diaconate that would serve only the needs of the church poor.

In Haarlem, the prince of Orange approved thirty-three magisterial candidates after the city joined the Revolt in August 1577. Of this number, nine were new members, and seventeen had served from 1572 to 1577 when Haarlem was under Spanish domination. Only seven had held their posts before 1572. Protestants also acquired significant representation in the magistracy. Of the sixteen whose religious inclinations can be detected, eleven were Protestant and five were Catholic.[48]

---

[48] Spaans, *Haarlem*, p. 53.

6.1 Jacob van Loo, *Allegory on the distribution of bread to the poor.*
Amsterdam Historical Museum, Amsterdam

The fact that twenty-four other members of the *vroedschap* left no record of their religious affiliation suggests perhaps that a majority of the members exhibited little outspoken affection for Calvinism.

While this observation must be taken somewhat tentatively, nevertheless the policies of the *vroedschap* attempted to safeguard the political power of Haarlem's leading families and to restrict the confessional influence of Calvinism. Joke Spaans has argued that the Haarlem magistracy worked to maintain a multi-confessional society during this period.[49] This magisterial policy was a continuation of a long tradition of patrician governance which upheld the notion that the city was a sacred and civic body under its direction. For this urban elite, the public church, be it Roman Catholic or Reformed, was to serve the interests of the city.

After 1577, the magistrates in Haarlem pursued a pluralistic religious policy that attempted to protect dissenting groups and place controls on the Reformed Church. Indeed, Haarlem maintained a reputation in the Low Countries as a Libertine city that protected all forms of worship from coercion by the Calvinist consistory. If the *vroedschap*'s religious policy stemmed from its conception of the civic community, it also was an attempt to revive domestic manufacturing through attracting skilled artisans from the southern Low Countries.[50] As a result, the city of Haarlem was home for a number of diverse confessional groups that experienced growth throughout the late sixteenth and early seventeenth centuries, which included Catholics, Mennonites, Lutherans, and later Remonstrants.

The anti-Catholic edicts passed by the *vroedschap* between 1581 and 1602 notwithstanding, practitioners of the Roman faith continued to make up a confessional majority of Haarlemmers after the emergence of the Reformed Church in 1578.[51] Sizable spiritual communities of lay Catholic women, called *klopjes*, numerous priests, and canons continued to abide in Haarlem and practice their faith largely undisturbed in *schuilkerken* (hidden churches) in the early 1600s. Haarlem was also a local center for an active Catholic missionary organization, known as the Holland Mission, which attempted to restore Hollanders to Holy Mother Church. As long as the *vroedschap* was assured that these missionaries were not a political threat to the Republic or the city, they could proselytize with little magisterial interference.[52]

Mennonites also boasted a large congregation in Haarlem throughout the early modern period and Haarlem was an important publication center for Anabaptist literature. The city government even permitted a small Jewish population, numbering around fifty families, to worship in a synagogue. In articulating their decision in this case to the outraged Reformed consistory, the *vroedschap* stated that the war against Spain was not fought for Calvinism but to defend the privileges of the city, which included religious freedom.[53] The Haarlem *vroedschap* envisioned

[49] *Ibid.*, pp. 52–3. [50] *Ibid.*, pp. 91–101; Briels, *Zuidnederlandse immigratie*, p. 132.
[51] Overmeer, *Haarlem*, pp. 121–2. [52] Spaans, *Haarlem*, pp. 75–9.
[53] Briels, *Zuidnederlandse immigratie*, pp. 132, 145.

the Reformed Church as the public religious body in the corporate civic community. And it attempted to ensure that the church functioned in that capacity.

In order to accomplish this aim, the magistracy allowed the consistory to discipline its congregation and the diaconate to provide alms to the church poor, as long as church officers confined these activities to members and as long as they did not exclude anyone from baptism, marriage, and public worship. Consequently, the Calvinist Church of Haarlem both supported the magistrates' ideal of a sacred civic community and maintained a confessional congregation for true believers.

Throughout this period, the Reformed diaconate in Haarlem operated independently alongside municipal poor relief. Funded through church collections, donations, and testaments, and from a portion of the former property of the Catholic Church, deacons attempted to provide assistance only to the needy within their eucharistic community.[54] In 1594, the ministers, elders, and deacons took on the additional responsibility of supporting southern immigrants who were Reformed Church members.[55] Since the early 1580s, the *vroedschap* had tried to attract skilled artisans from Flanders and Brabant in order to revive the city's flagging textile industry. By the mid-1580s though, this influx began to strain Haarlem's poor relief agencies, since many immigrants came into the city with few resources.[56] At least as early as 1586, the *vroedschap* had endeavored to accommodate these non-natives by creating a separate body of "southern almoners" to serve all immigrants from Flanders and Brabant regardless of religious persuasion. A percentage of the revenues from former monastic property was earmarked to support this poor relief effort. Eight years later, the consistory lessened the burden of the southern almoners by appointing the diaconate to serve southern immigrants who had belonged to the Reformed Church in their previous domicile.[57] Beyond alleviating the burdens of the southern almoners, the church's action signifies a Reformed understanding of community. The "household of faith" cut across national lines and incorporated all of the elect, those who embraced "the religion" and participated in the community's eucharistic meal.

In 1597, the *vroedschap* proposed that the consistory should incorporate the diaconate within municipal poor relief. According to this plan, a centralized college of almoners, including deacons, would be formed to meet the needs of all the poor in Haarlem. The consistory and deacons considered the proposal, but unanimously

[54] After 1581, deacons of the Dutch Reformed and Walloon Church received a portion of the incomes from monastic property. In the 1590s, this amount averaged 600 guilders per year, a sum that tripled by 1618 and continued to increase after 1620: Spaans, *Haarlem*, p. 182.
[55] *GAH. Kerkeraad*, vol. 1 (July 24, 1597).
[56] The city government also wanted to make sure that these newcomers did not supplant the political power of the leading families of Haarlem. The *vroedschap*, therefore, kept these non-Hollanders from gaining political influence in the city. In 1606, the *vroedschap* declared that all members of this exclusive college be native Haarlemmers, refusing to grant a seat to a Brabanter: Briels, *Zuidnederlandse immigratie*, p. 135.
[57] *GAH. Kerkeraad*, vol. 1 (July 29, 1594). The southern almoners continued to serve immigrants from Flanders and Brabant until 1598: Spaans, *Haarlem*, p. 176.

rejected centralization because the church officers believed it would undermine the apostolic integrity of the diaconate.[58] Subsequently, poor relief in Haarlem continued to be divided along communal lines, confessional and civic. Thus, throughout this period, the ministers, elders, and deacons remained committed to a confessional vision of poor relief, by consistently upholding an independent diaconate for members and by shouldering the burdens of Reformed refugees.

Internally, diaconal charity also exhibited the confessional orientation of Reformed charity present throughout Holland. Like all church members, the poor who received assistance from the deacons were subject to church discipline. For the poor, however, censure for moral transgressions could entail more than an interdiction from the Lord's Table; it could also mean a prohibition from church alms. Thus, discipline was a powerful mechanism to whip the community into shape and to compel those who received assistance to live in conformity to consistorial demands.

Joke Spaans has contended that all poor relief institutions in the city, municipal and ecclesiastical, conformed to the principles of humanistic poor relief. Furthermore, Spaans has argued that deacons categorized the "deserving poor" within their community and provided relief for their individual needs.[59] While this interpretation accurately depicts the dual structure of poor relief in Haarlem at the end of the sixteenth century, it obscures the internal operation of confessional charity. The humanist concept of the "deserving poor" was not synonymous with the confessional demands imposed upon poor members of the Reformed Church. According to the humanist definition, those who merited public assistance were incapacitated people or resident workers who through no fault of their own could not sustain themselves or their families. Recipients of poor relief, according to humanists, should attempt to employ themselves honestly and must not squander their alms in taverns, gambling houses, or brothels, or fall further into indebtedness.

The concept of the deserving poor and the behavioral guidelines for recipients fit those of the Reformed Church only to a certain point. These principles fell short of the church's demand that the poor must be members of the "household of faith." Centered on the doctrine of predestination, the Dutch Reformed Church perceived itself as a body of elected believers, atoned for by Christ's sacrifice, and set apart from a sinful world. Under the direction of the consistory, deacons of the Reformed church provided relief only to members who were in good standing. This status not only enjoined members from unseemly public behavior, but it also required that they hold to the doctrinal tenets of the Reformed faith. Consequently, poor relief was inextricably intertwined with discipline, and the function of the former cannot be understood outside the context of the latter. Those who violated the behavioral or doctrinal norms outlined by the church jeopardized simultaneously their membership in the community and their access to diaconal poor relief. Because the

---

[58] *GAH. Kerkeraad*, vol. I (March 23, 1597).   [59] Spaans, *Haarlem*, pp. 173, 181.

consistory in Haarlem, as elsewhere, envisioned poor relief as a means to achieve its community-forming objectives, the requirement of confessional identity was as important as the condition of poverty. Consequently, the consistory in Haarlem took steps to prevent poor people outside the congregation from receiving alms. Poor travelers had to produce an *attestatie*, indicating their home church, their good standing, and their specific travel plans. Later in 1613, the church council attempted to deter poor residents from joining the church simply to receive alms by resolving that a minister would interview all prospective members to determine if their motives were of a religious nature.[60]

Unlike the bitter relations in Leiden, the consistory and *vroedschap* displayed a much greater degree of cooperation in Haarlem. The *vroedschap* granted subsidies to both the Flemish and Dutch Reformed deacons and allotted portions for city-wide collections to each.[61] The notable exception to peaceful cooperation began around 1612 during the heightened religious tensions induced by the Remonstrant controversy. Opponents of Calvinism on the *vroedschap* charged the consistory with attempting to create a theocracy that precluded the traditional religious freedoms of Haarlemmers. As the *vroedschap* and the consistory vied for political leverage, the struggle centered around the issue of selecting ministers. In principle, the *vroedschap* held to the 1591 Church Ordinance that gave magistrates the right to approve a ministerial candidate before he would be given a call to local service. This ordinance was discussed but not adopted by the States of Holland, and was bitterly opposed by Calvinist church leaders. That the Haarlem *vroedschap* would cling to it suggests the pluralistic orientation of the magistracy. By virtue of their status as the Christian authority in the city, the members of the *vroedschap* maintained their prerogative to provide leadership in the public ecclesiastical institution that was to serve municipal community. For their part, the consistory rejected the legitimacy of this ordinance because they believed it gave the city government overweening power in purely religious matters.[62]

The conflict over the 1591 Church Ordinance came to a head in 1615 as church officers and city leaders labored to call two new ministers to Haarlem. While the consistory was divided over the 1591 Ordinance, the magistrates possessed a very definite desire that all new ministers would subscribe to it. In the ensuing negotiations, the magistrates approved of two orthodox candidates who supported the 1591 Ordinance: Daniel de Soutere and Dionisius Spranckhuysen. Although these ministers came to Haarlem, a pastor opposed to the statute, Adrian Jacobs Tetrode, and a number of elders came to resist the calling of Spranckhuysen. In January 1616, Tetrode denounced the *vroedschap* for overriding the church council's will in the selection procedure.[63] Subsequently, a few weeks later, the *vroedschap* dismissed

[60] *GAH. Kerkeraad*, vol. I (July 21, 1613).
[61] *GAH. Vroedschapresolutien*, vol. VII, fols. 223v–224r (November 25, 1595), 257 (October 12, 1596), 259r (November 5, 1596).
[62] Briels, *Zuidnederlandse immigratie*, pp. 133–5, 138.   [63] *Ibid.*, pp. 138–9.

the entire consistory in order to purge the strict Calvinist elements from the Reformed Church in Haarlem. Even though the other ministers attempted to reconcile Tetrode with Spranckhuysen and the city council, Tetrode began to administer communion in a separate service. This action initiated a split in the Reformed Church in Haarlem between the religious factions and their partisans that lasted until 1618. At that time, a stronger Contra-Remonstrant presence in the magistracy, which coincided with the Synod of Dordrecht, forced Spranckhuysen and supporters of the statute out of the Reformed Church in Haarlem.[64]

If these conflicts had any effect on Reformed poor relief, the financial result was positive. The greatest subsidy the *vroedschap* authorized for the diaconate came during the height of the bitterness. Between 1598 and 1616, the diaconate received less than 14 percent of the total allocations of the monastic property that went to poor relief. During the turbulent years from 1616 to 1618, the *rentmeester* of the spiritual property increased this allotment to 20 percent of poor relief appropriations. In terms of cold hard guilders, the diaconate received 1,200 guilders in 1616, 1,400 in 1617, and 1,800 in 1618 (200 of which went to the Walloon deacons). Furthermore, municipal subsidy for poor relief continued to rise dramatically after 1620, reaching an apex of 2,500 guilders in 1624. Spaans has surmised that the tensions between the *vroedschap* and consistory could have contributed to these increased subsidies, as the former tried to limit the damage of religious schism by pacifying the diaconate.[65] If the Haarlem *vroedschap* did try to mollify the diaconate during a period of strained relations, it was but one of many approaches among the cities of Holland. During the same controversy in Leiden, the magistrates placed greater limitations on the activity of the diaconate. Thus, the case of Haarlem shows that a city government's pluralistic religious policy could coincide with a consistory's efforts to control charity within the network of its ecclesiastical structure.

The relationship between the diaconate and municipal poor relief in Amsterdam paralleled Haarlem's settlement. Charity in both cities became split along confessional and civic lines. Yet, the political complexion of Amsterdam's magistracy was very different from that of Haarlem and the economic profile of Amsterdam was unique among the cities of Holland. Consequently, Amsterdam offers a case study of relations between Reformed charity and municipal poor relief in a city where a magistracy proved highly sympathetic to Calvinist confessional aims and where the Reformed diaconate was well endowed. In a city of great wealth and with a government supportive of Calvinism, wealthy patrons in the Amsterdam church equipped the diaconate with an enormous endowment that enabled it to operate unconstrained by financial impediments. The Reformed-friendly *vroedschap* posed no significant threat to an independent diaconate even during the Remonstrant controversy of the early seventeenth century.

[64] Spaans, *Haarlem*, pp. 211–19.   [65] *Ibid.*, p. 182.

Shortly after joining the side of William the Orange in 1578, the magistracy in Amsterdam was purged of the uncompromising Catholic faction (the *Dirkisten*) who had held power since 1538. The leader of this party, Hendrik Dirkszoon, never again sat on the *vroedschap* after 1578. Ten of the fifteen Protestant leaders who had opposed Dirkszoon in 1564 served as burgomasters between 1578 and 1588. In addition, Protestants filled all four burgomaster positions after the *alteratie*. In the new *vroedschap*, thirteen members were strong Calvinists who had fled Amsterdam in 1567 after the city chose to remain loyal to Philip II. Thirteen other members were moderate Protestants who had not been implicated in the tumultuous events of 1566 and 1567, and ten members were Catholics who had supported the rebellion.[66]

The composition of the new city government after 1578 provided a magistracy that was cooperative with the Amsterdam consistory and diaconate. The real political power in the magistracy was held by exiled Protestants such as Maarten Coster, Adriaen Cromhout, Dirck Janszoon de Graeff, and Adriaen Pauw. The Amsterdam city government was to all intents and purposes a closed oligarchy who continued to hold the reins of power by coopting family members into the *vroedschap*. Sixteen members of the 1578 *vroedschap* were followed by family members, while thirteen of the seventeen burgomasters from 1578 to 1590 were sons or sons-in-law of previous burgomasters.[67]

The *vroedschap*, however, was not originally dominated by strident Calvinists. The first generation of Reformers who sat on the *vroedschap*, called "old beggars," worked peacefully with Catholics loyal to the Republic who had matriculated back into regent circles to pursue the common interests of the merchant city.[68] Nevertheless, the dramatic changes in the city government after 1578 enabled Calvinist Reformers to establish close ties with a magistracy that would lend support to an independent Reformed diaconate.

At the turn of the century, a number of magistrates much more concerned with confessional orthodoxy assumed leadership in the city government. These magistrates came to power during the period in which theological disputes over predestination became intertwined with hotly contested political issues. The two primary antagonists were the stadholder, Prince Maurice of Orange, and Johannes Oldenbarnevelt, pensionary of the States of Holland. Maurice backed the Contra-Remonstrants and advocated war with Spain at the end of the Twelve Years' Truce (1621), whereas Oldenbarnevelt championed the Remonstrant cause and resisted renewal of the war. Amsterdam stood at the center of these conflicts. And the victory of Prince Maurice over Oldenbarnevelt in the northern Netherlands and the Contra-Remonstrant triumph at the Synod of Dort owed a great deal to the support of the triumphant Calvinist party in Amsterdam.

---

[66] Elias, *Amsterdamsche regentenpatriciaat*, pp. 6–9, 19–25.
[67] Carl Bangs, *Arminius: The World of the Dutch Reformation* (Grand Rapids, Mich., 1985), pp. 105–6.
[68] Elias, *Amsterdamsche regentenpatriciaat*, pp. 22–3, 28–9.

In terms of the local relationship between the magistracy and the consistory, regents such as Reynier Pauw, Gerrit Jacob Witsen, Barthold Cromhout, Frans Hendrickszoon Oetgens, and Claes Franszoon. Oetgens allied themselves with an orthodox church council led by Pieter Plancius and Jacob Trigland.[69] These magistrates, in concert with the consistory, promoted the Contra-Remonstrant cause in the Republic, launched an West Indies trading company, and supported Maurice's opposition to prolonging peace with Spain.[70]

The Remonstrants, however, also had support in the Amsterdam magistracy. The burgomaster C. P. Hooft, whose words were quoted at the beginning of this chapter, was one of the most vocal and prolific critics of confessional Calvinism. The most important Remonstrant historian of the seventeenth century, Geraerdt Brandt, relied heavily on Hooft's criticisms to portray Calvinists as intolerant, bloodthirsty schismatics.[71] Working alongside Hooft were Lauren Jacobszoon Real, Jacob Arminius' father-in-law, as well as P. C. Boom and C. van Teyligen, friends of Arminius.[72] These magistrates believed that asserting governmental control over the church would promote the measure of religious freedom necessary for a merchant city. Consequently, they became strong supporters of Oldenbarnevelt and fierce adversaries of confessional Calvinism.

The dominance of the Calvinists in the city government and a consistory committed to Reformed orthodoxy enabled the deacons to confine poor relief to church members and to count on a good deal of financial assistance from the government with no significant intervention. The Reformed diaconate in Amsterdam served poor members in the Dutch Reformed Church, not those of other Protestant congregations. This distinction often proved difficult to manage because several poor members were married to spouses from other congregations. The consistory negotiated an arrangement with the Walloon church, whereby the deacons of the respective congregation would provide relief to families of which the husband belonged to the particular church. In May 1595, the Dutch consistory extended this principle to widows, so that, if a husband who was a member of the Walloon church died, the Walloon deacons would continue to support his unmarried widow, even though she was a member of the Dutch congregation.[73]

Financially, the Amsterdam diaconate was unique in Holland in that it operated from a substantial chest, despite the fact that the *huiszitten meesters* continued to collect alms in the Nieuwe and Oude Kerken after the Reformation.[74] According to their annual accounts, the deacons never operated in the red after 1578 and usually

---

[69] Johan E. Elias, *De vroedschap van Amsterdam, 1578–1795*, 2 vols. (Haarlem, 1903), vol. I, p. lv.

[70] Elias, *Amsterdamsche regentenpatriciaat*, p. 50.

[71] Geraerd Brandt, *Historie der reformatie en andere kerkelijke geschiedenissen in en omtrent de Nederlanden*, 4 vols. (Amsterdam, 1671–1704), vol. II, pp. 248–9.

[72] Bangs, *Arminius*, p. 235.   [73] *GAA. Kerkeraad* (May, 25, 1595).

[74] The deacons did win the concession to take collections in Reformed churches built after 1578: Evenhuis, *Ook dat was Amsterdam*, vol. II, pp. 21, 77.

had a significant amount of surplus revenues.[75] The deacons obtained their revenues from voluntary donations, testaments, and house-to-house collections from members. The Amsterdam diaconate also received annual subsidies from the city government from a 1,000th penny on VOC (Dutch East India Company) transactions.[76] In addition, the magistracy made annual grants to the diaconate.[77] For this reason, the Amsterdam diaconate was able to provide occasional assistance to a number of other poorer congregations in the Low Countries throughout this period. From 1578 to 1587, they sent relief to Reformed churches in Schoonhooven, Oudewater (both in 1578), Enkhuizen (1581), Brussels, Oosteinde, Utrecht (all in 1583), Antwerp, Dordrecht (both in 1584), and Arnhem (1587).[78] For the purposes of this study, providing assistance to Reformed congregations outside the city, the province, and the Republic suggests a distinctive Calvinist vision of community. They envisioned Christian community to be the supralocal "household of faith"; consequently they provided relief to help maintain that body throughout the Low Countries.

Because of the Reformed sympathies on the *vroedschap* from 1578 to 1620, the diaconate worked comparatively smoothly with city authorities in Amsterdam. In 1583, the city government proposed a union of the diaconate with the *huiszitten meesters*, but when the consistory objected to the plan, the deacons were allowed to continue to operate independently of the municipal almoners. In fact, the deacons cooperated with the *huiszitten meesters* to ensure that poor relief recipients did not receive relief from both agencies. The deacons supported poor church members, while city almoners distributed charity to those who fit the definition of the "deserving poor."[79] Again in 1598, when Amsterdam magistrates centralized parish charity, the diaconate remained independent from municipal oversight.

Also working independently of municipal and Calvinist poor relief agencies were other religious organizations that included a wide spectrum of dissident groups consisting of foreign Protestant churches, Catholics, and Mennonites.[80] This

---

[75] In 1579, the deacons reported that receipts outpaced expenses by 536 guilders. This figure rose to 994 guilders in 1585, 3,306 guilders in 1595, and 25,289 guilders in 1605: Commelin, *Amsterdam*, vol. I, pp. 489–90.

[76] Evenhuis, *Ook dat was Amsterdam*, vol. II, p. 75; van Manen, *Armenpflege in Amsterdam*, p. 50.

[77] In the city treasury records, mention is made in 1621 that the annual subsidy to the deacons would be raised from 3,120 to 3,600 guilders, indicating the level of support the diaconate received from the city government: GAA. *Thesaurien*, nr. 1, *Resolutien, Notuleringen en Verbalen 1594–1657*, fol. 76v (February 19, 1621). In addition to these subsidies, the Reformed deacons received 100 Flemish pounds from the church wardens of the Oude Kerk and 1,200 Flemish pounds from the church wardens of the Nieuwe Kerk in 1602: Wagenaar, *Amsterdam*, vol. II, p. 151.

[78] On some occasions the consistory did appeal to the burgomasters to help them raise funds for these churches: GAA. *Kerkeraad* (October 9, 1578; December 30, 1578; January 6, 1581; April 28, 1583; October 4, 1583; December 18, 1583; January 24, 1584; November 7, 1584; February 21, 1587).

[79] Evenhuis, *Ook dat was Amsterdam*, vol. II, pp. 74, 78; van Deursen, *Bavianen*, p. 106; van Manen, *Armenpflege in Amsterdam*, p. 52.

[80] Evenhuis, *Ook dat was Amsterdam*, vol. II, p. 73. For a study of Mennonite poor relief in Amsterdam, see Mary Susan Sprunger, "Rich Mennonites, poor Mennonites: economics and theology in the Amsterdam Waterlander congregation during the golden age," Ph.D. thesis, University of Illinois (1993).

division of poor relief among the civic corporation on the one hand, and confessional communities on the other, signified the transition from the old ideal of the city as a unified corporate body into a society composed of different confessional groups under the protection of the magistracy.[81]

UNIVERSAL POOR RELIEF: DORDRECHT AND DELFT

The most important city in the southernmost corner of Holland during the late sixteenth century, Dordrecht became one of the most thoroughly Reformed municipalities during the Dutch Reformation. The success of the Calvinist Reformation in Dordrecht stemmed from the political support of an oligarchic magistracy that identified itself with the religious and social agenda of staunchly Reformed ministers, such as Hendrik van Corput, Johannes Roermond, Johannes Becius, and Jeremias Batinghuis.[82]

Before 1572, Dordrecht's city magistrates had remained loyal to the central government in return for the count of Holland's continued support for the staple privilege. When the Sea Beggars captured Den Brielle in April 1572, Dordrecht's river trade came to a halt, provoking a great deal of social unrest. A Protestant faction in the ruling elite, led by Adrian van Bleyenburg, Cornelis van Beveren, and Jacob Muys van Holy, used this turmoil and the anti-Spanish sentiments of the militia to stage a *coup d'état* in the city government. Van Bleyenburg appealed to Orange for assistance in June 1572 and, when the Beggar troops arrived, the militia refused to defend the city.[83]

The capitulation to the Orangist side enabled the Protestant families of van Beveren, de Witt, and Muys van Holy to tighten their grip their on political power and to oust their Catholic counterparts, the Oems and Drenckwaerts. In political terms, the Revolt and Reformation accelerated the movement toward a closed regent oligarchy, a process that had already been underway throughout the most of the sixteenth century.[84] Unlike many city governments in Holland, the ruling elite in Dordrecht embraced the strict confessional brand of Calvinism and worked to support its aims in the city. If a city's response to the 1574 Provincial Synod of Dordrecht serves as any sort of religious index, the city of Dordrecht was wholly Calvinist. The Dordrecht magistrates adopted it only days after the conclusion of the synod.[85] This Protestant oligarchy retained political power at least through the 1630s, a factor that ensured Calvinism's triumph and made Dordrecht one of its strongest centers in Holland.

This cooperative environment in Dordrecht was the result of two factors: the magistracy's preference for Reformed Calvinism and the social background of church officers. Throughout the Reformation period, the magistracy called ministers from regent backgrounds and the church elected officers from the social elite in

---

[81] See Roodenburg, *Onder censuur*, pp. 72–104.   [82] Elliott, "The classis of Dordrecht," pp. 154–5.
[83] *Ibid.*, pp. 146–8.   [84] *Ibid.*, pp. 149–69.   [85] Balen, *Dordrecht*, p. 850.

Dordrecht. From 1573 to 1579, an average of three magistrates (of fourteen) were elders and an even larger component of the militia were church officers. In addition, four church officers per year served on the magistracy from 1573 to 1589. This percentage continued to rise until it peaked at nine of fourteen during the first decade of the seventeenth century. Although most of the ministers came to Dordrecht from the southern Low Countries, they came from patrician families and many intermarried within the local elite in Dordrecht.[86] Consequently, pastors and regents in this city were united by social background, kinship ties, and religious confession.

During the same period in which the Leiden magistracy protected the "Libertine" minister Caspar Coolhaes from his confessional rivals, the city government in Dordrecht worked to exclude heterodox ministers. In 1582 the city council terminated the appointment of Herman Herbertszoon for failing to preach from the Heidelberg Catechism and for expressing latitudinarian opinions from the pulpit. It was at that point that Herbertszoon went to Gouda. The victor in this episode was Hendrik van der Corput, whom the magistrates called to Dordrecht in 1578. From a regent family in Breda, van der Corput served exiled Dutch Calvinist churches in the Palatinate before 1572.[87] He became the leading pastor in Dordrecht during the church's formative years and worked closely with the magistracy to implant confessional Calvinism in the Dordrecht church.

The Reformed church in Dordrecht grew relatively quickly from 368 communicants (out of a municipal population of 10,000) in 1573 to 800 in 1580.[88] The congregation continued to grow throughout the early seventeenth century, in part due to the influx of refugees from the southern Netherlands. It has been estimated that southern refugees made up one-third of Dordrecht's population in 1621. A cooperative relationship between the consistory and magistracy, combined with a burgeoning membership, enabled the church to dominate the social and religious life of Dordrecht and the surrounding region. The Mennonites in Dordrecht proved to be the strongest rival confession and even took members away from the Reformed Church until 1600, when the Calvinist church began to attract significant numbers of Mennonites.[89]

Conversely, the Catholic Church in Dordrecht had virtually no presence during the initial years of the Reformation. Priests left the area in the 1570s and the Holland Mission did not establish a foothold in Dordrecht until 1605.[90] By the end of the 1630s, Catholicism did begin to reassert itself, claiming 1,800 followers served by four clergy.[91] Despite the persistent complaints of Calvinist ministers, the Catholic revival in Dordrecht was dwarfed by Roman successes in other cities in Holland.

Even the most thorny dispute within Dutch Calvinism, the Remonstrant contro-

---

[86] Elliott, "The classis of Dordrecht," pp. 154–5.
[87] *Ibid.*, p. 154; van den Berg, "Herman Herberts," p. 21.
[88] Jensma, *Uw rijk kome*, p. 2; Elliott, "The classis of Dordrecht," pp. 157–8.
[89] Elliott, "The classis of Dordrecht," pp. 255–6.   [90] Rogier, *Katholicisme*, vol. II, pp. 382–5.
[91] Elliott, "The classis of Dordrecht," p. 304.

versy, did not play itself out dramatically in the city. A Calvinist clergy, supported by the magistracy, thwarted any significant doctrinal deviance and organization of an Arminian presence.[92] Thus, the city of Dordrecht, like the national synod that met there in 1618–19, stands out as a landmark of Dutch Calvinism's success in Holland.

It was in this context that the Reformed Church in Dordrecht established its diaconate. After the *overgang*, the church established a consistory and set about the task of implementing a diaconate. The earliest extant consistorial records indicate that in June 1573 both ministers and "some of the magistrates who had confessed their belief [in the Reformed religion]" nominated a double number of candidates for elders. Out of this number, the consistory would select the elders for the upcoming year. In the following month, the same process was used to select eight deacons.[93] At least from the consistory records, it appears that the ministers and lay leaders in the Dordrecht Church had no qualms about allowing magistrates to participate in the selection of church officers. This cooperation stands in stark contrast to situations in Leiden, Haarlem, and Delft where at certain moments during this period city governments and consistories clashed over the role of magistrates in the selection of church officers. The unity of the magistracy and consistory in Dordrecht indicates that, in political circumstances favorable to Calvinism, ministers permitted magisterial participation in important church matters, provided that those magistrates were of a Reformed persuasion.

Due to the strong Calvinist influence among the magistrates, poor relief in Dordrecht became a joint operation between the city government and the consistory. For their part, the magistrates conceded primary jurisdiction over the diaconate to the consistory. In 1578, the ministers and elders divided the city into quarters in order to establish greater supervision over discipline and poor relief. The deacons appeared every month to give a financial report to the consistory. Afterwards, a consistorial delegation would meet with a burgomaster, who was also a church member, to discuss the deacon's finances.[94] This arrangement reflected the relationship between Reformed poor relief and the Dordrecht magistracy. The city government recognized consistorial control over the diaconate, yet it collaborated with the consistory to ensure the financial well-being of Reformed poor relief.

While the ministers and elders superintended the affairs of the diaconate, the city government did give the deacons a significant amount of financial support. The burgomasters allocated revenues for the deacons and permitted them to take city-wide collections, at first on an *ad hoc* basis, and after 1604 every two months.[95] These revenues, combined with weekly church collections, bequeathed testaments, and donations from wealthy members, helped underwrite the burgeoning expenses of diaconal poor relief in Dordrecht.[96]

[92] *Ibid.*, pp. 205–8.   [93] Jensma, *Uw rijk kome*, p. 1 (June 14, 1573 [quote]); see also p. 3.
[94] *Ibid.*, pp. 69, 97–8, 156.   [95] Elliott, "The classis of Dordrecht," p. 363.
[96] In February 1578, the consistory decided to solicit the "rich brothers of the congregation" to meet the needs of church members. For this entry and several other examples of voluntary donations, testaments, and appeals to magistrates, see Jensma, *Uw rijk kome*, pp. 18, 97, 103, 157.

As a result of firm magisterial support in a city dominated by the Calvinist church, the Reformed deacons bore the lion's share of poor relief in the city. The deacons did not displace the traditional parish relief organ. Thus, while the *Heilige Geest* in Dordrecht made some significant contributions to the poor relief network in the city, it paled in comparison with the efforts of the diaconate. Throughout this period, the deacons assumed the primary responsibility for the *huiszitten* poor in Dordrecht. On at least one occasion, the consistory directed the deacons to meet with the *Heilige Geestmeesters* to coordinate their efforts and to try to devise more effective ways to help the poor.[97]

Despite its extensive efforts in municipal poor relief, the consistory made it clear to the deacons that their first task was to care for poor church members. In November 1574, several months after the Provincial Synod of Dordrecht which stipulated that only deacons could provide for members, the consistory reiterated this protocol for the Dordrecht deacons. The consistory gave them three instructions:

First, that above all they should give consideration to those needy members of our community so that they will be cared for. Secondly, that they should distribute alms without any suspicion. Thirdly, that they should specify in their accounts what people receive alms, so that the consistory will know whether or not the recipients are members and how the alms are spent.[98]

The diaconate provided relief to the poor of the entire city, while placing particular emphasis on needy church members. This classification indicates that the Dordrecht diaconate functioned simultaneously as a public charitable organization and the exclusive poor relief agency for members.

There is some evidence that the ministers were somewhat ambivalent about operating such a comprehensive poor relief program. For, in 1580, Hendrik van der Corput wrote Arent Corneliszoon asking him if the Delft deacons extended distributions to those outside the church or if they confined charity only to members.[99] While there is no record of any further discussion between van der Corput and Corneliszoon over this issue, van der Corput's query suggests that the burden for administering relief to most of the poor in the city was possibly an unintended consequence of the Calvinist demand to care for its own members.

Certainly the task of operating a relief system for all the city's inhabitants posed more difficulties for the deacons than confining charity only to members. And there are hints in the consistory records that financial problems weighed heavily on the diaconate and the consistory. In response to the deacons' financial complaints in August 1579, the consistory resolved to draw up a committee of deacons, elders,

---

[97] *GADR. Kerkeraad* (July 14, 1585).
[98] *Ibid.*, p. 24. The entry notes that some of the deacons expressed reservations about these instructions, although it is not clear what their particular objections were. The consistory agreed to discuss disputed issues over the next two weeks. If that discussion took place, there is unfortunately no record of it.
[99] Wouters and Abels, *Nieuw en ongezien*, vol. II, p. 212.

and ministers to formulate a better way to support the poor and to "teach them to be industrious."[100] Throughout this period, the consistory sought to find new sources of income to fund the diaconate. They frequently asked the magistrates for more support and for permission to take collections.[101] In addition, the consistory attempted to relieve the administrative load on the deacons by asking the magistrates to appoint extra officials to help with bookkeeping, beggars, and travelers.[102]

These demands, combined with van der Corput's request, suggests that the church officers had some reservations about the extensive character of diaconal poor relief in Dordrecht. They were clearly willing to assist non-members, but it was another matter altogether to assume responsibility for the *huiszitten* poor of the entire city. Yet the deacons shouldered this responsibility in order to ensure that an independent Reformed agency could provide charity to the poor in the "household of faith."

This particular arrangement in Dordrecht also resembled the poor relief arrangements in Delft, another relatively strong Calvinist city in southern Holland. Until 1614, when the deacons merged with the municipal institution, the *Kamer van Charitate*, an independent diaconate also played a strong role in the city's poor relief network. Like the Dordrecht diaconate, Delft deacons enjoyed a great degree of autonomy. Yet the dilemmas and difficulties that faced the Dordrecht diaconate became magnified in Delft, due to a higher level of poverty and a magistracy that was often less than sympathetic to Calvinism.

Like Leiden, Gouda, and Haarlem, Delft's city government was rather dubious about the public establishment of the Reformed Church.[103] Only three months before the *overgang* in August 1572, the *schepenen* had issued an ordinance against "songs and the outburst of rebellious language," which was no doubt aimed at Calvinists.[104] And very little displacement occurred in the magistracy in the aftermath of the Beggar triumph in Delft. Only six new members matriculated into the *vroedschap* and all regents maintained their previous positions.[105] Furthermore, after the *overgang*, one of the *schepenen*, four burgomasters, and eleven of the forty-member *vroedschap* were royalist and Catholic.[106] Even Christian van der Goes, the *schout* who prosecuted a number of heresy cases against Protestants in Delft, retained his post until 1577.[107] Delft magistrates also joined Leiden and

---

[100] Jensma, *Uw rijk kome*, p. 174.
[101] *GADR. Kerkeraad* (November 17, 1580; July 14, 1585; November 5, 1585; December 8, 1585; December 10, 1587; December 23, 1587).
[102] Elliott, "The classis of Dordrecht," p. 362. Incidentally, the consistory proposed to the magistrates in 1613 that the city institute a House of Discipline (*Tuchthuis*) to combat begging.
[103] Boogman, "De overgang," pp. 105–8.   [104] Quoted from Wijbenga, *Delft*, vol. II, p. 10.
[105] The prince of Orange intended to replace the entire college, but the *vroedschap* resisted, insisting that this wholesale replacement violated the original promises made before the city went over to the Orangist side: Boogman, "De overgang," p. 110. The six new regents were installed on December 18, 1572: Boitet, *Delft*, p. 83.
[106] Van Dijk, "Bedreigd Delft," p. 185.
[107] M. A. Kok, "Opkomst van protestantisme," p. 108; Boitet, *Delft*, pp. 131–2.

Gouda in blocking approval of the 1578 National Synod of Dordrecht in the States of Holland, because they believed that it granted the clergy far too much authority in the public church.[108]

The high level of continuity in the Delft magistracy meant that Reformed Church leaders had to work with a municipal government that had distanced itself from the Reformation before 1572. Continuity also confronted Delft Reformers with an age-old conception of the church's role in society that went against their confessional understanding of poor relief. Reminiscent of the Catholic Church's function in pre-Reformation Delft, the *vroedschap* considered the new church largely a public institution that should serve the needs of the entire community.

Despite the continuity in the city government after 1572, there was a greater degree of collaboration between the magistracy and the consistory in Delft than in Leiden and Gouda, albeit less cooperation than in Amsterdam and Dordrecht. J. J. Woltjer has attributed the stability to the personal and social connections between the two bodies. Thomas Tilius and Arent Corneliszoon, the two most prominent ministers, worked doggedly to sustain a favorable relationship with the *vroedschap*. The son of a Delft burgomaster, Corneliszoon grew up in Delft and returned in 1573 to shepherd the congregation there until his death in 1605. Corneliszoon, the church's most prominent minister, became the consistory's primary delegate in its relations with the magistracy.[109]

Beyond Corneliszoon's family connections to the regent class in Delft, a number of church officers also belonged to the magistracy. At least twenty-six church officers served in these municipal capacities from 1572 to 1620.[110] By 1584 one of the four burgomasters, three of the seven *schepenen*, and the *schout* served either as elders or as deacons. From 1584 until 1620, there were only six years in which at least one church officer did not serve as a burgomaster: 1586, 1587, 1601, 1608, and 1616. At no time, however, did church officials occupy a majority of the four burgomaster positions. After 1609, consistorial representation in the magistracy began to fall off dramatically. Between 1610 and 1620, church officers held more than two of twelve seats in the Wet (the combined college of burgomasters,

---

[108] Hibben, *Gouda in Revolt*, p. 108.

[109] Woltjer, "Een niew ende onghesien dingh," p. 12. Also see Jaanus, *Hervormd Delft*, pp. 94–5. The parallel social standing of church and civic leaders in Delft corresponded to the situation in most cities of Holland. A. Th. van Deursen has argued that the so-called conflict between church and state in Holland was usually confined to the regent class, as urban leaders staked out the boundaries of religious and temporal jurisdiction: van Deursen, *Bavianen*, p. 92.

[110] These dual officers were: Adrien Vincenten Sweys, A. Hendrickszoon van Giessen, Arent Gysbrechtszoon Stolk, B. Jacobszoon vander Dussen, B. Janszoon vander Block, C. van Adrichem, C. Hendrickszoon Verburch, Claes Teuniszoon Hodenpijl, Dirk Harmenszoon de Haen, D. Jacobszoon van Voorburch, Gerrit Franszoon Meerman, G. Janszoon van Graswinkel, H. F. Duyst van Voorhout, H. J. Bruynszoon vander Dussen, I. Lambrechtzoon vander Wel, Jacob Adrianszoon Pauw, Jacob Franszoon Duyst, Jan Janszoon Graswinckel, J. Pieterszoon Hoefijser, Joris Willemszoon, M. Willemszoon vander Hoeff, P. Joostenszoon van Ruyven, P. Wouterszoon vander Burch, Willem Arenszoon vander Burch, W. Jacobszoon van Voorburch, and W. Janszoon de Milde. See Boitet, *Delft*, pp. 307–492; Jaanus, *Hervormd Delft*, pp. 234–44.

schepenen, and *schout*) only once, in 1611. Church officers claimed two positions in 1610, 1612, 1613, 1615, and 1615 and only one in 1614, 1616, 1617, and 1620 (see appendix 6.1). By virtue of the presence of church officers in the city government, the Reformed Church had a significant degree of leverage in Delft. By no means, though, did this influence always enable Calvinists to get what they wanted. Most religious issues in Delft were settled only after extended negotiations between magistrates and ministers.

The consistory with which the magistracy had to negotiate remained solidly Calvinist throughout this entire period. From 1573 to 1605, Arent Corneliszoon played a leading role in trying to establish a Calvinist church order in the Reformed Churches of Holland and the Netherlands. Along with Reynier Donteclock, another Delft pastor, Corneliszoon sparred with more moderate Reformed ministers such as Caspar Coolhaes and Jacob Arminius. Likewise, in the early seventeenth century, orthodox Calvinists such as Henricius Arnoldi, Daniel van Dolegen, Albertus van Oosterwijck, and Josias Heinsius dominated the Delft consistory.[111]

The composition of the magistracy and the consistory's ties to the city government account for the relationship between the diaconate and charitable institutions in Delft. Throughout the period from 1572 to 1614, deacons carried out their duties under the authority of the consistory without any significant municipal oversight. They collected alms, decided who merited how much relief, kept a register of recipients, distributed charity, maintained records of their accounts, and gave monthly financial reports to the consistory.

In 1597, when the city government began to make plans to establish the *Kamer van Charitate*, the burgomasters proposed that the deacons merge with city almoners. Given the chronic deficits of the diaconate (discussed pp. 185–7), this proposal presented a dilemma for church leaders and in September 1597 they summoned an extraordinary meeting of all current officers as well as those who had served over the past two years to discuss the issue. After some deliberation, the consistory rejected the merger because the deacons maintained that it would violate "the apostolic example" of Reformed charity.[112]

The consistory opted for apostolic integrity over financial security, revealing the tenacity with which they would cling to their vision of a diaconate rooted in the offices of the church. For these ministers, elders, and deacons, Reformed charity was a function of the "household of faith" and an independent diaconate was crucial to maintaining its confessional character. The magistrates made it clear to the consistory that they were not altogether happy with the consistory's decision, but nevertheless they permitted them to remain independent.[113]

As the consistory began to lose representation in the city government in 1610, relations between the clergy and lay magistrates became increasingly strained. Arent Corneliszoon died in 1605 and the church officers who had entered the

[111] Bangs, *Arminius*, pp. 293, 312; Wouters and Abels, *Nieuw en ongezien*, vol. I, p. 164.
[112] *GAD. Kerkeraad* (September 26, 1597).   [113] *Ibid.* (September 29, 1597).

magistracy in the 1570s and 1580s also began to die off. Although other church officers entered the magistracy during the 1600s, their numbers were far fewer. While it is unclear whether this lack of representation was a cause or a result of local religious tensions in the 1610s, it is apparent that the weak financial base of Reformed charity led Delft magistrates to take a dim view of an independent diaconate. Consequently, in January 1614, the city government issued an ordinance that merged the diaconate with the *Kamer van Charitate* under magisterial authority.[114] Unfortunately, consistorial records between 1613 and 1616 are uncharacteristically meager, making it difficult to determine the attitude of church leaders. It is more than likely that the consistory felt that these measures and the principle of a merger compromised the confessional integrity of the diaconate that church leaders had defended throughout the past forty years.

The records do show, however, that in the ensuing negotiations related to the merger, the consistory fought tenaciously for several years to retain certain confessional characteristics of diaconal charity. The consistory sought to place the deacons on an equal footing with regents of the *Kamer* and to keep the church poor distinguished from non-members. In 1614, the city fathers had stipulated that eight deacons should serve alongside the twelve municipal regents. The unequal ratio meant that the deacons could be consistently outvoted by the city almoners over the administration of poor relief.[115] Not only did the deacons suffer from unequal representation, but in February 1616 the city government informed the consistory that the magistrates had decided to adopt the 1591 Church Order.[116] The consistory mounted a strong protest,[117] because the adoption of the 1591 resolution would give the city government control over the election of elders and deacons. Given the turbulent religious troubles in the Netherlands, the Delft magistracy, although firmly Contra-Remonstrant, decided to assert greater authority over the church.

The magistrate's decision fueled continued controversy over the relationship between deacons and almoners in the *Kamer*. The church officers sought to regain control over church elections, to place the diaconate on an equal footing with almoners, and to ensure that the deacons could maintain a separate system of relief for members. By the summer of 1617, the magistracy and consistory reached an accord on these issues. With respect to the election of church officers, the *vroedschap* allowed the consistory, with "assistance" from two magistrates, to nominate candidates. Before the consistory elected the officers, the burgomasters were to approve all nominees.[118] In the following month, the *vroedschap* granted the diaconate equal representation in the *Kamer*; six deacons would work in conjunction with six municipal almoners. Unfortunately for the consistory, however, the

[114] *GAD. Wetresoluties*, vol. 1, fols. 10v–11r (January 28, 1614).
[115] Wouters and Abels, *Nieuw en ongezien*, vol. 11, p. 245.
[116] *GAD. Kerkeraad* (February 22, 1616).   [117] See, for example, *ibid.* (February 26, 1616).
[118] *GAD. Burgermeesteren*, nr. 1165, *Accort tusschen de magistraten ende kerckenraet er stadt Delft opt beroepen van predikanten en aanstellen van ouderlingen en diaconen*, July 22, 1617.

vroedschap prohibited the deacons from administering charity for members separately and from giving additional assistance to church members.[119] Working within the framework of this resolution, the consistory countered a few days later with five provisions that would allow the diaconate to retain some semblance of confessional charity. The consistory proposed that: (1) six deacons would serve alongside six almoners; (2) deacons, with assistance from two almoners, would distribute charity to Reformed members on a separate day; (3) deacons and almoners would collectively revise the poor register for the winter and summer; (4) deacons could provide a maximum of twelve stuivers in extraordinary assistance to members in exceptional destitution; (5) deacons would send two deputies to assist the almoners with non-church members.[120] Despite the new provisions, the Reformed Church eventually lost any real control over poor relief for members. For it appears that, at least by 1621 and probably earlier,[121] the almoners had disregarded the provision that the deacons could give extraordinary stipends to members. The consistory protested to the almoners, but they responded that they treated all recipients equitably and that it was simply unnecessary for deacons to assist members outside the *Kamer*.[122]

Thus, by 1620, deacons and regents of the *Kamer van Charitate* worked collectively to administer all aspects of charity to the poor in Delft. The consistory was able to give deacons equal representation and to defend a separate day for distributions to church members. The *Kamer* distributed charity three times per week: Mondays and Fridays for non-members and Saturdays for church members.[123] The separate distribution for members suggests that the church leadership in Delft continued to maintain a distinction between the poor within "the household of faith" and the poor outside the religious community. But, by 1620, the special day was merely a symbol of the aspirations of Reformed charity: an independent diaconate for the eucharistic community. At the same time, it epitomized the blend of confessional identity and religious pluralism that shaped Dutch culture in the aftermath of the Reformation.

Underlying the particular institutional arrangement in Delft were two pressing issues that faced Reformed poor relief throughout late sixteenth-century Holland. Under what circumstances should deacons provide assistance to non-members? How was the diaconate to fund poor relief? The rich church archives in Delft reveal how one consistory confronted these problems, and they shed further light on the interaction between Calvinist charity and municipal poor relief.

From the outset of the church's public emergence in Delft, the church officers were not averse to giving charity to non-members. In October 1574 the consistory

[119] Wouters and Abels, *Nieuw en ongezien*, vol. II, p. 246.   [120] *GAD. Kerkeraad* (August 21, 1617).
[121] On two occasions in January 1620, the consistory appealed to magistrates for permission to administer charity separately to members, but the magistrates did not approve the requests: *ibid.* (January 3, 1620; January 27, 1620).
[122] Wouters and Abels, *Nieuw en ongezien*, vol. II, pp. 246–7.   [123] Wijbenga, *Delft*, vol. II, pp. 81–2.

donated 400 guilders for the purchase of shoes for the poor in the city.[124] And, in a petition for financial support to the magistrates in August 1580, three elders complained that half of the poor that the deacons supported "do not profess the religion."[125] Anton Wouters and Paul Abels have shown that the deacons took on an even more substantial role in assisting the *huiszitten* poor in the city by the early seventeenth century. In 1607, the year in which the deacons drew up a comprehensive poor relief register, three-quarters of the 633 recipients were not church members.[126]

Even though the deacons assumed a primary role in the city's poor relief network, their doing so was a consequence of the church's insistence on maintaining an independent diaconate that would aid the church poor. The 1574 Provincial Synod of Dordrecht, in which Arent Corneliszoon played a prominent part, indicated that Reformers throughout Holland intended for deacons only to assist church members and for the *Heilige Geest* to care for everyone else. After the selection of new deacons that summer, the consistory informed them of the duties of their office based on the provisions of the Dordrecht synod.[127] In spite of these resolutions, there is some evidence that the Delft consistory had already decided to permit diaconal charity for non-members. Wouters and Abels have argued that, either by the end of 1573 or the beginning of 1574, the consistory made a conscious choice to give assistance to non-members. They cite a notation written by Arent Corneliszoon on the back side of a letter written by Wessel Valck to the Delft ministers, which was dated November 18, 1573. The notation stated that

Since one should especially help and care for the household of faith with alms, the willingness and generosity of the hand at home should also extend to those outside the community if those who are outside are not assisted as the others. The brothers have decided that because of the circumstances those outside and inside will be helped equally. If those who are inside still come short, the well-to-do members of the community will be enjoined to [help] them. Because the members of Christ should especially demonstrate their beliefs out of love, just as it is especially important to assist the poor members.[128]

What were the "circumstances" that led the Delft consistory to decide that the deacons should offer relief to non-members? The war with Spain had devastated

[124] *GAD. Kerkeraad* (October 27, 1574).
[125] *Ibid.* (August 22, 1580). In an earlier article I have argued that the deacons gave charity only to non-members. Since the article was published, Anton Wouters and Paul Abels have shown that I was mistaken. They located a consistory resolution written on the back side of a piece of correspondence, which declared that the consistory did consent to provide relief to non-members. They also correlated a list of church members with a diaconal register of 1607 to show that most relief recipients were not church members. Although I was in error on this issue, the central argument of the article remains valid. The Dutch Reformed Church functioned both as a public church for everyone and an exclusive confessional community for members. For my previous argument, see Charles H. Parker, "Public church and household of faith: competing visions of the church in post-Reformation Delft, 1572–1617," *Journal of Religious History* 17 (1993), pp. 418–38.
[126] Wouters and Abels, *Nieuw en ongezien*, vol. II, pp. 238–9.
[127] *GAD. Kerkeraad* (August 1, 1574).   [128] Wouters and Abels, *Nieuw en ongezien*, vol. II, p. 215.

the lands of the *Heilige Geestmeesters* so seriously that their annual incomes fell from around 10,000 guilders before 1574 to 2,248 guilders in 1576.[129] Throughout the late sixteenth and early seventeenth centuries, Delft's economy suffered from blockaded rivers, meager harvests, outbreaks of the plague, and high rates of immigration from the southern Low Countries. Attempting to build a religious community that exemplified Christian love, the Reformed consistory could not neglect the plight of the poor in Delft.

The city government also put pressure on church leaders to relieve the needs of the poor in the entire municipal corporation. Magistrates considered it the duty of the public church to assist in providing for the welfare of all inhabitants, especially in these critical circumstances. In September 1573, they had allowed the church to select its own officers and to operate an independent diaconate supported by church collections. From time to time, the magistrates permitted the deacons to take city-wide collections to augment their deficient revenues. From the point of view of the magistracy, these privileges obligated the deacons to cooperate with the *Heilige Geest* and to assist the needy throughout the municipal community.[130] The consistory also recognized that it could not fund an independent diaconate for church members without the political and financial support of the city government.

The consistory was willing to concede such a burdensome task to the deacons in order to preserve the diaconate's exclusive relationship to the church poor. Corneliszoon underscored this mandate in justifying assistance to non-members in the consistory entry. Elsewhere Corneliszoon wrote that "the alms of Christ are collected and distributed so that the poor member of our Lord Christ will not be neglected."[131] The church officers, then, placed the highest priority on church members and distinguished them from the city poor.[132] To provide adequately for poor members, the consistory attempted to augment the diaconal chest by urging the congregation to give liberally, taking special collections, and reminding the sick to remember the church poor in their testaments.[133]

The consistory's assertion of an independent diaconate for church members carried a high price tag for the diaconate. Since the deacons received church collections and occasionally obtained a modicum of support from the city government, the Delft magistrates required that the deacons assume a primary role in providing outside relief. Thus, Delft deacons shouldered the primary burden for

---

[129] *Ibid.*, pp. 212–13.
[130] When the consistory appealed to the burgomasters for permission to take a collection in January 1579, they consented with the proviso that the alms should be distributed to all poor burghers and not just members of the Reformed Church: *GAD. Kerkeraad* (January 21, 1579).
[131] *GAD. ACC*, nr. 100.
[132] Johannes Uytenbogaert observed that the deacons in Delft, at least in the early seventeenth century, referred to non-member recipients as the "political poor": Uytenbogaert, *Historie*, p. 799.
[133] For examples, see *GAD. Kerkeraad* (August 24, 1573; March 8, 1574; August 22, 1578; December 31, 1578; November 13, 1581; September 1, 1586).

outside relief in the municipal community, mainly because they wished to assist the poor of the eucharistic community.

Another related problem the Delft deacons faced was inadequate funding. The diaconal balance sheet continuously operated in the red. From 1597 to 1609 expenditures outpaced receipts over 400 guilders per month, while the monthly deficit rose to over 600 guilders from 1610 to 1613.[134] Church officers and wealthy members of the congregation often had to make up these deficits through loans or outright donations. But the primary strategy the consistory used to increase the deacon's revenues was to petition the magistrates for financial help.

On a number of occasions, the city government did authorize city-wide collections or make grants for the deacons.[135] By the mid-1580s, the church officers, led usually by Corneliszoon, began to ask the burgomasters to devise a steady source of funding for the diaconate.[136] From 1586 to 1598, consistorial delegates came before the burgomasters regularly to appeal for a structural solution to their shortfall.[137] Often citing bad management on the part of the deacons, the burgomasters refused to create a municipal basis of financial support for the deacons.[138]

The only really serious comprehensive resolution the city government offered was to merge the diaconate with the *Kamer van Charitate* in 1597. As we have seen, the ministers, elders, and deacons rejected the proposal because it violated the "apostolic" character of the diaconate. The impasse meant that the diaconate would continue to shoulder the burden of not only poor members, but also an increasing percentage of the *huiszitten* poor in a period of economic difficulty in the city.

Between 1598 and 1614, the Reformed diaconate faced increasing deficits as they took on greater responsibilities for the *huiszitten* poor in the city. Heavily in arrears in 1600, the deacons complained to the consistory in March that there was little hope that the magistrates would cover their deficits. Furthermore, the deacons protested that, when they tried to shorten their register for the summer season, they were confronted with all sorts of complaints by the poor.[139] After discussing the matter in two separate meetings, the only suggestion the consistory could offer was to "use as much discretion as possible" to investigate the needs of the poor.[140] It does not appear that the deacons were successful in paring down their registers. For the number of recipients the deacons served continued to grow and they denied assistance only to recipients who had committed moral offenses.[141]

Nor was the consistory able to secure a significant financial commitment from

---

[134] Wouters and Abels, *Nieuw en ongezien*, vol. II, p. 235.
[135] For several examples, see *GAD. Kerkeraad* (October 4, 1577; December 24, 1578; January 21, 1579; September 28, 1579; December 19, 1583; September 24, 1582; July 2, 1584; February 27, 1589; February 25, 1591; May 22, 1595; December 22, 1609).
[136] *Ibid.* (December 20, 1586).
[137] *GAD. Resolutieboeck*, vol. II, fol. 80r (June 9, 1586); *GAD. Kerkeraad* (April 6, 1587; August 6, 1590; September 24, 1590; October 22, 1590; November 12, 1590; November 22, 1593; March 6, 1595; January 20, 1597; June 9, 1597).
[138] *GAD. Kerkeraad* (September 24, 1590).   [139] *Ibid.* (March 27, 1600).
[140] *Ibid.* (April 4, 1600; April 17, 1600).   [141] See ch. 5, apps. 5.3–5.5, pp. 152–4.

the burgomasters. In December 1608, the burgomasters consented to a one-time city-wide collection for the diaconate.[142] Two years later, the consistory asked the burgomasters to help fund the diaconate, but they refused, saying the elders and ministers should involve themselves more directly in poor relief matters.[143] Due to the increasing financial difficulty, the magistrates finally merged the deacons with the *Kamer van Charitate* in 1614.

URBAN POOR RELIEF AND CHRISTIAN COMMUNITY IN HOLLAND

The introduction of a Reformed diaconate in the cities of Holland necessitated an extensive reconsideration of municipal poor relief. For opponents of Calvinism, like Hooft and Uytenbogaert, exclusive charity for a eucharistic community shattered the ideal of civic solidarity. In spite of the two different types of settlements in Haarlem, Amsterdam, Dordrecht, and Delft, the resident poor became classified according to community, either religious or civic. Only in Leiden and Gouda, cities whose regents pursued a determined Libertine policy and whose consistories were divided or lacked a Calvinist presence, did magistrates preserve the traditional ideal of municipal charity.

Despite the different local outcomes, the arrangements that were worked out between 1572 and 1620 made the magistracies and the consistories joint partners and paralleled the distinct blend of municipal culture and church life that characterized Dutch society in the seventeenth century. This negotiated process was a reformation of both the old municipal corporation and confessional Calvinism. The pluralistic policies of municipal governments combined with the confessional aspirations of Calvinists led to the formation of a multi-confessional society in Holland.

Poor relief organization in the six cities also indicates that the economic crises and religious reformations did not inaugurate a secular approach to poverty. The sharp contrast between public (i.e., governmental) assistance and religious charity often used to analyze early modern poor relief simply does not work for Holland. Calvinist deacons worked alongside or under the authority of city officers, private benefactors contributed to municipal revenues allotted for poor relief, and parish almshouses continued to serve an important charitable function. Furthermore, the motivations for helping the poor remained as religious as they were social.

There was a distinction between confessional and municipal religious charity in seventeenth-century Holland. The negotiations that produced the three types of institutional arrangements difference did not erode the communal bases of charity

---

[142] *GAD. Keurboek*, vol. V, fol. 257 (January 4, 1609). From 1598 to 1614, the deacons did receive several additional income sources from a portion of excises on various goods, local fines, and voluntary donations at marriages: Wouters and Abels, *Nieuw en ongezien*, vol. II, p. 236. While the revenues from these sources were not insignificant, they were insufficient to meet the financial burdens of the diaconate. The deacons were forced to make up these deficits through loans and donations from wealthy benefactors.

[143] *GAD. Kerkeraad* (September 27, 1610; October 25, 1610; November 1, 1610).

that had characterized urban poor relief for centuries. The Dutch case, therefore, shows that the relationship between private charity and public welfare was a much more complex struggle, between a confessional and a sacral vision of Christian community. The late sixteenth century certainly marked a turning point in state involvement in social provision, but it did so in Holland with a great deal of conflict and collaboration with church authorities.

Appendix 6.1 *Number of church officers in the Delft magistracy, 1574–1620*

	Burgomasters (total number of officers: 4)	*Schepenen* (total number of officers: 7)	*Schout* (total number of officers: 1)	Heren van Wet (total number of officers: 12)
1574	1			1
1575	1	2		3
1576		1		1
1577		2		2
1578		2		2
1579	1	2		3
1580	1	1		2
1581	1	1		2
1582		1		1
1583	1	2		3
1584	1	3	1	5
1585	1	4	1	6
1586		3	1	4
1587		4	1	5
1588	1	3	1	5
1589	1	4	1	6
1590	1	2	1	4
1591	1	2	1	4
1592	1	2	1	4
1593	2	2	1	5
1594	2	1	1	4
1595	1	2	1	4
1596	2	1	1	4
1597	2	2	1	5
1598	1	2	1	4
1599	2	2	1	4
1600	1	4	1	6
1601		3	1	4
1602	2	4	1	7
1603	1	4	1	6
1604	1	5	1	7
1605	2	5	1	8
1606	2	3	1	6
1607	1	2	1	4
1608		3	1	4
1609	1	3	1	5
1610	1	1		2
1611	2	1		3
1612	1	1		2

Appendix 6.1 (*cont.*)

	Burgomasters (total number of officers: 4)	*Schepenen* (total number of officers: 7)	*Schout* (total number of officers: 1)	Heren van Wet (total number of officers: 12)
1613	2			2
1614	1			1
1615	1	1		2
1616	1			1
1617	1			1
1618	1	1		2
1619	?	?		?
1620	1			1

Source: Reinier Boitet, *Beschryving der stadt Delft* (Delft, 1729), pp. 83–6; H. J. Jaanus, *Hervormd Delft ten tijde van Arent Cornelisz. (1573–1605)* (Amsterdam, 1950), pp. 234–44.

7

The pillars of a new society: religious pluralism and confessional identity in Reformation Holland

In March 1591, Tanneken van Bruijssel, a member of the Reformed Church in Delft, asked the consistory for a loan of ten to twelve Flemish guilders so that she could satisfy her creditors. On some occasions, church officers had consented to provide short-term loans to members in similar situations, so van Bruijssel's petition was not that unusual. And the deacons had given her alms on previous occasions. But the consistory turned down this particular request on several grounds: (1) the church had assisted her in the past, but she had not shown any moral improvement; (2) other members, whom the church had turned down, would cause a commotion if the consistory granted her a loan; (3) the burgomasters would not be pleased if they learned of the grant.[1] These reasons that the consistory gave for turning down Tanneken van Bruijssel's request for a loan point to three features of Reformed charity in the late sixteenth and early seventeenth centuries. First, discipline framed Calvinist charity; secondly, ordinary members exerted their own agency in the church's ministries; and, thirdly, church officers depended upon the favor of city magistrates to carry out Reformed poor relief.

Discipline was an inherent part of Calvinist charity. In this particular case in Delft, van Bruijssel had in fact transgressed Reformed values and flouted social convention. Four years earlier, she had entered into a sexual relationship with Otto Thomiszoon only a few weeks after her husband had died. When summoned before the consistory, van Bruijssel admitted to sleeping with Thomiszoon, but refused to admit to any guilt, because she claimed that "she had taken him for her husband," even though they were not married. Nor does it appear that she had any change of heart. From February 1587 to October 1590, various ministers and elders intermittently admonished and threatened her, and denounced her from the pulpit.[2] So, by the time that van Bruijssel appealed to the consistory in March 1591, she had exhausted the goodwill of the ministers, elders, and deacons. Van Bruijssel's steadfast refusal to subject herself to the discipline of the church compelled the consistory to withdraw the helping hand of Christian charity.

---

[1] The consistory also included a more practical reason: when the church agrees to this type of request, it never seems to work very well (*GAD. Kerkeraad* [March 18, 1591]).

[2] *Ibid.* (February 9, 1587). For the discipline procedures taken against her, see *ibid.* (February 22, 1587; October 12, 1587; January 4, 1588; February 15, 1588; October 23, 1589; December 4, 1589; January 29, 1590; February 5, 1590; February 12, 1590; August 27, 1590; September 24, 1590; October 1, 1590).

As this case indicates, church officers throughout Holland imposed strict moral regulations on relief recipients. Yet, Dutch Calvinists have often received unwarranted criticism for using charity to serve the interests of the church rather than the needs of the poor.[3] Ministers, elders, and deacons displayed an extraordinary degree of forbearance with poor folk who begged, fell into debt, drank too much, quarreled, failed to attend church regularly, mistreated family members, and committed sexual misdeeds. But if these sins brought public scandal or if the accused proved recalcitrant, consistories would cut off church alms.

At the same time, church officers continued to support many recipients even as they were admonishing them to show moral improvement. Calvinists also recognized that some poor people probably affiliated with the Reformed Church for pecuniary reasons. They treated them as they did all other recipients; deacons provided assistance when they believed circumstances warranted it and ministers and elders subjected them to the discipline of the church. Thus, the moral demands of Calvinist charity should not be understood simply as social control or as an attempt to "protestantize" the poor. Rather, the interaction between recipients and church officers was a highly complex process in which Calvinists attempted to balance the pressing economic needs of the poor with the moral standards of the church.

The religious discipline that framed Calvinist poor relief came out of a Calvinist vision of Christian community. Indeed, Ben Kaplan has recently shown that discipline itself was more than a process to exclude the unworthy from communion. According to Kaplan, discipline was a "cultural idiom for a confessional mode of piety," characterized by "boundedness, uniformity, hierarchy, moral rigour, and theocracy."[4] Reformed congregations belonged to a supralocal confessional community centered around a pure communion table. Calvinists believed that, without Christian charity and precise moral boundaries, such a community could not exist.

Secondly, ordinary members exerted a significant degree of agency in poor relief and discipline. The Delft consistory observed that when other members learned that someone with Tanneken van Bruijssel's reputation had received a loan, it would cause a commotion. No consistory could ignore public opinion, even in cities with relatively large congregations, like Amsterdam, Dordrecht, and Delft. To do so would undermine the position of the public church and cast dishonor on the confessional community. Ordinary members and townsfolk were quite visible in bringing to light the transgressions of others and in corroborating rumors circulating in their neighborhoods. In these situations, consistories quickly took steps to investigate the case, to reconcile offending parties, and to publicize the church's response to offensive behavior. This interactive discourse suggests that consistories were not imposing an alien moral code onto their congregations. Instead, the

---

[3] See Hooft, *Memoriën en adviesen*, p. 54; Uytenbogaert, *Historie*, p. 799; Rogier, "Protestantiseering," pp. 330–3; Roodenburg, *Onder censuur*, p. 112; J. A. de Kok, *Nederland op de breuklijn*, p. 11; Briels, *Zuidnederlanders*, pp. 276–8; Nusteling, *Welvaart*, pp. 164–5.

[4] Kaplan, *Calvinists and Libertines*, pp. 28–67.

concern for moral governance owed a great deal to the social and religious values of common folk.

Poor people also asserted themselves with diaconates and consistories. They quarreled with church officers over the extent of their allowance and they routinely secured additional assistance with promises of good conduct. If no support was immediately forthcoming, they would often threaten to beg or leave the city. Given the forceful agency of recipients, diaconates and consistories had to consider the broader ramifications of individual poor relief decisions. In these ways, the poor exerted a degree of leverage in their negotiations with church leaders.

Thirdly, the reach of Reformed poor relief depended upon the will of the local city government. In February 1591, when the Delft consistory rejected van Bruij-ssel's request, the diaconate was in a difficult bind. The deacons lacked a secure financial base to cover the expenses of outside relief. Complaining about deacons' great burden of feeding the poor, Arent Corneliszoon repeatedly appealed to the burgomasters for a perpetual basis of support and for short-term grants and collections in the 1590s. Although the burgomasters did occasionally make some concessions, they often accused the deacons of managing their resources incompetently. A loan at this time, especially to a woman of ill repute, would have raised suspicions about Corneliszoon's claims and, thereby, jeopardize any further financial support. The Delft deacons were not alone in needing the financial and political support of the city government, for the fate of an independent diaconate in all of the six cities relief upon the goodwill of the magistracy.

The city governments of Dordrecht, Haarlem, Delft, Leiden, Amsterdam, and Gouda had established a long history of regulating most aspects of parish charity. Urban patricians endowed parish foundations, selected regents to govern them, and defined the criteria for granting and denying charitable assistance. These activities were rooted in the sacral and civic traditions of urban culture in late medieval Holland which continued to influence the periodic reorganization of charitable organizations throughout the sixteenth century. City regents designated parish charity for the poor who belonged to the civic community and worked to restrict assistance to outsiders.

The peculiar nature of the Calvinist Reformation in the Netherlands brought these two very different visions of Christian community into conflict. Both city magistrates and Calvinist church leaders demonstrated a great deal of resolve in maintaining their own communal characteristics of charity and in some cases accommodating them to new political realities. In every city with a viable Reformed consistory (i.e., all but Gouda), Calvinists fought for an independent diaconate to serve the poor of the "household of faith."

As long as local consistories could accomplish this aim, they exhibited a considerable flexibility in negotiating poor relief arrangements with city governments. In Dordrecht and Amsterdam, cities in which Calvinists enjoyed unwavering municipal support, church deacons experienced very different relationships with parish poor relief officers. The Dordrecht diaconate became the primary outside relief agency for the entire city, whereas deacons in Amsterdam served only poor church members. The consistory in Dordrecht was willing to extend charity beyond the religious community because church officers gained jurisdiction over poor relief. Even there, however, the consistory charged the deacons to keep separate registers for non-members and members. Diaconal poor relief in Dordrecht, therefore, corresponded to the dual role of the Reformed Church in Dutch society. It was a distinct confessional body of members and it was the public church supported by the magistracy. Perhaps the presence of Calvinist adversaries in the city government of Amsterdam persuaded the consistory to resist the *vroedschap*'s invitation to merge the diaconate with the *huiszitten meesters* in 1583 and 1597. It is certain that, in this favorable political climate, the Amsterdam consistory was able to protect the independence of the diaconate and to acquire a significant degree of municipal patronage.

In Leiden and Gouda, cities that had the strongest opposition to confessional Calvinism among the local regents, the diaconate became subjugated to municipal control soon after the Revolt. This stance suggests a direct correspondence between a suspicion of Protestant confessionalism and a hostility to an independent diaconate. That is, non-Reformed magistrates recognized that the Reformed diaconate manifested a confessional vision of community that was at odds with the sacral basis of the civic corporation. Since the consistory was divided and had little or no representation in the city government, it became subject to the most stringent restrictions on all church affairs. With respect to poor relief, the Calvinists on the consistory in Leiden were left with no political maneuverability. Their only viable strategy was to protest and to encourage the deacons to keep a special eye out for poor members, for which they received a sharp rebuke from the magistrates in 1586. The meager Calvinist presence in Gouda ensured that there would be no significant diaconate and that it certainly would not operate under the lone authority of the consistory. Thus, city magistrates were able to muzzle the confessional tendencies in Calvinist poor relief and to appropriate the diaconate for municipal purposes.

If these two groups of cities represented opposite ends of the political spectrum, Haarlem and Delft lay somewhere in the middle. In both cities, the consistory enjoyed a degree of representation or influence with the city government, yet there was also significant opposition to confessional Calvinism. Throughout most of this period, consistories and magistracies in both cities cooperated, albeit uneasily, in the administration of poor relief. Nevertheless, the city governments followed two different policies. The Haarlem magistracy allowed the consistory to maintain an independent diaconate exclusively for members, an arrangement that would circumscribe Reformed influence among poor non-members. Furthermore, this strategy squared nicely with the poor relief goals of church officers, because it enabled the diaconate to operate along the confessional boundaries set out in Reformed synods. The Delft magistrates, on the other hand, sought to take advantage of the new poor relief agency by requiring that it provide charity to everyone in the city. The consistory was willing to abide by this demand so that the deacons could become the exclusive relief organization for its membership. The religious tensions of the Remonstrant controversy and the financial straits of the diaconate brought this arrangement in Delft to an end in 1614, when the magistrates incorporated the diaconate within the *Kamer van Charitate*. For comparative purposes, it is instructive to note that these conflicts never surfaced in the Contra-Remonstrant stronghold of Dordrecht, the only other city in which an independent diaconate provided outside relief to all the poor. Thus, the political negotiations over poor relief in Delft, as elsewhere, was based upon fundamental differences between two rival views of Christian community. Although the various settlements in these two cites stemmed from local circumstances, they reveal the conflict between confessional Calvinism and traditional civic culture in Reformation Holland.

The interaction between those who promoted a confessional vision of community and those who held to the legacy of the municipal corporation also left its mark on early modern Dutch society. After 1620, Dutch law-makers continued to protect the traditional forms of social interaction in the parish and to make room for private religious dissent. As a result, the Dutch Republic became a refuge to a diverse array of Protestants, Catholics, Spiritualists, Jews, and free-thinkers of every variety.[5] By virtue of its religious pluralism, the Republic ranked as one of the leading intellectual centers in western Europe.[6] Even today, the Netherlands boasts one of the most open societies in the world.

If the Dutch demonstrated a remarkable degree of religious and intellectual freedom, the United Provinces was also a Protestant Republic whose public life and moral standards were heavily influenced by an intolerant brand of Calvinism. Ministers publicly humiliated sinners from the pulpit, sought to eliminate "superstitious" elements of popular culture, and upbraided authorities for loose morals. In 1654, even Rembrandt van Rijn, who helped make Dutch domestic simplicity so famous, found himself the target of a church investigation on the charge of adultery.[7] In modern times, Dutch laws and customs still bear witness to a distinct Protestant outlook.

This odd coexistence resulted from a conflict between the pluralistic policies of city magistrates and the religious demands of Calvinist leaders in the late sixteenth and early seventeenth centuries. Ultimately both Calvinists and non-Reformed political officials were able to achieve their most cherished ambitions. As Ben Kaplan has shown quite convincingly, Calvinists obtained the right to confessional-

---

[5] The Reformed Church itself did not even reach numerical parity with the Catholic Church until the middle of the seventeenth century, almost eighty years after the public establishment of the Reformed Church. Currently, the largest single denomination in the Netherlands is the Catholic Church: van Lieburg, "Pure church to pious culture," p. 412; Pat Seward, *Cultures of the World: Netherlands* (New York, 1995), p. 72.

[6] See Israel, *The Dutch Republic*, pp. 889–935.

[7] For this case, see Roodenburg, *Onder censuur*, p. 230.

ize the Reformed Church, but magistrates successfully defended civic solidarity and retained their authority over urban life.[8]

The pluralistic policies of urban magistrates, combined with the confessional goals of Calvinist leaders, established a pattern of social organization known as pillarization (*verzuiling*) which became formalized in the nineteenth century.[9] Originating out of distinct confessional identities, parallel social pillars have formed the basic institutions in modern Dutch society. Distinguished by people holding to a set of values, pillars organized its members into communities (e.g. Reformed, Catholic, Socialist) and provided them with social services and political representation. The pillars instituted welfare agencies, schools, political parties, unions, newspapers, television channels, health insurance groups, and fraternal clubs for their members. Until the post-war period, when pillarization began to go into decline, it was possible for a Dutch person to carry out the normal routines of his or her life with little reference to those of different pillars. The Dutch government encouraged this communal organization by providing financial support and regulating the activity of each pillar's institutions, such as schools, television programming, and insurance pools.

If social organization in the Netherlands blurred boundaries between the religious and the secular, Dutch poor relief arrangements also show that private charity formed the basis for public welfare. Since the late middle ages, magistrates managed parish foundations based on the ideal that the city was a sacral and civic community. Calvinists operated from a confessional vision of community and placed priority on the poor in the "household of faith." From these different religious motivations, both Reformed deacons and municipal almoners worked together to provide assistance. Many studies of early modern social welfare, especially those situated in Protestant lands, have either implied or explicitly argued that the sixteenth-century poor relief program desacralized poverty and rationalized charity under the auspices of civil authorities. According to this schema, secular welfare agencies eliminated the need for outdated religious charity.

Recent studies of Counter-Reformation Spain and France have shown, however, that religious values continued to motivate benefactors well into the eighteenth century.[10] Likewise, Brian Pullan has recently suggested that notions of the civic

---

[8] Kaplan, *Calvinists and Libertines*, pp. 302–3.

[9] For some important studies on *verzuiling* and its effects, see L. Apostel and M. Bots, *Pluralisme en verdraagzaamheid* (Antwerp, 1966); B. J. DeClerq, *Kritiek van de verzuiling* (Lier, 1968); Robert H. Cox, *The Development of the Dutch Welfare State: From Worker's Insurance to Universal Entitlement* (Pittsburgh, 1993), especially pp. 58–95; A. Lijphart, *Verzuiling, pacificatie en kentering in de Neder-landse politiek*, 3rd edn. (Amsterdam, 1979); Harry Post, *Pillarization: An Analysis of Dutch and Belgian Society* (Brookfield, Vt., 1989).

[10] Flynn, *Sacred Charity*, pp. 144–5; Norberg, *Grenoble*, pp. 301–2. See also Colin Jones, *The Charitable Imperative: Hospitals and Nursing in Ancien Régime and Revolutionary France* (New York, 1989), and William J. Callahan, "The poor, the privileged, and the church in eighteenth-century Spain," in *Religion in the Eighteenth Century*, R. E. Morton and J. D. Browning, eds. (New York, 1989), pp. 103–16. An older but still important article on this theme is by Emmanuel Chill, "Religion and mendicity in seventeenth-century France," *International Review of Social History* 7 (1962), pp. 400–25.

"public good" and religious "good works" were complementary forces in the reform of charitable institutions throughout early modern Italy.[11] If religious philanthropy did indeed die out in Protestant lands, then poor relief in Holland bears a closer resemblance to charity in Catholic territories than to social welfare in Protestant ones. Confraternities, religious orders, and clerics in cities such as Toledo, Zamora, Grenoble, Paris, and Venice cooperated with civil authorities and contributed to municipal relief, yet attempted to retain control over distinctly religious charitable agencies. Calvinist leaders in the cities of Holland did much the same thing and also fought for an independent diaconate under ecclesiastical authority.

Thus, the fundamental social, economic, and religious changes of the sixteenth century did not forge a new frontier between private religious charity and public assistance in Holland. Poor relief organization in the cities of Holland drew from the dynamic communal character of parish life and the confessional aims of Calvinist charity. As such, negotiations over poor relief constituted a reformation of community that has left an indelible imprint on social life in Holland.

[11] Brian Pullan, "Private charity and public relief in early modern Italy," paper presented at "From Poor Laws to the Modern Welfare State: Private Charity and Public Assistance in Historical Perspective," Saint Louis University (St. Louis, Mo.), August 16, 1996. At the same conference, Anthony Brundage pointed out that old charitable impulses, informed by religious motivations, mitigated the effects of the 1834 Poor Law at the local level in Victorian England: Brundage, "Private charity and the 1834 Poor Law."

Sources cited

ARCHIVAL SOURCES

Amsterdam

GAA. Kerkeraad.
GAA. Keurboek, vols. F–H.
GAA. Memorialboek.
GAA. Predikanten.
GAA. Thesaurien, Resolutien, Notuleringen en Verbalen, 1594–1657.
GAA. Vroedschapresoluties, vols. IV–V, 1578–88.

Delft

GAD. ACC, nr. 99, *Beschrijvinghe des Ampts der ouderlinghen inder Ghemeijnte J. Christi.*
GAD. ACC, nr. 100, *Gebeden ende Meditaties*
GAD. ACC, nr. 300, *Wijkboekje van Arent Cornelisz. Crusius.*
GAD. Burgermeesteren.
GAD. Kamer, nr. 43, *Wetten en besluiten van overheidinstanties, memorien, en documenten, 1577–1777.*
GAD. Kamer, nr. 50, *Bedelaer boek, 1597–1610.*
GAD. Kerkeraad.
GAD. Keurboek, vols. III–VI, 1566–1623.
GAD. KrCor.
GAD. Memorialboek, vols. I–III, 1537–1653.
GAD. Memorialen.
GAD. Regle.
GAD. Resolutieboeck, vols. II–III.
GAD. Wetresoluties, vols. I–II, 1609–1719.

Dordrecht

GADR. Kerkeraad, Notulen van de vergaederingen van de Algemene Kerkeraad.

Gouda

GAG. Vroedschapboeken, vols. XLIV–XLVII, 1559–1624.

Sources cited

Haarlem

GAH. *Kerkeraad*, vol. I, 1589–1601.
GAH. *Kerkeraad, Predikanten*.
GAH. *Vroedschapresolutien*, vols. II, IV, VII–IX, 1522–1617.

Leiden

GAL. *Kerkeraad*.

PUBLISHED PRIMARY SOURCES

Breen, J. C., ed., *Rechtsbronnen der stad Amsterdam*, 2nd series, nr. 4, 's-Gravenhage, 1902.

Bucer, Martin, *De Regno Christi*, in *Melanchthon and Bucer*, Wilhelm Pauck, ed., Philadelphia, 1969, 155–394.

Calvin, John, *Institutes of the Christian Religion*, 2 vols., John T. McNeill, ed., Ford Lewis Battles, trans., Philadelphia, 1960.

Couquerque, L. M. Rollin, and van Embden, A. Meerkamp, eds., *Rechtsbronnen der stad Gouda*, 2nd series, nr. 18, 's-Gravenhage, 1917.

Eeghen, I. H. van, ed., *Dagboek van broeder Wouter Jacobsz. (Gualtherus Jacobi Masius) prior van Stein. Amsterdam 1572–1578, en Montfoort 1578–1579*, 2 vols., Groningen, 1959.

Elias, Johan E., *De vroedschap van Amsterdam, 1578–1795*, 2 vols., Haarlem, 1903.

Enschedé, A. J., and Gonnet, C. J., eds., *Kuerboeck der stadt Haerlem*, 's-Gravenhage, 1887.

Fruin, J. A., ed., *De oudste rechten der stad Dordrecht en van het baluwschap van Zuid Holland*, series 1, nr. 4, 2 vols., 's-Gravenhage, 1892.

Hooft, Cornelis Pieterszoon, *Memoriën en adviesen*, Utrecht, 1871.

Huizinga, J., *Rechtsbronnen der stad Haarlem in werken der vereeniging tot uitgraaf der bronnen van het Oud-Vaderlandsche Recht*, 2nd series, nr. 13, 's-Gravenhage, 1911.

Iterson, P. D. J. van, and Laan, P. H. J. van der, eds., *Resoluties van de vroedschap van Amsterdam, 1490–1550*, Amsterdam, 1986.

Jansma, Th. W., ed., *Uw rijk kome: acta van de kerkeraad van de Nederduits Gemeente te Dordrecht, 1573–1579*, Dordrecht, 1981.

Joosting, J. G. C., and Muller, S., eds., *Bronnen voor de geschiedenis der kerkelijke rechtspraak in het Bisdom Utrecht in de middeleeuwen*, vol. III, 's-Gravenhage, 1912.

Keuren ende ordonnantien opt backen van broot binnen deser stadt Leyden: opgelezen den negenden Decembris vijftien-hondert zes ende tnegentich, Leiden, 1596.

Kurtz, G. H., ed., *Haarlemsche stadsrecht van 1245: tekst der oorkonden*, Haarlem, 1945.

Laan, Ph. J. van der, ed., *Oorkondenboek van Amsterdam tot 1400*, Amsterdam, 1975.

Luther, Martin, *The Babylonian Captivity of the Church* (1520), vol. XXXVI of *Luther's Works*, Abdel Ross Wentz, ed., Philadelphia, 1959.

Reitsma, J., and Veen, S. D. van, *Acta der provincial en particuliere synoden, gehouden in de Noordelijke Nederlanden gedurende de jaren 1572–1620*, 8 vols., Groningen, 1892–98.

Resolutiën van de Staten van Holland, 278 vols., n.p., 1524/43–1793, vol. VI.

Rutgers, F. L., ed., *Acta van de Nederlandse synoden der zestiende eeuw*, 's-Gravenhage, 1889.

Salter, F. R., ed., *Some Early Tracts on Poor Relief*, London, 1926.

Sources cited

Schreveli, Theodorus, ed., *Haarlemias of eerts stichting der stad Haarlem*, 3 vols., Haarlem, 1754.

Soutendam, J., ed., "Het oudste keurboek van Delft," *Nieuwe Bijdragen van Regtsgeleerheid en Wetgeving*, new series, 2 (1876), 481–555.

SECONDARY SOURCES

Abel, Wilhelm, *Massenarmut und Hungerkrisen im vorindustriellen Europa: Versuch einer Synopsis*, Berlin, 1974.

Ailly, A. E. D', ed., *Zeven eeuwen Amsterdam*, 9 vols., Amsterdam, n.d.

Allan, F., *Geschiedenissen bescrijving van Haarlem van de vroegste tijden tot onze dagen*, 4 vols., Haarlem, 1883; reprint edn., 1973.

Alves, Abel Athouguia, "The Christian social organism and social welfare: the case of Vivès, Calvin, and Loyola," *Sixteenth-Century Journal* 20 (1989), 3–22.

Ampzing, Samuel, *Bescryvinge ende lof der stad Haerlem in Holland*, Haarlem, 1628; republished edn., 1974.

Andrew, Donna T., *Philanthropy and Police: London Charity in the Eighteenth Century*, Princeton, 1989.

Apostel, L., and Bots, M., *Pluralisme en verdraagzaamheid*, Antwerp, 1966.

Appleby, Andrew B., *Famine in Tudor and Stuart England*, Stanford, 1978.

Aston, T. H., and Pilpin, C. H. E., eds., *The Brenner Debate: Agrarian Class Structure and Economic Development in Pre-Industrial Europe*, Cambridge, 1984.

Aydelotte, Frank, *Elizabethan Rogues and Vagabonds*, New York, 1913.

Baart, J. M., "De materiële stadscultuur," in Baart, et al., *De Hollandse stad*, 93–112.

Baart, J. M., de Boer, D. H., Herwijnen, G. van, et al., eds., *De Hollandse stad in de dertiende eeuw*, Zutphen, 1988.

Balen, Jansz. Matthys, *Beschryvinge der stad Dordrecht*, Dordrecht, 1677.

Bangs, Carl, *Arminius: The World of the Dutch Reformation*, Grand Rapids, Mich., 1985.

Barrois, G., "On medieval charities," in McCord and Parker, *Service in Christ*, 65–79.

Bataillon, Marcel, "J. L. Vivès: réformateur de la bienfaisance," *Bibliothèque d'humanisme et Renaissance* 14 (1952), 141–59.

Becker, Marvin B., "Aspects of lay piety in early renaissance Florence," in Trinkhaus and Oberman, *Pursuit of Holiness*, 177–99.

Beeck Calkoen, Jan Frederik van, *Onderzoek naar den rechtstoestand der geestelijke en kerkelijke goederen in Holland na de reformatie*, Amsterdam, 1910.

Beier, A. L., *Masterless Men: Vagrants and Vagrancy in England, 1580–1640*, Cambridge, 1987.

Benedict, Philip, "The historiography of continental Calvinism," in *Weber's Protestant Ethic: Origins, Evidence, Context*, Hartmut Lehman and Kenneth F. Ledford, eds., Cambridge, 1993, 305–26.

Berg, A. J. van den, "Herman Herberts (ca. 1540–1607) in conflict met de gereformeerde kerk," in *Kerkhistorische opstellen aangeboden aan Prof. dr. A. J. van den Berg*, C. Augustijn, P. N. Holtrop, G. A. M. Postuhumus Meijes, and E. G. E. van der Wall, eds., Kampen, 1987, 20–9.

Bernoulli, Wilhelm, *Das Diakonenamt bei J. a Lasco*, Grifense, 1951.

Beuningen, B. van, *Het geestelijk kantoor van Delft*, Arnheim, 1870.

Biéler, André, *La Pensée economique et sociale de Calvin*, Geneva, 1959.

Biesterveld, P., Lonkhuizen, J. van, and Rudolph, R. J. W., *Het diaconaat: handboek ten dienste der diaconieen*, Hilversum, 1907.

Bleyswijck, Dirck van, *Beschryvinge der stadt Delft*, 2 vols., Delft, 1667.

Blickle, Pieter, *Gemeindereformation: die Menschen des 16. Jahrhunderts auf dem Weg zum Heil*, Munich, 1987.

Bloch, Camille, *L'Assistance et l'état en France à la vielle de la Révolution*, Geneva, 1909.

Blockmans, W. P., "Mobiliteit in stadsbesturen 1400–1550," in de Boer and Marsijle, *De Nederlanden in de late middeleeuwen*, 236–60.

Blockmans, W. P., Pieters, G., Prevenier, W., and Schaik, R. W. M. van, "Tussen crisis en welvaart: sociale veranderingen 1300–1500," in *NAGN*, vol. IV, 42–86.

Blockmans, W. P., and Prevenier, W., "Armoede in de Nederlanden van de 14e tot het midden van de 16e eeuw: bronnen en problemen," *Tijdschrift voor Geschiedenis* 88 (1975), 501–38.

Blok, P. J., *Geschiedenis eener Hollandsche stad: een Hollandsche stad onder de Republiek*, 's-Gravenhage, 1916.

Boer, D. H. de, "Op weg naar volwassenheid," in Baart, et al., *De Hollandse stad*, 28–43.

Boer, D. H. de, Boone, M. H., and Hessing, W. A. M., *Nederlands verleden in vogelvlucht. Delta I de middeleeuwen: 300 tot 1500*, Leiden, 1992.

Boer, D. E. H. de, and Marsijle, J. W., eds., *De Nederlanden in de late middeleeuwen*, Utrecht, 1987.

Boitet, Reinier, *Beschryving der stadt Delft*, Delft, 1729.

Bonenfant, P., "Les Origines et le charactère de la réforme de la bienfaisance publique aux Pays-Bas sous le règne de Charles-Quint," *Revue Belgique de philologie et d'histoire* 5 (1926), 887–904; 6 (1927), 207–30.

Boogman, J. C., "De overgang van Gouda, Leiden, Dordrecht, en Delft in de zomer van 1572," *Tijdschrift voor Geschiedenis* 57 (1942), 81–112.

Boom, H. ten, "De diaconie der gereformeerde kerk te Tiel van 1578–1795," *Nederlands Archief voor Kerkgeschiedenis NS* 55 (1975), 32–69.

De reformatie in Rotterdam 1530–1585, 's-Gravenhage, 1987.

Bossy, John, "Blood and baptism: kinship, community and Christianity in western Europe, fourteenth to the seventeenth century," in *Sanctity and Secularity: The Church and the World*, Derek Baker, ed., Oxford, 1973, 129–43.

"Review article: holiness and society," *Past and Present* 75 (1977), 119–37.

"The mass as a social institution, 1200–1700," *Past and Present* 92 (1983), 29–60.

Bouwsma, William, *John Calvin: A Sixteenth-Century Portrait*, Oxford, 1988.

Brady, Thomas A., Jr., "Luther and the state: the reformer's teaching in its social setting," in *Luther and the Modern State in Germany*, James D. Tracy, ed., Kirksville, Mo., 1986, 31–44.

Ruling Class, Regime and Reformation in Strasbourg 1520–1555, Leiden, 1978.

Brandt, Geraerd, *Historie der reformatie en andere kerkelijke geschiedenissen in en omtrent de Nederlanden*, 4 vols., Amsterdam, 1671–1704.

Braudel, Fernand, *Civilization and Capitalism, Fifteenth–Eighteenth Century*, 3 vols., Sian Reynolds, trans., New York, 1981.

Sources cited

Bredero, Adriaan H., *Christenheid en christendom in de middeleeuwen: over de verhouding van godsdienst, kerk, en samenleving*, 2nd edn., Kampen, 1987.

"De Delftse begijn Gertrui van Oosten (ca. 1320–1358) en haar niet-erkende heiligheid," in de Boer and Marsijle, *De Nederlanden in de late middeleeuwen*, 83–98.

Bremmer, R. H., *Reformatie en rebellie: Willem van Oranje, de calvinisten en het recht van opstand tien onstuimige jaren, 1572–1581*, Franeker, 1984.

Briels, J. G. C. A., *Zuidnederlanders in de Republiek, 1572–1630: een demografische en cultuurhistorische studie*, St. Nicholas, 1985.

Zuidnederlandse immigratie in Amsterdam en Haarlem omstreeks 1572–1630, Utrecht, 1976.

Brokken, H. M., *Het ontstaan van de Hoekse en Kabeljauwse twisten*, Zutphen, 1982.

Brown, Dorothy M., and McKeown, Elizabeth, *The Poor Belong To Us: Catholic Charities in American Welfare*, Cambridge, Mass., 1997.

Bruine, M. C. C. Slotemaker de, *Het ideaal van de navolging van Christus ten tijde van Bernard van Clairvaux*, Wageningen, 1926.

Brundage, Anthony, "Private charity and the 1834 Poor Law," paper presented at "From Poor Laws to the Modern Welfare State: Private Charity and Public Assistance in Historical Perspective," Saint Louis University (St. Louis, Mo.), August 16, 1996.

Burke, Peter, *Popular Culture in Early Modern Europe*, New York, 1978.

Burnett, Amy Nelson, "Church discipline and moral reformation in the thought of Martin Bucer," *Sixteenth-Century Journal* 22 (1991), 439–56.

Cahen, Leon, *Le Grand Bureau des pauvres des Paris au milieu du XVIIIe siècle*, Paris, 1904.

Callahan, William J., "The poor, the privileged, and the church in eighteenth-century Spain," in *Religion in the Eighteenth Century*, R. E. Morton and J. D. Browning, eds., New York, 1989, 103–16.

Cavallo, Sandra, *Charity and Power in Early Modern Italy: Benefactors and Their Motives in Turin, 1541–1789*, Cambridge, 1995.

Chevalier, Bernard, *Les Bonnes Villes de France du XIV au XVI siècle*, Paris, 1982.

Chill, Emmanuel, "Religion and mendicity in seventeenth-century France," *International Review of Social History* 7 (1962), 400–25.

Chrisman, Miriam U., *Strasbourg and the Reform: A Study in the Process of Change*, New Haven, 1967.

Cipolla, Carlo, *Before the Industrial Revolution: European Society and Economy, 1000–1700*, 2nd edn., New York, 1980.

Clark, G. N., *The Wealth of England from 1496 to 1760*, London, 1946.

Commelin, Caspar, *Beschryvinge van Amsterdam*, 2 vols. Amsterdam, 1691.

Cox, Robert H., *The Development of the Dutch Welfare State: From Worker's Insurance to Universal Entitlement*, Pittsburgh, 1993.

Crew, Phyllis Mack, *Calvinist Preaching and Iconoclasm in the Netherlands, 1544–1569*, Cambridge, 1978.

Critchlow, Donald T., "Philanthropic foundations and the modern welfare state," paper presented at "From Poor Laws to the Modern Welfare State: Private Charity and Public Assistance in Historical Perspective," Saint Louis University (St. Louis, Mo.), August 16, 1996.

Dalen, J. L. van, *Geschiedenis van Dordrecht*, 2 vols., Dordrecht, 1931–33.

Sources cited

Davids, K., and Noordegraaf, L., eds., *The Dutch Economy in the Golden Age*, Amsterdam, 1993.

Davis, Natalie Zemon, "Ghosts, kin, and progeny," *Daedalus* 16 (1977), 87–114.

"Humanism, heresy, and poor relief in sixteenth-century Lyon," in Davis, *Society and Culture*, 17–64.

"The reasons of misrule," in Davis, *Society and Culture*, 97–123.

"The rites of violence," in Davis, *Society and Culture*, pp. 152–88.

Society and Culture in Early Modern France, Stanford, 1975.

'The sacred and the body social in sixteenth-century Lyon," *Past and Present* 90 (1981), 40–70.

DeClerq, B. J., *Kritiek van de verzuiling*, Lier, 1968.

Delumeau, Jean, *Le Catholicisme entre Luther et Voltaire*, Paris, 1971.

Deursen, A. Th. van, *Bavianen en slijkgeuzen: kerk en kerkvolk ten tijde van Maurits en Oldenbarnevelt*, Assen, 1974.

"Kerk of parochie? De kerkmeesters en de dood tijdens de Republiek," *Tijdschrift voor Geschiedenis* 89 (1976), 531–7.

Het kopergeld van de gouden eeuw, 4 vols., *Dagelijks brood*, vol. I, *Hel en hemel*, vol. IV, Assen and Amsterdam, 1978–80.

Plain Lives in a Golden Age: Popular Culture, Religion and Society in Seventeenth-Century Holland, Maarten Ultee, trans., Cambridge, 1991.

Dickens, A. G., *The English Reformation*, New York, 1964.

Diefendorf, Barbara, *Beneath the Cross: Catholics and Huguenots in Sixteenth-Century Paris*, New York, 1991.

Dijk, J. H. van, "Bedreigd Delft," *Bijdragen voor Vaderlandsche Gescheidenis en Oudheidkunde*, 6th series, 6 (1928), 177–98.

Duke, Alastair, "The ambivalent face of Calvinism in the Netherlands, 1561–1618," in *International Calvinism 1541–1715*, Menna Prestwich, ed., Oxford, 1985, 109–34.

Reformation and Revolt in the Low Countries, London, 1990.

Ehrle, Franz, *Beiträge zur Geschichte und Reform der Armenpflege*, 1881.

"Die Armenordnungen von Nürnberg (1522) und von Ypern (1525)," *Historisches Jahrbuch* 9 (1888), 450–79.

Elias, Johan E., *Geschiedenis van het Amsterdamsche regentenpatriciaat*, 's-Gravenhage, 1923.

Elliott, John P., "Protestantization in the Northern Netherlands, a case study: the classis of Dordrecht 1572–1640," Ph.D. thesis, Columbia University, 1989.

Elton, Geoffrey, "An early Tudor poor law," *Economic History Review*, 2nd series, 6 (1953), 55–67.

Estèbe, Janine, and Vogler, Bernard, "La Genèse d'une société protestante: étude comparée de quelques registres consistoraux languedociens et palatins vers 1600," *Annales ESC* 31 (1976), 362–88.

Evenhuis, R. B., *Ook dat was Amsterdam: de kerk de hervorming in de gouden eeuw*, 5 vols., Amsterdam, 1965–71.

Everts, Johannes, *De verhouding van kerk en staat in bijzonder ten aanzien der armverzorging*, Utrecht, 1908.

Fairchilds, Cissie C., *Poverty and Charity in Aix-en-Provence, 1640–1789*, Baltimore, 1976.

Farr, James R., *Hands of Honor: Artisans and Their World in Dijon, 1550–1650*, Ithaca, 1988.

Sources cited

"The pure and disciplined body: hierarchy, morality, and symbolism in France during the Catholic reformation," *Journal of Interdisciplinary History* 21 (1991), 391–414.

Fehler, Timothy G., "Social welfare in early modern Emden: the evolution of poor relief in the age of reformation and confessionalization," Ph.D. thesis, University of Wisconsin–Madison, 1994.

Flynn, Maureen, *Sacred Charity: Confraternities and Social Welfare in Spain, 1400–1700*, Ithaca, 1989.

Foucault, Michel, *Discipline and Punish: The Birth of the Prison*, Alan Sheridan, trans., New York, 1977.

Madness and Civilization: A History of Insanity in the Age of Reason, Richard Howard, trans., New York, 1965.

Galpern, A. N., "The legacy of late medieval religion in sixteenth-century Champagne," in Trinkhaus and Oberman, *Pursuit of Holiness*, 141–76.

The Religions of the People in Sixteenth-Century Champagne, Cambridge, 1976.

Garrisson-Estèbe, Janine, *Protestants du Midi, 1559–1598*, Toulouse, 1980.

Gascon, R. "Economie et pauvreté aux XVI et XVII siècles: Lyon exemplaire et prophétique," *Etudes sur l'histoire de la pauvreté*, M. Mollat, ed., Paris, 1974, 747–60.

Gavitt, Philip R., *The Ospedale degli Innocenti, 1410–1536*, Ann Arbor, Mich., 1990.

Gelder, H. A. Enno van, *De levensbeschouwing van Cornelis Pieterszoon Hooft, burgermeester van Amsterdam, 1547–1626*, Amsterdam, 1918.

Geselschap, J. E. J., "De ontwikkeling van het kerkelijk leven in Gouda vanaf de hervorming," in *Gouda zeven eeuwen stad*, 287–331.

"Het verenigde Wees- en Aalmoezeniershuis te Gouda 1495–1948," in *Gouda zeven eeuwen stad*, 241–86.

Geyl, Pieter, *The Revolt of the Netherlands 1555–1609*, 2nd edn., London, 1958.

Gouda zeven eeuwen stad, Gouda, 1972.

Gouw, Johannes ter, *Geschiedenis van Amsterdam*, 8 vols., Amsterdam, 1879–93.

Greyerz, Kaspar van, "Städt und Reformation: Stand und Aufgaben der Forschung," *Archiv für Reformationsgeschichte* 76 (1985), 6–63.

Grimm, Harold, "Luther's contributions to sixteenth-century organization of poor relief," *Archiv für Reformationsgeschichte* 61 (1970), 222–34.

Groenhuis, G., *De predikanten: de sociale positie van de gereformeerde predikanten in de Republiek der Vereenigde Nederlanden voor 1700*, Groningen, 1977.

Gutton, Jean-Pierre, *La Société et les pauvres en Europe (XVIe–XVIIIe siècles)*, Paris, 1974.

La Société et les pauvres: l'exemple de la généralité de Lyon, 1534–1789, Paris, 1971.

Haestens, Henrick, Oorlers, Jan, and Marie, Jan, *Beschrijvinge der stad Leyden*, Leiden, 1614.

Hagemeijer, Pauline, "Devote vrouwen in Holland omstreeks 1400," in Jansma, *Schaduw van de eeuwigheid*, 224–41.

Hall, Basil, "Diakonia in Martin Butzer," in McCord and Parker, *Service in Christ*, 94–100.

Herwaarden, Jan van, "Middeleeuwse aflaten en Nederlandse devotie," in de Boer and Marsilje, *De Nederlanden in de late middeleeuwen*, 31–68.

Herwaarden, Jan van, Boer, Dick de, Kan, Fred van, and Verhoeven, Gerrit, *Geschiedenis van Dordrecht tot 1572*, Hilversum, 1996.

Herwijnen, G. van, "Stad en land in het graafschap Holland en Zeeland in de dertiende eeuw," in Baart, et al., *De Hollandse stad*, 18–27.

Sources cited

Hibben, C. C., *Gouda in Revolt: Particularism and Pacificism in the Revolt of the Netherlands, 1572–1588*, Utrecht, 1983.

Hoffman, Philip, *Church and Community in the Diocese of Lyon, 1500–1789*, New Haven, 1984.

Höpfl, Harro, *The Christian Polity of John Calvin*, Cambridge, 1982.

Houtte, J. A. van, "Hervorming van de armenzorg," in *AGN*, vol. IV, 245–9.

Hsia, R. Po-Chia, *Social Discipline in the Reformation: Central Europe 1550–1750*, New York, 1989.

Israel, Jonathan I., *The Dutch Republic: Its Rise, Greatness, and Fall 1477–1806*, Oxford, 1995.

Jaanus, H. J., *Hervormd Delft ten tijde van Arent Cornelisz. (1573–1605)*, Amsterdam, 1950.

James, Mervyn E., "Ritual drama and the social body in the late medieval English town," *Past and Present* 98 (1983), 3–29.

Jansen, H. P. H., "Holland's Advance," *Acta Historica Neerlandica* 10 (1978), 1–20.

Jansma, T. S., "De betekenis van Dordrecht en Rotterdam omstreeks het midden der 16e eeuw," in Jansma, *Tekst en uitleg*, 146–77.

   "Het economische overwicht van de laat-middeleeuwse stad t.a.v. haar agrarische omme-land, in het bijzonder toegelicht met de verhouding tussen Leiden en Rijnland," in Jansma, *Tekst en uitleg*, 35–53.

   "Holland en Zeeland onder de Bourgondische hertogen, 1433–1477," in *AGN*, vol. II, 313–41.

In de schaduw van de eeuwigheid: tien studies over religie en samenleving in laatmiddeleeuws Nederland aangeboden aan prof. dr. A. H. Bredero, Utrecht, 1986.

   "De oudste geschiedenis van Rotterdam," in Jansma, *Tekst en uitleg*, 1–34.

Tekst en uitleg: historische opstellen aangeboden aan de schrijver bij zijn aftreden als hoogleraar aan de Universiteit van Amsterdam, 's-Gravenhage, 1974.

Jensma, Theunis Watzes, *De Grote- of Onze Lieve Vrouwekerk van Dordrecht*, Dordrecht, 1987.

Jones, Colin, *The Charitable Imperative: Hospitals and Nursing in Ancien Régime and Revol-utionary France*, New York, 1989.

Jones, Eric L., *The European Miracle: Environments, Economies, and Geopolitics in the History of Europe and Asia*, 2nd edn., Cambridge, 1987.

Jones, Rosemary, "De Nederduitse gereformeerde gemeente te Leiden in de jaren 1572–1576," *Leidse Jaarbook* 66 (1974), 126–44.

Jongkees, A. G., "Holland in Erasmus' tijd," in de Boer and Marsijle, *De Nederlanden in de late middeleeuwen*, 379–92.

Jordan, W. K., *Philanthropy in England 1480–1660: A Study of the Changing Pattern of English Social Aspirations*, London, 1959.

Jütte, Robert, "Poor relief and social discipline in sixteenth-century Europe," *European Studies Review* 11 (1981), 25–52.

Poverty and Deviance in Early Modern Europe, Cambridge, 1994.

Kan, F. J. W. van, *Sleutels tot de macht: de ontwikkeling van het Leidse patriciaat tot 1420*, Hilversum, 1988.

Kaplan, Benjamin J., *Calvinists and Libertines: Confession and Community in Utrecht 1578–1620*, Oxford, 1995.

"Dutch particularism and the Calvinist quest for holy uniformity," *Archiv für Reformationsgeschichte* 82 (1991), 239–56.

"'Remnants of the papal yoke': apathy and opposition in the Dutch Reformation," *Sixteenth-Century Journal* 25 (1994), 653–69.

Kesper, L. A., "De Goudsche vroedschap en de religie," *Bijdragen voor Vaderlandsche Geschiedenis en Oudheidkunde*, series 4, 2 (1902), 391–428.

Kiernan, V. G., *State and Society in Europe, 1550–1650*, New York, 1980.

Kingdon, Robert M., "The control of morals by the earliest Calvinists," in *Renaissance, Reformation, Resurgence*, Peter de Klerk, ed., Grand Rapids, Mich., 1976, 95–106.

"The control of morals in Calvin's Geneva," in *The Social History of the Reformation*, L. P. Buck and J. W. Zophy, eds., Columbus, Ohio, 1972, 3–16.

"The deacons of the Reformed Church in Calvin's Geneva," in *Mélanges d'histoire du XVIe siècle offerts à Henri Meylan*, Geneva, 1970, 81–90.

"Social welfare in Calvin's Geneva," *American Historical Review* 76 (1971), 50–69.

Kistemaker, Renee, and Gelder, Roelof van, *Amsterdam: The Golden Age 1275–1795*, New York, 1983.

Knappert, L., *De opkomst van het protestantisme in eene Noord-Nederlandsche stad*, Leiden, 1908.

Knetsch, F. R. J., "Diakonaat als ambtelijke armenzorg I," *Nederlands Archief voor Kerkgeschiedenis NS* 64 (1984), 144–59.

Kok, J. A. de, *Nederland op de breuklijn Rome-Reformatie*, Assen, 1964.

Kok, Jacobus, *Amsteldamsche Jaarboeken*, 3 vols., Amsterdam, 1781.

Kok, M. A., "Het geestelijk leven te Delft," in *De stad Delft*, vol. I, 106–08.

"Opkomst van het protestantisme," in *De stad Delft*, vol. I, 108–12.

Kooi, Christine Jane, "The Reformed Community of Leiden, 1572–1620," Ph.D. thesis, Yale University, 1993.

Kriedte, Peter, *Peasants, Landlords, and Merchant Capitalists: Europe and the World Economy, 1500–1800*, New York, 1980.

Kruisheer, Jaap, *Het ontstaan van de stadsrechtoorkonden van Haarlem, Delft, Alkmaar*, Amsterdam, 1985.

"Stadsrechtbeoorkonding en stedelijke ontwikkeling," in Baart, et al., *De Hollandse stad*, 44–54.

Lambert, Audrey, *The Making of the Dutch Landscape: An Historical Geography of the Netherlands*, 2nd edn., London, 1985.

Lamet, Sterling, "The *vroedschap* of Leiden 1550–1600: the impact of tradition and change on the governing elite of a Dutch city," *Sixteenth-Century Journal* 12 (1981), 15–42.

Lampe, G. W. H., "Diakonia in the early church," in McCord and Parker, *Service in Christ*, 49–59.

Laslett, Peter, *The World We Have Lost, Further Explored*, 3rd edn., New York, 1984.

Le Roy Ladurie, Emmanuel, *The Peasants of Languedoc*, John Day, trans., Urbana, Ill., 1974.

Leeuwen, H. W. van, "Bestuurlijke en rechterlijke organisatie," in *De stad Delft*, vol. I, 24–9.

Lely, Willem van der, *Beschryving van de Kamer van Charitaten, de diakonie en het leprooshuis*, 1732.

Leupen, P. H. D., "Heer en stad, stad en heer in de dertiende eeuw," in Baart, et al., *De Hollandse stad*, 9–17.

Sources cited

Lesger, Clé, "Intraregional trade and the port system in Holland, 1400–1700," in Davids and Noordegraaf, *Dutch Economy*, 185–217.

Lieburg, Fred A. van, "From pure church to pious culture: the further reformation in the seventeenth-century Dutch Republic," in *Later Calvinism: International Perspectives*, Fred W. Graham, ed., Kirksville, Mo., 1994, 409–29.

Ligtenberg, Christina, *Armezorg te Leiden tot het einde van de 16e eeuw*, 's-Gravenhage, 1908.

Lijphart, A., *Verzuiling, pacificatie en kentering in de Nederlandse politiek*, 3rd edn., Amsterdam, 1979.

Lindberg, Carter, *Beyond Charity: Reformation Initiatives for the Poor*, Minneapolis, 1993.

  "The liturgy after the liturgy: welfare in the early reformation," in *Through the Eye of a Needle: Judeo-Christian Roots of Social Welfare*, Emily Albu Hanawalt and Carter Lindberg, eds., Kirksville, Mo., 1994.

  "'There should be no beggars among Christians': Karlstadt, Luther, and the origins of Protestant poor relief," *Church History* 46 (1977), 313–34.

  "Through a glass darkly: a history of the church's vision of the poor and poverty," *Ecumenical Review* 33 (1981), 37–52.

Lis, Catharina, and Soly, Hugo, *Poverty and Capitalism in Pre-Industrial Europe*, Atlantic Highlands, N.J., 1979.

Loenen, Jacques van, *De Haarlemse brouwindustrie vóór 1600*, Amsterdam, 1950.

McCord, James I., and Parker, T. H. L., eds., *Service in Christ: Essays Presented to Karl Barth on His 80th Birthday*, London, 1966.

McKee, Elsie Ann, *John Calvin on the Diaconate and Liturgical Almsgiving*, Geneva, 1984.

Maltby, William S., *Alba: A Biography of Fernando Alverez de Toledo Third Duke of Alba, 1507–1582*, Berkeley, 1983.

Manen, Ch. A. van, *Armenpflege in Amsterdam in ihrer historischen Entwicklung*, Leiden, 1913.

Margry, P. J., *Amsterdam and het mirakel van het heilig sacrament: van middeleeuwsche devotie tot 20-eeuwse stille omgang*, Amsterdam, 1988.

Marsijle, J. W., "De geografische, institutionele en politieke ontwikkelingen," in *Deugd boven geweld: een geschiedenis van Haarlem, 1245–1995*, G. F. van der Ree-Scholtens, ed., Hilversum, 1995, 19–45.

  "Het Haarlemse klerkambt in de 15e eeuw," in de Boer and Marsijle, *De Nederlanden in de late middeleeuwen*, 182–98.

Martz, Linda, *Poverty and Welfare in Hapsburg Spain: The Example of Toledo*, Cambridge, 1983.

Méjan, François, *Discipline de l'Eglise Réformée de France annotée et précédée d'une introduction historique*, Paris, 1947.

Mentink, G. J., "Armenzorg en armoede in de archivische bronnen in de Noordelijke Nederlanden, 1531–1854," *Tijdschrift voor Geschiedenis* 88 (1975), 551–61.

Mentzer, Raymond A., "Disciplina nervus ecclesiae: the Calvinist reform of morals at Nîmes," *Sixteenth-Century Journal* 18 (1987), 89–115.

  "Ecclesiastical discipline and communal reorganization among the Protestants of southern France," *European History Quarterly* 21 (1991), 163–83.

  "Marking the taboo: excommunication in the French Reformed churches," in *Sin and the Calvinists: Morals Control and the Consistory in the Reformed Tradition*, R. A. Mentzer, ed., Kirksville, Mo., 1995, 97–128.

Sources cited

"Organizational endeavour and charitable impulse in sixteenth-century France: the case of Protestant Nîmes," *French History*, 5 (1991), 1–29.

Michielse, H. C. M., "Policing the poor: Juan Luis Vivès and the sixteenth-century origins of modern social welfare administration," *Social Service Review* 64 (1990), 1–21.

Moeller, Bernd, *The Imperial Cities and the Reformation: Three Essays*, H. C. Erik Midelfort and Mark U. Edwards, Jr., eds., Durham, N.C., 1982.

Monter, E. William, *Calvin's Geneva*, New York, 1967.

Muchembled, Robert, *Culture populaire et culture des élites*, Paris, 1978.

Muir, Edward, *Civic Ritual in Renaissance Venice*, Princeton, 1981.

Mulier, E. O. G. Haitsma, "Grotius, Hooft and the writing of history in the Dutch Republic," in *Clio's Mirror: Historiography in Britain and the Netherlands*, A. C. Duke and C. A. Tamse, eds., Zutphen, 1985, 55–72.

Muller, Sheila D., *Charity in the Dutch Republic: Pictures of Rich and Poor for Charitable Institutions*, Ann Arbor, Mich., 1985.

Naphy, William G., *Calvin and the Consolidation of the Genevan Reformation*, Manchester, 1994.

Niermeyer, J. F., "Henegouwen, Holland, en Zeeland onder het huis Wittelsbach," in *AGN*, vol. III, 92–117.

Nijenhuis, W., "Varianten binnen het Nederlandse Calvinisme in de zestiende eeuw," *Tijdschrift voor Geschiedenis* 89 (1976), 358–72.

Nolf, J., *La Réforme de la bienfaisance publique à Ypres au XVIe siècle*, Ghent, 1915.

Noordegraaf, Leo, "Dearth, famine, and social policy in the Dutch Republic at the end of the sixteenth century," in *The European Crisis of the 1590s: Essays in Comparative History*, Peter Clark, ed., London, 1985, 67–83.

"Dutch industry in the golden age," in Davids and Noordegraaf, *Dutch Economy*, 131–57.

Hollands welvaren? Levensstandaard in Holland 1450–1650, Bergen, 1985.

Noordegraaf, Leo, and Valk, Gerrit, *De gave Gods: de pest in Holland vanaf de late middeleeuwen*, Bergen, 1988.

Noordham, Dirk Jaap, *Geringde buffels en heren van stand: het patriciaat van Leiden, 1574–1700*, Hilversum, 1994.

Norberg, Kathryn, *Rich and Poor in Grenoble, 1600–1814*, Berkeley, 1985.

Nusteling, Hubert, *Welvaart en werkgelegenheid in Amsterdam, 1540–1860*, Amsterdam, 1985.

Oberman, Heiko, "*Europa afflicta*: the reformation of the refugees," *Archiv für Reformationsgeschichte* 83 (1992), 91–111.

Oestreich, Gerhard, *Neostoicism and the Early Modern State*, Brigitta Oestreich and H. G. Koenigsburger, eds., David McLintock, trans., Cambridge, 1982.

Olson, Jeannine, *Calvin and Social Welfare: Deacons and the Bourse Française*, London, 1989.

One Ministry, Many Roles: Deacons and Deaconesses Through the Centuries, St. Louis, 1992.

Oosterbaan, D. P., "Kroniek van de Nieuwe Kerk te Delft," *Bijdragen voor de geschiedenis van het Bisdom Haarlem* 65 (1958), 5–313.

Het Oude en Nieuwe Gasthuis te Delft, Delft, 1954.

De Oude Kerk te Delft gedurende middeleeuwen, 's-Gravenhage, 1973.

Overmeer, W. P. J., *De hervorming te Haarlem*, Haarlem, 1904.

Sources cited

Overvoorde, J. C., "Advies van burgermeesters en gerecht van Leiden aan de Staten van Holland over de acta van de 1578 te Dordt gehouden," *Nederlands Archief voor Kerkgeschiedenis* 9 (1912), 117–49.

Ozment, Steven, *The Reformation in the Cities: The Appeal of Protestantism to Sixteenth-Century Germany and Switzerland*, New Haven, 1975.

Parker, Charles H., "Public church and household of faith: competing visions of the church in post-reformation Delft, 1572–1617," *Journal of Religious History* 17 (1993), 418–38.

Parker, Geoffrey, *The Dutch Revolt*, Ithaca, 1977.

    Europe in Crisis, 1598–1648, Brighton, 1980.

Peristiany, J. G., ed., *Honor and Shame: The Values of a Mediterranean Society*, London, 1965.

Pettegree, Andrew, *Emden and the Dutch Revolt: Exile and the Development of Reformed Protestantism*, Oxford, 1992.

    "Exile and the development of Reformed Protestantism," paper presented to "Sixteenth-Century Studies Conference," Toronto, Ontario, October 28, 1994.

    Foreign Protestant Communities in Sixteenth-Century London, Oxford, 1986.

Pinkse, V. C. C. J., "Het Goudse kuitbier: Gouda's welvaren in de late middeleeuwen," in *Gouda zeven eeuwen stad*, pp. 91–128.

Pirenne, Henri, *Histoire de Belgique*, 3 vols., 2nd edn., Brussels, 1912.

Piven, Frances Fox, and Cloward, Richard A., *Regulating the Poor: The Functions of Public Welfare*, New York, 1971.

Pontanus, Johannes Isaac, *Historische beschrijvinghe der seer wijt beroemde coop-stadt Amsterdam*, Amsterdam, 1614.

Post, Harry, *Pillarization: An Analysis of Dutch and Belgian Society*, Brookfield, Vt., 1989.

Post, R. R., *Kerkelijke verhouding in Nederland vóór de Reformatie van 1500 tot 1580*, Utrecht, 1954.

Postan, M. M., *Essays on Medieval Agriculture and General Problems of the Medieval Economy*, Cambridge, 1973.

Posthumus, N. W., *De geschiedenis van de Leidsche lakenindustrie*, 2 vols., 's-Gravenhage, 1939.

Prinsen, J., "Armenzorg te Leiden in 1577," *Bijdragen en Mededeelingen van het Historische Genootschap te Utrecht* 26 (1905), 113–60.

Pullan, Brian, "Private charity and public relief in early modern Italy," paper presented at "From Poor Laws to the Modern Welfare State: Private Charity and Public Assistance in Historical Perspective," Saint Louis University (St. Louis, Mo.), August 16, 1996.

    Rich and Poor in Renaissance Venice: The Social Institutions of a Catholic State, Cambridge, 1971.

    "Catholics and the poor in early modern Europe," *Transactions of the Royal Historical Society*, series 5, 26 (1976), 15–34.

Querido, A., *Godshuizen en gasthuizen*, Amsterdam, 1960.

Ratzinger, Georg, *Geschichte der Armenpflege*, 2nd edn., Freiburg-im-Breisgau, 1884.

Reegen, O. F. ter, *De sacramentsprocessie: onderzoek naar de bronnen van het processie-ceremonieel in het ceremoniale episcoporum*, Brussels, 1965.

Reid, J. K. S., "Diakonia in the thought of John Calvin," in McCord and Parker, *Service in Christ*, 101–9.

Sources cited

Rich, E. E., and Wilson, C. H., *The Cambridge Economic History of Europe*, vol. IV, *The Economy of Expanding Europe in the Sixteenth and Seventeenth Centuries*, Cambridge, 1967.

Riemsdijk, B. W. F. van, *Historische beschrijving van het klooster van Sinte Agatha met het Prinsenhof te Delft*, 's-Gravenhage, 1894.

Roelink, A. J., "Het calvinisme," in *AGN*, vol. IV, 281–304.

Rogier, L. J., *Eenheid en scheiding: geschiedenis der Nederlanden*, Utrecht, 1968.

Geschiedenis van het katholicisme in de Noordelijke Nederlanden in de 16e en 17e eeuwen, 3 vols., Amsterdam, 1945–7.

"De protestantiseering van het Noorden," in *AGN*, vol. V, 326–65.

Roodenburg, Herman, *Onder censuur: de kerkelijke tucht in de gereformeerde gemeente van Amsterdam, 1578–1700*, Hilversum, 1990.

Salgado, Gamini, *The Elizabethan Underworld*, London, 1977.

Schama, Simon, *The Embarassment of Riches: An Interpretation of Dutch Culture in the Golden Age*, Berkeley, 1978.

Schepper, H. de, "De burgerlijke overheden en hun permanent kaders 1480–1579," in *NAGN*, vol. V, 312–49.

Schilling, Heinz, "Calvinistische Presbyterien in Städten der Frühneuzeit: eine kirchliche Alternativeform zur bürgerlichen Repräsentation? (Mit eine quantifizierenden Untersuchung zur Holländischen Stadt Leiden)," in *Städtische Führungsgruppen und Gemeinde in der werdenden Neuzeit*, W. Ehbrecht, ed., Cologne, 1980, 385–444.

Civic Calvinism in Northwestern Germany and the Netherlands, Sixteenth to Nineteenth Centuries, Kirksville, Mo., 1991.

"'History of crime' or 'history of sin'? Some reflections on the social history of modern church discipline," in *Politics and Society in Reformation Europe: Essays for Sir Geoffrey Elton on His Sixty-fifth Birthday*, E. I. Kouri and Tom Scott, eds., London, 1987, 289–310.

"Reformierte Kirchenzucht als Sozialdisziplinierung? Die Tätigkeit des Emder Presbyteriums in den Jahren 1557–1562," in *Niederlande und Nordwestdeutschland: Studien zur Regional- und Stadtgeschichte Nordwestkontinentaleuropas im Mittelalter und in der Neuzeit*, Wolfgang Ehbrecht and Heinz Schilling, eds., Cologne and Vienna, 1983, 261–327.

Schoffer, I., "The Batavian myth during the sixteenth and seventeenth centuries," in *Geschiedschrijving in Nederland: studies over de historiographie van de nieuwe tijd*, vol. II, P. A. M. Geurts and A. E. M. Janssen, eds., 's-Gravenhage, 1981, 85–109.

Schwartz, Robert, *Policing the Poor in Eighteenth-Century France*, Chapel Hill, N.C., 1988.

Scribner, R. W., "Civic unity and the reformation in Erfurt," *Past and Present* 66 (1975), 29–60.

"Cosmic order and daily life: sacred and secular in pre-industrial German society," in *Religion and Society in Early Modern Europe*, Kaspar van Greyerz, ed., London, 1984, 17–35.

"Ritual and popular religion in Catholic Germany at the time of the reformation," *Journal of Ecclesiastical History* 35 (1984), 47–77.

Sels, J., *Beschrijving der stad Dordrecht*, Dordrecht, 1853.

Seward, Pat, *Cultures of the World: Netherlands*, New York, 1995.

Sources cited

Soly, H., "Economische ontwikkeling en sociale politiek in Europa tijdens de overgang van middeleeuwen naar nieuwe tijden," *Tijdschrift voor Geschiedenis* 88 (1975), 584–97.

Spaans, Joke, *Haarlem na de reformatie: stedelijke cultuur en kerkelijk leven, 1577–1620*, 's-Gravenhage, 1989.

Spalding, James, "Discipline as a mark of the true church in its sixteenth-century Lutheran context," in *Piety, Politics, and Ethics: Reformation Studies in Honor of George Wolfgang Forell*, Carter Lindberg, ed., Kirksville, Mo., 1984, 119–38.

Spierenburg, Pieter C., *The Spectacle of Suffering: Executions and the Evolution of Repression from a Pre-Industrial Metropolis to the European Experience*, Cambridge, 1984.

Spiker, Willem van 'T, *De ambten bij Martin Bucer*, Kampen, 1970.

Sprunger, Mary Susan, "Rich Mennonites, poor Mennonites: economics and theology in the Amsterdam Waterlander congregation during the golden age," Ph.D. thesis, University of Illinois, 1993.

De stad Delft: cultuur en maatschappij, 2 vols., Delft, 1981.

Sterck, J. F. M., *De Heilige Stede in de geschiedenis van Amsterdam*, Hilversum, 1938.

Sudeck, Elisabeth, *Bettlerdarstellungen am Ende des XV. Jahrhunderts bis zu Rembrandt*, Strasbourg, 1931.

Sunshine, Glenn S. "Geneva meets Rome: the development of the French reformed diaconate," *Sixteenth-Century Journal* 26, 2 (1995), 331–47.

Taal, J., *De archieven vande Goudse kloosters*, 's-Gravenhage, 1957.

Tawney, R. H., *Religion and the Rise of Capitalism*, New York, 1926.

Tierney, Brian, *Medieval Poor Law: A Sketch of Canonical Theory and Its Application in England*, Berkeley, 1959.

Tobriner, Alice, *A Sixteenth-Century Urban Report*, Chicago, 1971.

Tracy, James D., "The Calvinist church of the Dutch Republic, 1572–1618/19," in *Reformation Europe: A Guide to Research* II, William S. Maltby, ed., St. Louis, 1992, 253–80.

A Financial Revolution in the Hapsburg Netherlands: Renten and Renteniers in the County of Holland, 1515–1565, Berkeley, 1985.

Holland Under Hapsburg Rule, 1506–1566: The Formation of a Body Politic, Berkeley, 1990.

"A premature counter-reformation: the Dirkist government of Amsterdam, 1538–1578," *Journal of Religious History* 13 (1984), 150–67.

Trigland, Jacobus, *Kerckelycke geschiedenissen*, Leiden, 1650.

Trinkhaus, Charles, and Oberman, Heiko A., eds., *The Pursuit of Holiness in Late Medieval and Renaissance Religion*, Leiden, 1974.

Troeltsch, Ernst, *The Social Teaching of the Christian Churches*, 2 vols., 2nd edn., Olive Wyon, trans., New York, 1960.

Tukker, C. A., *De classis van Dordrecht van 1573 tot 1609: bijdrage tot de kennis van in- en extern leven van de gereformeerde kerk in de periode van haar organisiering*, Leiden, 1965.

Unger, W. S., "De economische en sociale structuur van Dordrecht in 1555," *De Economist* 64 (1916), 947–84.

Uytenbogaert, Johannes, *Kerckelijcke historie*, Rotterdam, 1647.

Verhoeven, G., "De cultus van het heilig hout te Dordrecht: het onstaan van een bedevaart in de late middeleeuwen," in Jansma, *Schaduw van de eeuwigheid*, 200–20.

Sources cited

Devotie en negotie: Delft als bedevaartplaats in de late middeleeuwen, Amsterdam, 1992.

Vries, Jan de, "The labour market," in Davids and Noordegraaf, *Dutch Economy*, 55–78.

Vries, Jan de, and Woude, Ad van der, *Nederland 1500–1815: de eerste ronde van moderne economische groei*, 2nd edn., Amsterdam, 1995.

Wagenaar, Jan, *Amsterdam in zyne opkomst, aanwas geschiedenissen*, 3 vols., Amsterdam, 1760.

Waite, Gary K., *David Joris and Dutch Anabaptism, 1524–1543*, Waterloo, Pa., 1990.

Wallerstein, Immanuel, *The Modern World-System* I: Capitalist Agriculture and the Origins of the European World-Economy in the Sixteenth Century, New York, 1974.

Walton, Robert C., *Zwingli's Theocracy*, Toronto, 1967.

Walvis, Ignatius, *Beschryving der stad Gouda*, 2 vols., Gouda, 1713.

Walzer, Michael, *The Revolution of the Saints: A Study in the Origins of Radical Politics*, Cambridge, Mass., 1965.

Wandel, Lee Palmer, *Always Among Us: Images of the Poor in Zwingli's Zurich*, Cambridge, 1991.

Watt, Jeffrey, "The reception of the Reformation in Valangin, Switzerland, 1547–1588," *Sixteenth-Century Journal* 20 (1989), 89–104.

Weber, Max, *The Protestant Ethic and the Spirit of Capitalism*, 2nd edn., Talcott Parsons, trans., London, 1930.

Weismann, A. W., "Het tuchthuis en spinhuis te Amsterdam," *Oud Holland* 26 (1908), 335–40.

Werveke, H. van, "De opbloei van handel en nijverheid," in *AGN*, vol. II, 417–47.

"De steden: rechten, instellingen en maatschappelijke toestanden," in *AGN*, vol. II, 374–415.

Wijbenga, D., *Delft: een verhaal van de stad en haar bewoners*, 2 vols., Elmar, 1984.

Winckelmann, Otto, "Über die ältesten Armenordnung der Reformationszeit," *Historische Vierteljahrschrift* 17 (1914/15), 361–440.

Woltjer, J. J., "Dutch privileges, real and imaginary," in *Britain and the Netherlands*, J. S. Bromley and E. H. Kossman, eds., London, 1975, 19–35.

"Een Hollands stadsbestuur in het midden van de 16e eeuw: brouwers en bestuurders te Delft," in de Boer and Marsijle, *De Nederlanden in de late middeleeuwen*, 261–79.

"Een niew ende onghesien dingh: verkenningen naar de positie van de kerkeraad in twee Hollandse steden in de zestiende eeuw," Afschiedscollege, Rijksuniversiteit te Leiden, 1985.

"De plaats van de calvinisten in de Nederlandse samenleving," *Zeventiende Eeuw* 10 (1994), 3–23.

Wouters, A. Ph. F., and Abels, P. H. A. M., *Nieuw en ongezien: kerk en samenleving in de classis Delft en Delfland, 1572–1621*, 2 vols., Delft, 1994.

Zanden, Jan Luiten van, "Economic growth in the golden age: the development of the economy of Holland, 1500–1560," in Davids and Noordegraaf, *Dutch Economy*, 5–26.

Index

Index

CAMBRIDGE STUDIES IN EARLY MODERN HISTORY

ADQ-7921

4/19/99

App

BX
9474.2
P37
1998